Trailer Life's
RV Repair & Maintenance Manual

OTHER BOOKS BY TRAILER LIFE

RVing America's Backroads

California	*Arizona*
Florida	*Idaho/Montana*
New York	*Texas*

Six information-packed four-color travel guidebooks designed *specifically* for recreational vehicle owners! Each book takes you on spectacular backroads tours, lavishly illustrated with gorgeous color photography by award-winning photojournalists. Clear, accurate maps of suggested backroads tours show easy access from the major interstates...fact sheets list annual events, museums, restaurants. Don't plan an RV vacation without these exciting new books.
8½ x 11, 128 pages
$15.95 each

Full-time RVing: A Complete Guide to Life on the Open Road
Bill and Jan Moeller

The answers to all the questions anyone who dreams of traveling full time in an RV may have can be found in this remarkable new source book. *Full-time RVing* takes the mystery out of fulltiming and makes it possible to fully enjoy this once-in-a-lifetime experience.
7¼ x 9¼, 352 pages
$14.95 ISBN: 0-934798-14-1

RX for RV Performance & Mileage
John Geraghty and Bill Estes

In 32 chapters, this book covers everything an owner must know about how an engine (particularly a V-8) works, vehicle maintenance, propane and diesel as alternative fuels, eliminating engine "ping," improving exhaust systems and fuel economy, and much more.
7¾ x 9¼, 359 pages
$14.95 ISBN: 0-934798-08-0

The Good Sam RV Cookbook
Edited by Beverly Edwards and the editors of *Trailer Life*

Over 250 easy and delicious recipes, including 78 prize-winners from the Good Sam Samboree cook-offs around the country. Also contains tips, ideas, and suggestions to help you get the most from your RV galley.
7¼ x 9¼, 252 pages
$14.95 ISBN: 0-93478-17-6

These books are available at fine bookstores everywhere. Or, you may order directly from Trailer Life. For each book ordered, simply send us the name of the book, the price, plus $2 per book for shipping and handling (California residents please add 6½% sales tax). Mail to:

Trailer Life Books, P.O. Box 4500, Agoura, CA 91301

You may call our Customer Service representatives if you wish to charge your order or if you want more information. Please phone, toll-free, Monday through Friday, 6:30 A.M. to 5:30 P.M.; Saturday, 7:30 A.M. to 12:30 P.M. Pacific Time, **1-800-234-3450.**

Trailer Life's

RV REPAIR & MAINTENANCE MANUAL

EDITED BY
Bob Livingston

TRAILER LIFE BOOKS
AGOURA, CALIFORNIA

Trailer Life Book Division

President: Richard Rouse
Vice President/General Manager: Ted Binder
Vice President/Publisher, Book Division: Michael Schneider
General Manager, Book Division: Rena Copperman
Assistant Manager, Book Division: Cindy Lang

Cover design: Robert S. Tinnon and Kaufman/Kane
Editor/production manager: Rena Copperman
Production coordinator: Robert S. Tinnon
Art assistant: Mary Andert
Assistant editors: Judi Lazarus, Bob Howells
Indexer: Becky Goodman
Cover and interior illustrations: Miyake Illustration
Cover separations: Western Laser Graphics

This book was set in ITC Times Roman by Andresen Typographics
and printed on 50-pound Edition Matte by R.R. Donnelley and
Sons in Willard, Ohio.

ISBN 0-934798-12-5

Library of Congress Cataloging-in-Publication Data

Livingston, Bob, 1949-
    Trailer life's RV repair & maintenance manual/Bob Livingston and
  the editors of Trailer Life.
        p.   cm.
    Includes index.
    ISBN 0-934798-12-5 : $19.95
    1. Recreational vehicles—Maintenance and repair—Handbooks,
manuals, etc.   I. Trailer Life.   II. Title.   III. Title: Trailer
life's RV repair and maintenance manual.   IV. Title: RV repair &
maintenance manual.   V. Title: RV repair and maintenance manual.
TL298.L59   1989
629.28'76—dc20   89-4637
                                                         CIP

Contents

Chapter 17

Illustrations
(Selected List)

Tables

Troubleshooting Guides

Foreword

Some RV owners would regard an easily accessible encyclopedia of RV technical knowledge merely as an insurance policy—essential when you need it, but not the most scintillating of reading matter.

For many thousands of others, including Bob Livingston, the editor of this book, anything of a technical nature involving RVs is on their personal bestseller lists.

RV owners tend to fall into three categories: those who want the vehicle to work every time and have no interest in what makes it tick; those who want it to work and to know how it ticks; and those who want to personally be able to make it tick. Livingston and the contributors to this book are in the latter class—RV owners who enjoy travel but who also enjoy collecting and using knowledge about everything from amperage to zerk fittings. RV tinkering, in other words, is a hobby unto itself. It's something Livingston and I and the contributors to this book have enjoyed for many years.

I think you'll find that a book of this caliber could only have been assembled by someone who enjoys the technical side of RVing rather than regarding it as a necessary evil. Thus, *Trailer Life's Repair and RV Maintenance Manual* is much more than an insurance policy. It's your ticket to the satisfying feeling that comes from dramatically improved knowledge of how your RV works, how it should be maintained, and how it should be repaired if it breaks. Even RV owners who have no intention of doing any of the work should be armed with the best, most complete, RV repair and maintenance information when dealing with mechanics.

Having just made the best possible move by acquiring this book, you're on the way to more enjoyable, less expensive RV travel.

BILL ESTES
Associate Publisher
Trailer Life/MotorHome

Introduction

Recreational vehicles are complex. Unlike automobiles, RVs are equipped with multiple systems, including the proverbial kitchen sink, and can develop a multitude of service and maintenance problems. And when something goes wrong, it can happen at an unknown location, far from home. There's nothing worse than throwing yourself at the mercy of the local repair shop, especially when the vacation-time clock continues to tick.

The key to successful RV travel is having a basic understanding of the systems that make these vehicles livable. *Trailer Life's RV Repair & Maintenance Manual* consists of 17 chapters, divided primarily by systems. Each chapter is designed to allow the RV owner to become more familiar with a particular system in any trailer, motorhome or camper, from electrical to plumbing to drivetrain.

Beyond the basic primers, this book is designed to instruct the owner in the proper procedures for preventive maintenance, a crucial element for troublefree RV travel. The use of a large number of appliances and associated equipment inside a single vehicle creates an environment best left to the expert tinkerers of the world. Unless the RV is maintained meticulously, even the die-hard shade-tree mechanic can become frustrated. Checklists throughout this book provide the necessary information for service and inspections so that the owner can stay one step ahead of failures and breakdowns.

Sometimes the best-laid plans can go awry, or in severe cases, the RV owner becomes victimized by Murphy's Law. Unfortunately, things will break or cease to function, even if maintained properly. If, indeed, an appliance or a system becomes temporarily inoperative, the Troubleshooting Guides should lead the owner to the source of the problem. In addition, the accompanying text will describe the repair procedures, supported by detailed illustrations, photographs, and tables. Owners who are not adept at wielding tools can use this information to give them an upper hand when dealing with service technicians.

Hopefully the information contained in this repair manual will guide the RV owner through most procedures. Although your exact appliance or accessory may not be described, the repair or service procedure is usually applicable with minor variations.

The information in *Trailer Life's RV Repair & Maintenance Manual* would not be possible without the excellent cooperation of the manufacturers who continually supply the appliances and accessories to the RV industry. Special thanks goes to Dometic, Norcold, Onan, Kohler, Tekonsha, Kelsey-Hayes, Atwood Mobile Products, Hewitt Tubular, Magic Chef, Arco Solar, Reese, Eaz-Lift, GNB Batteries, Thetford, SeaLand, Microphor, Joseph Pollack, Theodore Bargman, Jabsco, Shurflo, Sure Power, Thin-Lite, Intec, and Macedon. Without these and other companies, there would be no RV industry, and certainly no RV repair manual.

Assembling a manual of this magnitude is no easy feat. It took a team of dedicated RV enthusiasts to assist in digesting the material from the various manufacturers, integrating the information with personal experience, knowledge, and talent, and finally interpreting and communicating this information to you, the reader. The efforts of Rich Johnson, Brian Robertson, and Bill Estes are greatly appreciated; without their help this book simply would not be possible. Rena Copperman deserves the credit for putting all the pieces together, but moreover, the clean design and easy readability of this manual are a tribute to her expertise in book publishing. Special thanks goes to art director Bob Tinnon, who really put his heart into the project and worked into the wee hours accommodating our changes.

After perusing *Trailer Life's RV Repair & Maintenance Manual* please take a few moments and fill out the Reader's Survey in the back of this book. Your valued input will enable us to update this manual periodically with information you find most important.

While this book may not be entertaining in the true sense of the word, it is comforting to know that the information you need to get you back on the road again is here. There's nothing less entertaining than being broken down without help—but nothing more rewarding than to be able to fix it yourself.

May your travels be trouble-free and enjoyable.

CHAPTER 1

Electrical Systems

Recreational vehicles use 12-volt direct current (DC) and/or 120-volt alternating current (AC) power from one of three sources: onboard 12-volt storage batteries, 120-volt AC campground hookups, or 120-volt AC auxiliary generators. Twelve-volt power is also provided by means of the power converter when connected to campground hookups. The 120-volt AC in an RV is similar to that in a home and, other than periodic checks for low voltage, it usually requires little or no maintenance.

All 120-volt AC wiring for appliances and accessories is protected by a series of circuit breakers located inside the RV. The 120-volt system is potentially dangerous and should not be modified unless the user has sufficient understanding of AC electricity.

Proper Use of 12-Volt DC Power

Twelve-volt power presents little danger of electrical shock. Still, care must be taken when dealing with 12-volt systems because DC power is capable of producing large amounts of current. A short circuit or an overloaded circuit can generate a lot of heat, melting insulation off wiring, damaging appliances, and creating potential for fire. To protect against possible short circuits or fire, all circuits must contain some type of over-current protection device (OCPD) that is rated no higher than the conductor's maximum ampere rating. Ideally, the OCPD (fuse or circuit breaker) should be within 18 inches of the power source.

Although troubleshooting RV electrical systems may seem somewhat mysterious, most of these systems can be checked with simple tools. Interruptions in current flow are the most common problems faced by the RV owner. And these interruptions can be diagnosed by use of an inexpensive 12-volt test light or a multimeter. While a test light indicates when voltage exists, a multimeter can help identify breaks or shorts in circuits without the existence of voltage. A multimeter also will show exact voltage.

■ Using a Test Light

Checking power at a 12-volt appliance or light fixture can be easily accomplished by using a 12-volt test light (see Figure 1.1).

CAUTION: Be *certain* that you have properly differentiated between 12-volt DC and 120-volt AC appliances. Inserting the probe of a 12-volt DC test light into a 120-volt AC wall outlet can cause a dangerous electrical shock.

Most test lights consist of a plastic handle with a small bulb inside. A wire lead with an alligator clip at the end protrudes from the handle. The "business" end of the tester is a sharp probe. To test for power:

1. Touch the probe to the positive post of the battery and the alligator clip to the negative post. The bulb should illuminate, confirming that the tester is functioning.
2. Connect the alligator clip to a good ground or to the cold (negative) side of the item to be

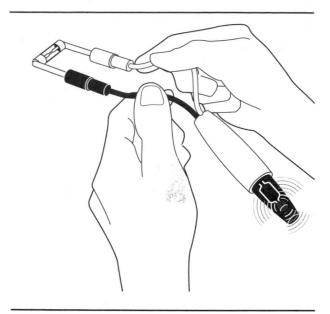

■ FIGURE 1.1 ■
Checking for voltage with a common test light

checked, for example the switch, light socket, or wire.
3. With the power on, touch the probe to the hot (positive) terminal or connection that you wish to test. When checking wiring, the probe must break the insulation.
4. If the bulb illuminates, power is confirmed.

■ Using a Multimeter

As its name suggests, a multimeter has many functions, making it one of the most versatile tools available to the do-it-yourselfer (see Figure 1.2). A multimeter can be used to check for voltage in either 120-volt AC or 12-volt DC circuits. The ability to read the exact voltage allows the owner to check battery condition, battery-charging effectiveness, and voltage available to appliances and fixtures regardless of whether the power source is a campground hookup or an onboard AC generator. Before using a multimeter, the battery inside the device should be checked (battery-check position on scale) and the meter should be zeroed according to manufacturer's instructions.

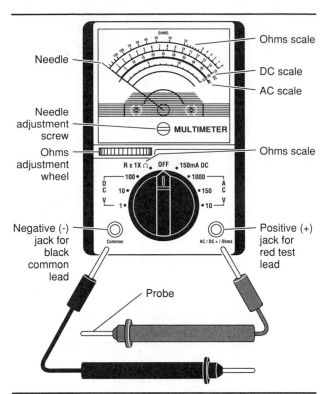

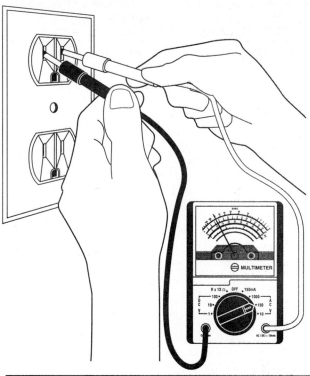

■ FIGURE 1.2 ■■■■
Typical analog multimeter has scales to read 12-volt DC, 120-volt AC, and ohms.

■ FIGURE 1.3 ■■■■
Checking 120-volt AC current with a multimeter

Checking AC Voltage

To check AC voltage, follow these steps (see Figure 1.3):

1. Connect the multimeter probes to the multimeter, as instructed by the manufacturer. Set the range selector to 150 volts AC.
2. Hook the RV electrical cord to campground power or start the generator.
3. Insert the red probe into the larger wall socket slot and the black probe into the other. Read voltage.
4. Voltage range should be between 110 and 127 with no load on the system. Voltage will rarely exceed 120 in campgrounds, but AC generators may produce upward of 130 with no load, and will drop when a load is switched into the system. If voltage falls below 100 volts AC, motor-driven appliances will be damaged, and 12-volt DC converters may cease to function. Voltage monitored at the wall sockets should be the same as that of the appliances and accessories.

Checking DC Voltage

To check DC voltage, follow these steps:

1. Connect the multimeter probes in the appropriate slots for DC power. Set the range selector to 15 DCV.
2. Touch the red probe to the positive side of the switch, accessory, or wire and the black probe to the negative side.
3. With the power on, read the voltage. Voltage will vary from near 0 (dead battery) to nearly 15 (output of a GM alternator in cold weather), depending on conditions and the type of equipment used. For example, a fully charged battery that is not connected to a load will produce voltage readings of about 12.6. Appliances will not operate properly when voltage drops to about 10.5. RV converters (battery chargers) will produce 13.8 to 14 volts and alternator output will vary from 13.5 to 15, depending on how much current the alternator is producing and the ambient temperature.

See Figure 1.4 for diagrams of typical use of a multimeter in circuit.

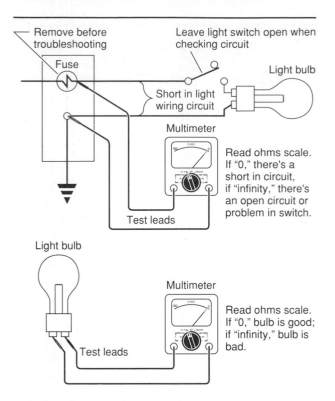

Remove before troubleshooting

Leave light switch open when checking circuit

Fuse

Short in light wiring circuit

Light bulb

Multimeter

Read ohms scale. If "0," there's a short in circuit, if "infinity," there's an open circuit or problem in switch.

Test leads

Light bulb

Multimeter

Read ohms scale. If "0," bulb is good; if "infinity," bulb is bad.

Test leads

■ **FIGURE 1.4**
Multimeters can be used for locating shorted circuits or for checking a light bulb.

Checking Continuity and Resistance with a Multimeter

The ability to check for resistance to current flow is important in diagnosing electrical problems. If the flow of current is impeded by broken, corroded, shorted, or poorly soldered or connected wires, resistance occurs. To check for resistance:

1. Connect the multimeter probes in the corresponding slots for DC/ohms. Set the range selector to R × 1K ohms.
2. Touch the probes together; the K ohms scale should read 0. Zero means that there is no resistance while holding the two probe tips together; current is moving freely (see Figure 1.5).
3. To check resistance in a wire, touch one probe to one end of the wire and the second probe to the other end. The meter should read 0. If it does not, resistance may be caused by wire damage, corrosion, or poor connections (see Figure 1.6).

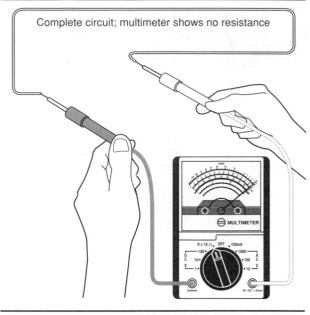

Complete circuit; multimeter shows no resistance

■ **FIGURE 1.5**
A complete circuit will show no resistance on the multimeter.

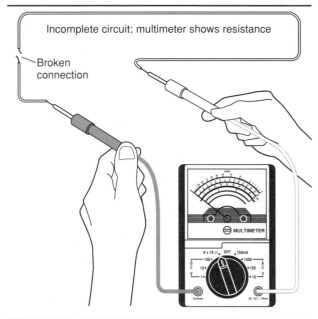

Incomplete circuit; multimeter shows resistance

Broken connection

■ **FIGURE 1.6**
Broken circuits will show resistance on the multimeter.

4. To check for resistance in a solder joint or solderless connection, touch the probes to both sides of the connection and read the scale. Zero means the connection is good; any other position of the needle means the solder joint is cold or corroded and/or the connector is bad or badly crimped.

■ **TABLE 1.1**

Amperage Load in Circuit

Gauge	1	1.5	2	3	4	5	6	7	8	10	12	15	20	24	30	36	50	100	150	200
							Allowable Conductor Length—Feet in Circuit Before 1 Volt Loss													
20	106	70	53	35	26	21	17	15	13	10	8	7	5	4	3	3	2	1	0	0
18	150	100	75	50	37	30	25	21	18	15	12	10	7	6	5	4	3	1	1	0
16	224	144	112	74	56	44	37	32	28	22	18	14	11	9	7	6	4	2	1	1
14	362	241	181	120	90	72	60	51	45	36	30	24	18	15	12	10	7	3	2	1
12	572	381	286	190	143	114	95	81	71	57	47	38	28	23	19	15	11	5	3	2
10	908	605	454	302	227	181	151	129	113	90	75	60	45	37	30	25	18	9	6	4
8	1452	967	726	483	363	290	241	207	181	145	120	96	72	60	48	40	29	14	9	7
6	2342	1560	1171	780	585	468	390	334	292	234	194	155	117	97	78	65	46	23	15	11
4	3702	2467	1851	1232	925	740	616	529	462	370	307	246	185	154	123	102	74	37	24	18
2	6060	4038	3030	2018	1515	1212	1009	866	757	606	503	403	303	252	201	168	121	60	40	30
1	7692	5126	3846	2561	1923	1538	1280	1100	961	769	638	511	384	320	256	213	153	76	51	38
0	9708	6470	4854	3232	2427	1941	1616	1388	1213	970	805	645	485	404	323	269	194	97	64	48

The above table is computed for a 68°F (20°C) ambient temperature.

5. To check for resistance in a fuse, touch the probes to the metal ends or tabs of the fuse and read the scale. The needle should point to 0. Bulbs can be checked by probing the contact(s) and case and reading the scale. The needle should point to 0.

■ Wiring

In many cases 12-volt DC appliances and accessories will suffer operational losses when improper wiring size and/or improper wiring techniques are used during installation. The heart of the RV 12-volt electrical system is primary wire, which differs from 120-volt wire because it is comprised of many smaller strands of copper wire, bundled together to form a specific gauge (size). Although primary wire generally ranges from 10- to 22-gauge (the smaller the number, the larger the wire), most RVs are wired with either 10-, 12-, or 14-gauge wire. Larger wire, such as 8-gauge, is also used in many cases, especially when connecting the battery or batteries to a fuse box or when wiring a charge line from a tow vehicle to a trailer.

To determine the proper wire size for a specific application, it is necessary to know the current or ampere requirement of the appliance or accessory and the length of wire needed for installation. Wire that is too small for the rated amperage of the appliance will cause a voltage drop (lower voltage at the terminus of the wire than at the power source), which will lead to underperformance and possible damage to the appliance. Most RV appliances and accessories will have a label that displays the rated amperage or wattage. Amperage can be determined from known wattage by using the following formula:

$$\frac{\text{watts}}{\text{volts}} = \text{amps}$$

Once amperage (power capacity) is determined, the proper wire can be selected using tables established in the *National Electrical Code Handbook* (see Table 1.1).

Caution must be exercised when using the amperage load chart because under certain circumstances the wire may be capable of handling a specified load for a specified distance but will not conform to recreational vehicle industry standards. For example, Table 1.1 shows that a 16-gauge wire can be used to operate an appliance that is within 11 feet of the power source. However, to meet RV industry standards, a 12-gauge wire must be used—based on Section 551 of the *National Electrical Code Handbook* (see Table 1.2).

■ **TABLE 1.2**

National Electrical Code Amperage

Wire Size	Amperage Rating
18	6
16	8
14	15
12	20
10	30
8	40
6	55

Source: *National Electrical Code Handbook*, (Quincy Mass.: National Fire Protection Association, 1981), 70–494.

A typical circuit in an RV consists of a wire running from the positive terminal of the battery to a fuse (or circuit breaker) and then to the appliance or accessory (see Figure 1.7). A second wire equal in size to the positive wire must then be used to ground the appliance or accessory to the negative side of the battery. In some cases the RV chassis may be used as a ground-circuit conductor. When the circuit is completed, electrons flow through wiring to the appliance and return to the battery.

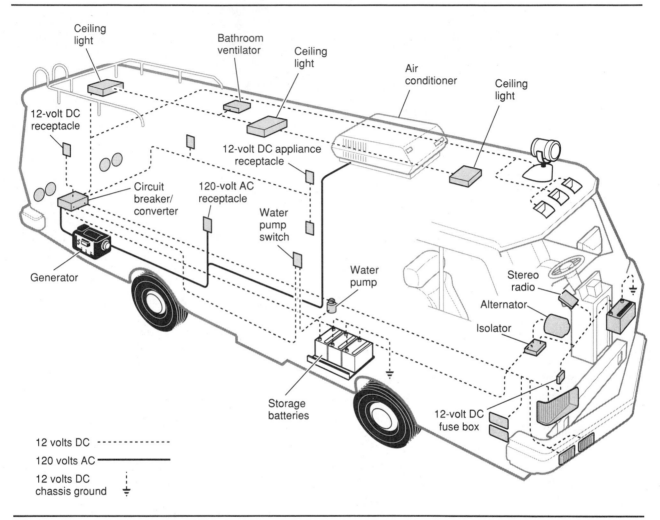

■ FIGURE 1.7 ■

A typical RV has 12-volt DC and 120-volt AC wiring circuits. The power converter and batteries supply 12-volt DC power; generator and campground hookups supply 120-volt AC power.

Although wiring is relatively easy to work with and consists of no moving parts, installation inconsistencies can cause failures. When possible, all wiring should be routed inside conduit or wiring looms. Grommets must be used where wires are routed through walls or bulkheads, although silicone sealant, if used properly (see Figures 1.8 and 1.9), works well in providing abrasion protection.

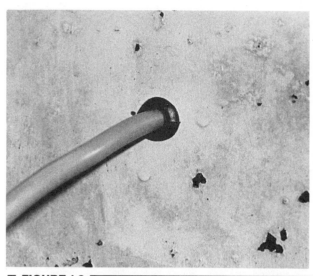

■ FIGURE 1.8 ■
A grommet should be used when routing wiring through metal surfaces.

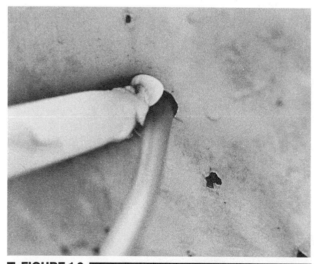

■ FIGURE 1.9 ■
Silicone can be used to protect a wire if a grommet is not available.

■ Wire Terminals

Modern wire terminals have made soldering virtually unnecessary, but improper use of these connectors can cause a number of problems. The electrical industry has established standards for wire terminals and uses the following color coding: red terminals can be used on 22- to 18-gauge wire, blue represents 16- to 14-gauge, and yellow is for 12- to 10-gauge. There are a number of terminals available for almost any wiring job. The most common are *ring spade, tongue spade, butt splice*, and *faston* terminals (see Figure 1.10).

Terminals are made up of three or four parts, depending on the type and quality: *wire barrel, tongue, insulation*, and *strain-relief sleeve*. When crimping a terminal, the wire barrel tends to spread at the seam, so it's best to look for a terminal in which the seam is brazed shut or one that is seamless. This allows the seam to remain closed so that a second crimp can be made for strain relief.

Automotive terminals have either nylon or polyvinyl chloride (PVC) insulation. Nylon is easier to work with and allows a visual inspection of the crimp, but PVC is less susceptible to cuts and moisture. Nylon may be necessary when using the terminals in an environment where certain chemicals are present. Moisture can be sealed out of a terminal by using a small length of shrink tubing over a portion of the wire and terminal. Some terminals have shrink tubing built into the insulation, which is doubly advantageous, although these connectors are more expensive.

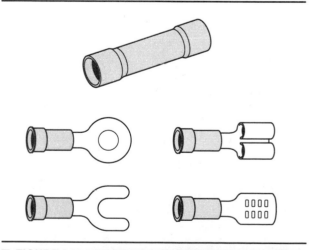

■ FIGURE 1.10 ■
Common solderless terminals include butt splice, ring spade, tongue spade, and faston connectors.

How to Crimp a Terminal

Although solderless terminals offer superior connections, they are useless if the crimp is poorly executed. Terminals should not be installed with pliers, vise-grips, or a rock. A proper crimping tool is required, preferably one that is made by the terminal manufacturer. If the tool punctures the insulation during the crimping procedure, the terminal should be discarded. Once the proper connector and wire have been matched, the following procedure should be used:

1. Strip the wire so that the bare wire will protrude $\frac{1}{32}$ to $\frac{1}{16}$ inch past the wire barrel of the terminal. Some tools have indicators inscribed into the tool (see Figure 1.11).
2. Place the terminal into the tool in the correct die according to wire size. Apply gentle pressure to hold the terminal in place.
3. Place the wire into the terminal (see Figure 1.12).
4. Close the tool completely. Some tools have two points that must be touched, indicating a proper crimp.
5. Move the tool to the strain-relief sleeve (if supplied on terminal) and close the tool completely (see Figure 1.13).
6. If using terminals with heat-shrink tubing (Figure 1.14), apply propane torch, match, or electric heat source after crimping. Stop heating when sealant inside the tubing begins to ooze out of the terminal insulation (see Figure 1.15).

■ **FIGURE 1.11**
Typical crimping tools have inscribed indicators to assist the user.

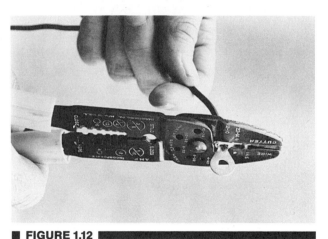

■ **FIGURE 1.12**
Terminals are placed in corresponding slots for crimping.

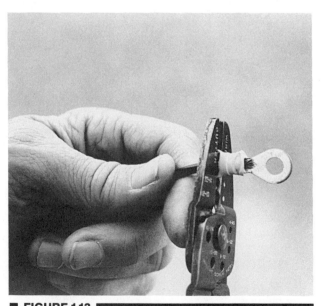

■ **FIGURE 1.13**
It's important to crimp the strain-relief portion of the terminal.

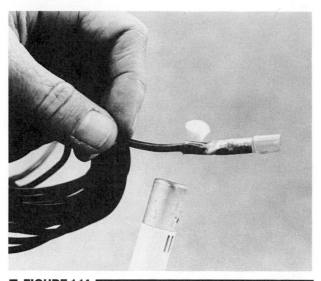

■ FIGURE 1.14 ▬▬▬▬▬▬
Terminals with heat shrink built in must be heated to complete the seal.

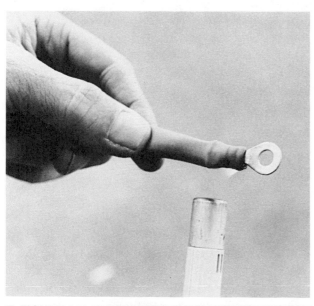

■ FIGURE 1.15 ▬▬▬▬▬▬
Shrink tubing can be used over any terminal to protect against moisture and corrosion.

Batteries

Recreational vehicles are equipped with two types of wet-cell batteries: *engine starting* and *deep cycle*. The starting battery employed by either the tow vehicle or motorhome engine is designed to provide high-amperage discharges for short periods, as required by the starter motor. Deep-cycle batteries are designed for low-amperage discharges to operate accessories such as furnaces, lights, and entertainment systems. Plates in deep-cycle batteries are constructed of higher-density lead, which allows frequent deep discharges without the accelerated shedding of material from the plates that occurs when starting batteries are subjected to this type of use. Starting batteries will fail rapidly if repeatedly discharged heavily.

■ Battery Ratings

Reserve capacity is the amount of time the battery can sustain a discharge at a specified level. Different levels are used to rate different batteries. For example, the level for deep-cycle golf-cart batteries is 75 amperes. Battery reserve capacity is stated in two ways. A battery rating stated in minutes means that the battery will sustain a 25-ampere load for the given number of minutes before voltage drops to 10.5 (12-volt battery). For example, the common Group 27 RV deep-cycle battery may be rated at 160 minutes. This same battery also may carry the old-style ampere-hour rating—in this case 105 ampere-hours. The amp-hour rating is a measure of reserve capacity and only approximately 60 percent of that capacity is usable.

■ How Batteries Work

Lead-acid or *wet-cell* batteries are constructed of plates made of lead oxide, sulfuric acid, water, and fibers bonded together into a paste. One plate is positive and the other is negative. Inside the case is electrolyte, a mixture of sulfuric acid and water. As the battery delivers power (discharging), the acid in the electrolyte enters the positive and negative plates. The electrolyte becomes weaker as the acid is depleted until the battery cannot deliver power at a useful voltage. By reversing the current flow (charging), the sulfuric acid is returned to the electrolyte from the plates (see Figure 1.16).

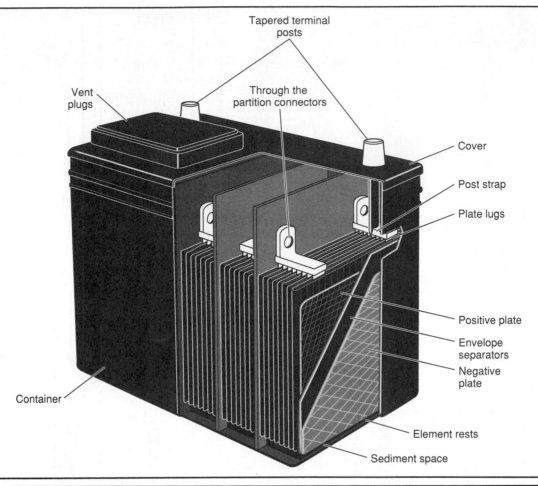

■ FIGURE 1.16 ■■■■■■■■

Components of a lead-acid, wet-cell battery used in RVs

Electrolyte management (maintaining proper water levels), combined with proper charging techniques and intervals, can make the difference in performance and battery longevity. Maintenance-free and sealed batteries do not require water replenishment.

■ Testing the Battery

The three methods for testing a battery are: checking electrolyte with a hydrometer, voltage measurement, and load testing. A *hydrometer* measures the battery's state of charge by comparing the weight of the electrolyte to the weight of water (specific gravity). Because temperature affects specific gravity, a temperature-correcting hydrometer must be used. An adjustable *battery condition/load tester* takes all the guesswork out of checking a maintenance-free battery. Load testers are usually only available at repair facilities, but maintenance-free battery condition can be determined by reading open-circuit voltage and comparing it to a table (see Table 1.3).

■ TABLE 1.3 ■■■■■■■■

Open-Circuit Voltage

Volts	State of Charge (%)
12.6 or higher	100
12.4	75
12.2	50
12.0	25
11.7	0

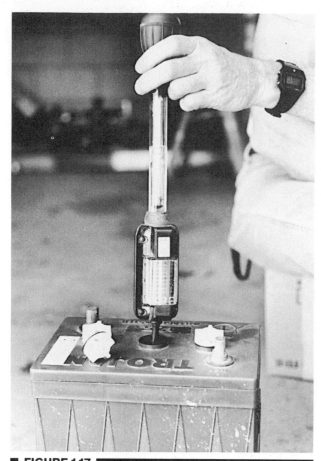

■ **FIGURE 1.17** ■
Checking battery specific gravity with a hydrometer

Using a Hydrometer

To check a battery using a hydrometer, follow these steps (see Figure 1.17):

1. Remove battery caps.
2. Insert syringe into cell and extract electrolyte.
3. Hold at eye level and read specific gravity (see Table 1.4).
4. Return electrolyte to cell.

CAUTION: Battery acid is corrosive and can damage painted surfaces, metal parts, clothing, skin, or eyes. If spilled, use baking soda and water to neutralize the acid. Flush immediately and seek medical attention if acid is accidentally spilled on skin or squirted in eyes.

■ **TABLE 1.4** ■
Specific Gravity Values

Charge Level (%)	Specific Gravity
100	1.265
75	1.225
50	1.190
25	1.155
Discharged	1.120

Open-Circuit Voltage Test

To check a battery's open-circuit voltage, follow these steps:

1. Perform test only if battery has not been charged within the previous 8 to 10 hours (so surface charge will dissipate).
2. Remove negative battery cable (to make sure no load is on the battery).
3. Read voltage with accurate voltmeter.
4. Reconnect battery cable.

Battery state of charge can be determined by comparing voltage to the percentage of charge listed in the open-circuit voltage chart (see Table 1.3). For example, if the voltage read at the voltmeter is 12.6 volts or higher, the battery is fully charged. A battery is completely discharged at 11.7 volts.

■ Charging the Battery

Recreational vehicle batteries are most commonly charged by the vehicle's engine alternator. The alternator will do a good job of charging both the starting and house battery(s) provided it is rated high enough to supply the demands of appliances and accessories being operated while driving and still have a surplus for battery charging. All batteries should be returned to a full state of charge before storing the RV. Extended driving with an alternator that is producing voltage levels of 14 to 15 (depending on temperature) will usually bring a battery to a full state of charge. Batteries that become depleted can be restored to a full state of charge by using a portable charging unit found in many auto parts stores. Most portable units are designed to taper the charge as battery condition improves, but the use of a nonautomatic charger with a constant, small amperage output (about 5 percent of the battery's rated amp-hour capacity) also is effective (see Table 1.5).

■ **TABLE 1.5** ▬▬▬▬▬▬▬

**Battery-Charging Guide
for Fixed-Rate External Chargers**

Rated Reserve Capacity* (in Minutes)	Slow Charge	Fast Charge
80 or less	10 hrs. at 5 amps 5 hrs. at 10 amps	2.5 hrs. at 20 amps 1.5 hrs. at 30 amps
80 to 125	15 hrs. at 5 amps 7.5 hrs. at 10 amps	3.75 hrs. at 20 amps 1.5 hrs. at 50 amps
125 to 170	20 hrs. at 5 amps 10 hrs. at 10 amps	5 hrs. at 20 amps 2 hrs. at 50 amps
170 to 250	30 hrs. at 5 amps 15 hrs. at 10 amps	7.5 hrs. at 20 amps 3 hrs. at 50 amps
Over 250	24 hrs. at 10 amps	6 hrs. at 40 amps 4 hrs. at 60 amps

Note: These charging rates and times are guidelines and should only be used if battery manufacturer's recommendations are not available.
*indicates the number of minutes the battery will sustain a 25-ampere load before voltage falls to 10.5 (12-volt battery).

CAUTION: Careful attention must be paid to prescribed limits of charging time when using a non-automatic charger. Substantial overcharging can cause case meltdown or serious gassing, (release of hydrogen and oxygen), which can cause an explosion.

■ Overcharged Batteries

Overcharging is a common reason for premature battery failure. A faulty voltage regulator is usually the culprit. Designed to limit the output voltage of the alternator, it turns the field current on and off so that constant voltage is attained. A voltage regulator can either be an internal part of the alternator or an external piece of equipment.

Electrical converters built into RVs also can cause overcharging over long periods by providing voltage levels that are high enough to cause continual battery gassing. Voltage of the converter should not be higher than 13.8 for long-term use with conventional open-cell batteries. It can be about 14 volts when maintenance-free or sealed batteries are being used. Voltage output of battery chargers intended for short-term use may be slightly higher.

■ Undercharged Batteries

Undercharging is the most common cause of battery failure. The voltage regulator or a slipping fan belt can be the reason. Fan belts should be tightened to allow for about 1 inch of deflection at the center. Belts should be free from cracks, brittleness, and glazing. It's important to check belts periodically and replace them at the first sign of weakening. During cold weather, batteries will not accept a charge as easily. If the vehicle is used for short trips during winter, the battery may never gain the necessary charge to be effective.

■ Sulfated Batteries

Batteries become sulfated when allowed to remain in a discharged state for too long. Lead sulfate forms on negative plates during the normal process of battery discharge. Problems occur only when the sulfate remains on the plates too long and hardens; this begins within a month if the battery is left in a discharged state. The hard coating acts like varnish, restricting the electrolyte's ability to penetrate the plates. Battery capacity is reduced as sulfation increases. Moderate sulfation may be broken by slow-charging the battery for 24 hours at a 6- to 8-ampere rate. This is not effective, though, in severe cases. Once a battery becomes badly sulfated, it should be discarded.

Analysis of voltage output can be helpful in diagnosing problems with insufficient battery-reserve power. Voltage can be checked at the batteries, while the engine is running, to determine the proper output of the alternator. Using a multimeter, check voltage of each battery; the voltage with the engine running should be between 14 to 14.8. Voltage checks should not be performed when the battery is in a low state of charge.

■ Installing a Battery

To install a battery, follow these steps:

1. Make sure battery is filled with the proper amount of electrolyte (if not a maintenance-free type). Never add electrolyte after the first filling; add only distilled water.
2. Clean terminal posts with a wire brush until the metal shines.

3. Turn off all power draw, including lights and accessories. If the negative cable sparks during removal, a draw is still present.
4. Notice position of battery in tray in relation to polarity.
5. Disconnect cables, negative first, and remove old battery.
6. Make sure carrier and hold-down hardware are free of corrosion.
7. Check terminals and cables.
8. Install terminals, observing polarity.
9. Install hold-down hardware. **Note:** Vibration can destroy batteries so make sure battery is secure.
10. Observe polarity before starting engine or activating battery switch in motorhomes or trailers. Reverse polarity can damage the battery, electrical system, alternator, and voltage regulator.

Be sure to properly discard old batteries. Most service stations and auto parts stores will take the battery in trade, or require its return in lieu of a core charge.

◼ Hooking up Multiple Batteries

Parallel hookup is the common wiring method when more than one 12-volt battery is used to operate appliances and accessories in a motorhome or trailer. This is accomplished when the two positive posts are connected to each other, and the two negative posts are also connected. The load is connected to either battery. The number of batteries is usually dependent on electrical needs, recharging capability, and available space. Batteries connected in parallel should be the same brand and type to minimize the interaction that reduces long-term capacity (see Figure 1.18).

Series connection of batteries produces higher voltage. For example, two 6-volt batteries wired in series produce 12-volt output. In a series hookup, the negative cable from one battery is attached to the positive cable of the other. The remaining two posts are connected to the load (see Figure 1.18). A common practice is to connect two 6-volt golf-cart (electric-vehicle) batteries in series. Electric-vehicle batteries usually have high reserve capacity ratings and can withstand deeper discharges over a longer period of time.

◼ Battery Cables

The selection of battery cables is determined by the size of the battery and the proper routing length (see Table 1.6). Battery cables are available as custom or ready-made assemblies. Caution must be exercised when choosing a ready-made cable because a thick insulation may be concealing a much smaller gauge wire. For example, many booster cable sets are only 8-gauge wire even though the insulation appears as thick as a battery cable used in engine compartments.

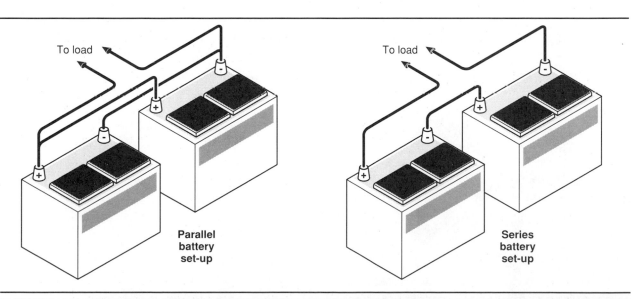

◼ **FIGURE 1.18**
Twelve-volt batteries are wired in parallel and 6-volt batteries are wired in series in RVs.

■ TABLE 1.6 ■

Recommended Wire and Cable Sizes for Charging Systems

| Alternator Output Maximum Amperes | | | | | | Wire Size (AWG) |
To 40	40–60	60–80	80–100	100–130	130–160	
Maximum Distance Alternator to Battery						
5						14
7	5					12
12	8	6				10
18	12	9	8			8
30	20	15	12	9		6
45	30	23	19	14	12	4
	50	38	30	24	20	2
		50	40	30	25	1
			48	38	30	0

Cables can be custom made one of three ways: using bolt-on terminals, soldering, or crimping. Bolt-on terminals should be avoided except for emergency situations because they cannot be properly attached or sealed to prevent corrosion. Corrosion that starts in a terminal can travel, in time, the entire length of the cable. Soldering works well, but the integrity of the connection is only as good as the mechanic; a cold solder joint can cause resistance, which leads to voltage loss. Crimping usually can only be performed by a qualified mechanic because the tools required to attach solderless terminals to a battery cable cost hundreds of dollars and are not likely to be part of an owner's toolbox (see Figure 1.19). Custom cables should be finished with approximately 1½ inches of sealant-filled shrink tubing to protect the cable ends from moisture and corrosion (Figure 1.20).

■ **FIGURE 1.19** ■
Special crimpers are used to connect a battery terminal to the appropriate cable.

■ **FIGURE 1.20** ■
Shrink tubing is used to seal the connection of the battery terminal to the cable.

Care of Cables and Terminals

Cables are the main links to the battery. If a terminal is loose, dirty, or broken, power can be disrupted or become erratic. Periodic inspection should include the following:

☑ CHECKLIST ■

- ☐ Check cables for breaks, corrosion, or stripped insulation.
- ☐ Check terminals for tightness.
- ☐ Make sure terminals are securely fitted to cable.
- ☐ Remove terminals, negative first, and clean with solution of baking soda and water.
- ☐ Clean terminal posts with baking soda and water.
- ☐ Replace all suspect cables and terminals.
- ☐ Apply thin layer of petroleum jelly or commercial protectant to posts; connect terminals, observing polarity.

■ Using Jumper Cables

Although the practice of using a booster battery from one vehicle to start the engine of a second vehicle with a dead battery seems elementary, many people are injured by not following safe procedures (see Figure 1.21).

1. Make sure terminals on both batteries are tight.
2. Turn off ignition keys and place gear selector in Park, or manual shifter in Neutral.

TROUBLESHOOTING the Battery

Problem	Possible Cause	Correction
Excessive use of water, lead deposits on caps, excessive case heat, warped or broken plates, active material shedding, damaged separators	Overcharging	Check regulator. Check converter. Replace battery.
	Excessive vibration	Repair hold-down.
Not holding a charge	Undercharging	Check regulator. Check converter.
	Loose fan belt	Tighten fan belt.
	Sulfation	Perform slow charge.
	Bad battery	Replace battery.
	Low electrolyte	Replenish.
Won't start engine	Low voltage	Recharge battery. Load-test.
	Low electrolyte	Replenish.
	Loose cable terminal	Tighten terminals.
	Bad cable terminal	Replace terminal.
	Corroded terminals	Clean corrosion.
	Worn or broken cables	Replace cable(s).
	Cold/hot weather	Use larger battery.
Will not operate appliances and accessories	Low voltage	Recharge battery. Load-test.
	Low electrolyte	Replenish.
	Loose cable terminal	Tighten terminals.
	Bad cable terminal	Replace terminal.
	Corroded terminals	Remove corrosion.
	Break in wiring	Check wiring.
	Bad battery	Replace battery.
	No power	Check battery. Clean terminals. Check wiring. Check fuse box.
	Low output from alternator or converter	Check charging sources.

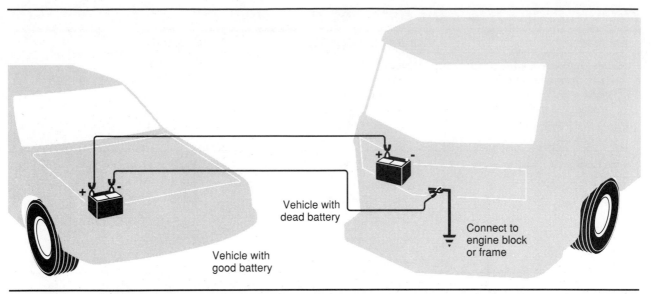

■ **FIGURE 1.21** ■
Jump-starting a vehicle with a dead battery requires a safe hookup to avoid the possibility of explosion.

3. Attach the end of one cable to the positive terminal on the discharged battery.

4. Attach the other end of the first cable to the positive post on the booster battery.

5. Attach one end of the second cable to the negative terminal on the booster battery.

6. Attach the other end of the second cable to a good ground source such as the engine block or frame. Do not connect to the negative terminal of the discharged battery.

7. Attempt to start the stalled car's engine. If it does not turn over, start the booster-battery engine and hold at a fast idle for a few minutes, or until the stalled engine starts.

8. Once started, disconnect cables in *exact* reverse order as above.

Battery Isolators

Recreational vehicles usually have at least two batteries, one for starting the motorhome or tow vehicle engine and one (or more) for operating the 12-volt house systems. An *isolator* is used to separate the batteries, allowing only the house battery to be discharged when the engine is not running (see Figure 1.22). Separating the batteries is called *isolation* and is achieved by using one of two types of equipment: a solid-state isolator or an electrically activated mechanical solenoid switch.

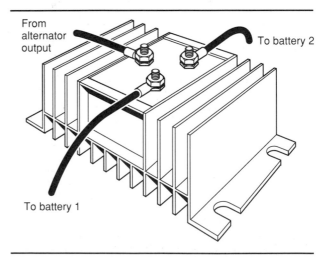

■ **FIGURE 1.22** ■
Wiring hookup for a multi-battery, solid-state isolator

TROUBLESHOOTING *the Multiple-Battery Isolator*

Problem	Possible Cause	Correction
Battery boils or overcharges	Shorted diode	Replace isolator.
All batteries go dead	Defective solenoid contacts	Replace solenoid.
	Open diode	Replace isolator.
One battery not charging	Open diode	Replace isolator.
Low battery voltage	Defective diode	Replace isolator.

■ How Isolators Work

The simplest and least durable method of isolating a battery is with a solenoid switch (see Figure 1.23). These switches have three terminals, one for each battery and one for connection to an ignition-switched 12-volt source. When the power flows to the switch terminal on the solenoid (by turning the ignition switch to the "on" or "start" position), the solenoid connects the batteries in parallel. When the switch terminal is deactivated, the batteries are separated and only the auxiliary battery can be discharged by RV appliances. There is an inherent disadvantage with the solenoid switch: If the switch contacts become damaged and are locked together, the owner may assume that the batteries are separated, when, in fact, they are not, causing a dead starting battery. During extended use, contact points of the switch typically become pitted, causing voltage drop (loss of potential to transmit current) and reducing the ability of the alternator to charge the house batteries.

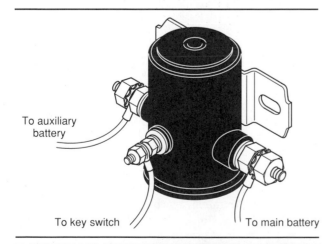

To auxiliary battery

To key switch   To main battery

■ **FIGURE 1.23** ■
Wiring hookup for a dual-battery, mechanical solenoid

■ Solid-State Isolators

Solid-state isolators separate two or more batteries using diodes that are one-way check valves. Each battery receives current from the alternator, but the batteries are never connected in parallel. When the auxiliary battery is being discharged, a diode keeps the starting battery from being discharged as well. Current can only flow from the alternator. When the engine is started, the isolator controls current flow to both batteries, charging each as its needs dictate. The solid-state isolator allows effective, independent charging of batteries by the same alternator.

Typically a diode will cause a voltage drop of about 0.5 volt, but the device triggers higher output from the alternator to compensate. Thus, voltage available to the house batteries is not reduced, compared to a direct hookup that does not utilize diodes.

■ Installing a Multiple-Battery Isolator

To install a multiple-battery isolator, follow these steps (see Figures 1.24 and 1.25).

1. Remove negative terminals from all batteries.
2. Mount isolator in convenient location away from exhaust manifolds or other sources of high heat.
3. Locate the BAT terminal on the alternator (usually the largest wire), remove it, and attach to terminal 1 on the isolator (see Table 1.7 for proper wire sizes).
4. Crimp terminals on appropriate length of wire to reach from isolator to alternator. Attach one end of wire to terminal A on isolator and the

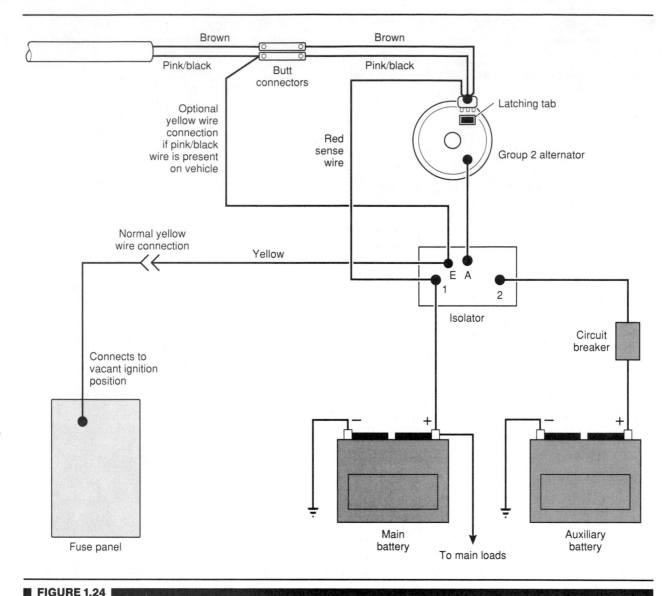

Wiring diagram for installing a multi-battery isolator in vehicles with Group 2 alternators

other to the BAT terminal on the alternator. For engines with Delcotron CS Series Type 100 alternators follow step 5. For engines manufactured in 1985 and later follow step 6. For all others jump to step 7.

5. Delcotron CS Series Type 100 alternators require an external exciter that is wired from a separate terminal on the isolator, usually marked ''E.'' Locate a source of 12-volt power controlled by the ignition switch; if a pink/black wire is present on the alternator, it may

be used for such a source. Connect a wire from the 12-volt source or the pink/black wire to the E terminal on the isolator. Be sure *not* to use the accessory position of the ignition switch as a source of 12-volt power. The use of a kit such as Sure Power's Model K0144 is necessary to connect the sense wire to the alternator. Proceed to step 7.

6. Certain late-model Ford alternators do not have a BAT terminal, but instead have a plug-in terminal (see Figure 1.26). To wire the isolator,

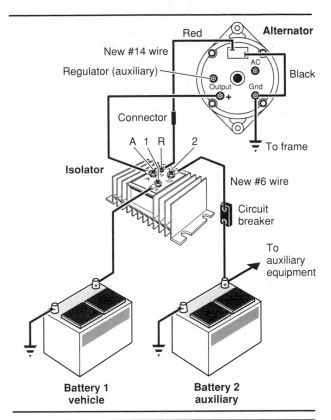

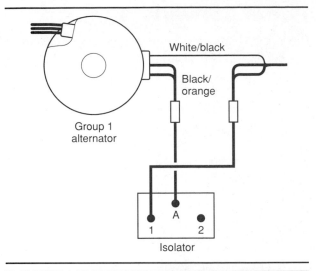

■ **FIGURE 1.25**

Wiring diagram for installing a multi-battery isolator in vehicles with Group 3 alternators

■ **FIGURE 1.26**

Wiring diagram for installing a multi-battery isolator in Ford vehicles using alternators with plug-in connections

first disconnect the battery. Locate the connector on the alternator with one light wire and two heavy black wires. Cut the black/orange wires, leaving approximately 2 inches to allow for a butt connector.

CAUTION: Damage may occur if wire is cut beyond cabling. Attach a wire to both cut wires from the alternator (use butt connector) and connect the other end to the A terminal on the

isolator. Attach a wire to both cut wires leading from the harness and connect the other end to terminal 1 on the isolator. Proceed to step 7.

7. Attach a length of wire to terminal 2 on the isolator and to one terminal on an appropriately sized circuit breaker (see Table 1.8). Attach one end of a length of wire long enough to reach from the isolator to the auxiliary battery to the unattached terminal of the circuit breaker and the other to the positive terminal of the battery.

8. Repeat step 5 for each additional battery when using three- and four-battery isolators.

9. Reconnect negative terminals on all batteries.

■ **TABLE 1.7**

Determining Proper Wire Size

Alternator Rating	Wire Gauge				
	10 ft.	11–15 ft.	15–20 ft.	20–25 ft.	25–30 ft.
Up to 70 amp	10	8	8	6	6
70 to 95	8	8	6	6	4
95 to 120	6	6	4	2	1
120 to 160	4	4	2	2	0

■ **TABLE 1.8**

Circuit Breakers for Charging Systems

Alternator Rating	Expected Load	Recommended Breaker
Up to 90 amps	40 amps	50-amp
Up to 120 amps	70 amps	80-amp
Up to 150 amps	110 amps	120-amp
Up to 200 amps	140 amps	150-amp

Power Converters

Modern recreational vehicle appliances and accessories operate on two electrical systems: 12-volt DC and 120-volt AC power. In order to avoid duplication of fixtures and some appliances, a power converter is used to transform 120-volt AC power to 12-volt DC power when the RV is plugged into a campground receptacle or when connected to the output of an AC generator. The converter supplies 12-volt DC power to items such as interior lights, fans, and the water pump, while the 120-volt AC input to the RV provides household current to the wall outlets, air-conditioner, refrigerator, etc. The converter also charges the batteries, although the amperage output often is too low to be effective for short-term charging. Converters may also incorporate 120-volt AC circuit breakers and a 12-volt DC fuse panel.

CAUTION: Internal converter repairs should be left to a qualified service technician.

There are two types of power converters: *switching* and *battery floater*. The switching-type converter uses automatic relays and separate output circuits to provide 12-volt power for appliances and to charge the batteries (see Figure 1.27). The switching converter has a specifically rated battery-charge capability and a separately rated output for appliances. This type of converter can only deliver a specified charging output regardless of battery condition and charging needs.

A battery-floater converter usually has a higher rating and has only one output circuit (see Figure 1.28). All this output is directed to the battery. The amount of power required by appliances is subtracted from the output available for battery charging. Thus when demands of appliances are low, the battery charge capability is high, and vice versa. The charging circuit will automatically taper off as the battery becomes closer to a full state of charge.

Low-voltage output can be checked using a multimeter set to the DC voltage function. When the battery

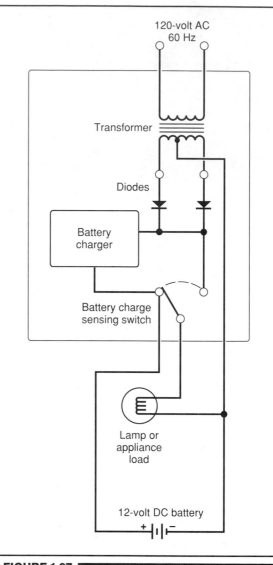

■ FIGURE 1.27 ■
Switching-type power converter with automatic relays

is at full charge, the output of the converter should be 13.8 to 14 volts. If lower voltage is detected, the manufacturer may be able to make necessary adjustments. The converter should be checked for signs of corrosion, and its mounting location should be kept free from stored supplies, especially flammables. Converters create heat and require adequate ventilation.

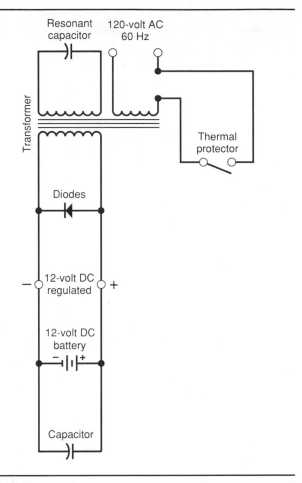

■ **FIGURE 1.28** ■
Battery-floater power converter

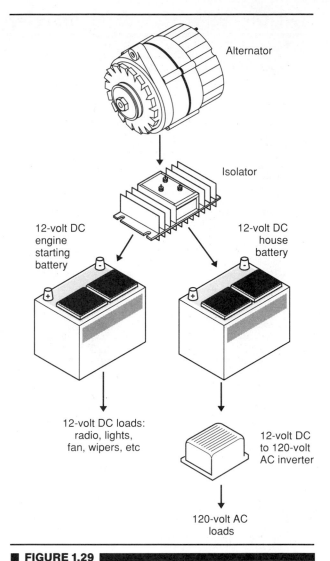

■ **FIGURE 1.29** ■
Inverters transform 12-volt DC power to 120-volt AC power

Inverters

Inverters transform 12-volt DC power into regular (120-volt AC) household current (see Figure 1.29). Inverters allow use of 120-volt AC convenience items without the need to operate an AC generator or to connect to campground power. The most common use of an inverter is to power color television sets, stereos, food processors, microwave ovens, and computers, with only a specific number of appliances used at one time, depending on the inverter's output rating and the amount of power required by the appliance. Teamed up with good deep-cycle batteries and an adequate charging system, an inverter provides continuous noise-free power. Inverters pull a great amount of energy from a battery, so judicious use is required.

To determine the size inverter for your particular needs, you first must list the continuous power ratings in watts of all the appliances you intend to operate (see Table 1.9 for appliance and accessory ratings). Unless you plan on operating more than one appliance at a time, the inverter's size can be dictated by the appliance with the highest draw. When using multiple appliances, the wattage ratings must be totaled to determine the minimum inverter rating. Wattage can also be determined by multiplying the amperage times the voltage. For example, if a 120-volt AC color television is rated at 1 ampere, the continuous wattage rating is 120.

TROUBLESHOOTING *the Inverter*

Problem	Possible Cause	Correction
No DC power at appliances	Blown fuse	Replace fuse.
	Bad battery cable	Replace cable.
	Discharged battery	Charge battery.
	Tripped load protector	Reset load protector.
Load protector continues to trip	Appliance overload	Reduce appliance load.

Note: Inverters should be repaired internally only by qualified service technicians. If repairs are needed, seek help from an appropriate repair facility.

CAUTION: When connecting the battery to the inverter, it is important to pay close attention to polarity. Some inverters do not have polarity protection and if the terminals are miswired, the inverter can be damaged.

■ **TABLE 1.9** ■

Continuous Power Consumption for Typical 120-Volt AC Appliances

Appliance	Wattage
Blender	1000
Coffee maker	1380
Computer	60–100
Drill motor, ⅜-inch	360
Electric blanket	120
Freezer	500
Hair dryers	1500
Ice maker	600–700
Microwave oven	800–1500
Popcorn popper, hot-air	1400
Refrigerator	600
Satellite dish	200–250
Soldering iron	40
Stereo	200
Television, 9-inch color	480
Toaster	1800
Trash compactor	800–1000
VCR	20
Washing machine	600

When calculating the proper size inverter, surge ratings must be considered. Surge power is the additional wattage required to start the appliance; appliances with motors usually need much more power to start than to operate continuously. Surge-power ratings may be available from the manufacturer of the appliance. A good rule of thumb is to allow two times the rating for televisions, blenders, microwaves, entertainment systems, and drill motors, and four times the continuous rating for large appliances such as air compressors, freezers, washing machines, trash compactors, and refrigerators.

Solar Power

Solar power is the production of electricity when sunlight strikes a photovoltaic module, which is made up of a series of solar cells that respond to sunlight by creating electrical current (see Figure 1.30). The current can charge batteries used to operate a variety of appliances.

Higher current is produced as the intensity of light increases. Available sunlight and environmental conditions affect photovoltaic module performance. For instance, an Arco Solar M61 photovoltaic module will generate 11.64 ampere-hours per day in Albuquerque, New Mexico, and only 4.76 ampere-hours per day in Pittsburgh, Pennsylvania.

By including an inverter in the system, a wide variety of appliances and systems can be operated without a 120-volt AC land line or use of an AC generator.

■ Determining Solar Power Requirements

The number of modules (panels) needed depends on individual situations. Power consumption must be calculated by determining the number of hours each appliance will be operated and the total amperage required (see Table 1.10). Multiply the consumption rate of the individual appliance by the hours per day it will most likely be operated to arrive at the total ampere-hours per day. Total the ampere-hours per day and divide that figure by the average output of module(s) in your area (see Table 1.11). You can then determine how many modules will be needed to meet your individual demands.

Since photovoltaic modules do not store energy, batteries are integral in any solar system. Good battery-reserve capacity is the key to utilizing a solar system. A large deep-cycle 12-volt battery will suffice in some cases, while several batteries may be needed in others.

The number of cells in each photovoltaic module determines its voltage output. Modules that produce

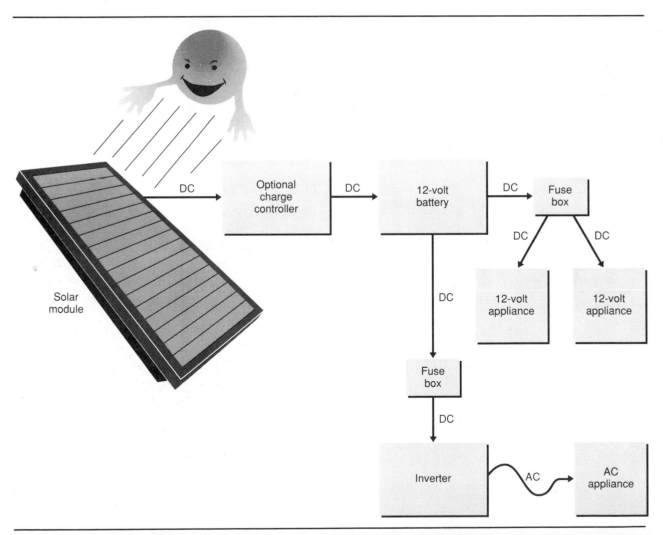

■ FIGURE 1.30 ■
Solar-power modules wired into the 12-volt DC circuit of an RV can be used to charge batteries and operate appliances.

■ **TABLE 1.10**

Approximate Average Power Consumption of Widely Available 12-Volt DC Appliances

Description	Amps
Lighting	
15-watt fluorescent light	1.0
16-watt slimline fluorescent light	1.2
Dual 8-watt fluorescent tubes	1.2
20-watt standard fluorescent light	1.5
30-watt slimline fluorescent light	2.0
Kitchen	
Coffee percolator	11.5
Toaster	15.0
Slow cooker	20.0
Range hood, fan and light	5.0
Vent fan	2.5
Refrigerator	5.0
Household	
Travel iron	10.0
Electronic bug killer	2.5
Electric razor	1.3
Vacuum cleaner, hand portable	5.0
Electric toothbrush	1.0
Tools	
Winches (for light use)	10.0–100.0
Air compressor	3.5–9.0
Chain saw, 14″ blade	100.0
Drill	12.0–15.0
Communications	
TV, B&W, 12″	1.4
TV, color, 9″	4.0
CB radio	0.5
Digital clock	0.1
Tape recorder	0.5
Amplifier (30 watt)	2.0
DC turntable	0.5

Formula to Compute Amp-Hours	
Light	1.5 amps × 6 hours = 9.0 amp-hrs
Coffee maker	11.5 amps × 1 hour = 11.5 amp-hrs
TV	1.4 amps × 3 hours = 4.2 amp-hrs
Total (of this example)	24.7 amp-hrs

higher voltage at no load require the use of a voltage regulator to prevent battery overcharging; this type is suitable for RV use. Self-regulating panels will not produce enough voltage to overcharge a battery. While this enables the panel to function without a regulator, it is less efficient in reduced solar-light conditions. For optimum effectiveness, photovoltaic systems should include one battery for each module.

■ Wiring a Photovoltaic System

Although photovoltaic modules can be wired in series to produce 24 or 36 volts, they are wired for 12-volt service in RVs. A typical one-module system will require one battery of at least 105 ampere-hour rating, a fuse or circuit breaker, and a length of wire (see Figure 1.31a). The panels are wired by routing lengths of wire from the positive and negative terminals of the module to the corresponding terminals of the battery, which is connected to the load. The positive lead is routed from the module through a fuse or circuit breaker, then to the battery. A second module (or more modules) can be wired in parallel (see Figure 1.31b). Although the charts may show that smaller wire can be used, it is best to use at least 10-gauge wire throughout any photovoltaic system. The wire length should kept as short as possible.

■ Module Location

Photovoltaic modules work best when faced directly at the sun. It's impractical to use a tracking system in RVs, so the modules usually are mounted flat on the roof. This somewhat restricts their output—which makes proper load management necessary. The use of a good ampere meter will allow you to monitor the electricity production rate and allow you to alter appliance usage, depending upon the solar conditions each day.

If you are parked for an extended period of time, try to position your RV so that the modules face south, the recommended position for the northern hemisphere.

■ **TABLE 1.11** ■
Solar Performance Table

Lat.	Location	Amp-Hrs.*	Tilt Angle	Lat.	Location	Amp-Hrs.*	Tilt Angle
32N	AL, Montgomery	7.55	55S	39N	MO, St. Louis	7.11	60S
61N	AK, Bethel	6.41	60S	47N	MT, Great Falls	7.85	70S
65N	AK, Fairbanks	5.19	90S	41N	NM, N. Omaha	8.09	60S
62N	AK, Matanuska	5.60	75S	36N	NV, Las Vegas	10.89	45S
33N	AZ, Phoenix	10.50	45S	40N	NJ, Seabrook	6.55	65S
35N	AR, Little Rock	7.29	60S	35N	NM, Albuquerque	11.64	40S
39N	CA, Davis	8.27	60S	41N	NY, New York City	6.26	65S
37N	CA, Fresno	8.42	60S	39N	NC, Ely	10.81	50S
34N	CA, Los Angeles	9.57	50S	36N	NC, Greensboro	7.43	60S
34N	CA, Riverside	10.28	45S	47N	ND, Bismarck	8.51	65S
40N	CO, Boulder	8.40	50S	41N	OH, Cleveland	6.08	65S
40N	CO, Granby	10.27	40S	35N	OK, Oklahoma City	9.21	50S
39N	D.C., Washington	6.74	60S	42N	OR, Medford	7.20	65S
30N	FL, Gainesville	8.72	45S	40N	PA, Pittsburgh	4.76	65S
26N	FL, Miami	9.25	30S	41N	RI, Newport	6.68	65S
34N	GA, Atlanta	7.80	55S	33N	SC, Charleston	7.95	55S
21N	HI, Honolulu	9.74	35S	44N	SD, Rapid City	9.39	55S
44N	ID, Boise	8.17	65S	36N	TN, Nashville	6.85	60S
42N	IL, Chicago	4.57	65S	32N	TX, Big Spring	9.20	45S
40N	IN, Indianapolis	6.46	65S	33N	TX, Fort Worth	8.95	50S
42N	IA, Ames	7.10	65S	41N	UT, Salt Lake City	8.24	65S
38N	KN, Dodge City	10.27	45S	38N	VA, Richmond	6.61	60S
39N	KN, Manhattan	7.35	60S	47N	WA, Seattle	5.43	70S
38N	KY, Lexington	8.09	60S	48N	WA, Spokane	7.37	70S
30N	LA, New Orleans	6.35	55S	43N	WI, Madison	6.88	65S
32N	LA, Shreveport	7.32	55S	43N	WY, Lander	11.03	45S
44N	ME, Portland	7.49	65S				
42N	MA, Boston	5.92	65S				
43N	MI, E. Lansing	6.29	65S				
46N	MN, St. Cloud	7.50	70S				

*Generated by one M-61 Arco Module per day

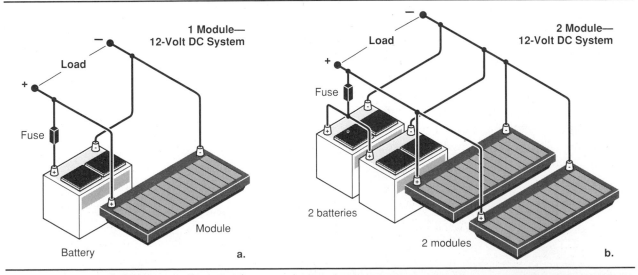

■ **FIGURE 1.31** ■
Any number of solar-power modules can be wired into an RV, but the most common use is either a one- (*a*) or two-module (*b*) system.

TROUBLESHOOTING the Incandescent Lighting Fixture

Problem	Possible Cause	Correction
Fails to light	Burned-out bulb	Replace bulb.
	No power	Test voltage and restore power. Check and charge battery.
	Corroded bulb connections	Clean with crocus cloth and reinstall.
Low light	Improper voltage	Check and charge battery.
	Fogged lens	Replace fixture lens.
	Bad fixture socket	Replace fixture.

■ Maintenance

Photovoltaic modules require minimal service. When the module becomes dirty, clean it with a sponge or soft cloth and water. If necessary, a mild nonabrasive detergent may be used. Connections, wiring, and mounting hardware should be inspected every six months to assure integrity. Do not walk on or drop items on the modules; broken glass on a module can become an electrical hazard and can cause injury.

Modules are not designed to be serviced internally by the user; damage to the cells or diodes can result. Nor should the user wear jewelry when working on photovoltaic modules. It is also important to maintain batteries connected to any photovoltaic system. See "Batteries" (page 9) for instructions.

12-Volt DC Lighting

Most RVs are equipped with either incandescent or fluorescent fixtures as the primary type of lighting. Some motorhomes and trailers have 120-volt AC lighting, but this type of lighting is usually used to complement 12-volt DC lighting or used for aesthetics in luxury coaches. Other than occasional bulb replacement, interior lighting fixtures are usually trouble free. On the other hand, outside marker lights require constant attention.

■ Checking for Low Voltage at Light Fixture

If the light is dim, the voltage at the fixture must be checked using the following steps:

1. Using a multimeter, read voltage at battery.
2. Remove lens from fixture.
3. Unscrew fixture from ceiling or wall.
4. Using a multimeter, touch the positive lead to the black wire and the negative lead to the white wire. If wire nuts are used to connect the wires, remove them; otherwise probe the multimeter leads through the wire insulation.
5. With the bulb/tubes in place and the switch in the "on" position, read voltage. Voltage should compare to that read at battery.

If voltage is low or incandescent lights are dim or not working, proceed with the following steps:

1. Check and clean terminals on bulb and socket. Clean with crocus cloth. If outside marker light sockets are corroded, clean and coat surface with a thin layer of silicone diaelectric grease.
2. Check terminals for proper connections.
3. Rewire to fixture if necessary, using proper gauge wire.
4. If voltage is okay at connections but lower at socket, replace fixture.

User maintenance on fluorescent fixtures is limited to changing tubes and ballasts. Circuit board and internal inverter require factory service.

TROUBLESHOOTING the Fluorescent Lighting Fixture

Problem	Possible Cause	Correction
Fails to light	Reversed polarity	Rewire with black wire to positive, white to negative.
	Bad tubes	Replace tubes.
Tube ends turning black	Frequent on/offs	Limit on/offs.
	Low voltage	Check and recharge battery. Check connections.
	Bad tube	Replace tube.
Frequent ballast failure	Failure to replace bad tubes	Replace ballast and tubes.
	Low voltage	Check and recharge battery. Check connections.
	High transient voltages (spikes)	Check power converter.

Back-up Monitors

Back-up monitors allow the driver to view the area at the rear and portions of the sides of a motorhome, and in some cases, a travel trailer. These relatively new marvels in video technology have virtually eliminated rear blind spots, giving the driver exceptional visibility when backing up. They utilize a small television-type monitor mounted on, or close to, the dashboard and a camera affixed to the upper rear of the motorhome (or trailer). Miniaturization of the cameras has made flush-mount installations possible, which greatly reduces the risk of camera damage.

Although back-up monitors are relatively trouble free in operation, periodic checks of the cable, camera, and monitor will prevent possible failure.

■ Checking the Back-up Monitor Installation

To check the back-up monitor installation, include these items (see Figures 1.32, 1.33, and 1.34):

☐ Inspect the coaxial cable that leads from the camera to the monitor. Check for chafing, cracks, and bare spots. This specially shielded cable must be completely intact to offer perfect reception.

☐ Inspect the leads from the monitor used to power the system. Most systems use a red wire for the 12-volt DC power, a black wire for the ground, and either a blue, purple, or red/white wire for the connection to the back-up light circuit. The connection to the back-up lights allows the unit to operate automatically when the transmission shifter is placed in reverse.

☐ Inspect the ground wire. Make sure it is securely attached to a clean portion of the chassis. This connection must be free from dirt and corrosion, and away from painted surfaces.

☐ Make sure the camera is clean. Driving in rain or snow causes the camera to become covered with dirt, severely limiting vision. The lens cover should be cleaned with window cleaner and a soft rag.

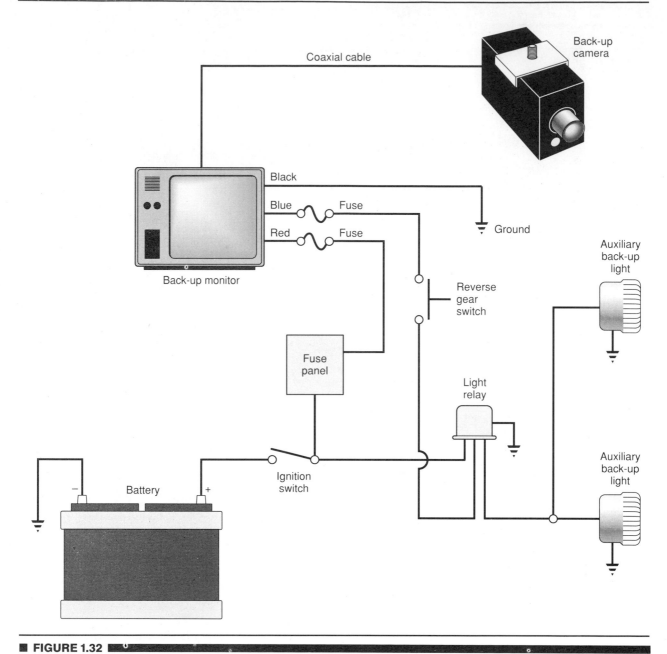

■ **FIGURE 1.32**
Wiring diagram for the Intec Car Vision back-up monitoring system

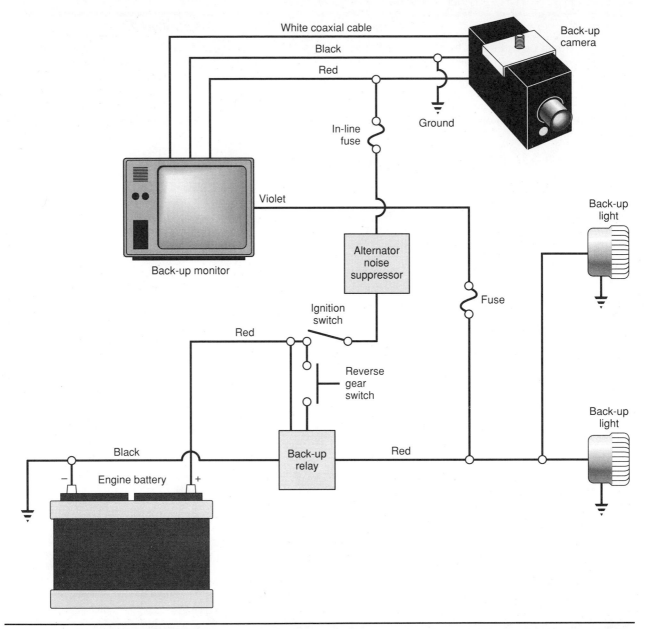

■ **FIGURE 1.33**
Wiring diagram for the Macedon Safety Vision back-up monitoring system

TROUBLESHOOTING the Back-up Monitor

Problem	Possible Cause	Correction
Monitor lights up but no picture appears	Loose or dirty connections	Check coaxial cable for break or looseness; tighten or replace cable.
	Beam out of adjustment	Adjust beam on monitor.
Monitor does not turn on	Faulty wiring	Check wiring for proper connection to power and ground.
	Wire shorting	Repair shorted wire.
	Main cable shorting	Check for short in cable between pin locations in connectors.
Picture blurry, distorted, too dark, or too light	Monitor needs adjustment	Adjust beam and focus on monitor.
	Bad cables and connectors	Inspect and repair or replace.
	Faulty wiring	Inspect and repair or replace.
	Dirty camera lens	Clean camera lens.
Unwanted noise bars, stripes, or dots appear on monitor screen	Faulty ground	Inspect and repair contact points for dirt, corrosion, and paint. Secure wire if necessary.
	Ignition coil interference	Make sure capacitor on vehicle engine-ignition coil is connected between positive terminal and chassis ground.
	Alternator interference	Install alternator suppressor between ignition switch and fuse in red wire that powers camera and monitor.
	Spark plug interference	Install resistor-type spark plugs in engine.
	Interference from automotive accessories	If necessary (extreme cases), install suppressor capacitors across windshield-wiper motor, electric fuel pump, or electric clock.

Note: Back-up monitors and cameras are not user serviceable. If proper picture cannot be gained by checking above items, send camera and monitor back to manufacturer or take vehicle to authorized service center for repair.

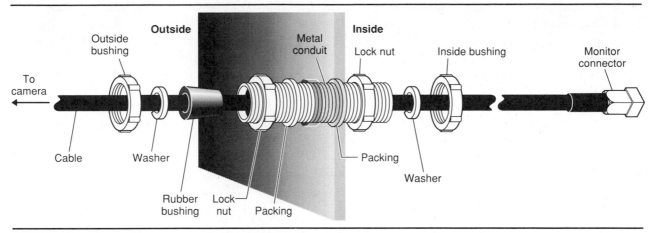

FIGURE 1.34

Cable entry fitting for coaxial cables used in back-up monitoring systems

Wiring a Tow Vehicle

In order to operate the marker/taillights, brake lights, electric brakes, and back-up lights, a tow vehicle must be wired so that the trailer plug can be temporarily connected when towing. A charge line must also be routed to the plug receptacle so that the tow vehicle alternator can charge the trailer batteries. Most lighting and brake actuation failures are attributable to faulty wiring or wiring that has become shorted, corroded, or disconnected (see Figure 1.35).

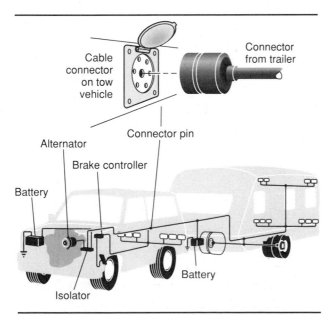

FIGURE 1.35

The tow vehicle must be wired so the marker lights, turn signals, brake lights, and electric brakes can operate and the batteries charge in the trailer.

■ Installing the Trailer Plug Connector
The Charge Line

To prevent voltage drop (restriction of current flow), a No. 8 charge line should be used. Proper connections will insure that the trailer battery or batteries will receive a good charge.

To install the charge line, follow these steps:

1. Route a No. 8 automotive, stranded copper wire from the tow vehicle's engine compartment to the rear bumper. Route the wire so that it cannot be chafed by the chassis or other sharp edges found under a vehicle. Secure with black (ultraviolet-protected) tie wraps so the wire does not sag at any point. Make sure the wire is away from sources of extreme heat such as the exhaust system.

2. Connect the wire lead in the engine compartment to one side of a 50-ampere circuit breaker that has been mounted either on the fender well or engine firewall.

3. Connect another length of No. 8 wire to the other side of the 50-ampere circuit breaker and connect the other end to the battery terminal on the alternator. The charge line wire may also be attached to the positive terminal of the starting battery.

■ Brake Lights, Marker/Taillights, and Back-up Lights

For brake lights, marker/taillights lights, and back-up lights, follow these steps:

1. Locate the wiring harness in the vicinity of the tow vehicle's taillights.
2. Using a 12-volt test light or a multimeter, turn on taillights, and left and right turn signals, one at a time, and probe the wires in the harness until the light indicates presence of current. Back-up-light wires must also be located if trailer is so equipped. Probing can be avoided if you have a service manual that identifies the wiring code.
3. Connect a length of No. 16 automotive wire to each of the wires of the taillight, right and left signal, and back-up-light wires using quick connectors. **Note:** Quick connectors will cause erratic operation if not used properly. A good way to prevent a quick connector from collecting moisture and corrosion is to coat the con-

nector with RTV silicone sealant after it has been locked into place on the wire. If possible, make your wiring additions the same color as the original wiring in the vehicle.

■ Grounding Wires

To ground wires, attach one end of a length of No. 8 automotive wire to a clean portion of the chassis in the proximity of the receptacle. This should be accomplished using at least a ¼-inch bolt and corresponding ring terminal. Sheet-metal screws or smaller bolts attached to the receptacle bracket are not adequate sources of a good ground.

■ Trailer Plug Receptacle

Most trailers use a 7-way Bargeman or Pollak flat pin plug and receptacle (see Figure 1.36). Trailers equipped with Dometic 3-Way Automatic Energy Selector refrigerators require a 9-way version of the same type of

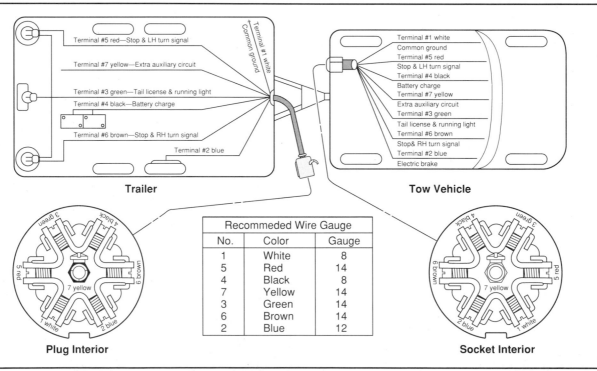

Recommended Wire Gauge		
No.	Color	Gauge
1	White	8
5	Red	14
4	Black	8
7	Yellow	14
3	Green	14
6	Brown	14
2	Blue	12

■ **FIGURE 1.36** ■

Wiring diagram for 7-way plug and receptacle used for most travel trailers

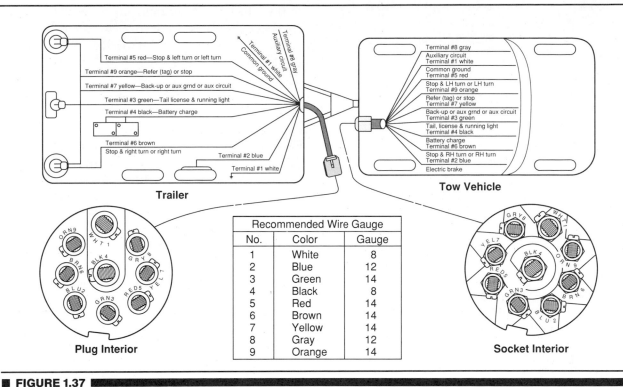

Trailer

Terminal #5 red—Stop & left turn or left turn
Terminal #9 orange—Refer (tag) or stop
Terminal #7 yellow—Back-up or aux grnd or aux circuit
Terminal #3 green—Tail license & running light
Terminal #4 black—Battery charge
Terminal #6 brown
Stop & right turn or right turn
Terminal #2 blue
Terminal #1 white
Terminal #8 gray
Auxiliary circuit
Terminal #1 white
Common ground

Tow Vehicle

Terminal #8 gray
Auxiliary circuit
Terminal #1 white
Common ground
Terminal #5 red
Stop & LH turn or LH turn
Terminal #9 orange
Refer (tag) or stop
Terminal #7 yellow
Back-up or aux grnd or aux circuit
Terminal #3 green
Tail, license & running light
Terminal #4 black
Battery charge
Terminal #6 brown
Stop & RH turn or RH turn
Terminal #2 blue
Electric brake

Plug Interior

Socket Interior

Recommended Wire Gauge		
No.	Color	Gauge
1	White	8
2	Blue	12
3	Green	14
4	Black	8
5	Red	14
6	Brown	14
7	Yellow	14
8	Gray	12
9	Orange	14

■ **FIGURE 1.37** ■
Travel trailers with automatic refrigerators will require a 9-way plug and receptacle.

receptacle (Figure 1.37). Receptacles should be mounted below the rear bumper, on the left side of the hitch receiver. **Note:** Mounting the receptacles in such locations is standard in the RV industry, but makes them highly susceptible to moisture, dirt, and corrosion. If the wire attachments are connected properly, they should not work loose or break off. A coating of RTV silicone to the back portion of the receptacle helps prevent moisture and dirt from entering the connections, greatly improving durability of the receptacle.

■ Wiring the Dometic AES Refrigerator

In order to operate Dometic's 3-Way Automatic Energy Selector on 12-volt DC power, a connection must be made between the tow vehicle or motorhome ignition system and the block marked ING LOCK in the

back of the refrigerator (Figure 1.38). When power from the alternator is desired, a low-current 12-volt DC signal is directed into the refrigerator's control system from the vehicle's ignition system. If wired correctly, the refrigerator will operate on 12-volt DC only when the engine is running. Normally a switch is installed under the dash so the driver can turn off the 12-volt DC section if refrigerator operation on only LP-gas or 12-volt AC electricity is desired. When operating on 12-volt DC power the refrigerator will draw from 20 to 23 amperes, depending on the model.

If the connection to the engine ignition system is not made, the refrigerator will not operate on 12-volt DC and will function on LP-gas whenever 12-volt AC power is not available.

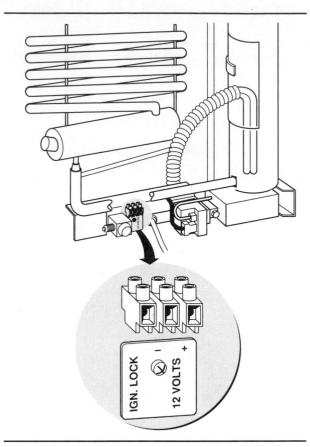

CAUTION: A battery must be included in the 12-volt circuit; if it is powered only by the converter, operation of the 12-volt DC refrigerator control system will be erratic. See Figure 1.39 for wiring diagrams for travel trailers and motorhomes.

The refrigerator must be connected to the 12-volt DC circuit with adequate size wire; otherwise, voltage drop will affect refrigerator operation. See Table 1.12 for correct wire size and length. The 12-volt DC circuit must be fused using the following maximum sizes: 30 amps for Model RM 763 and 40 amps for Model RM 1303. No other equipment or accessories can be connected to the 12-volt DC refrigerator circuit.

■ **FIGURE 1.38**
Connection location in Dometic AES refrigerator for providing 12-volt DC power for vehicle ignition

■ **TABLE 1.12**

Wiring Guide for Dometic AES Refrigerators

Wire Gauge AWG	Model RM763	Model RM1303	Model RM663
10	13 ft.	*	19 ft.
8	22	19 ft.	31
6	34	31	49
4	55	50	79

*Not recommended

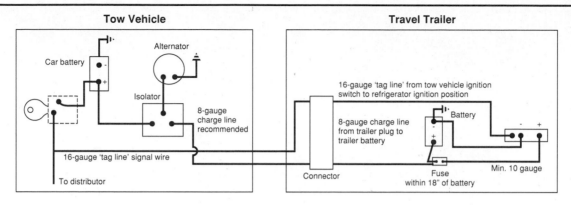

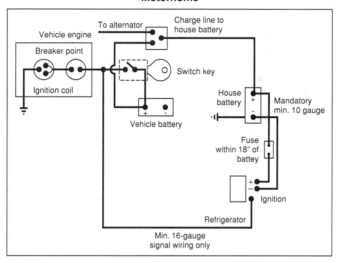

■ FIGURE 1.39
Dometic AES wiring diagrams for tow vehicles, travel trailers, and motorhomes

CHAPTER 2

LP-Gas Systems

Both butane and propane are derived from the distillation of crude oil into lighter products such as gasoline. Each gas exhibits distinctly different properties. Although the flame each gas produces is nearly the same, the physical qualities of the raw gas are quite different (see Figure 2.1).

Propane (chemical formula C_3H_8) is most widely used since it will perform well in all climates. *Butane* (chemical formula C_4H_{10}) has the disadvantage of freezing at 31°F, making its use in climates where the temperature drops below freezing impractical. Propane is usable down to −44°F.

Both gases are easily liquefied under moderate pressure (150 psi), which makes their storage easy. Because they are stored in liquid form and are petroleum products, they are both referred to as *liquid petroleum gas* or *LP-gas*. Containers are constructed to hold pressure, and because the gas is concentrated in liquid

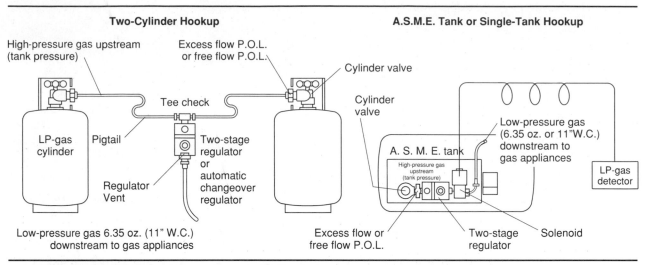

Two-Cylinder Hookup   **A.S.M.E. Tank or Single-Tank Hookup**

■ **FIGURE 2.1**

Travel trailers typically use a two-cylinder LP-gas system with a two-stage regulator or automatic changeover regulator. Motorhomes use an ASME tank and two-stage regulator.

form, there is an abundance of heat potential in a relatively small package. Approximately 92,000 Btu's of heat are contained in one gallon of propane; butane is slightly higher at 103,000 Btu's. Even a small 5-gallon cylinder of propane offers 460,000 Btu's of heat; this is enough to operate a 25,000-Btu/hour heater continuously for 18.4 hours.

The specific gravity of these gases makes them heavier than air. If air equals 1, propane's specific gravity is 1.53, while butane checks in at 2.00. This creates a safety hazard if there is a leak. The gases tend to pool much like water, seeking the lowest point. Because they do not dissipate easily, a spark in the immediate vicinity can cause an explosion. That is why gas-leak detectors are mounted near the floor level.

Both gases are colorless and odorless, which, combined with their tendency to settle in low places, make them difficult to detect. To make detection easier they are odorized at the time of manufacture. The smell, sometimes described as a "rotten egg" odor, is a sign of a possible leak. At the first sign (smell) of a leak, open doors and windows, do not turn a light switch on or off, extinguish all flames, and turn off the cylinder supply valve. Many RV leak detectors automatically shut off the cylinder supply via an electronic solenoid when a gas concentration at the sensor reaches the danger level.

These gases are heavier than air, but they are lighter than water. Propane is only one-half the weight of water, with a liquid specific gravity of .51 (water equals 1.0). **Note:** The weight of propane, 4.25 pounds per gallon, should be taken into account when you are weighing an RV to determine usable load capacity.

As a motor fuel, propane has less Btu's, or heat value, than gasoline (about 12% less); therefore it reduces the power output of any given engine by that amount. The big advantage of propane lies in its high-octane rating (near 120), which reduces ping (detonation). Many vehicles were converted to propane or gasoline/propane (dual fuel) in the early 1970s to circumvent the skyrocketing cost of gasoline and long lines at service stations. Since then, propane cost has matched that of gasoline and, with the reduction of power and poorer availability of propane, it lost its advantage.

Safety

Safety around flammable LP-gas should be your number one priority. Leaks are serious. Never use an open flame to check for leaks; always use a solution of soapy water. In the following Checklist are a few common sense rules when filling, removing, or installing an LP-gas cylinder in an RV.

✓ CHECKLIST

☐ Close valves on appliances and pilot burners.

☐ Make sure regulator coupling nut is tight between the regulator and the cylinder valve. This nut has a left-hand thread. Be sure to use a properly fitting wrench to prevent deforming the brass nut (Figure 2.2).

☐ Slowly open the cylinder valve.

☐ Check for leaks with soapy water solution at fittings and connections (Figure 2.3).

☐ Relight pilots and check them for proper flame (light blue—no yellow).

☐ Light main burners to check for proper flame color.

☐ Check to see that the regulator vent is clear and free of debris (Figure 2.4).

☐ Close the cylinder valve when appliances will not be used.

☐ Never store cylinders indoors in an unvented enclosed area or near an open flame or source of sparks.

■ FIGURE 2.2 ■
The regulator coupling nut has a left-hand thread and can be deformed easily if forced in the opposite direction.

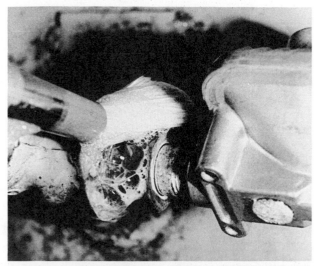

■ FIGURE 2.3 ■
LP-gas leaks should only be checked with soap and water.

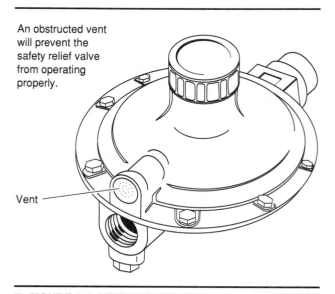

An obstructed vent will prevent the safety relief valve from operating properly.

Vent

■ FIGURE 2.4 ■
Regulator vent location

Storage Tanks

Liquid-petroleum gas tanks are the means by which RVers carry a supply of fuel for cooking, heating, and refrigeration. The tanks are constructed to rigid standards established by the Department of Transportation (DOT) or American Society of Mechanical Engineers (ASME).

DOT cylinders are mounted on the RV in a way that allows them to be removed for filling. DOT cylinders also utilize the same port for filling as for withdrawing gas. ASME tanks have a separate filling port and are designed to be bolted permanently to the RV's frame; they must be filled in place. All frame-mounted tanks and portable tanks that are enclosed in compartments must be clearly marked on the outside

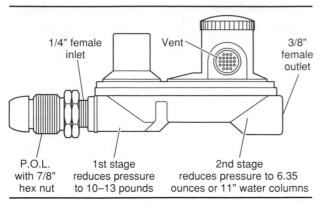

■ **FIGURE 2.5**
Two-stage regulators are designed to reduce LP-gas pressure to 11 inches water column.

of the RV with the one-inch-high letters *LPG* indicating the location of the tank.

LP-gas tanks are equipped with an outlet valve that dispenses gas in vapor form to the RV's appliances through a *regulator* (see Figure 2.5). This regulator is attached to the valve via a left-hand-threaded connection known as a *POL connector*. The hex portion of the fitting has a small groove machined around its circumference indicating that it has left-hand threads.

Pressure in a full cylinder is about 150 pounds per square inch (psi). This pressure is necessary to keep the gas in liquid form within the tank and will vary with temperature changes. As pressure is reduced during withdrawal, the gas vaporizes and exits the tank through the regulator. Improper positioning of a tank may allow liquid fuel to flow into the regulator. Since the regulator is designed for gas, not liquid, damage to the regulator could occur. Excessive gas quantities could enter the appliance, causing dangerous flareups. The appliances in an RV are designed to operate at a much lower pressure level (about .4 psi or 11 inches of water-column [W.C.] pressure). The regulator is designed to reduce the high cylinder pressure to a steady 11 inches water-column pressure for the appliances to operate correctly.

Regulators

Propane cylinders contain pressure of 100 to 200 psi in order to keep the gas in liquid form. Since the appliances in your RV are designed to operate on 11 inches of water-column pressure (.4 psi), the regulator is needed to reduce the pressure. Regulators are durable instruments, but once in a while they may get out of adjustment.

In order to adjust the pressure, a gauge called a *manometer* is used (see Figure 2.6). This gauge accurately measures very low pressure readings in what is called inches of water column. A *water-column gauge* consists of a glass or plastic tube bent in a U-shape filled midway with water. Pressure is applied to one end of the tube, which displaces the water. The total displacement is measured in inches of water column. Most RV appliances work best when the regulator is set to 11 inches of pressure. The water in the gauge is

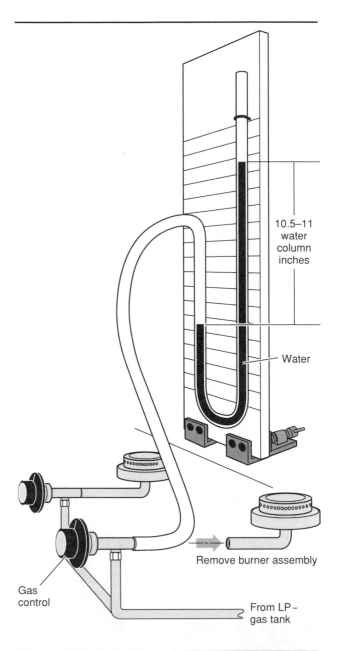

■ **FIGURE 2.6**
LP-gas pressure is checked with a manometer or water-column gauge.

TROUBLESHOOTING the Regulator

Problem	Possible Cause	Correction
Regulator freeze-up	Overfilled tank	Seek qualified help to bleed excessive pressure from tank.
	Clogged regulator vent	Clean vent opening.
	Water in tank	LP-gas facilities can inject alcohol to absorb moisture.
Pilot lights fail	Low regulator pressure	Check regulator output pressure, set to 11″ water-column pressure.
	Low LP-gas level	Replenish supply.
	Clogged regulator vent	Clean vent opening.
	Defective thermocouple	Install new thermocouple.
Regulator vent clogs	Road dirt and debris	Install shield to protect regulator from debris.

pushed down 5½ inches in one tube, which pushes the water up the other tube 5½ inches. The total displacement is 11 inches. Most commercial gauges do not use a glass tube with water, but a special low-pressure dial gauge that is calibrated to water-column pressure. Never attempt to adjust pressure with a conventional gauge calibrated in pounds per square inch. As stated earlier, 11 inches of water-column pressure is only .4 psi, a number that would hardly register, even on a low-psi type of gauge. Commercial gauges are available. One sold through NAPA auto parts stores (Part No. 700-1411) sells for $40.

Pressure is checked by slipping a connector over an appliance gas outlet (usually the galley stove burner) that leads to the water-column pressure gauge. The appliance is turned on and a direct pressure reading is taken. If an adjustment is necessary, the protective cover on the regulator cap is removed to reveal the pressure-adjusting screw. Turning the screw clockwise increases the pressure; counterclockwise reduces the regulator's pressure output.

■ Service and Repair

The *diaphragm vent* is located in the top cover of the regulator and is designed to allow air to enter and exit from the spring side of the diaphragm. If this vent becomes blocked by dirt, insects, or road debris, the regulator can be rendered useless and/or dangerous. A small blockage may cause enough pressure drop to allow pilot lights to blow out, or the condition could

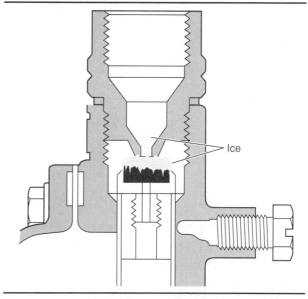

Ice

■ FIGURE 2.7
Regulator freeze-up during extremely cold temperatures can prevent LP-gas from flowing.

lead to excessive gas pressure being forced to the appliances, causing a safety hazard. The vent is covered with a fine-mesh screen that should be checked and cleaned periodically (see Figure 2.4).

Driving in icy or freezing rain conditions may cause water to enter the vent and freeze the opening shut (see Figure 2.7). If these weather conditions bring about odd behavior of propane appliances, a clogged vent may be the culprit. Regulators that lie horizontally are most apt to have the vent fill with

TROUBLESHOOTING the LP-Gas Tank

Problem	Possible Cause	Correction
Propane (rotten egg) odor	Leaking gas	Leak-test all connections and fittings with soapy water. Check connection tightness with a wrench. If tightening the connection does not solve the problem, turn off gas until repairs are made.
Tank will not fill	Defective stop-fill valve	Have replaced by qualified technician.
	Incorrect valve installation	Install as per stop-valve manufacturer's instructions.
Low tank capacity	Misadjusted stop-fill	Have valve adjustment done by qualified technician.
	Surging of fuel	Allow fuel to stabilize and resume filling.
Tank overfills	Defective stop-fill valve	Have replaced by qualified technician.
	Improper filling procedure	Follow correct fill routine.

water and ice. A shield or hood can be constructed that will protect vents.

Another problem can arise when water enters the tank and causes the regulator to freeze from the inside. The pressure-control valve inside the regulator will freeze if water is present in the propane tank. As propane is vaporized from liquid to gas it becomes very cold. If there is water present, it is possible for the temperature inside the regulator to drop to below 32°F. This results in regulator freeze-up. Water can enter the tank through a contaminated supply, or through a tank valve that is left open by the consumer when the tank is empty. If it is determined that moisture has entered the tank, methyl alcohol can be injected along with propane by the supplier on the next fill-up. The alcohol absorbs the moisture and allows it to be carried out of the tank without causing freeze-ups.

Leak Detectors

LP-gas leaks are serious business. Many RVs come equipped with electronic leak detectors. These units have sensors mounted low to the floor (propane gas is heavier than air and will seek the lowest level) that "sniff" constantly to detect the presence of gas. When gas is detected, they sound an alarm and, in many cases, send a signal to a tank-mounted electric-solenoid shut-off valve that will immediately shut the gas off at the cylinder.

Stop-Fill Valves

Recently, many LP-gas-tank manufacturers have been equipping their products with *stop-fill valves* (see Figures 2.8 and 2.9). LP-gas tanks are designed to be filled to 80% of their total capacity. Cylinders are equipped with a small *bleed valve* that has a tube connected to the back side of the valve. This tube drops into the tank and stops at the 80%-of-capacity level. When a cylinder is filled, the bleed valve is opened. At first only vapor is released, but as the liquid level rises up to the 80% level, it flows up the tube and appears at the external bleed valve as a white spray. This is a sign that the cylinder is filled to its proper capacity. The propane fill-station operator

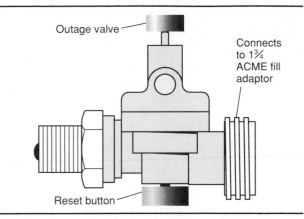

Outage valve

Connects to 1¾ ACME fill adaptor

Reset button

■ **FIGURE 2.8**

The Auto Stop stop-fill valve automatically stops the flow of LP-gas when the tank becomes 80% filled.

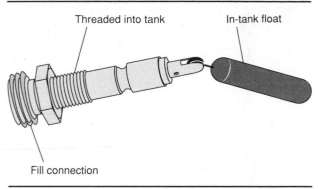

Threaded into tank

In-tank float

Fill connection

■ **FIGURE 2.9**

The Ceodeux stop-fill valve uses an in-tank float to prevent LP-gas overfilling.

should immediately shut off the fill hose. Filling or "topping off" the cylinder past the 80% point should not be attempted.

The 20% of air space remaining allows room for expansion of the gas as the temperature rises. A cylinder that is too full could allow liquid to pass through the regulator and feed too much gas to an appliance, possibly causing a dangerous flare-up. An overfilled cylinder can also cause the pressure relief valve to frequently "pop off," releasing large quantities of gas to the atmosphere; in the presence of a spark or open flame, this could be disastrous.

Many times a cylinder without a stop-fill valve will be overfilled by an inattentive service attendant. Stop-fill valves eliminate the guesswork or the ignorance of station attendants by automatically stopping the propane flow when the level reaches the 80% mark. The most common stop-fill valves operate like the float mechanism in a residential toilet bowl. The float is simply pushed up by the rising liquid entering the tank. At the 80% level, the float exerts enough pressure on the valve to stop the flow of gas from the fill-station pump.

CHAPTER 3

Water Systems

The freshwater system probably does more to make an RV like a home than any other feature. You'd think that a system that provides so much convenience would be difficult to maintain and repair, but it's not. Many people have a mental block when it comes to plumbing, but the RV's water system can be maintained and repaired easily with a little thought and a few basic tools.

An RV's water system consists of a metal or plastic water-storage tank, a connection for city water, copper tubing or plastic water lines, a 12-volt DC-powered water pump or air compressor, an accumulator tank, a strainer system, check valves, a water-filter system, and faucets to control water flow (see Figure 3.1). A particular system may contain all or just a few of these components.

Basically there are two types of water systems. The most common is the *demand* system, where water is available "on demand" by either a hand vacuum pump pulling the liquid from a storage tank, or by opening a

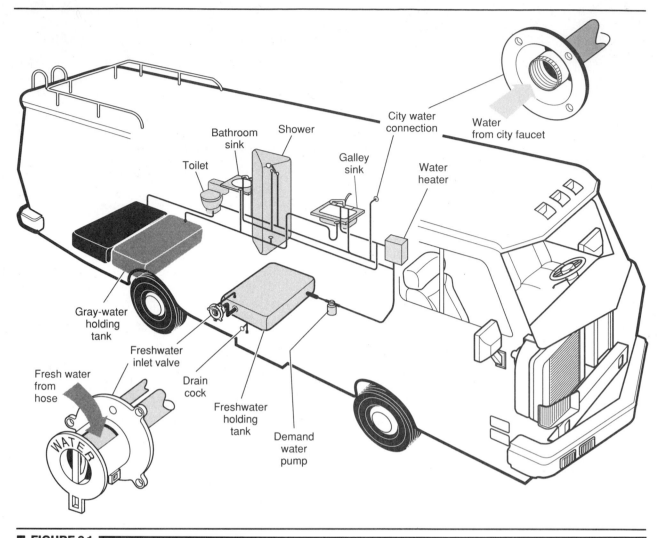

■ **FIGURE 3.1**
A typical RV water system

valve and allowing an electric pump to push water to the fixture. The other type of system, no longer popular with manufacturers, operates by *air pressure*. In this type of system, an air compressor pressurizes a tank filled with water, forcing water through the system to each valve or faucet.

A hand-pump system uses a handle that is physically pumped back and forth until water is drawn to the fixture. An electric demand pump has a telltale whirring pump motor that comes on almost instantly as a faucet is opened. The air-compressor system, on the other hand, will delay several seconds, or if a small amount of water is drawn, several minutes, before the compressor can be heard.

Water Tanks

Most RVs utilize plastic water tanks. They are lightweight, durable, impact resistant, sanitary, and easily manufactured in a variety of shapes and sizes.

RVs with air-pressure systems are most likely to have a metal tank of stainless steel or aluminum. Some of the high-line motorhomes feature stainless-steel metal tanks in concert with a demand system. The average RV water-tank capacity is about 40 gallons. This translates to about 340 pounds of liquid weight that the tank must contain. When 340 pounds of water are sloshed around due to road movement, the forces that the tank must contend with are considerable. Even so, water tanks seldom require repair.

Maintenance consists of keeping the tank fresh by sanitizing with chlorine and making sure that nothing is stored near the water tank that could puncture it.

TROUBLESHOOTING the Water Tank

Problem	Possible Cause	Correction
Tank will not fill	Vent hose clogged	Clear vent hose.
Tank leaks	Loose hose or tubing	Check and tighten.
	Crack in tank	Repair or replace tank.
	Freeze damage	Repair or replace tank.
Odor or bad taste	Bacteria	Sanitize water system.

It's also important to drain the water system or install potable antifreeze during cold winter months to prevent severe damage to the water tank and to the rest of the system.

■ Tank Removal

The most difficult service procedure involving water tanks is the removal of the tank itself. Although many repairs can be made to tanks while they are in the RV, it is best to remove the tank for leak repair.

■ Repairing the Freshwater Tank

Cracks or holes may appear in the freshwater tank if severe impact or abrasion is encountered. After many miles of travel, the constant vibration may cause a crack to appear. Plastic tanks can be repaired with a special epoxy resin and fiberglass patch following these steps:

1. Drain the tanks so the crack area is dry. If the crack is in an inaccessible area, the tanks must be removed.
2. A small hole (⅛-inch diameter) should be drilled at each end of the crack. This prevents the crack from propagating from under the patch you will apply.
3. Sand the area around the crack until the tank surface is roughed up to allow a good adhesive bond.
4. Cut a fiberglass patch about 1 to 2 inches larger than the crack in all directions.
5. Mix the epoxy resin with its catalyst. After the catalyst is added there are only about 15 minutes of working time before the resin "sets up" and starts to harden.
6. With a small brush, dab a layer of resin over the area that was rough-sanded. Then lay the fiberglass-cloth patch over the resin. Pat the

patch with the brush until all the fiberglass is soaked with resin.
7. Add more resin to the patch area until it takes on a glossy appearance and the cloth fibers are covered.
8. The resin will become tacky in about 15 to 20 minutes and will fully harden in a few hours. The tank can be filled with water and leak inspection performed.

Some plastics can be welded with a hot-gas procedure and special plastic welding rod. This is a specialized method that is used most often in plastic-tank manufacture. Many RV repair shops are equipped to perform this type of repair (see Figure 3.2).

Metal tanks, stainless steel, or aluminum should not be repaired with the fiberglass/epoxy method. The best way is by welding. Since stainless steel and aluminum are difficult to weld, they are best repaired by a professional with Gas Tungsten Arc (sometimes known as Heliarc or TIG) welding. The tank should be removed from the RV before welding.

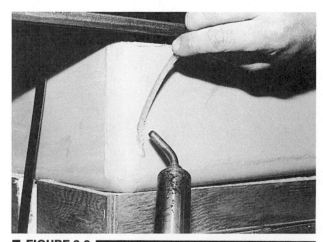

■ **FIGURE 3.2** ■
Polyethylene tanks can be repaired with a special plastic welding rod and heat gun.

Tanks that have been damaged by freezing can be repaired if the damage is not too severe. Permanent bulges, long cracks, or split tank seams warrant tank replacement. Although temporary repairs may be made, this type of damage often will cause the tank to fail in a relatively short period of time.

■ Vent Hose Inspection and Repair

A water tank will fill slowly (or not at all) if the vent hose is clogged. The vent hose is usually made of a vinyl plastic section that leads from a fitting on the top of the tank to a fitting that terminates at the outside water-fill door (Figure 3.3). The usual problem is that the hose becomes bent and kinked, making it impossible for air to pass. The problem can be remedied by either shortening the hose to remove the kink, or by replacing the hose if it is too short. In both cases, the hose should make a smooth transition from the top of the tank to the outside fill port. It is also important not to store objects on the water tank that could restrict the vent hose's ability to allow air to flow.

■ Leaking Hose Connections and Fittings

Since the water in the tank and the associated plumbing on the suction side of the pump cannot be pressure-tested (except for air-pressure systems), leaks can be deceptive. Small leaks may go unnoticed until water damage has been done to the RV.

Hose connections to the water tank can be the cause of a leak (Figure 3.4). Depending on the situa-

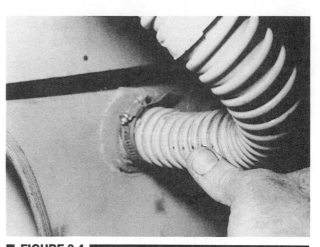

■ FIGURE 3.4 ■
The hose connection from the water fill to the tank should be checked for leaks or kinking.

tion and type of fitting, repairs can usually be performed while the tank is in the RV. If fittings are damaged by freezing, the tank may have to be removed for fitting replacement. If there is inadequate room near the tank to position a wrench to rotate a fitting, the entire tank has to be removed.

Check hoses and fitting connections for excessive side pressure. If a hose is routed around a sharp bend or abrupt turn, the pressure may be enough to deflect the hose fitting and cause a leak. Hoses should be rerouted so that pressure is not applied to the fittings or hose. Most RVs are plumbed with either plastic poly or soft-copper tubing. The plastic tubing uses plastic barb fittings to make connections and bends. The tubing is generally crimped to the fitting with a special tool. If a leak is detected at one of these connection points, the crimped fittings cannot be tightened. They can, however, be removed and worm-gear-type hose clamps installed in their place.

Copper tubing uses compression-type connectors that can be tightened if a leak appears (Figure 3.5). The leak may also be caused by damage to the compression ring (Figure 3.6). The seating surface on the fitting must be clean and free from nicks and scratches. If the sealing surface is damaged, the fittings should be replaced.

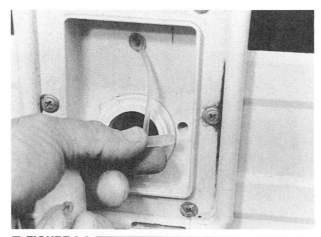

■ FIGURE 3.3 ■
Opening the water-fill vent plug facilitates the job of adding water.

■ **FIGURE 3.5** ■

Compression-tank connectors on copper tubing must be tightened if a leak occurs.

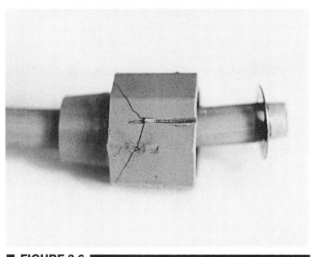

■ **FIGURE 3.6** ■

Overtightening plastic fittings usually results in breakage.

■ Water System Sanitization

It is not uncommon for RV owners to complain of bad water. The first sign of a contaminated water system is usually a bad taste, followed by strange odors emanating from the water supply. Bacteria may have built up in the water tank, especially if the water tank's supply has not been used frequently and not been replenished with fresh, clean water on a regular basis. When a rig comes out of storage, or is being used extensively on a city-water connection, the tank and entire water system should be sanitized before use. *Some of the bacterial buildup can cause serious illness; don't take chances!*

Here are the steps to water tank sanitization:

1. Drain water tank completely, then refill halfway with clean, fresh water.
2. Mix ¼ cup of household bleach for every 15 gallons of tank capacity in a container with a gallon or two of clean water.
3. Pour this mixture into the water tank.
4. Top off the water tank with fresh water. Drive the rig around the block to mix the solution.
5. Pump water through each faucet so that all the lines are filled with the water/bleach mixture from the tank. Usually, running a quart of water out each faucet is adequate.
6. The hot-water tank holds at least 6 gallons of water. Run the hot-water faucets until this much solution has passed to insure that the old water has been purged from the hot-water tank, and it is now filled with the water/bleach solution from the water tank.
7. Let the water stand for several hours.
8. Drain the entire water system, hot-water tank included.
9. To remove the bleach odor, mix ½ cup of baking soda with a gallon of water and pour into the freshwater tank.
10. Fill the tank completely and pump this solution through the water heater and rest of the water lines. This solution can sit in the system for a few days. Driving the rig around the block will slosh water around and thoroughly clean the tank.
11. Drain the entire system and refill with fresh, clean water.

Water Pumps

Water pumps seem to be the biggest cause of RV water-system difficulties. The pump is the most-used component in the water system; it's mechanical, electrical, and has moving parts.

There are a variety of electric pumps on the market; make it a point to be familiar with the one installed in your RV. Most RV pumps use a type of rubber diaphragm driven by a 12-volt DC electric motor. Some manufacturers of pumps use a rotary-impeller system. The diaphragm pump's main advantage is that it operates more quietly than the rotary-impeller design and will not be damaged if accidentally run dry.

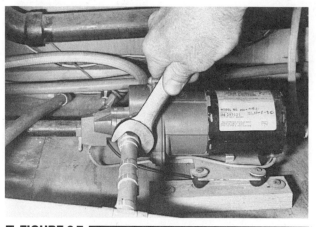

■ **FIGURE 3.7** ■
If the pump connections are not tight, air may be drawn in, allowing the pump to lose its prime.

■ Service and Repair

Servicing a water pump is easy with a few basic tools: A couple of screwdrivers (Phillips and flat), a set of small wrenches and sockets (¼-inch through ½-inch), an adjustable-end wrench that will open to 1 inch, pliers, a pair of water-pump pliers, and a multimeter for checking electrical components.

If the water pump runs but fails to deliver water, the cause is most often a restriction in the suction or inlet side of the pump.

Testing the Suction Water Line

To evaluate the condition of the suction water line, follow these steps:

1. Carefully follow the line from the pump inlet back to the water tank. Look for any signs of pinching or kinks in the line. If necessary, re-route the line to avoid this condition.
2. Check the tightness of all connections from the water tank to the pump. A leak here will allow air to be drawn in with the water flow, causing the pump to lose its prime.
3. If an in-line backflow valve is installed in the line, it may be stuck closed, shutting off water flow to the inlet side of the pump. Remove the check valve from the line. An arrow should indicate the direction of water flow (see Figure 3.7). Blow through the valve in the direction of the arrow (Figure 3.8). Air should pass this way but not in the opposite direction. If air fails to pass through the valve, it should be replaced.

■ **FIGURE 3.8** ■
Checking the water-pump backflow valve with air will determine its integrity.

If it is determined that water is reaching the pump through the suction line from the water tank, the lack of water flow could be caused by a broken drive belt. If the RV is equipped with a Jabsco belt-drive pump, make sure the belt has not broken or slipped off the pulleys (Figure 3.9). This belt is a toothed, positive-drive belt that is easily replaced. Simply slip a new belt into position, making sure that the teeth of the belt mesh with the cogs of the pulleys.

If water still fails to flow, check the pump's wiring (see Figure 3.10). If the 12-volt DC leads are reversed, the pump will run backward, failing to pump water. Reverse the pump-motor wires and operate the pump. If water now pumps, permanently connect the wiring leads in this position; if water still fails to pump, return the leads to their original position and check the pump diaphragm. A defective diaphragm can cause failure to pump, low water volume, and intermittent cycling when all faucets are turned off.

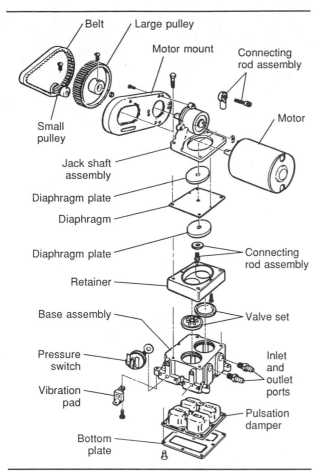

■ **FIGURE 3.9**

Exploded view of the Jabsco belt-drive water pump

■ **FIGURE 3.10**

Water pump will run backward if 12-volt DC wiring polarity is reversed.

Overhauling the Water Pump

To inspect the pump diaphragm, the pump assembly should be disconnected and removed from the RV (see Figure 3.11). All pump manufacturers supply a service kit that contains a new diaphragm, pump check valve, drive belt (if needed), and gaskets. Purchase this service kit before you start to overhaul the pump. To overhaul the water pump:

1. Remove electrical connections from the pump, marking the wires for their correct location.

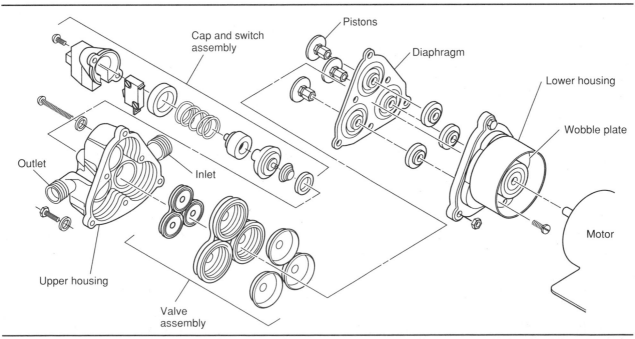

■ **FIGURE 3.11**

Exploded view of the Shurflo water pump

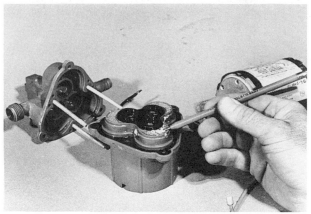

■ **FIGURE 3.12** ■
The Shurflo water pump diaphragm can be accessed after removing the cover screws.

■ **FIGURE 3.13** ■
The water-pump diaphragm should be inspected for cracks or defects after removal.

2. Drain the water tank and hot-water tank to keep water from flowing out of the inlet line when it is removed.

3. Remove the inlet and outlet lines from the pump housing. Use a proper-size wrench so that fittings are not damaged.

4. Remove pump-housing mounting bolts and rubber vibration pads from the mounting location on the RV.

5. When the pump is free from the RV, take it to a clean work area for disassembly.

6. All pumps have retaining screws that hold the diaphragm cover in place. By removing these screws, the diaphragm can be removed (Figure 3.12). Jabsco pumps require that the motor and jack-shaft assembly be removed before the diaphragm screws can be reached. Shurflo pumps have the pressure-sensing switch located in the diaphragm cover. The switch and the pressure spring will pop out when the cover is removed.

7. With the diaphragm removed, inspect the rubber for cracks and defects (Figure 3.13). Check the small flapper-check valves for signs of sticking or foreign objects that may prevent them from seating fully (Figure 3.14). If the pump has an internal filter screen on the inlet side, replace the screen or clean it before reassembly.

8. Replace the diaphragm. Reassemble the pump and mount it back in the RV. Connect the inlet and outlet water lines and 12-volt DC wiring.

9. To test the pump, fill the water tank, inspect connections for leaks, turn on the water-pump switch and open a faucet. The pump should

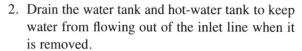

■ **FIGURE 3.14** ■
Debris can prevent the flapper-check valves in the water pump from seating.

start, prime, and pump water. Run water from each fixture until the air is bled from the system. The pressure switch should automatically turn off the pump when pressure builds.

Testing Other Components of the Water Pump

A pump that fails to operate may have a defective master control switch, or simply low battery voltage. To check these components a multimeter is needed. Follow these steps:

1. Battery condition can be determined by taking a voltage reading across the positive and negative terminals or by trying other 12-volt DC appliances. Low voltage will prevent the pump from operating. Voltage at the battery should be not less than 11 volts.

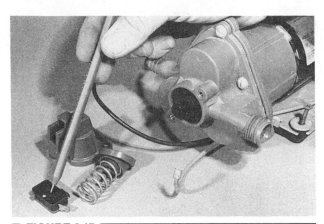

■ FIGURE 3.15 ■
The pressure switch can be checked for condition after its removal from the water pump.

■ FIGURE 3.16 ■
The use of rubber mounts will minimize noise and vibration during water-pump operation.

2. If voltage is normal, locate the 12-volt DC fuse that protects the water pump. See if the fuse is intact. Using the multimeter (volts), check to see that there is voltage on both sides of the fuse. If not, replace the fuse and recheck.

3. With the pump's master control switch in the "on" position, voltage should be present to one side of the pressure-sensitive control switch. If not, the master switch is defective or there is a break in the wiring from the switch to the pump.

4. If there is voltage to the switch and the pump still will not function, the pressure switch should be removed to test it. On Jabsco belt-drive pumps, the pressure switch is located on the outside of the pump housing and can be removed without removing the pump housing. On Shurflo pumps the pressure switch is located under the pump housing's diaphragm cover, which must be removed.

5. With the switch removed from the pump, the test can be done with a multimeter (Figure 3.15). These pressure switches are normally closed: The circuit is complete without pressure. After calibrating the multimeter, touch the leads to each side of the switch; there should be zero resistance reading on the multimeter (ohms). If not, replace the switch, reassemble the pump, and turn on the master switch to test the pump. The motor should run until pressure is established and then the pump should shut off.

This same test procedure should be done if the pump fails to shut off. The pressure switch may fail to open as pressure builds. The switch will test with a zero ohm reading even when pressure is applied. Replace the switch if it will not open with pressure applied.

Another common cause of pump run-on is low battery voltage. When the battery is low, the pump motor cannot produce sufficient pressure to open the pressure-sensing switch. This can lead to motor overheating and potentially permanent damage to the motor and pump. Wiring that is too small a gauge may also cause this condition. Make sure that the correct gauge wiring, as recommended by the pump manufacturer, is used.

Reducing Pump Noise

Excessive pump-motor noise is a common complaint among RV owners. Here are some tips to reduce pump noise.

☑ CHECKLIST ■■■■■■

☐ Make sure the pump is mounted on a solid surface that is not flimsy or prone to vibration; the RV floor is usually the best surface since it is likely to be the most rigid.

☐ Mount the pump on the manufacturer's rubber mounts; they are designed to minimize noise (Figure 3.16).

☐ Make sure all mounting connections, pulleys, and associated drive mechanism are tight.

☐ The compartment where the pump is located can be insulated with fiberglass or Styrofoam to provide a sound barrier.

TROUBLESHOOTING the Water Pump

Problem	Possible Cause	Correction
Pump runs but no water flows at outlets	Low water level in tank	Replenish supply.
	Clogged water lines	Locate, remove obstruction.
	Kink in suction line	Straighten line.
	Air leak in suction line	Repair air leak.
	Loose hose clamps on suction side of pump	Tighten clamps.
	Stuck pump-check valve	Repair or clean valve.
	Punctured diaphragm	Replace diaphragm.
	Cracked pump housing	Replace pump housing.
	Stuck backflow valve	Replace backflow valve.
	Broken pump-drive belt	Replace belt.
	Worn pump impeller	Replace impeller.
	Pump running backward	Reverse pump wiring.
	Plugged in-line filter	Replace element or screen.
Pump cycles off and on with faucets closed	Water leak in plumbing	Locate and repair.
	Leaking faucet sets	Repair faucet sets.
	Defective toilet valve	Repair valve.
	Internal leak in pump	Install pump-repair kit.
	Failed pressure switch	Replace pressure switch.
Pump motor fails to run	Blown fuse	Locate and replace.
	Master switch off	Turn on master switch.
	Low battery charge	Charge battery.
	Loose wiring connection	Check all connections.
	Poor ground	Check ground connection.
	Defective pump motor	Replace motor.
Pump fails to shut off when faucet closed	Empty water tank	Replenish water supply.
	Low voltage condition	Charge batteries.
	Leaking faucets	Repair faucets.
	Failed pressure switch	Replace pressure switch.
Excessive pump noise or vibration	Restricted intake line	Clear suction hose.
	Inadequate pump mounting	Mount per manufacturer's specs.
	Loose mounting bolts	Tighten bolts.
	Worn mount bushings	Replace with new bushings.
	Failed pulsation damper	Replace with new damper.
	Loose drive pulleys	Tighten pulleys.
	Worn pump bearings	Replace bearings.

TROUBLESHOOTING the Water Pump (continued)

Problem	Possible Cause	Correction
Inadequate water flow	Air leak at pump suction	Check suction line.
	Undersized suction line	Replace with larger line.
	Kinked outlet line	Straighten line.
	Clogged intake strainer	Clean strainer.
	Leaking pump diaphragm	Replace diaphragm.
	Inadequate pump wiring	Rewire with larger wire.
Sputtering water flow	Air leak in suction line	Repair leaks.
	Air not bled from lines	Bleed air from lines.
	Air in water heater	Bleed hot-water lines.
Pump will not prime	Empty water tank	Fill water tank.
	Air leak in suction line	Repair suction line.
	Restricted suction line	Clear obstruction.
	Defective pump diaphragm	Replace diaphragm.
	Defective pump impeller	Replace impeller.
	Broken pump-drive belt	Replace drive belt.
	Clogged intake strainer	Clean strainer.
	Defective check valve	Clean or replace valve.

It's not common, but an older pump may have defective motor- or drive-mechanism bearings. If the pump becomes progressively noisy with age, it is likely the pump needs to be replaced.

Hot-Water Tanks

An RV hot-water tank consists of an insulated water tank (usually 6, 8, 10 or 12 gallons), a flue assembly for routing hot gases through a passage in the tank so that heat transfers to the water, a gas burner, a gas control valve, and an electronic direct spark ignition, electric pilot light ignition, or manual gas pilot ignition system (see Figure 3.17). Some water heaters may be both gas and electric units to take advantage of the best source of fuel supply. Electric (120-volt AC) is used when hooked up in campsites, while gas is used when hookups are not available. Both fuel sources can be used simultaneously for fast recovery rates.

Water heaters are rated for Btu input and the rate of 100° rise (the number of gallons of water per hour that the heater can raise 100°). Water heaters require little maintenance, but should be subject to periodic tank flushing, winterizing, and minor burner adjustments.

■ Service and Repair

Consistent pilot-light outage may be caused by a number of things, most often a weak pilot caused by a dirty orifice and/or low gas pressure. Check gas pressure (see LP-gas section, pages 40–41), to confirm that it is 11 inches of water-column pressure.

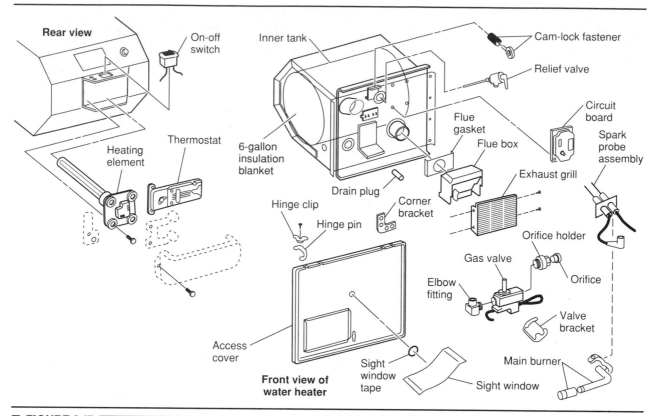

■ FIGURE 3.17 ■
Exploded view of Atwood 6-gallon direct spark ignition hot-water tank

Cleaning the Pilot

Cleaning the orifice is a delicate job since the hole the gas passes through is only slightly larger than the diameter of a human hair. Do not attempt to clean the orifice with any metal object; the hole will be enlarged and the pilot flame will be too large. Cleaning can be done with rubbing alcohol and a wooden toothpick.

To clean the pilot, follow these steps:

1. Remove pilot tube and orifice from the main burner assembly (Figure 3.18).
2. Soak orifice end in alcohol.
3. Use a toothpick to clean orifice hole (Figure 3.19). Be careful not to break any wood off in the hole.
4. Reinstall pilot tube and burner assembly and try to relight. If there still is inadequate flame and the orifice is clogged, replace the tube and pilot burner assembly.

5. Dirt and debris lodged in the pilot burner can also create a frequent pilot-outage situation. Make sure the air passage around the pilot burner is clean—free of dirt, insects, and corrosion.

Replacing the Thermocouple

Many times a pilot light will go out almost immediately after lighting. Here are some simple checks and remedies for this problem:

1. Make sure that the thermocouple is given adequate time to heat, at least 30 seconds. If more than 30 seconds are required, replace the thermocouple.
2. The thermocouple is removed with a ⅜-inch open-end wrench at the gas control valve. The other end is held in a spring-clip arrangement that allows the thermocouple to be pulled straight out of the holder (Figure 3.20).

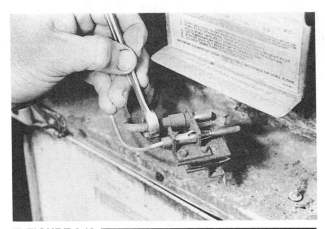

FIGURE 3.18
The pilot tube can be removed from the hot-water tank burner assembly with a line wrench.

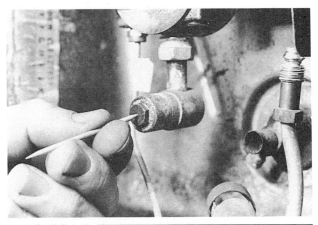

FIGURE 3.19
A toothpick should be used to clean the pilot orifice.

FIGURE 3.20
The thermocouple can be removed from the gas control valve with a ⅜-inch wrench.

FIGURE 3.21
The main burner in the hot-water tank is adjusted by sliding the air shutter valve.

3. Slip the new unit into the holder until one-third of the end will be exposed directly to the pilot flame. The other end is tightened finger-tight in the gas control valve. Then tighten one quarter-turn with the wrench. Do not overtighten or undertighten, or the unit will not function.

4. Open the gas valve to the pilot position, depress the pilot light button, and hold while lighting the flame. Release the button after 30 seconds; the pilot should remain lit.

Main Burner Adjustment

The main burner flame can also affect the pilot flame and determine the overall performance of the water heater. The proper steps for adjustment are as follows:

1. Slide the air shutter valve so that it is about one quarter of the way open (Figure 3.21).
2. The flame should burn predominantly blue with a short tip of yellow.
3. If the flame is too yellow, open the shutter slightly until only a tip of yellow is visible. *This may be necessary for optimum heater performance at high elevations.*
4. The flame should not roar excessively. If it does, it is likely that the air shutter is open too far and the gas mixture is too lean. Close the shutter slightly until you see a slight tip of yellow on a blue flame. Tighten the shutter-locking screw or nut.
5. If the flame will not adjust, it is possible that the main burner jet is clogged, incorrectly centered in the burner tube, or the burner tube itself contains dirt and obstructions.

TROUBLESHOOTING the Hot-Water Tank

Problem	Possible Cause	Correction
Pilot outage	Poor pilot flame	Replace pilot orifice.
	Fluttering pilot flame	Clean or replace orifice.
	Weak thermocouple	Replace thermocouple.
	Insufficient gas pressure	Adjust to 11 inches water-column pressure.
	Weak gas control magnet	Replace control unit.
	Obstructed air intake	Clean intake tube.
	Improper air adjustment	Adjust air shutter.
Pilot extinguishes itself when attempting to light flame	Thermocouple needs more time to heat	Wait 30 seconds.
	Loose thermocouple	Tighten connection.
	Weak thermocouple	Replace thermocouple.
	Weak gas control magnet	Replace gas control.
No spark (direct ignition heaters)	Spark gap incorrect	Adjust gap.
	Corroded terminals	Clean terminals.
	Cracked insulators	Replace electrodes.
	Cracked wires	Replace lead wire.
	Overly long high-voltage wire	Shorten lead.
	Dirt and dust on wires	Clean system.
Flame will not establish (direct ignition)	Wrong spark gap adjustment	Adjust spark gap.
	Malfunctioning valve	Replace valve.
Early lockout	Reversed polarity	Reverse wires to power and ground.
	Poor ground	Establish good ground.
	High gas pressure	Lower to 11 inches water-column pressure.
	Sensor probe	Adjust position in flame.
Erratic burner flame	Blocked burner orifice	Clean orifice.
	Misaligned main burner	Align burner tube.
	Obstruction in burner	Remove obstruction.
	Improper air adjustment	Adjust air shutter.
	Insufficient gas pressure	Adjust gas pressure.
	Poor gas supply	Replace gas in tank.
Yellow-colored flame	Improper air mixture	Adjust air shutter.
	Plugged burner orifice	Clean orifice.
	Obstruction in tube	Clear burner tube.
	Wrong gas pressure	Adjust to 11 inches water-column pressure.
	Obstructed heater grill	Clear grill.
	Misaligned burner jet	Align burner jet.

TROUBLESHOOTING the Hot-Water Tank (continued)

Problem	Possible Cause	Correction
Smoking and/or sooting	Improper air mixture	Adjust air shutter.
	Misaligned main burner	Align burner jet.
	Obstruction in main jet	Clear main burner jet.
	Poor gas supply	Replace gas supply.
Main burner will not light	Blocked burner jet	Clear burner jet.
	Improper air adjustment	Adjust air shutter.
	Defective gas control valve	Replace control valve.
Excessive and/or insufficient water temperature	Misaligned burner jet	Align burner jet.
	Blocked burner jet	Clear burner jet.
	Improper air setting	Adjust air shutter.
	Obstruction in tube	Clear obstruction.
	Incorrect thermostat setting	Set higher or lower.
	Defective gas control	Replace control valve.
Relief valve leaks	Foreign material in seat	Flip valve handle to clear.
	Air in system	Purge all air from system.
	Defective valve	Replace valve.

6. Turn off the flame, loosen the burner tube hold-down screws, and remove the tube from the end of the gas control valve (Figure 3.22).

7. The burner jet is located in the end of the gas control valve and is removable with a small wrench. Check to see that the jet is clear. It can be cleaned in alcohol and a wooden toothpick can be inserted in the hole to remove any dirt accumulation.

8. Clean the inside of the burner tube (Figure 3.23).

9. Install the jet and burner tube and attempt to light, and adjust the air shutter to attain a proper flame.

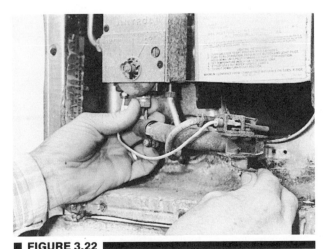

■ **FIGURE 3.22** ■
The burner jet in the hot-water tank is located in the end of the gas control valve.

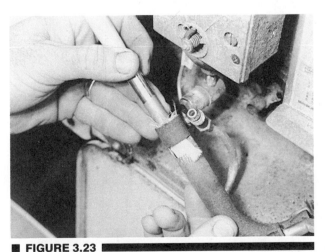

■ **FIGURE 3.23** ■
The burner jet should be inspected for any accumulation of dirt.

Main Burner Alignment

The burner jet must align with the center of the burner tube for the gas to mix properly with the incoming air (Figure 3.24). Check to see that the center of the jet is parallel with the center of the burner tube. If it is not, the tube can be loosened and rotated slightly up or down until the jet is parallel. Tighten tube hold-down screws.

Tank Cleaning

If the hot-water tank is used a great deal during the year you may want to flush it out a number of times to remove accumulation of dirt and scale that can shorten tank life. To clean the tank:

1. Turn off the main water supply—either the city supply or the 12-volt DC pump.
2. Drain the tank by opening the wing-shaped drain petcock on the outside of the tank (Figure 3.25).
3. Open the relief valve to admit air to speed draining (Figure 3.26).
4. If the drain valve becomes clogged while draining, a small wire, such as a coat hanger, pushed through the drain opening will dislodge any scale blocking the water's path.
5. With the city water connected and turned on, flush the heater for about 5 minutes through the drain valve. This will dislodge and flush corrosive scale particles from the tank.
6. Close the drain; open a hot-water faucet inside the RV to bleed air from the tank. Close the faucet; the tank is now clean and flushed.

■ FIGURE 3.24 ■
Check that the center of the burner jet is parallel with the center of the burner tube.

■ FIGURE 3.25 ■
The hot-water tank can be drained by opening the petcock, accessed through the outside door.

■ FIGURE 3.26 ■
Draining the hot-water tank can be facilitated by opening the relief valve.

Winterizing the Water System

Winterizing the RV's water system is necessary to protect all components from freezing. There are two ways to accomplish the job:

1. Drain all water from the system and use compressed air to blow out remaining water that may lie in low spots within the system.
2. Fill the system with a potable nontoxic antifreeze until all water is removed from the system.

In each case the hot-water tank must be drained. When a nontoxic winterizing fluid is used, it is best to install a winterizing kit that allows the system to bypass the hot-water tank so that expensive antifreeze is not needed to fill the heater.

■ **FIGURE 3.27**
A homemade adapter can be fabricated to purge the water system with compressed air.

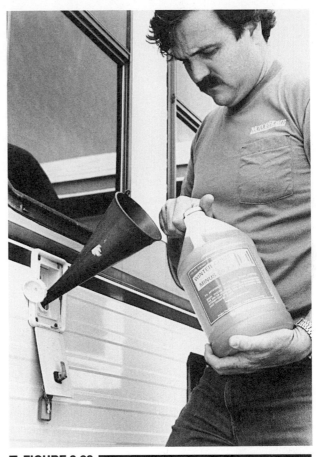

■ **FIGURE 3.28**
Nontoxic antifreeze will prevent pipes from bursting during extremely cold temperatures.

■ Winterizing Using Compressed Air

To winterize using compressed air, follow these steps:

1. Open all drains in the system, including the hot-water tank.
2. If you are going to use the compressed-air method, purchase an air-fitting adapter for the city water connection so that you can blow the air from that location (Figure 3.27).
3. Operate the 12-volt DC pump with a faucet open until it runs dry.
4. Connect the air fitting to the city water hookup and open the faucet farthest from the water pump. Close all drains in the system except the hot-water tank. Blow air through the city hookup line until only air comes out.

5. Open another faucet and then close the first one and blow out that line until it is clear. Continue this procedure throughout the rig until all lines have been blown clean.
6. Close all faucets, turn off water pump, and close all drains; the system is winterized.

■ Winterizing Using Nontoxic Antifreeze

If you choose to fill the system with nontoxic antifreeze there are a couple of methods you can use (Figure 3.28). Installation of a hot-water-tank bypass kit will avoid having to fill the entire water heater with antifreeze.

Pour a couple of gallons of potable nontoxic antifreeze directly into the freshwater tank of the RV. Operate the water pump so that the solution will flow through all the lines starting with the faucet farthest from the pump. Leave the faucet open until the antifreeze is visible (usually pink in color). Operate each faucet in the same fashion until all lines are filled with the fluid.

Another method requires less fluid, since you do not pour it into the water tank. A connection is made at the inlet side of the water pump and the antifreeze is drawn from the container through the pump, filling all the lines and accessories in the water system. You must make sure that the freshwater tank and the hot-water tank are drained completely.

Shut off all faucets and turn off the water pump; the system is winterized. After the winter storage period, the hot-water bypass must be switched so that water will flow through the tank, and city pressure water connected so that the antifreeze solution can be flushed out. The fluid is tasteless, odorless, and nontoxic, but it's a good idea to sanitize the system after a winter-long storage stint.

CHAPTER 4

Sanitation Systems

Three types of toilets are used in RV applications: freshwater, recirculating, and portable. The most common type of toilet, the *freshwater*, is mounted permanently, flushing with clean water from the RV's onboard tank. The flushing mechanism, whether a foot-operated pedal or a hand-operated lever, allows a valve in the bottom of the bowl to open, permitting the contents to be flushed into the holding tank. A stream of water under pressure from the RV's water system swirls around the bowl, cleaning it and flushing the contents into the holding tank. Most models have two levers, each working independently of the other so the bowl can be filled with water prior to use.

Freshwater toilet bowls are made of either durable plastic or porcelain, depending on the brand. These toilets flush using simple, dependable components. A vacuum breaker (back-flow restrictor) mounted at the rear of the toilet prevents water from the toilet from

TROUBLESHOOTING *the Thetford Aqua-Magic IV Toilet*

Problem	Possible Cause	Correction
Water keeps running into bowl	Sticking levers	Make sure levers return all the way to left.
	Sticking slide valve	Remove foreign material from blade or seat. Replace if cleaning does not work.
Toilet leaks on floor	Leaking water-supply line	Tighten as necessary.
	Loose closet-flange nuts	Tighten as necessary.
	Wrong closet-flange height	Make sure flange height is between ¼ and $^{7}/_{16}$ inch.
	Defective closet flange	Replace seal.
Poor flush	Flush duration too short	Hold levers open for at least 2 to 3 seconds.
	Bad water flow	Adjust flow rate to 10 quarts per minute.

backing into the RV's freshwater system. The vacuum breaker works by creating a vacuum in the toilet water supply line so that water flowing to other faucets in the RV will not suck water from the toilet.

Maintaining the Freshwater Toilet

While freshwater toilets require little maintenance, certain precautions must be taken to prolong the life of the mechanisms, especially the slide ball, or flapper valve. The first rule of thumb is to make sure all the contents are removed from the bowl before closing the valve. If toilet paper gets caught between the valve and seal, the toilet may emit odors from the holding tank. If paper or contents become lodged in the seal, the cleaning process is not pleasant. Do not use a sharp object to clean the seal area since damage may occur.

To clean the toilet, use a nonabrasive cleaner and a soft rag or paper towel. Do not use a highly concentrated or high-acid-content household cleaner. Scouring powder or other abrasives can damage the seal and other plastic parts in the toilet mechanism.

■ Thetford Freshwater Toilets

If the toilet must be removed to replace a leaky flange seal, proceed with the following steps for the various models of Thetford freshwater toilets.

Replacing the Aqua-Magic IV Model Toilet

To replace the Aqua-Magic IV model toilet (see Figure 4.1):

1. Turn off the water supply to the toilet.
2. Disconnect the water-supply line from the water valve located at the rear of the toilet. Hold the water-valve hex nut with a $1^{1}/_{16}$-inch wrench while loosening the water-line fitting. Be careful not to exert too much force or the fitting can become damaged.
3. Remove the mounting flange bolts.
4. Lift toilet from the mounting flange.
5. Reverse procedure when replacing toilet.
   CAUTION: Do not overtighten the water-line fitting or damage will result.

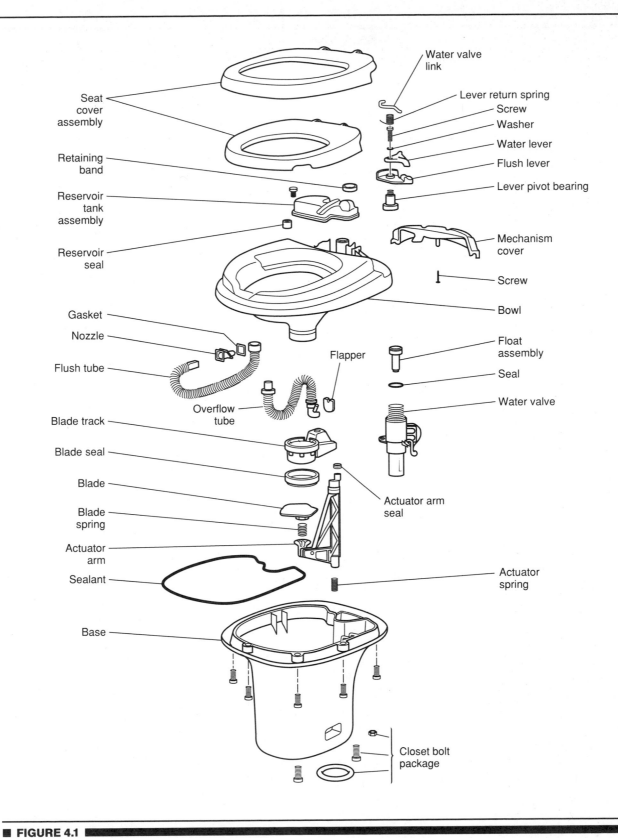

■ **FIGURE 4.1**
Exploded view of Thetford Aqua-Magic freshwater toilet

TROUBLESHOOTING the Thetford Galaxy and Starlite Toilets

Problem	Possible Cause	Correction
Water keeps running into bowl	Slide valve is not seated	Clean all foreign material in groove where valve blade seats when closed.
Leaks	Leaking water-supply line	Tighten as necessary.
	Leaking vacuum breaker	Replace vacuum breaker. Replace ball valve if vacuum breaker leaks without flushing.
	Defective bowl-to-mechanism seal	Replace seal.
	Defective closet flange-to-floor seal	Tighten flange nuts. Remove toilet and check flange height. Adjust to $1/4$–$7/16$ inch above floor. Replace flange seal.
Harder than normal foot pedal or sticking blade	Mounting bolts too tight	Check for overtight condition and adjust.
	Restricted valve blade	Apply light film of silicone spray on blade. **CAUTION:** Do not use hydrocarbon-based lubricants; damage to seals and other surfaces can occur.

Replacing Aqua-Magic Galaxy or Starlite Models

To replace Aqua-Magic Galaxy or Starlite model toilets (see Figure 4.2):

1. Turn off water supply to the toilet.
2. Insert a $2^1/2$-inch object to prop open the slide valve in the flush hole. Attach a cord or wire to keep it from falling into the holding tank. Use a 12-point, $1/2$-inch ratcheting box-end wrench to reach the front bolt through the opening above the foot pedal.
3. Remove rear bolt, positioned at about 11 o'clock, using the ratcheting box-end wrench if there is room between the toilet and wall. If there is not adequate room, the bolt can be reached via the access hole in the top of the toilet. Pry the plug open with a coin and insert a deep $1/2$-inch socket and universal swivel attached to a 12-inch extension to remove the nut.
4. Lift toilet from mounting flange.
5. Reverse procedure when replacing toilet.
   CAUTION: Do not overtighten the water-line fitting or damage will result.

Winterizing Thetford Freshwater Toilets

The water-supply line can be drained by propping open the slide valve in the flush hole. This can be accomplished by using a soft-drink bottle or like object to hold the valve open. Attach a cord or wire to keep object from falling into holding tank.

CAUTION: If compressed air is used to purge the water from the RV system, the toilet valve must be held in the open position.

RV antifreeze can also be used to winterize the toilet, following the directions from the antifreeze manufacturer.

CAUTION: Do not attempt to flush the toilet if it contains ice. Doing so will damage the toilet's internal valves.

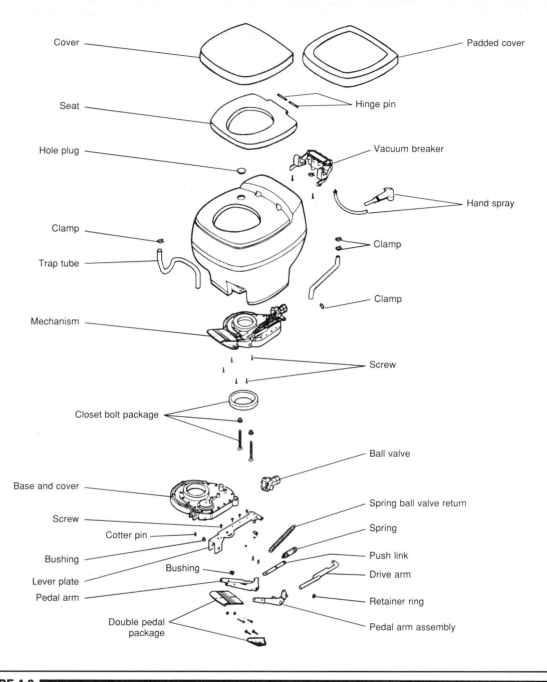

Exploded view of Thetford Aqua-Magic Galaxy freshwater toilet

TROUBLESHOOTING *the SeaLand Traveler Toilet*

Problem	Possible Cause	Correction
Water will not stay in bowl	Loose clamp ring	Tighten clamp-ring adjusting nut.
	Improper flush-ball seal	Inspect flush ball and underside of Teflon seal and clean dirt or debris.
	Worn or damaged seals	Replace both seals.
	Worn or damaged flush ball	Replace flush ball.
	Cracked half-clamps	Replace half-clamps.
Plastic flush ball will not close completely	Overtight clamp ring	Loosen clamp ring.
	Weak or defective spring	Let up on flush ring suddenly. If lever does not snap back, re-place spring, cam, and plate with new spring cartridge.
	Worn or damaged flush ball or shaft	If lever snaps back, but flush ball will not close completely, replace flush ball and shaft.
Toilet overflows	Dirt in water-valve seal	Disassemble and clean water valve.
	Bent cam strap; holds water valve open	Bend up front of cam strap $1/16$ inch.
	Worn or defective water valve	Replace valve assembly.
	Worn or defective spring	Replace spring, cam, and plate with new spring cartridge.
Water does not enter bowl properly	Low water pressure	Check and adjust water pressure.
	Clogged water valve	Remove and clean filter screen on inlet of water valve.
	Defective water valve	Replace water valve.
	Worn or defective flush lever	Replace flush lever.
	Leaking vacuum breaker	Replace vacuum breaker.
	Plugged wash holes in rim	Clean holes.

■ SeaLand Traveler Freshwater Toilets

The SeaLand Traveler is a freshwater toilet (see Figures 4.3, 4.4, 4.5, and 4.6). If the Traveler toilet needs to be removed to replace a defective flange seal or to remodel the bathroom, proceed with the following steps.

Replacing the SeaLand Traveler Freshwater Toilet

To remove and/or replace the SeaLand Traveler toilet, follow these steps:

1. Remove shroud near floor by reaching behind edges and pulling outward while shroud is

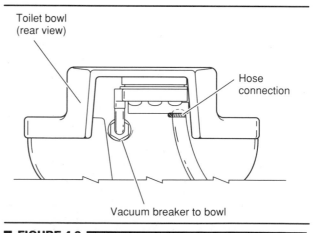

■ **FIGURE 4.3**
SeaLand Traveler freshwater toilet vacuum breaker assembly

TROUBLESHOOTING *the SeaLand Traveler Toilet* (continued)

Problem	Possible Cause	Correction
Water leaking from water valve	Loose connection	Tighten bottom cap, inlet fitting, and outlet-hose clamp.
	Worn or defective water valve	Replace water valve.
	Worn or missing seal	Replace water valve.
	Cracked valve body	Replace water valve.
Water leaking from bottom of toilet base	Loose toilet	Tighten toilet-mounting bolts.
	Worn or defective toilet-mounting floor seal	Replace sponge-rubber seal between floor flange and toilet base.
	Worn or defective base	Replace base assembly.
	Worn or defective floor flange	Replace floor flange.
Water leaking from rear of toilet bowl	Loose hose connection	Tighten hose connections.
	Loose vacuum breaker	Tighten vacuum breaker-to-bowl connection.
	Worn or defective vacuum breaker	Replace vacuum breaker assembly.
	Cracked or defective toilet bowl	Replace toilet bowl.

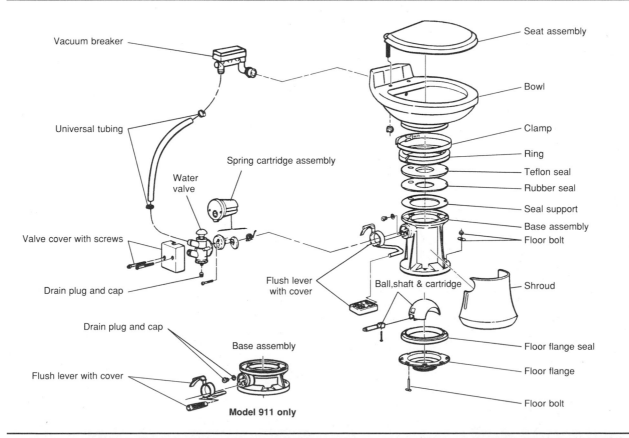

■ **FIGURE 4.4** ■
Exploded view of SeaLand Traveler models 910 and 911 freshwater toilets

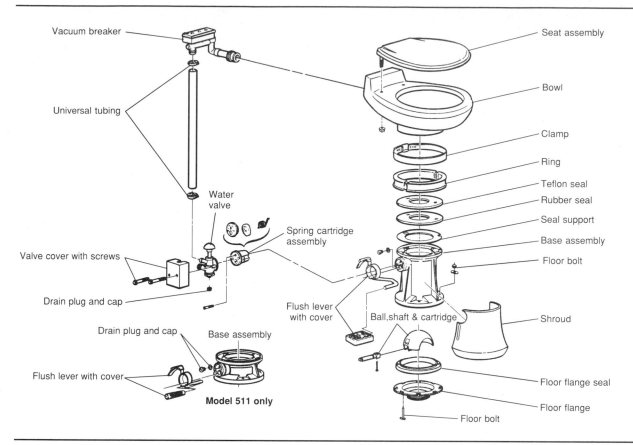

Exploded view of SeaLand Traveler models 510 and 511 freshwater toilets

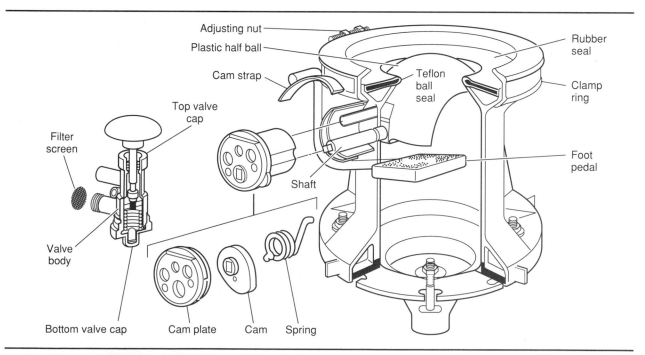

Exploded view of SeaLand Traveler freshwater toilet base

pulled forward. Do not force; shroud should be removed with light pressure.

2. Disconnect the water-supply line by loosening the ½-inch fittings.
3. Remove the 4 flange nuts.
4. Lift and remove toilet.
5. Reverse order to reinstall.

CAUTION: Do not overtighten supply-line fittings; damage can occur.

Winterizing the SeaLand Traveler Toilet

To winterize the SeaLand Traveler toilet, follow these steps:

1. Clean and flush toilet.
2. Shut off the water supply in RV.
3. Remove drain plug.
4. Remove drain cap from bottom of water valve in Models 910 and 510 (See Figure 4.7).
5. Depress flush lever until all water is drained from the system.

CAUTION: Do not flush toilet if water is frozen; damage to valves can occur.

■ Microphor Microflush Toilets

The Microphor Microflush freshwater toilet is usually found only in high-line coaches and trailers. The toilet is similar in size and style to a home model, but uses both water pressure and compressed air to operate. Air pressure is used to expel wastewater over the

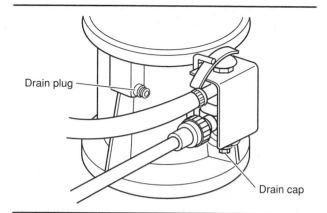

Drain plug

Drain cap

■ FIGURE 4.7 ■
Location of water-valve drain cap in SeaLand Traveler freshwater toilets

trapway to the holding tank. The compressed air reduces water consumption by almost 90%. Microphor toilets, when installed and adjusted properly, are rated to flush with only a half-gallon of water.

The Microflush uses the following sequence to flush (see Figure 4.8): The handle is pressed, opening a flapper valve and allowing the water in the bowl to flow into the lower chamber. Clean water enters from around the rim, washing the bowl. After a few seconds, the flapper valve closes, and clean water continues to flow into the bowl, ready for the next use. After the flapper valve is closed, compressed air is released into the lower chamber, forcing the contents out the discharge line (see Figure 4.9).

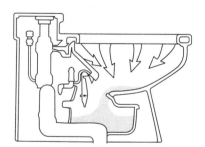

When the handle is pressed, the flapper valve opens, allowing the water in the bowl to flow into the lower chamber. Clean water enters from around the rim, thoroughly washing the bowl.

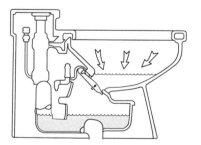

After a few seconds, the flapper valve closes. Clean water continues to flow into the bowl, where water remains until the next flush.

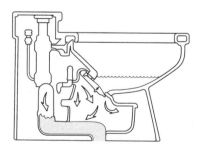

When the flapper valve has closed, compressed air is released into the lower chamber, forcing the contents out through the discharge line. Models are available for either rear or downward discharge.

■ FIGURE 4.8 ■
Microphor Microflush freshwater toilets use compressed air and water pressure to complete the flushing cycle.

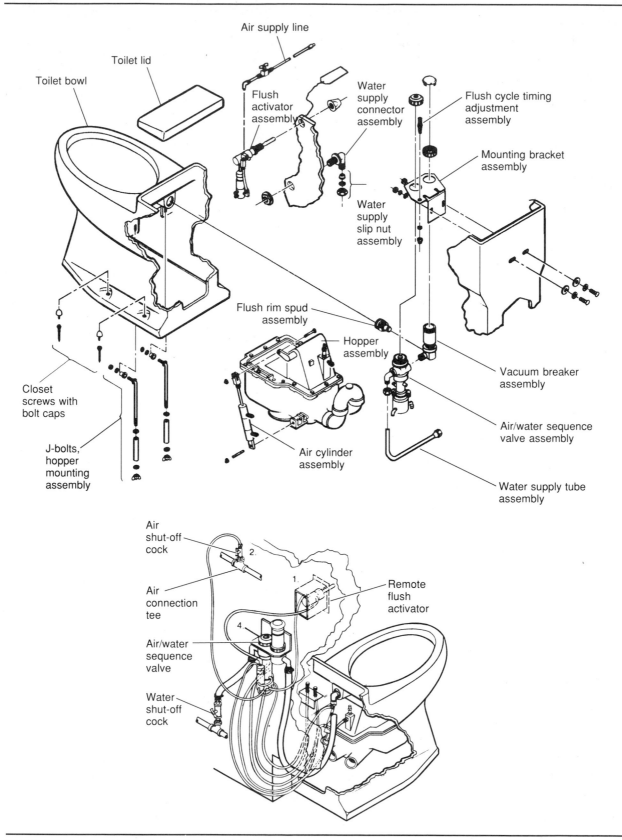

Air supply line

Toilet lid

Toilet bowl

Flush activator assembly

Water supply connector assembly

Flush cycle timing adjustment assembly

Mounting bracket assembly

Water supply slip nut assembly

Flush rim spud assembly

Hopper assembly

Vacuum breaker assembly

Closet screws with bolt caps

Air cylinder assembly

Air/water sequence valve assembly

J-bolts, hopper mounting assembly

Water supply tube assembly

Air shut-off cock

Remote flush activator

Air connection tee

Air/water sequence valve

Water shut-off cock

■ **FIGURE 4.9** ■
Exploded view of Microphor Microflush freshwater toilet

Adjusting the Microflush Toilet

To adjust the Microflush toilet, follow these steps (see Figure 4.10):

1. Turn on water to toilet.
2. Adjust flapper cycle to 5 to 7 seconds by turning the flush-cycle timing adjustment: to lengthen cycle, turn timing adjustment clockwise; to shorten, turn counterclockwise.
3. Adjust water level in bowl to top edge of flapper opening by turning the water-shutoff valve (angle stop) next to the toilet.

Cleaning the Microflush Toilet

To properly clean the Microflush toilet, follow these steps:

1. Depress the flush activator, turn off water, and allow bowl cleaner to flow to lower chamber while activator continues to be depressed. Any liquid toilet bowl cleaner is acceptable, but do not use caustic drain openers.
2. Insert bowl brush into lower chamber and agitate.
3. Remove brush and release the flush activator.
4. Turn on water and flush twice to rinse thoroughly.

Routine Maintenance of Microflush Toilet

Water pressure should be maintained at levels below 50 psi. Air pressure should be regulated at 60 psi. The air-operated flush valve requires lubrication every five years. The Microflush toilet becomes more complicated when installed in RVs. Internal repairs and adjustments other than listed above should be performed by an authorized service center.

Recirculating Toilets

A *recirculating* toilet (Figure 4.11) requires no pressure-water connection or holding tank. This type of toilet uses a 12-volt DC pump and a system of filters to recirculate the contents. The liquid portion is separated from the solid contents and used to flush the toilet. When the contents fill the internal holding tank, the toilet must be dumped by use of a 3-inch termination valve, similar to those used to dump holding tanks. A holding tank can be installed to increase toilet capacity.

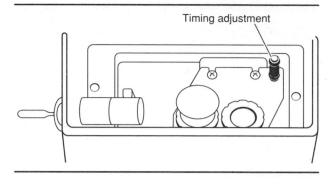

■ **FIGURE 4.10** ▬▬▬▬▬▬
The flush cycle in the Microphor Microflush is controlled by the timing adjustment under the toilet lid.

■ The Thetford Electra Magic Toilet

One popular type of recirculating toilet is the Thetford Electra Magic.

Replacing the Electra Magic Toilet Fuse

To replace a fuse in the Thetford Electra Magic toilet, follow these steps:

1. Remove the 2 cover-mounting screws and motor cover.
2. Check fuse with multimeter.
3. Replace if defective.

Replacing the Electra Magic Toilet Switch

To replace the Electra Magic toilet switch, follow these steps:

1. Disconnect lead wires from power source.
2. Remove the 2 cover-mounting screws and motor cover.
3. Remove switch retaining nut and remove wires from switch terminals.
4. Check with multimeter.
5. Replace if defective.

Replacing the Electra Magic Toilet Pump

To replace the Electra Magic toilet pump, follow these steps:

1. Disconnect lead wires from power source.
2. Remove the 2 cover-mounting screws and motor cover.

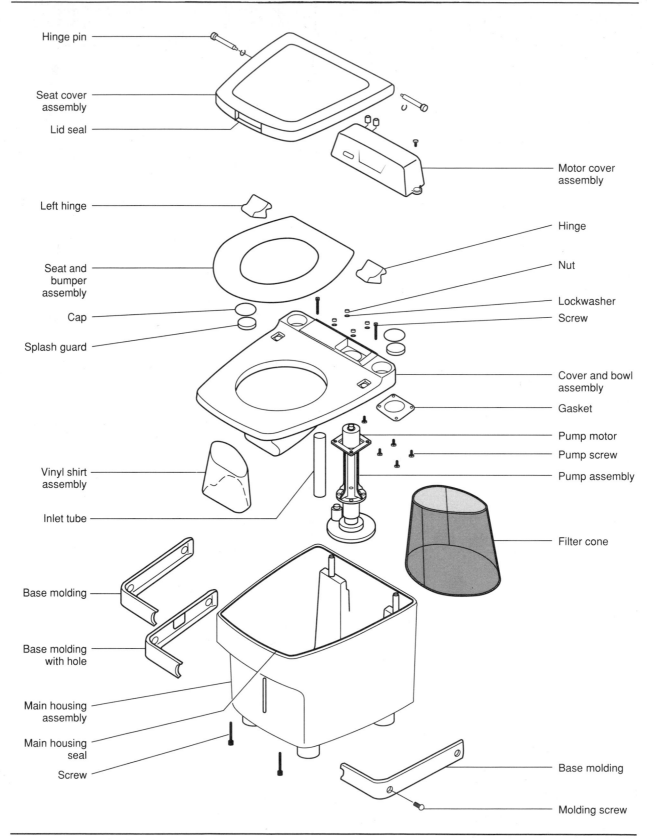

Hinge pin

Seat cover assembly

Lid seal

Left hinge

Seat and bumper assembly

Cap

Splash guard

Vinyl shirt assembly

Inlet tube

Base molding

Base molding with hole

Main housing assembly

Main housing seal

Screw

Motor cover assembly

Hinge

Nut

Lockwasher

Screw

Cover and bowl assembly

Gasket

Pump motor

Pump screw

Pump assembly

Filter cone

Base molding

Molding screw

■ **FIGURE 4.11**
Exploded view of Thetford Electra Magic recirculating toilet

TROUBLESHOOTING the Thetford Electra Magic Recirculating Toilet

Problem	Possible Cause	Correction
Toilet wobbles	Closet flange too high; mounting surface too high	Check by laying straightedge across flange and measuring gap to floor at four leg locations. Height should be $\frac{1}{4}$ to $\frac{7}{16}$ inch.
Flush action too weak or noisy	Pump running backward	Check wire polarity: black is positive, white is negative.
	Cycling without sufficient water	Charge with 3 gallons of water or to charge-level indicator lens.
	Pump damaged by continuous dry operation	Replace pump assembly.

3. Remove cover and bowl-assembly screws in rear from top side and the 2 screws from bottom side; remove cover and bowl assembly.
4. Remove the 4 pump-mounting screws.
5. Disconnect flush tube from pump outlet.
6. Remove pump assembly.
7. Replace if defective.

Replacing the Electra Magic Slide-EZ Valve

To replace the Electra Magic Slide-EZ Valve, follow these steps (Figure 4.12):

1. Disconnect lead wires from power source.
2. Empty toilet completely.
3. Remove cotter pin and extension handle if so equipped.
4. Remove the 2 molding-mounting screws and remove the 2 base moldings.
5. Remove slides by catching tabs with a hooked instrument and pulling forward.
6. Lift toilet from closet flange and invert unit.
7. Remove the 4 screws and remove valve.
8. Replace if defective.

Cleaning the Electra Magic Toilet

The bowl and outside of the Electra Magic toilet can be cleaned using the same type of nonabrasive cleaners specified for freshwater toilets (see page 64). For cleaning the tank, use Thetford's Aqua Bowl or diluted household laundry detergent (2 to 4 ounces to 1 gallon of water).

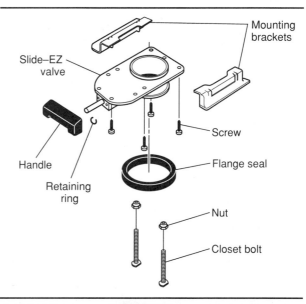

FIGURE 4.12
Thetford Electra Magic recirculating toilet Slide-EZ Valve

Winterizing and Storing the Electra Magic Toilet

To winterize the Electra Magic Toilet, follow these steps:

1. Completely empty unit via termination valve.
2. Refill unit to bottom of bowl with fresh water.
3. Add 8 ounces (1 cup) of Aqua Bowl or diluted solution of laundry detergent.
4. Cycle 3 times by depressing flush button for 10 seconds each cycle.

5. Let stand for a few minutes.
6. Completely empty unit via termination valve.
7. Add one-half charge with propylene glycol-type antifreeze for winterizing toilet.

Portable Toilets

Portable toilets are used in smaller RVs that are not equipped with holding tanks and the appropriate plumbing. This type of toilet is commonly found in folding trailers or in truck campers that are not self-

contained. Portable toilets are very simple to use and can be dumped into a conventional toilet, pit toilet, or at a dump station. Most portables are comprised of two pieces: a top half consisting of a bowl, seat, and freshwater reservoir, and a bottom half containing the slider valve and handle, waste-holding tank, and evacuation tube. Various models offer larger holding tanks (see Figure 4.13).

Other than periodic cleaning, the only maintenance needed is to keep the slider valve and seal clean of debris. The holding tank should be thor-

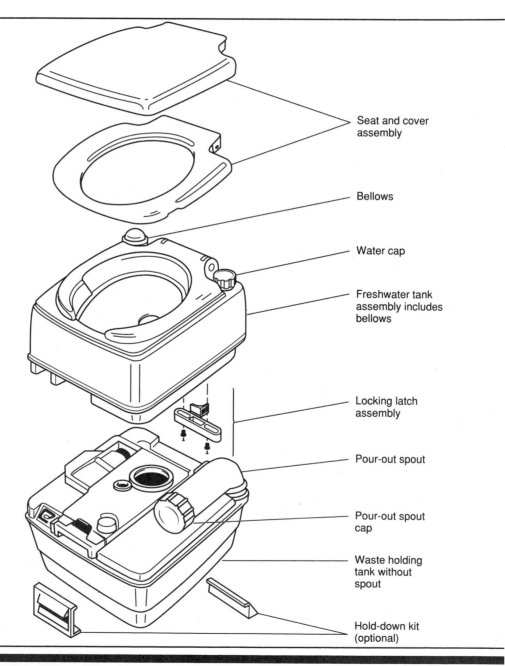

Seat and cover assembly

Bellows

Water cap

Freshwater tank assembly includes bellows

Locking latch assembly

Pour-out spout

Pour-out spout cap

Waste holding tank without spout

Hold-down kit (optional)

■ FIGURE 4.13 ■
Exploded view of Thetford Porta-Potti portable toilet

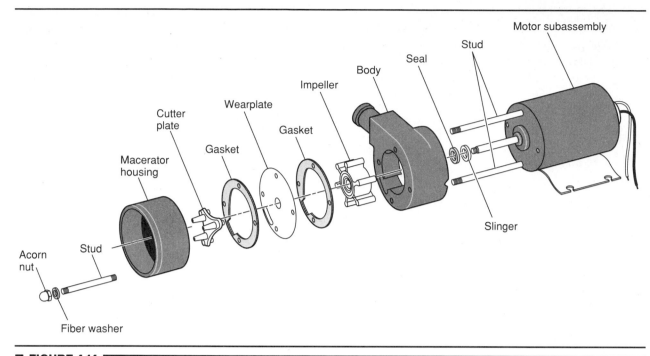

Acorn nut · Stud · Fiber washer · Macerator housing · Cutter plate · Wearplate · Gasket · Gasket · Impeller · Body · Seal · Stud · Motor subassembly · Slinger

■ **FIGURE 4.14**

Exploded view of ITT Jabsco Par macerator pump

oughly rinsed before storing the toilet. To winterize, simply add propylene glycol-type antifreeze to the freshwater holding tank.

Macerator Pumps

Macerator pumps are designed to aid in emptying a holding tank by grinding waste down to a particle size no larger than ⅛ inch and pushing it out a 1-inch discharge hose. This pump can handle body wastes, toilet tissue, and facial tissue, but not hard, solid objects, sanitary napkins, or rags. The ITT Jabsco Par macerator pump, for example, will empty a typical 30-gallon waste-holding tank in 3 minutes (Figure 4.14).

A macerator pump will perform properly if the following recommendations are followed:

☑ CHECKLIST

☐ Flush the holding tank with several gallons of water after each pump-out.

☐ Do not run the motor dry.

☐ Operate pump only when battery is fully charged or outside hookups are available.

☐ Do not run the motor for more than 15 minutes in continuous duty.

☐ Be sure the pump is wired with 10-gauge wire for distances up to 20 feet and 12-gauge wire for distances under 10 feet. Use a 20-amp fuse.

Note: After long periods of non-use, the pump may not turn freely. Pour a cup of water down the pump-discharge line to help free impeller.

■ Replacing the Seal, Impeller, and Gasket in the Par Macerator Pump

To replace the seal, impeller, and gasket in the Par Macerator pump, follow these steps:

1. Remove acorn nuts and inlet housing.
2. Unscrew cutter plate from shaft by turning the facing cutter blades counterclockwise. Hold motor shaft behind plate to prevent turning.
3. Remove gaskets, wearplate, and slide-pump assembly from mounting studs.
4. Remove seal by pushing out evenly with screwdriver from impeller-bore side of body.
5. Remove gasket and impeller.
6. Replace with new gasket and impeller.
7. Reassemble seal by coating the outside of the metal case lightly with sealant and pressing into body with lip facing impeller.

8. Press star retaining washer (with concave side up) into seal bore and against seal case.

9. Apply a light coating of grease to impeller bore and wearplate to aid in initial start-up.

10. Reassemble body, impeller, gaskets, wearplate, housing, and acorn nuts.

Holding Tanks and Drainpipes

Self-contained RVs have a system of plastic pipes that allow the sinks, shower, and toilet to drain into holding tanks. In most RVs, the shower and sinks drain into one holding tank, and the toilet waste is routed into a separate holding tank. The drain water goes into what is known as the gray-water holding tank, and wastes end up in the black-water holding tank. Toilet-waste holding tanks can also be referred to as *sewer* or *waste* tanks (Figure 4.15).

Both holding tanks terminate at a 3-inch dump valve that is usually under the motorhome or trailer (or somewhere close to the floor area) on the left side, within 16 feet of the rear bumper (Figure 4.16). Although only one dump valve is the norm (some coaches use two dump valves, one for each holding tank), the contents from each tank are separated by individual slide valves. A typical RV system will have a section of 3-inch pipe from the black-water holding tank connected to a 3-inch slider valve and the main

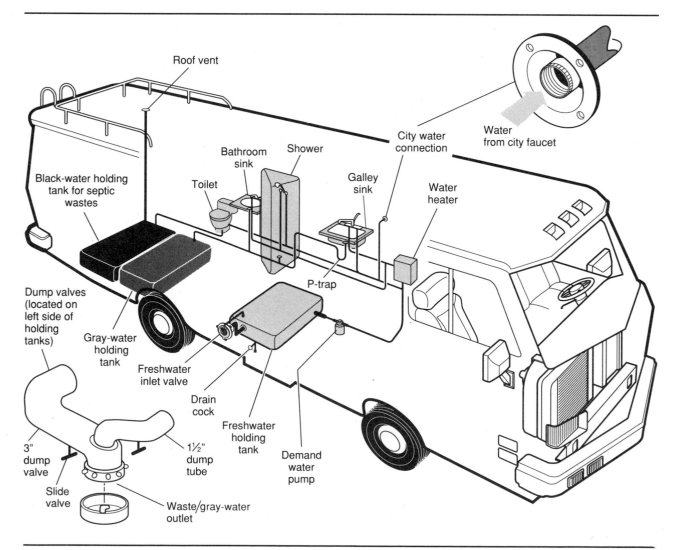

■ FIGURE 4.15 ■

RVs are equipped with two holding tanks: One for collecting gray water from the sinks and shower and the other for storing the waste from the toilet. Dump valves are used to control removal of contents from individual tanks.

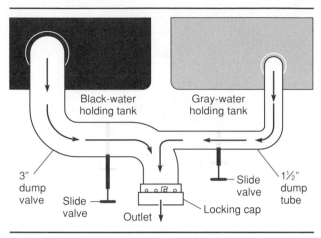

■ FIGURE 4.16 ▬▬▬▬▬▬▬▬▬▬▬
Holding tanks terminate at a 3-inch exit pipe that is fitted with a 3-inch slide valve for the black-water tank and a 1½-inch slide valve for the gray-water tank.

dump connection. A 1½-inch pipe with a separate slide valve will be routed from the gray-water holding tank to a point right after the main slider valve.

■ Dumping the Holding Tank

The main dump valve is fitted with extruded pins that allow the attachment of a flexible holding-tank hose. The hose is then routed to a 4-inch pipe in a dump station or campsite hookup. To properly dump the holding tanks, the black water should be evacuated first. After the black-water tank finishes draining, the gray-water tank should be emptied. This allows the gray water to rinse the hose. Make sure the smaller slide valve is closed when draining the black-water holding tank so that waste material cannot be forced into the gray-water plumbing.

When hooked up to a campsite sewer, the black-water valve should remain closed until the tank is at least three-quarters full. The tank cannot be flushed properly unless there is a sufficient amount of material to gravity-flow from the tank. Clogging of the termination valve can result if an insufficient amount of waste is flushed. After dumping, the black-water holding tank should be filled with fresh water and dumped again to clean the tank completely.

Normally only a couple of holding-tank rinses are needed before storing the RV. After prolonged usage it may be necessary to clean the tank with a holding-tank cleaner and fresh water. Holding-tank cleaners are available in most RV-supply stores.

CAUTION: Do not use household detergents or cleaning compounds when cleaning holding tanks. These may contain chemicals that could damage the drain system or termination valves; cleaners that contain petroleum distillates can damage toilet seals and termination valves.

■ Repairing the Holding Tank

Holding-tank leaks are a messy proposition. Most holding tanks are made from black ABS, which is very durable. But holes and breaks can be caused by flying rocks, or by dragging on steep driveways and rough terrain. If a crack develops, the ends of the crack should be drilled to keep it from getting any longer before repairing (see Figure 4.17).

Obviously, holes or cracks that are too large cannot be repaired, and the holding tank must be replaced. Smaller holes and cracks can be repaired using a commercially available patch kit. Another good method is to use fiberglass cloth and a gap-filling cyanoacrylate adhesive, such as Slo-Zap, found in most hobby shops. This glue is similar to Super Glue but is much thicker and takes longer to set—sometimes as long as two minutes. The thicker adhesive allows adequate time to cover the crack or break. The key to using gap-filling cyanoacrylate adhesive is the accelerator compound, such as Zip Kicker, that will instantly set

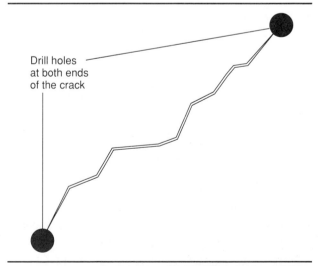

Drill holes at both ends of the crack

■ FIGURE 4.17 ▬▬▬▬▬▬▬▬▬▬▬
A crack in the holding tank can be stopped by drilling holes in each end of the damaged area.

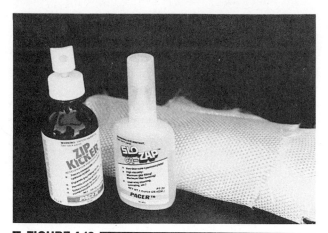

■ **FIGURE 4.18** ■
Cyanoacrylate adhesive, found in most hobby stores, can be used to fix holding tanks.

■ **FIGURE 4.19** ■
Seal-N-Place, a kit designed to repair ABS or polyethylene tanks, is available commercially.

the glue (see Figure 4.18). The owner has enough time to saturate the fiberglass cloth, position it over the break, and then zap it with accelerator to instantly set the glue. Use the following steps to fix a holding-tank break.

1. Empty holding tank and, when dry, clean the area around the damage.
2. Cut a piece of fiberglass cloth a couple of inches larger than the damaged area.
3. Saturate the fiberglass cloth with the cyano-acrylate adhesive.
4. Place the saturated fiberglass cloth over the damaged area. Smooth out with hands (use disposable gloves for this job).
5. When fiberglass is in position and smooth, zap the area with the accelerator. The fiberglass cloth and adhesive will bond instantly to the damaged area.

The preceding procedure can be used to make emergency repairs to ABS pipes, tanks, or exterior fiberglass.

Repairing Polyethylene Tanks

Polyethylene tanks (translucent) can be repaired with a commercially available kit, Seal-N-Place, or by "welding" (heat). The welding process is more complicated and requires specialized equipment and the expertise available at larger RV repair shops (see also pages 47–48).

The Seal-N-Place kit (Figure 4.19) is designed for permanent repairs but must be used quickly because the resin mixture begins to harden in 6 to 8 minutes. The resin is cured in 20 minutes. The resin can be used in temperatures down to 30°F. Allow yourself 5 minutes to make the repair after mixing the material so that you will have a slight time cushion before the resin hardens. Repairs can be made using the Seal-N-Place kit and following these procedures:

1. Remove grease, road dirt, tar, and any oil from the repair surface.
2. Rough up the surface with the sandpaper.
3. Cut enough of the fiberglass cloth to overlap the damaged area.
4. Break off the tip on the metal tube within the plastic bag holding the resin.
5. Using the key over the metal tube, empty hardener from tube into plastic bag.
6. Knead the plastic bag until the resin and hardener are thoroughly mixed (approximately 20 seconds).
7. Brush a layer of resin over the area to be covered by the fiberglass.
8. Lay the cut fiberglass over the resin-coated area.
9. Brush on a heavy coat of resin over the fiberglass until it is completely saturated. Flare out the edges of the resin.

Note: Seal-N-Place kits can also be used for repairing ABS, polypropylene, and other plastic surfaces.

■ Toilet Chemicals

Unlike home sewage that drains into a large underground septic system or a city sewer, the waste in RV holding tanks remains in close proximity to the living quarters. To eliminate offensive odors, chemicals must be used in the black-water holding tank. Normally the tank is charged with a dose of toilet chemicals after dumping. But during hot summer days, additional chemicals may be necessary. Products are also available to freshen gray-water holding tanks.

Many municipalities require that biodegradable chemicals, devoid of formaldehyde, be used. Therefore, a wide variety of environmentally safe chemicals is available. There are many home remedies that have surfaced during evening campfire conversations, but some of these household products may damage the toilet seals, plumbing, or termination valves. It is always safer to use a commercially available toilet chemical.

Although it is not absolutely necessary, it is advisable to use single-ply, white toilet paper in all RV toilets. Not only is the bulk limited because the paper is thin, but it also tends to break down faster, which is easier on the plumbing system, especially the termination valves.

■ Drainpipes

An RV's plumbing system, which drains the water from the sinks and shower, is comprised of a series of black ABS pipes, configured much the same as a home system. Pipes fitted to the sinks and shower are routed to nearby P-traps and then on to the holding tanks. P-traps are U-shaped curves in the pipe that allow columns of water to remain temporarily trapped until the next amount of water is drained. This column of water prevents the gases in the holding tank from backing up into the sinks and shower, preventing nasty smells from entering the living quarters. Traps can become clogged with accumulated hair, grease, and other small food particles. To break a clog, hot water can be flushed down the drain. If this does not work, the P-trap can be dismantled by unscrewing the fittings on each end. Do not use sharp objects to free a clog, or damage to the pipe may result.

Pipes made of ABS are usually hardy enough to last the life of the RV. Occasionally a leak will develop or a break will be caused by a heavy item that has fallen on the pipe. Repairing or rerouting is fairly easy, requiring only a hacksaw, new ABS pipe sections, connectors, and ABS cement to dissolve the surfaces of the pipes to be connected, allowing two sections to be welded together. The cementing process is fast and requires forethought and organization before proceeding.

Slide valves usually must be replaced if a jam or break develops. This is also an easy process since termination valves are universal and often are only attached to the pipe with large hose clamps. If that is the case, the hose clamp can be removed, the valve twisted off, and a new one attached. If the valve is ABS-cemented to the pipe, it must be cut and a new valve installed, using appropriate couplers.

CHAPTER 5

Generators

AC generators, the type primarily found in most RVs, are compact powerplants designed to provide 120-volt, 60-cycle-per-second alternating current to household appliances when outside hookups are not available. Generators are either single- or multi-cylinder 4-cycle engines powered by gasoline, propane, or diesel fuel.

Generators are sized and classified by the amount of power they are able to produce, expressed in kilowatts (thousands of watts). Those for RVs range from 2.5-kw to diesel-powered 12.5-kw units. Determining the type and power rating of your generator is easy. A nameplate with all pertinent information affixed to the side of the unit contains the following information: model and serial number (both are necessary to order parts), AC voltage output, phase, kilowatts (sometimes expressed as KVA), ampere rating, hertz or cycles per second, engine-governed RPM, and type of fuel required.

Maintenance of AC Generators

It's important to keep the AC generator well maintained for optimum performance. Refer to Table 5.1 for the proper schedule.

■ **TABLE 5.1**

AC Generator Maintenance Schedule

	At startup	At 50 hrs.	At 100 hrs.	At 500 hrs.
Check RV battery	X			
Check oil level	X			
Check fuel supply	X			
Check air inlet and outlet	X			
Check compartment for debris	X			
Check air cleaner (Figure 5.1)	X			
Lubricate governor linkage		X		
Change oil			X	
Replace oil filter			X	
Clean fuel filter			X	
Replace spark plug			X	
Check breaker points			X	
Check electrical connections			X	
Check mounting bolts			X	
Adjust carburetor			X	
Check brushes				X
Service cylinder heads				X

Service and Repair

■ Battery

Without a fully charged battery and clean, tight electrical connections, starting the generator will be impossible. The battery electrolyte level should be checked regularly.

Removing Battery Corrosion

Follow these steps to remove battery corrosion:

1. Remove terminals from battery posts using a battery terminal puller if necessary.
2. Soak terminals in a mixture of 1 quart of water and ½ cup of baking soda.
3. Mix another quart of water and ½ cup baking soda and pour over battery top to remove corrosion.

4. Rinse the terminals and battery top with clean water, then dry.
5. A battery post/terminal brush should be used to thoroughly clean the inside of the terminal fitting and the outside of the posts.
6. Use a light grease or commercially available terminal protectant on the terminals and posts; install terminals to posts and tighten firmly.

If battery problems persist see "Batteries," page 9 for additional information.

■ Cooling System Intake/Outlet

Check and clean the air-inlet screen. Cooling air is drawn over the generator, then exits by passing over the engine. Make sure there is no debris such as leaves or paper that may block the flow of air.

For liquid-cooled generator units, check the radiator for any signs of debris buildup.

■ Crankcase Oil Level

When checking the oil level make sure you follow the generator manufacturer's recommendations. Kohler generators require that the level be checked with the oil cap resting on the oil-shaft collar; do not thread the cap on (Figure 5.2). Onan requires the opposite method: the cap should be screwed in to its fully seated position before reading the dipstick.

Changing the Oil and Filter

Oil change should be performed every 100 hours or once every 12 months. Drain oil while engine is warm, after running the generator at half load for 30 minutes.

To drain the oil and change the filter:

1. Stop generator.
2. With drain pan under generator, remove drain plug if so equipped, or open drain valve (Figure 5.3a).
3. Remove old oil filter (Figure 5.3b).
4. Clean filter base on engine.
5. Wipe a film of clean oil on the new filter's gasket.
6. Screw new filter to base until gasket contacts, then tighten an additional half turn.
7. Replace drain plug or close drain valve.

■ FIGURE 5.1 ■
The air filter should be checked periodically for debris.

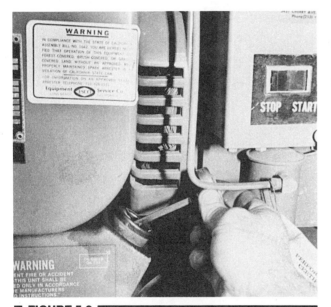

■ FIGURE 5.2 ■
The generator oil level should be checked at the outset of each trip.

■ FIGURE 5.3 ■
(*Top*) A drain plug or petcock (shown) is used to drain the oil from generators. (*Bottom*) Removing the old oil filter should be part of the oil-change maintenace program.

8. Refill crankcase to proper level with the recommended grade and weight oil for the operational service temperature expected (see Figure 5.4).
9. Start engine and run for a few minutes, checking for leaks at filter base and drain plug or valve.
10. Record the generator's hour-meter time of the oil change in a log to keep for future reference.

■ Setting Ignition Points and Timing

Follow these steps to set ignition points and timing (see Figures 5a and b):

1. The battery cables, negative cable first, should be removed to prevent accidental engine start-up during point adjustment procedure.
2. The points are found under a sheet metal cover on the engine block or governor.
3. Point contact surfaces should be clean and smooth. If points are rough and pitted, they will require replacement.
4. Gap settings vary greatly, depending on the make and model of the generator, but generally are between .016 and .025 inch (see Figures 5.6 and 5.7).
5. Point gap must be set with the points in their fully open position. Rotate the engine by turning the generator shaft to open the points. Onan

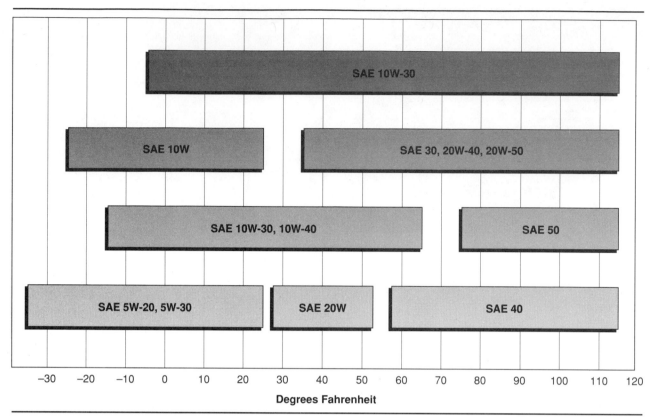

■ FIGURE 5.4 ▨
Recommended oil grade and weight for various operational temperatures

requires a ⅜-inch hex socket to turn the shaft in a clockwise direction until the points open. For Kohler, a ¾-inch socket is used to turn the shaft in the same clockwise direction.

6. In both cases a clean, flat feeler gauge of the recommended thickness should be used to check the gap.

7. If the gap is incorrect, loosen the hold-down screws and move the stationary member of the points until the proper gap is attained.

8. Tighten the hold-down screw, replace cover, and reconnect the negative battery terminal.

Some of Kohler's 2.5-kw gen-sets (after Serial No. 159482) have an electronic ignition system and do not use a point breaker set. Onan's ignition timing is determined by the point gap setting. Once the correct gap has been established the timing is automatically correct. Kohler units require shifting a setting on the engine's governor with a timing light. Kohler recommends that the procedure be done only by a qualified service technician.

■ FIGURE 5.5 ▨
(*Top*) Points for this Onan generator are located under a box that is easily accessed. (*Bottom*) An automotive feeler gauge is used to set point gap.

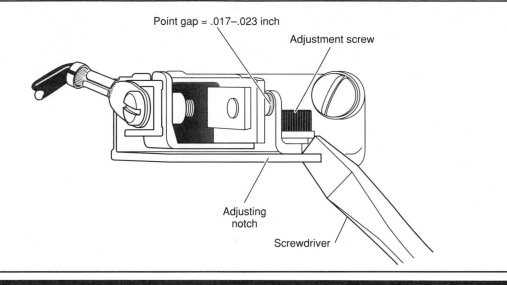

Point gap = .017–.023 inch

Adjustment screw

Adjusting notch

Screwdriver

■ **FIGURE 5.6**
Point gap for Kohler generators should be set between .017 and .023 inch.

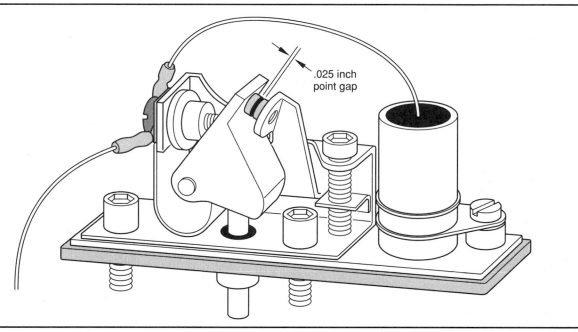

.025 inch
point gap

■ **FIGURE 5.7**
Point gap for Onan generators should be set at .025 inch.

TROUBLESHOOTING *the AC Generator*

Problem	Possible Cause	Correction
Will not start	Low battery	Charge or replace.
	Out of fuel	Replenish.
	Bad battery connection	Clean terminals.
	Clogged fuel filter	Replace filter.
	Dirty air cleaner	Clean or replace.
	Faulty ignition points	Clean, adjust, replace.
	Worn or dirty spark plug	Clean or replace.
	Faulty ignition coil	Replace.
	Oil too heavy	Replace with lighter grade.
	Stuck carburetor choke	Clean and adjust.
	Blown starting-circuit fuse	Check and replace.
	Fuel shutdown solenoid	Replace or remove.
Hard to start	Stale fuel	Replace.
	Wrong carburetor adjustment	Adjust.
	Incorrect point setting	Adjust gap.
	Dirty air cleaner	Replace.
	Worn spark plug	Replace.
	Engine running too hot	Check cooling system.
	Faulty fuel pump	Replace.
Engine runs, then stops	Low fuel level	Replenish supply.
	Low oil pressure	Check/add oil.
	Oil level too high	Check/remove oil.
	Wrong fuel mixture	Adjust.
	Faulty spark plug	Clean or replace.
	Clogged fuel filter	Clean or replace.
	Fuel shutdown solenoid	Replace or remove.
Emits black smoke	Rich fuel mixture	Adjust carburetor.
	Clogged air cleaner	Replace element.
	Choke stuck closed	Clean and adjust.
Engine lacks power	Clogged air cleaner	Replace element.
	Rich fuel mixture	Adjust carburetor.
	Overloaded engine	Reduce electrical load.
	Bad or stale fuel	Replenish with fresh fuel.
	Dirty or faulty spark plug	Clean or replace plug.
	Engine carbon buildup	Service/clean carbon.
	Ignition points	Adjust or replace points.
	Overheated engine	Check cooling system.

TROUBLESHOOTING the AC Generator (continued)

Problem	Possible Cause	Correction
Engine surges	Clogged air cleaner	Clean or replace.
	Worn ignition points	Replace.
	Worn spark plug	Replace.
	Fuel starvation	Check filter and pump.
	Incorrect carburetor adjustment	Adjust.
	Stale fuel	Replace with fresh fuel.
	Sticking linkage	Clean and lubricate.
Engine overheats	Clogged airflow ducts	Clean inlet and outlet.
	Carburetor mixture too lean	Enrich mixture.
	Incorrect point adjustment	Adjust.
No AC current output	Tripped circuit breaker	Reset breaker.
	Breaker continues to trip	Reduce load.
	Breaker still trips	Short in wiring.
	Internal generator defect	Seek service center.
Low AC output	Engine speed too low	Adjust carburetor or governor.
	Power overload	Reduce load.

■ Air Cleaners

Virtually all generators use a pleated paper air filter element that requires service approximately every 50 hours (see Figure 5.8). The element can be cleaned after the first 50 hours by lightly tapping it against a flat surface to dislodge any loose dirt and debris. Paper elements should not be washed in any type of solvent solution since damage to the element will occur. Replace the element every 100 hours, but if the generator is operated in extremely dusty or dirty environments, replace the element more often.

■ Spark Plugs

Spark plugs should be replaced after approximately 100 hours of running time or, if upon inspection, they show signs of burning or heavy deposits of carbon. Spark plugs that show heavy, black-colored deposits could indicate excessive oil consumption or a carburetor that is adjusted so the mixture is too rich.

Replacing Spark Plugs

To replace spark plugs follow these steps:

1. Remove spark plug with spark plug socket, either a ⅝-inch or ¹³/₁₆-inch, depending on the spark plug type.
2. Make sure that the gasket seating surface of the cylinder head is clean.
3. Set plug gap to .025 inch.
4. Tighten plug carefully, 18 to 22 foot-pounds torque. Since most generators use an aluminum cylinder head, the threads are prone to stripping if overtightened.

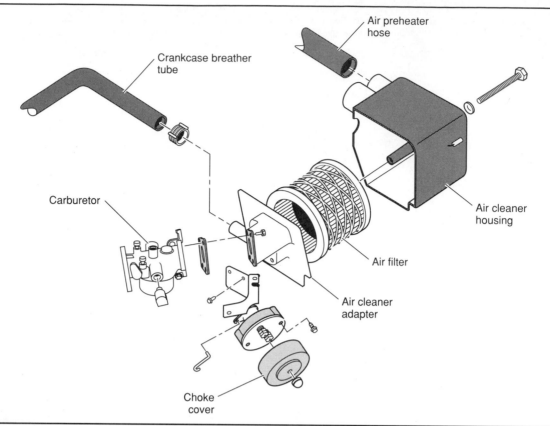

The Onan generator uses a pleated paper air filter element.

■ Fuel Filters and Pumps

Generator fuel pumps are either electrically operated by 12-volt power or are mechanically actuated by an eccentric lobe on the engine's camshaft (see Figure 5.9). The electronics are not serviceable; only the diaphragm and filter assembly may be repaired. The diaphragm can be replaced in mechanical pumps.

Cleaning the Electric Pump Filter

To clean electric pump filters (for Kohler and pre-June, 1986, Onan; Onan electric pumps after June, 1986, do not have filters), follow these steps:

1. With a ⅝-inch wrench, loosen the cover on the pump and remove by hand.
2. Remove the cover, gasket, and filter assembly.
3. Wash the filter in clean solvent to remove debris, then blow dry with low-pressure compressed air.

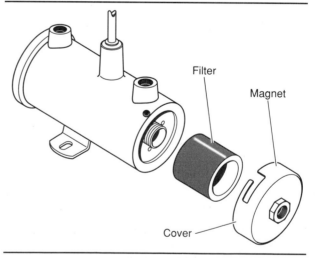

■ **FIGURE 5.9** ■■■■■■■■■■
Generator fuel pumps can be either mechanical or electric, such as this one used in Onan products.

Testing the Electric Pump

For electric pump testing, Kohler and pre-June 1986 Onan, follow these steps:

1. Remove fuel-outlet line to carburetor and install a fuel-pressure gauge.
2. Press the ''start'' switch and hold until a pressure reading is constant.
3. The pressure should read between 4 and 5 psi. Pressure should stay constant or drop off very slowly.
4. June 1986 and later Onan pumps will have a lower pressure reading of 3½ to 5 psi. These pumps are not serviceable; if the pump fails to perform properly, the entire assembly must be replaced.

■ Fuel-Shutdown Solenoid

Kohler equips its carburetors with a fuel-shutdown solenoid that prevents run-on (dieseling) after the engine is shut down. The solenoid is mounted on the top of the carburetor and is energized by battery current when starting the engine. When the engine is shut down the solenoid is de-energized, dropping a plunger to stop fuel flow. If the solenoid fails, fuel cannot reach the engine.

Bypassing the Solenoid

To bypass the solenoid temporarily, it can be removed, the plunger removed from the solenoid, and the solenoid reinstalled. Follow these steps:

1. Turn main fuel adjustment in until it bottoms.
2. Record number of turns in.
3. Then turn main screw out far enough to shift the solenoid retaining bracket.
4. Lift out the solenoid and remove the plunger.
5. Reinstall the solenoid and its retaining bracket.
6. Turn the main fuel adjustment screw in until it bottoms.
7. Back the screw out the recorded number of turns.
8. Minor adjustments may have to be made in the fuel mixture.

■ Carburetor Adjustments

There are three main carburetor adjustments: main fuel mixture, idle fuel mixture, and the choke setting. Improper carburetor adjustment can lead to serious engine trouble. A mixture that is too rich can wash away lubricating oil from the cylinder walls, causing accelerated piston ring wear. A mixture that is too lean can cause overheating and burned valves and pistons.

Main Fuel Mixture (Kohler)

The main fuel-mixture adjustment screw is centered on the top of the carburetor except for the 2.5-kw generator, which has the screw centered on the bottom (see Figure 5.10). For 2.5-kw generators:

1. Turn main mixture screw in clockwise until it lightly bottoms.
2. Back screw out 1¼ turns.
3. Minor adjustments may have to be made with the engine running at full load to achieve maximum power.

For all other Kohlers:

1. Turn main fuel-mixture screw in until it lightly bottoms.
2. Back screw out 2½ turns.
3. With engine thoroughly warmed up and running under full-rated load, turn screw in until engine slows down (lean setting).
4. Turn screw out (rich setting) until the engine regains speed and then starts to slow down.

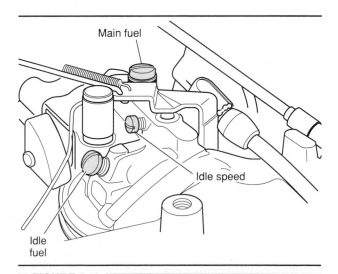

Main fuel

Idle speed

Idle fuel

■ **FIGURE 5.10**
Adjusting the main fuel mixture screw in Kohler generator carburetors

5. Turn screw back in until the position is halfway between rich and lean.

6. Engine should operate with a steady, smooth governor action.

Main Fuel Mixture (Onan)

Onan generators have the main mixture screw centered on the bottom of the carburetor (see Figure 5.11). To adjust an Onan, follow these steps:

1. Start the generator and apply full-rated load; run for 10 minutes.

2. Connect a multimeter (voltage) to the AC output.

3. Turn the adjustment screw inward until voltage drops.

4. Turn the screw outward until voltage drops again.

5. Locate the point where voltage is the highest.

6. From this setting turn the screw out an additional ¼ turn.

Idle Fuel Mixture Adjustment (Kohler)

The idle circuit of the carburetor only functions as the engine comes up to speed through the idle range and if there is no load on the generator. The correct method for Kohler's 2.5-kw set is:

1. Locate idle screw on upper side of carburetor.

2. Turn screw in until it lightly bottoms.

3. Back screw out ¾ turn.

4. No further adjustment is necessary.

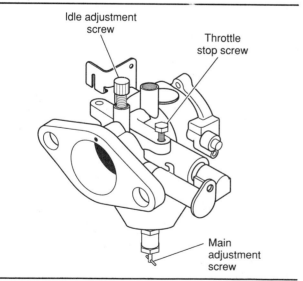

Idle adjustment screw

Throttle stop screw

Main adjustment screw

■ FIGURE 5.11 ■

Adjusting the main fuel mixture, idle, and throttle stop screws in Onan generator carburetors

For Kohler's other generators, the screw is on the top of the carburetor offset from center and is slightly smaller than the main adjustment screw.

1. Turn screw in until it lightly bottoms.

2. Back out 2½ turns.

3. No further adjustment is necessary.

Idle Fuel Mixture Adjustment (Onan)

Onan generators are slightly different:

1. Run the generator until warmed up, about 10 minutes.

2. Remove all load.

3. Connect multimeter (voltage) to AC output.

4. Turn screw inward until voltage drops and engine begins to run roughly.

5. Back out screw until engine runs smoothly without any surging.

6. Add and remove full load several times to make sure engine does not bog or surge.

■ Carburetor Overhaul

Many carburetor problems can be corrected by adjusting the mixture or float, but to effectively clean gummed-up fuel passages and/or worn internal parts, a complete overhaul is necessary. The instructions that follow for overhauling a carburetor pertain to Onan's BGE model, but represent the same type of service necessary for rebuilding carburetors found in most generators.

Carburetor Removal and Disassembly

To remove and disassemble the carburetor, follow these steps (see Figure 5.12):

1. Remove crankcase breather hose and air preheater hose from air-cleaner housing.

2. Remove air-cleaner-housing center cap screw and lift off housing and air filter.

3. Remove choke cover retaining nut and lift off choke cover.

4. Disconnect choke lead wires at choke terminals.

5. Remove the 3 cap screws that secure air-cleaner adapter to carburetor and lift off adapter. Choke linkage must be disengaged from choke assembly.

6. Disconnect fuel line and governor control linkage from carburetor.

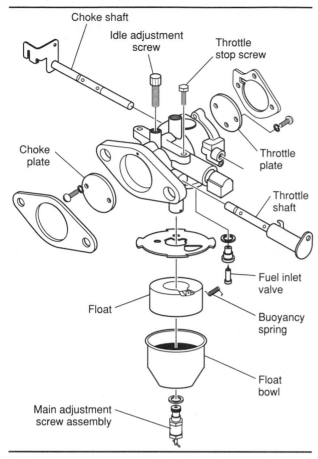

■ FIGURE 5.12 ■
Exploded view of Onan generator carburetor

7. Remove intake manifold cap screws and lift off carburetor preheater. Lift off carburetor and manifold as one assembly.

8. Remove the 2 intake manifold gaskets and plug the intake ports with a rag to prevent loose parts from entering ports.

9. Remove the 2 cap screws that secure the carburetor and choke pull-off assembly to the intake manifold. Disengage choke pull-off linkage from the carburetor and carefully separate the carburetor from the intake manifold (see Figure 5.13).

10. Remove air-cleaner adaptor and automatic choke assembly.

11. Remove throttle and choke-plate retaining screws and plates. Carefully pull out throttle and choke shafts making sure not to damage the Teflon coating.

12. Remove the main and idle-mixture screw assemblies.

13. Separate the fuel bowl (lower section of the carburetor) from the fuel bowl cover (lower section).

14. After noting the position of the float assembly, slide out the retaining pin and remove float assembly, springs, clips, and needle valve.

15. Unscrew and remove needle and valve seat.

16. Soak all metal parts in carburetor cleaner that are not replaced by the repair kit. Most automotive parts stores carry carburetor cleaner in a can that has a wire basket. Make sure not to soak nonmetal parts such as the float itself. Soak for the time prescribed by the manufacturer of the cleaner.

CAUTION: Carburetor cleaner is flammable and should not be used around flames or while smoking.

17. Clean the carbon deposits from the carburetor bore, especially where the throttle and choke plates seat. Make sure the idle or main fuel ports do not become plugged.

18. Blow out all the passages with compressed air. Do not clean with a wire or other metallic object that may increase the size of the orifices.

19. Check condition of needle valve and float (Figure 5.14). Replace the needle valve if damaged, and the float if saturated with fuel or damaged. Needle valves and floats may not be part of the repair kit and may have to be purchased separately.

20. Check condition of choke and throttle shafts for excessive play in their bore and replace if necessary.

21. Replace old components with new parts from repair kit.

Reassembly of Carburetor

Reassemble the carburetor when parts are clean and dry, following these steps:

1. Slide in throttle shaft and install throttle plate using new screws (if supplied in repair kit). The plate must be centered in the bore before tightening. To center, back off the throttle lever. Seat the plate by gently tapping with a small screwdriver, then tighten screws.

2. Install the choke shaft and plate using same procedure as step 1.

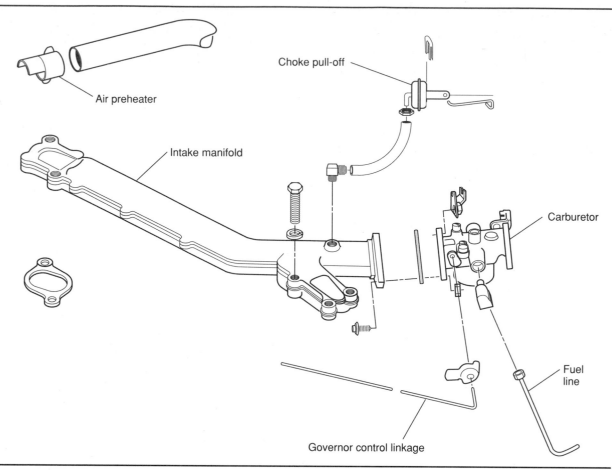

■ FIGURE 5.13
Carburetor and intake manifold assembly in Onan generators

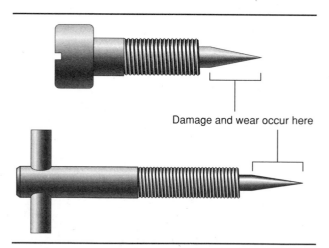

■ FIGURE 5.14
The condition of the needle valve should be checked when performing a carburetor overhaul.

3. Install idle-mixture screw assembly. Turn the screw in until it becomes lightly seated and then out one turn, plus or minus ¼ turn for Onan, or the number of turns specified by the generator manufacturer. Do not force the mixture adjustment screw; overtightening can damage the needle and seat.

4. Install the needle and seat, fuel-bowl gasket, and float assembly (Figure 5.15). Make sure the clips and springs are properly placed and the float can move freely.

5. Invert the float and needle valve assembly and check float level between float and gasket (see Figure 5.16). The full weight of the float should be resting on the needle valve and spring. The distance between the float and the bowl flange gasket should be ¹/₁₆ inch, plus or minus ¹/₃₂ inch. This figure is for the Onan; other measurements will vary depending on generator manufacturer. To achieve the proper

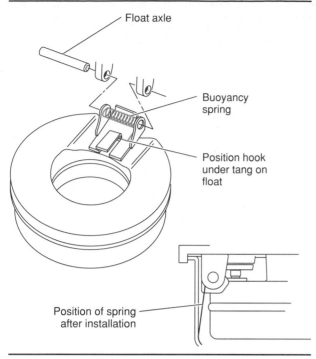

■ FIGURE 5.15 ■

Procedure for installing a float and a needle and seat assembly in Onan generator carburetors

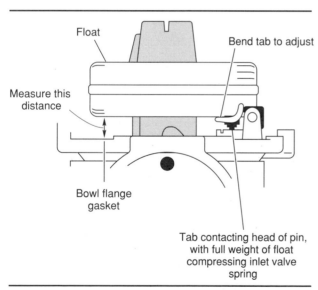

■ FIGURE 5.16 ■

Adjusting the carburetor float level in Onan generators

distance, remove the float and bend the tap, but only at the point specified by the float manufacturer (marked on float). The needle and seat can become damaged if the float is adjusted while in the carburetor.

6. Install the float bowl and main mixture screw assembly. Turn screw in until lightly seated, then out two turns, plus or minus ¼ turn for Onan or the specified figure for other manufacturers.

7. Reverse steps 1–9 under Carburetor Removal and Disassembly (page 92) to reassemble carburetor, manifold, and air cleaner.

8. Readjust mixture screws as described on pages 91–92.

■ Choke Adjustment (Kohler)

Generators utilize a 12-volt DC electric-choke system (Kohler's 2.5-kw unit has a manual, hand-operated choke) to enrich the fuel mixture when the engine is cold. To adjust choke:

1. Loosen the two screws securing choke assembly to its bracket.
2. When properly set, choke plate will be within 5°F to 10°F of full open at 70°F.
3. Rotate choke housing to attain this setting.
4. Tighten retaining screws.

■ Choke Adjustment (Onan)

To adjust Onan models:

1. Allow engine to completely cool.
2. Remove plastic choke cover and mounting nut.
3. Loosen heating element screws.
4. Rotate element housing until choke plate is halfway open.
5. Slowly rotate cover counterclockwise while tapping the carburetor choke lever and making the choke lever bounce slightly. Continue rotation until tapping the lever no longer makes it bounce. This is the fully closed position and becomes the reference position.
6. Refer to Table 5.2 to determine the number of degrees the cover must be rotated from the reference position. Marks on housing are in 5-degree increments.
7. Rotate cover as specified in the chart, depending on air temperature.
8. Tighten screws and move lever back and forth to check for binding.
9. Install choke cover and tighten mounting nut.

■ **TABLE 5.2**

Choke Adjustments

Ambient Air Temperature	Rotation from Reference Mark*
40°F (4°C)	0°
45°F (7°C)	4°CW
50°F (10°C)	8°CW
55°F (13°C)	12°CW
60°F (16°C)	16°CW
65°F (18°C)	20°CW
70°F (21°C)	24°CW
75°F (24°C)	27°CW
80°F (27°C)	32°CW
85°F (29°C)	35°CW
90°F (32°C)	39°CW
95°F (35°C)	43°CW
100°F (38°C)	47°CW

*Each mark on choke housing equals 5° angular rotation.

■ **TABLE 5.3**

Kohler Voltage and Frequency Specifications

No load	62–63 Hz	1800 rpm	120 volts, plus or minus 5 volts
Full load	59–60 Hz	1800 rpm	120 volts, plus or minus 5 volts

■ **TABLE 5.4**

Onan Voltage and Frequency Specifications

Maximum no load	63 Hz	1890 rpm	132 volts
Minimum full load	57 Hz	1710 rpm	108 volts
Normal no load	62 Hz	1800 rpm	127.5 volts, plus or minus 4.5 volts

■ Governor Adjustment

Voltage output and frequency of the generator are affected by engine speed, which is controlled by the governor. Increasing engine speed increases voltage and frequency, and vice versa. The governor maintains constant engine speed as the load conditions vary so that voltage and frequency remain within factory parameters. The most popular generators operate at 1800 RPM at a voltage range between 120 and 132 volts and a frequency range between 59 and 63 hertz. The owner should limit adjustment of the governor to checking voltage by changing the linkage position.

Adjusting the frequency requires instrumentation not normally available to the average mechanic. If voltage is too high or too low after checking with a multimeter (see Chapter 1, page 2), the governor linkage can be adjusted to temporarily improve voltage. A factory-certified service center should fine-tune voltage and frequency as soon as possible (see Tables 5.3 and 5.4).

Adjusting the Kohler Governor

To adjust the Kohler governor, follow these steps (see Figure 5.17):

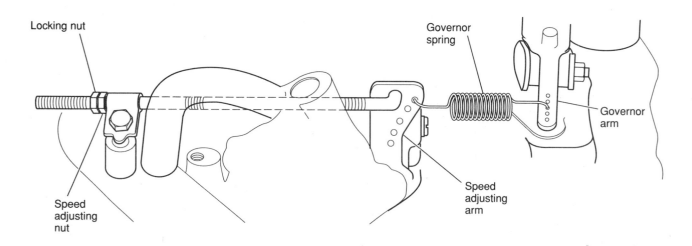

■ **FIGURE 5.17**

Adjusting the governor in Kohler generators

1. Probe the closest 120-volt AC plug receptacle to the generator using a multimeter.
2. Make sure all appliances and circuit breaker to the power converter are off.
3. Start the generator and read voltage.
4. If adjustment is necessary, shut down the generator and loosen the outside locking nut on the speed adjusting arm.
5. Restart generator.
6. To increase speed and voltage, turn the adjusting nut (next to the locking nut) so that it tightens or draws back the speed adjusting arm.
7. To decrease speed and voltage, loosen the adjusting nut.
8. Tighten the locking nut after proper voltage is achieved.
9. Open circuit breaker(s) for the power converter and appliances.

If the governor is too sensitive, engine speed will surge as the load changes. If a big drop is noticed when a normal load is applied, the governor must be set for greater sensitivity. This is accomplished by changing the position of the governor spring in the governor arm holes. Move the spring in to make the governor control more sensitive or out to make it less sensitive. Recheck engine speed after changing sensitivity.

Adjusting the Onan Governor

To adjust the Onan governor, follow these steps (Figure 5.18):

1. Run generator for 10 minutes under light load to allow engine to reach normal operating temperature.
2. Make sure all appliances and circuit breaker to power converter are off.
3. Probe the closest 120-volt AC plug receptacle to the generator using a multimeter.
4. Make sure the carburetor is properly adjusted.
5. Adjust the length of the governor linkage and check for binding or looseness.
6. Adjust the length so that the stop on the throttle shaft assembly almost touches the stop on the side of the carburetor. This should be done

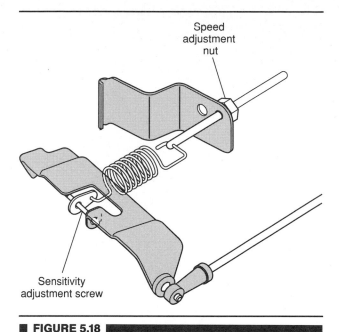

■ **FIGURE 5.18**
Adjusting the governor in Onan generators

with the engine stopped and with tension on the governor spring. The adjustment is correct if one more turn on the ball joint will allow the throttle shaft stop to touch the carburetor. Tighten lock nut.

7. With the generator running at no load, turn the speed adjusting nut in to increase speed and voltage, or out to decrease speed and voltage. Then check voltage under load (open circuit breakers and turn on 120-volt AC appliances) using the same technique.
8. The sensitivity adjustment screw must be set to insure minimum (or no) speed and voltage difference between no load and full load, without causing the engine to hunt. To increase sensitivity or allow closer regulation, turn the screw counterclockwise; to decrease sensitivity, turn the screw clockwise.
9. Recheck speed and voltage after readjusting sensitivity.

CHAPTER 6

Heating Systems

With the exception of a few luxury motorcoaches, all RVs use a propane-fired furnace for comfort heating. The most common type is the *forced-air ducted furnace*. This type of furnace functions in a similar way as the home-type furnace in that it heats air in a heat exchanger, and a blower pushes it through a series of ducts located at various points in the RV. A ducted furnace is most likely found in RVs over 19 feet.

Another type of RV furnace is the *undercounter unit*, where air is heated by a heat exchanger and is blown into the RV directly from the furnace, without the use of ducts. These undercounter units are often found in smaller RVs, such as pickup campers, where heat distribution over a wide area is not required.

Catalytic heaters are a third source of heat. Catalytics mix gas and air in a silica wool pad that is impregnated with platinum. Platinum is the catalyst that allows combustion to take place without a flame. This flameless unit produces heat that warms objects and people, not the air. Catalytic heaters are nearly 100% efficient, but they use oxygen and therefore require ventilation in all cases; forced-air units operate at about an 80% level. Catalytic heaters are normally used as an auxiliary heat source.

A fourth type is the *perimeter heating system*, found only in a few large, luxury motorhomes. It requires that the living area be specifically designed for use of the system. These systems heat water and circulate it through pipes with a small electric pump around the perimeter of the RV's floor. The heat given off is very even and feels natural.

Forced-Air Furnaces

All forced-air furnaces share the same operating principles and design characteristics (see Figure 6.1). The term *forced air* comes from the fact that outside air is force-fed to a sealed combustion-chamber assembly while interior air is moved through a heat exchanger. There are three types of ignition systems. The first is a *manual match-lit pilot* (called a *standing pilot*) that remains on until it is manually turned off. The second is a *piezoelectric spark ignition* to light the standing pilot (this eliminates the need for a match). The third is an *electronic ignition* whereby a transformer generates a spark to light the main burner upon demand from the thermostat (this is a fully automatic, pilotless lighting system).

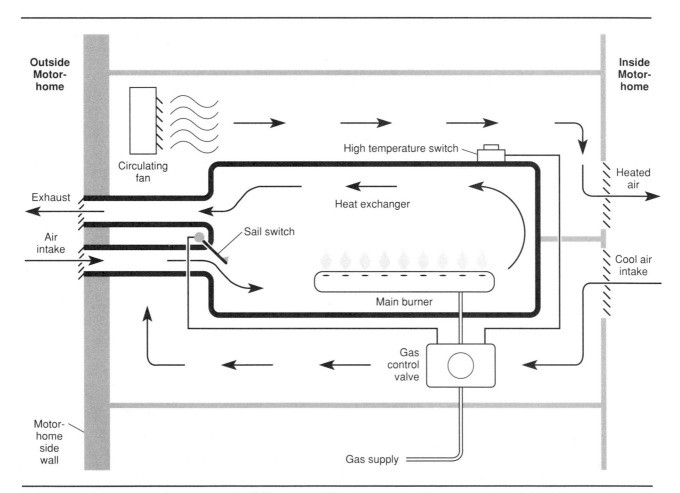

■ FIGURE 6.1 ■
Operation and flow of a typical RV heating furnace

Furnace operation is controlled by a wall-mounted thermostat. The thermostat monitors the interior temperature of the RV and tells the furnace when to turn on and off. It does this through a set of contacts that open and close. When the room temperature drops below that of the setting on the dial, the contacts close, energizing the furnace circuitry that will set the heating cycle into motion. In standing pilot furnaces, the gas control valve opens and exposes propane to the pilot flame and the burner is lit. In electronic-ignition furnaces, the gas control valve opens and a spark is generated to light the main burner.

Gas-burning furnaces are oxygen-consuming appliances and must be vented to the outside so that oxygen inside the RV is not consumed. The flame burning in the combustion chamber heats the air in a sealed heat exchanger. A fan pulls cold air from inside the RV through the heat exchanger where it is heated and forced back into the living compartment. It is this separation of combustion and inside air that makes the furnace safe.

Safety of the forced-air furnace is further enhanced by the addition of other features. The most prominent is the *thermocouple*, a heat-sensing device that detects a level of heat and generates a small electrical current in response. This small current is sent to the gas control device that will turn off the gas supply if current is not available. If, for instance, the pilot flame were to blow out, the thermocouple would sense the lack of heat and fail to produce an electrical current which in turn would signal the control valve to shut off the gas supply.

Another safety feature is a special switch called a *sail* (or sometimes called an *air-prover*), so-called because it is sensitive to airflow much like a sail on a boat. The sail switch is designed to detect proper airflow to the burner assembly. If the airflow is inadequate to the combustion chamber, the sail switch will not allow the gas control valve to open and the main burner cannot be lit. In cases where the air supply to the burner is blocked, restricted, or caused by slow fan speed due to low-system voltage, the sail switch will prevent the furnace from functioning.

Forced-air furnaces also feature a *temperature limit switch*. This safety switch, which is normally closed, will open when the furnace assembly becomes overheated. When the switch opens it causes the gas control valve to close, shutting off the gas flow to the main burner. In the case of a blocked furnace outlet, which could cause overheating, the limit switch comes into play, shutting the system down.

A *furnace fan switch* serves to cool the heat exchanger and purge the combustion chamber at the end of a heating cycle. When the interior space is warm enough, the contacts open in the thermostat, which shut off the gas controller, stopping the flame. But the combustion chamber and heat exchanger remain hot. The fan switch will allow the fan to operate for several minutes, or until the assembly is cool, before shutting off; the furnace is now ready to relight upon demand from the thermostat. A malfunction in any of these integrated safety systems could cause a problem with the furnace operation. A logical course of troubleshooting can spot the defective component.

■ Service and Repair of Forced-Air Furnaces

RV furnaces cannot perform properly if voltage is lower than 10.5 (see Figure 6.2). Many times operational difficulties are as simple as a low battery level. See pages 10–11 to determine the battery's state of charge.

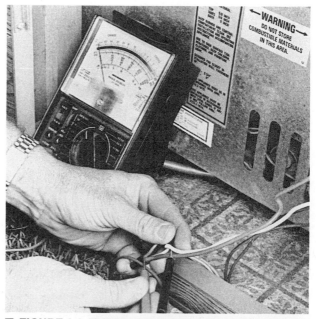

■ FIGURE 6.2 ■
Voltage to the furnace should be checked with a multimeter.

For safety's sake, furnaces should not be serviced or repaired if you are uncertain of the procedures. Major repairs should be done by professional service technicians.

Furnaces that use electronic ignitions systems produce high voltages to create a spark to light the main burner. This voltage can cause severe shock. Keep hands and tools away from the igniter area when testing.

Correcting Pilot-Light Failure

One of the most common furnace problems is pilot-light failure. Check the following to correct this difficulty:

☑ **CHECKLIST**

☐ Make sure that there is an adequate amount of fuel in the propane tank. Check to see that the gas cylinder valve is open and the manual valve to the furnace is in line with the gas supply tubing (open position).

☐ Make sure the gas control valve (in furnace) is turned to the "on" position and that the pilot light button is fully depressed.

☐ Check that the gas pressure regulator is set to 11 inches of water-column pressure with the propane tank filled (see page 40).

☐ If the furnace in question utilizes a piezoelectric spark lighter for the flame, there must be a spark present when the lighter is energized. If not, check the gap from the spark electrode to ground. It should be about 1/16 inch.

☐ If the gas supply has been shut off during prolonged storage, the lines may be full of air (see Figure 6.3). Try lighting other appliances to purge air from the system. It may take several minutes and attempts before the gas reaches the pilot orifice.

☐ The pilot gas orifice is very small and is prone to clogging. To check for a clogged orifice, place a small amount of soapy water solution over the end of the orifice and push the pilot light button on the gas control valve. If no bubbles appear, the orifice is clogged.

☐ Pilot orifices are so small that it is best to replace them instead of cleaning. Do not try to insert any metal object through the orifice; the precision-size hole in soft brass may become deformed.

■ **FIGURE 6.3** ■
The LP-gas supply to the furnace is controlled by an in-line valve.

☐ Manual pilots usually have an adjustment screw located behind a cover screw in the gas controller. This screw is to adjust the height of the pilot flame. If it is closed too far, the flame will not light. Remove the cover screw (there will be a small O-ring located under this screw). It must be in place when the cover screw is returned or gas will leak into the interior of the RV. Once the pilot flame is established, it should be adjusted to envelop the end of the thermocouple.

Correcting Pilot-Light Outage

Many times the pilot is easy to light, but not easy to keep going. If constant pilot outage is the problem, there are several areas that can be checked and serviced.

☑ **CHECKLIST**

☐ The flame can be adjusted in two ways: with the flame adjustment screw on the gas control valve (Figure 6.4a) or by slightly bending the pilot flame mounting bracket with needlenose pliers to direct the flame at the thermocouple (Figure 6.4b). The flame should be pointed so that the entire end of the thermocouple is covered.

☐ If the pilot still goes out, it is likely the thermocouple is defective (Figure 6.4c). It is inexpensive and easy to change. Turn off the gas

■ FIGURE 6.4 ■

Pilot flame adjustment can be made by turning the screw in the gas control valve (*top*) or by slightly bending the pilot flame mounting bracket with needlenose pliers so that the flame is directed to and covers the thermocouple (*center*). Removing a defective thermocouple is easy when using a line wrench (*bottom*).

supply at the propane tank and, using a tubing wrench, remove the connector nut where the thermocouple's tube goes into the gas control valve. Remove the connection between the thermocouple tip and the furnace's combustion chamber.

☐ To replace the unit, reverse the above procedure, making sure that the tip of the thermocouple is set at the correct distance from the pilot flame orifice. Tighten the tubing nut into the gas control valve finger-tight, plus one quarter turn. Do not over-tighten since it will damage the end of the tube and destroy the thermocouple.

☐ Relight the pilot; the flame should continue to burn.

Checking for a Leaking Control Valve

Other reasons for pilot outage may be lack of venting, incorrect gas pressure, a leaking control valve, or improper pilot flame adjustment. A leaking control valve allows a very small amount of raw gas to enter the chamber, where over a period of time it consumes the oxygen in the chamber, eventually causing the pilot to go out. To check for a leaking control valve:

☑ CHECKLIST

☐ Observe the main burner assembly when it is shut off. The presence of even a small flame will cause the pilot to fail.

☐ If there is a flame present other than the pilot flame, the gas controller should be replaced.

Replacing the Gas Controller

To replace the gas controller (Figure 6.5):

1. Make sure that you have obtained an exact replacement as stated in the furnace owner's manual. Install a controller designed for your specific application.
2. Shut off the propane supply at the main tank.
3. Carefully remove and mark all control wires so that they are installed in the correct location on the new valve assembly.
4. With a tubing wrench, remove the propane inlet, the outlet to the main burner, the thermocouple, and the pilot tube from the control valve.
5. The control valve is now free from the furnace and can be removed.

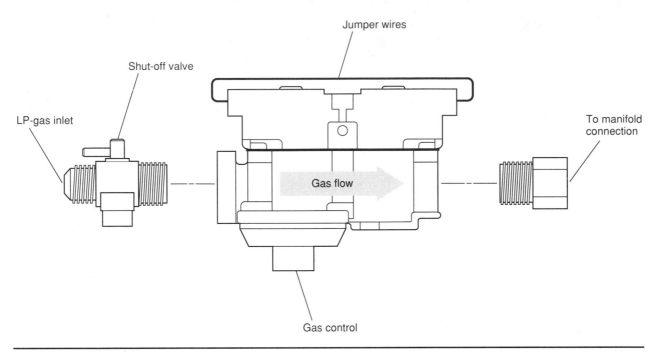

Jumper wires

Shut-off valve

LP-gas inlet

To manifold connection

Gas flow

Gas control

■ **FIGURE 6.5**
The gas control valve in the furnace must be replaced with the identical part specified by the manufacturer.

6. Some furnaces may have the burner manifold assembly connected directly to the gas valve. If this is the case, the burner assembly should be removed with the valve assembly so that the valve can be placed in a bench vise to remove the burner.

7. Replace the new valve in the reverse order, connect wires, turn on gas, and check all connections with soapy water for leaks.

8. If there are no leaks, turn on the control valve, light and adjust the pilot, and adjust the thermostat so that the main burner will light. Check condition of the pilot flame and main burner flame. When the main burner cycles off, the pilot should continue to burn.

If any gas pressure fluctuation occurs, erratic furnace performance will result. Outside temperature and level of fuel in the propane tank also determine the ultimate gas pressure. Here's what Duo-Therm has to say about the importance of proper gas pressure:

Low gas pressure can lead to unsatisfactory furnace operation (nuisance lockouts, high-pitched noise during operation, reduced heat output and pilot outages etc.) Be sure that the gas-line pressure at the furnace is 11 inches (water column) pressure during furnace operation. This line pressure will result in a 9.5 to 10.5 manifold pressure at the gas valve manifold outlet tap. Low gas-line pressure can be corrected by adjusting the propane tank regulator. This adjustment should be made by a qualified service person.

At low temperatures partially filled propane tanks may not be able to deliver sufficient gas to maintain adequate line pressure. For example, a 50-percent-full, 30-pound (7½-gallon) propane tank at 0°F can only supply 22,600 Btu's of gas each hour, a 30-percent-full tank will further reduce this supply to 17,600 Btu's per hour and a 50-percent-full tank at −10°F will deliver only 11,300 Btu's per hour. When the demand on the system is greater than it can supply, line pressure will be reduced which will adversely affect the operation of the appliance.

Checking for Other Burner-Light Failures

Once it is established that the pilot is operating properly, the main burner can still fail to light. Here are some areas that can be checked:

☑ **CHECKLIST**

☐ Make sure the thermostat is turned on and set to a temperature high enough to activate the gas control valve.

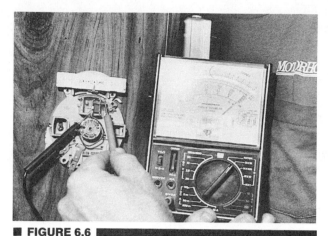

■ FIGURE 6.6 ■

The wall thermostat that controls the furnace can be checked with a multimeter.

■ FIGURE 6.7 ■

The burner assembly must be removed from the furnace to clean the main burner jet.

☐ To check the thermostat, disconnect the thermostat wires from the furnace. Then, connect the leads from a multimeter (ohms) across these two wires. When the thermostat contacts close (thermostat set to high temperature), there should be a zero ohm reading; when the contacts open (thermostat set to low temperature) there should be an infinite ohm reading (see Figure 6.6). If this does not occur, replace the thermostat with an exact duplicate. There are many different types of thermostats used in the RV industry; an incompatible replacement may render the furnace inoperable.

☐ Low battery voltage will not allow the furnace fan to operate fast enough to close the airflow (sail) switch. Make sure voltage is at least 10.5.

☐ A stuck sail switch that does not respond to airflow will not allow the gas control valve to open. The furnace must be removed from its compartment to gain access to the switch and associated linkage. The sail switch can be checked with a multimeter (ohms). It should be in the closed position (zero ohm) normally, and open only when excessive heat is encountered. If the switch is open when it is cold it will require replacement.

☐ Reversed battery polarity will cause the fan motor to operate in reverse. This will not allow the sail switch to close and activate the burner.

☐ If the furnace is ducted, make sure that the ducting and register grates are not blocked or kinked. If airflow cannot escape the furnace at an adequate rate, the limit switch will overheat, causing the gas control valve to shut down the burner.

☐ The burner intake and outlet on the exterior of the RV must be free and clear. Any blockage here will reduce airflow to the combustion chamber, making the flame nearly impossible to light. Check for animal nests or other obstructions in the vent inlet and outlet.

☐ If the furnace has electronic ignition, the lighting spark may not be adequate to start the gas burning. Check to see that the electrode gap is correct. For all models of furnaces the gap should be ⅛ inch, plus or minus 1/32 inch. If there still is no spark, check the electrode lead for cracks and broken insulation. If there are high voltage leaks, the spark will fail to appear.

☐ The spark is controlled by a modular printed circuit board. It is important that the board's wiring connections and terminals be clean. Corrosion and dirt at these terminals can cause the spark ignition to fail. Remove the connections and check for dirt and corrosion. A cotton swab and alcohol can be used to clean the terminal connections.

☐ If the main burner still fails to light, the problem could be a clogged main burner jet. To clean the jet, the burner assembly must be removed from the gas control valve (Figure 6.7). Do not attempt to clean the jet with a metal object as the jet can become damaged, producing an incorrect amount of gas flow. Clean the jet with a wooden or plastic toothpick (Figure 6.8). If the clog cannot be removed by this method, a new jet should be purchased and installed.

TROUBLESHOOTING *the Forced-Air Furnace*

Problem	Possible Cause	Correction
Pilot will not light	Empty LP-gas supply	Replenish.
	Wrong LP-gas pressure	Adjust to 11 inches water-column pressure.
	Defective piezo lighter	Replace lighter assembly.
	Incorrect spark gap	Set spark gap.
	Clogged pilot orifice	Clean or replace.
	Air in gas line	Purge gas line.
	Adjustment screw wrong	Adjust pilot screw.
Pilot will not stay lit	Defective thermocouple	Replace thermocouple.
	Air leakage	Check for leakage.
	Lack of air	Check for venting.
	Leaking control valve	Check control valve.
	Incorrect gas pressure	Set to 11 inches water-column pressure.
	Clogged pilot orifice	Clean or replace orifice.
	Pilot adjustment screw	Adjust pilot flame level.
Noisy operation	Low input voltage	Charge or replace battery.
	Unbalanced blower wheel	Replace blower wheel.
	Loose blower wheel	Tighten wheel.
	Loud burner	Adjust air shutter.
	Rubbing blower wheel	Check clearance with housing.
Main burner will not light	Thermostat off	Turn on thermostat.
	Thermostat contacts open	Reset thermostat.
	Gas off	Turn on gas supply.
	Empty propane tank	Replenish supply.
	Low gas level in tank	Refill tank.
	Low gas pressure	Adjust to 11 inches water-column pressure.
	Low battery voltage	Charge battery.
	Stuck sail switch	Clean switch.
	Defective sail switch	Replace switch.
	Defective limit switch	Replace limit switch.
	Reversed battery polarity	Check wiring.
	Blocked ducting	Check duct hoses.
	Blocked air intake	Check air intake.
	Blocked burner exhaust	Clear burner exhaust.
	No igniter spark	Check electrode lead.
	Incorrect spark gap	Reset spark gap.
	Dirty module connections	Clean connections.
	Clogged main burner jet	Replace or clean jet.

TROUBLESHOOTING *the Forced-Air Furnace* (continued)

Problem	Possible Cause	Correction
Burner lights but shuts off (lockout)	Misaligned flame sensor	Adjust flame sensor.
	Loose sensor wire	Tighten connections.
	Dirty sensor probe	Clean probe.
	Defective sensor	Test sensor.
	Defective module board	Replace board.
	Low gas pressure	Set to 11 inches water-column pressure.
	Low gas level in tank	Refill tank.
Main burner will not shut off	High thermostat setting	Reduce temperature setting.
	Stuck thermostat points	Check points.
	Defective gas valve	Replace gas valve.
Blower will not run	No or low voltage	Check voltage at furnace.
	Blown 12-volt fuse	Check fuse and replace.
	Reversed battery polarity	Check wire connections.
	Open thermostat points	Check points for closing.
	Locked motor	Rotate by hand to check.
	Defective motor relay	Replace relay.
	Defective motor	Replace motor.
No igniter spark	Improper input polarity	Check 12-volt wiring.
	No voltage present	Check voltage at furnace.
	Poor electrode ground	Check ground connection.
	Corroded connections	Clean connections.
	Loose connections	Tighten connections.
	Wrong spark gap	Set spark gap.
	Broken electrode lead	Replace electrode lead.
	Cracked insulators	Replace insulators.
	Faulty module board	Replace module board.

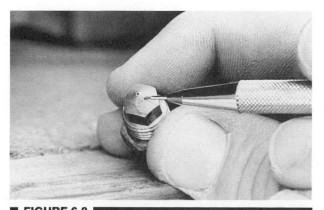

■ FIGURE 6.8
The burner jet should only be cleaned with a toothpick; metal objects can damage the jet.

■ Checking for Burner Lockout (Electric Ignition Furnaces Only)

Burner lockout occurs only in electronic ignition furnaces. It is noticeable when the main burner momentarily lights, then goes out. The furnace must be shut off for several minutes while it resets, then relight can be attempted. Chronic lockout is attributable to several causes:

☑ CHECKLIST

☐ Instead of a thermocouple, the electronic furnace utilizes a flame sensor. The flame sensor is mounted next to the spark-ignition system and is exposed to the main burner when it lights. If the sensor is not exposed directly to the flame, it will cause lockout. The sensor can be bent slightly to aim it into the flame area.

☐ If the sensor tip is dirty and corroded, it can be cleaned with steel wool or crocus cloth for better heat contact.

☐ The electronic sensor and control board require special testing equipment that can measure microamps of current. Seek help at a qualified service center.

☐ Low gas pressure can reduce the flame output to a level that is too low to activate the heat sensor. Have gas pressure set to 11 inches of water-column pressure.

■ Checking for Burner Shutoff Failure

The opposite problem of lockout is failure for the main burner to shut off. If this situation occurs check the following:

☑ CHECKLIST

☐ The thermostat must be set to a lower setting. If this does not correct the problem, the points in the thermostat may be stuck closed.

☐ The points can be examined by pulling off the cover of the thermostat.

☐ They can also be checked with a multimeter (ohms). If the multimeter reads zero when the thermostat is turned to its lowest temperature, the points are stuck closed. They probably are pitted and will stick again, even if they are manually pushed apart. Replacement of the thermostat is recommended.

☐ If the thermostat responds to temperature, the problem may be in the gas control valve. Remove the wires from the control valve while the main burner is activated. This should allow the valve to shut immediately. If it does not, the valve is defective and should be replaced.

☐ The thermostat also contains a small internal adjustment called a *heat anticipator*, which can delay furnace shutdown if it is set too high (Figure 6.9). The normal setting for most thermostats is about .3 on the small dial. By moving a small lever you can change this setting. A move toward a smaller number will cause the furnace to shut off

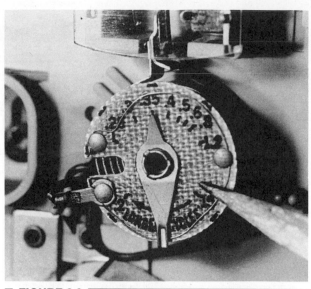

■ **FIGURE 6.9** ■
Furnace heating cycles can be controlled by adjusting the heat anticipator in the wall thermostat.

sooner (a shorter heating cycle) and a move to a larger number will cause the heater to run longer (a longer heating cycle.) Experiment to see which settings give the best results.

■ Checking for Blower Motor Failure

Another furnace problem that may crop up is the failure for the blower motor to start. If the blower cannot operate, the sail switch cannot close and the main burner cannot light. Here are some things to look for if the blower motor fails to start:

☑ CHECKLIST

☐ Check the 12-volt fuse protecting the furnace. If the fuse is blown, replace it with the proper amperage fuse. Continual fuse blowing is an indication of a problem that may require expert assistance.

☐ Low battery voltage can cause the furnace to become inoperable. Make sure that at least 10.5 volts are present at the furnace.

☐ Crossed wires may cause the blower to fail to operate. Make sure that polarity is observed.

☐ Check the thermostat points (Figure 6.10). If they fail to close, the motor cannot start (Figure 6.11). The points can be manually closed with a small screwdriver and they can be checked with a multimeter (ohms) to insure that when they do

■ FIGURE 6.10 ■
The points in the wall thermostat should be checked with a multimeter to insure that good contact is being made.

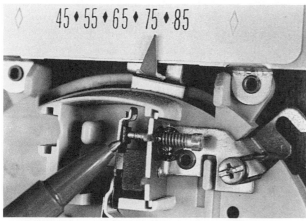

■ FIGURE 6.11 ■
The furnace motor cannot operate if the thermostat points fail to close.

make contact, a good connection occurs. With the wires to the thermostat removed from the heater, there should be a zero-ohm reading on the meter when the points are closed.

☐ Some furnaces have a motor relay that can fail. Check with an authorized service center for your brand of furnace.

☐ If all else is determined to be good, the motor should be removed from the furnace and tested. If it will not function with a direct 12-volt hookup, it is defective and should be replaced.

■ Checking for Noise

If noise is the primary complaint, it generally comes from the blower-fan assembly but can also be caused by an improperly burning flame or low battery voltage. Check the following:

☑ CHECKLIST

☐ Low voltage can cause the fan motor to run at a less than optimal speed. The noise generated is generally a low-frequency groan. The low blower speed can also affect the combustion in the burner chamber, allowing the flame to make a roaring noise. The problem is easily solved by charging the battery, replacing it if necessary, or using campground hookups.

☐ In rare cases the blower wheel may be out of balance or loose on the motor shaft. If this is the case, the entire furnace must be removed and disassembled to gain access to the fan.

☐ A metallic scraping sound may indicate that the blower is rubbing the surrounding housing. The furnace must be removed and disassembled to correct this problem.

■ Checking for Spark Failure

Electronic ignition furnaces utilize a high-voltage spark jumping a gap, much like a spark plug, to ignite the propane-air mixture in the combustion chamber. There are several things that you can do if the spark fails to fire:

☑ CHECKLIST

☐ Check the input polarity and voltage.

☐ Corrosion of the electrode terminal connections can create a poor ground. The sparker assembly has a side electrode that must have a good ground in order for the spark to jump across. Check the electrode assembly mounting screws for tightness. Make sure that they are clean to insure a good ground.

☐ Any connection terminals to the modular printed circuit board must also be clean. Dirt and grime can cause a no-spark situation. Remove the terminal connections and make sure that both the male and female parts of the plug are clean.

☐ Check to see that the spark gap between the electrode and side electrode is ⅛ inch, plus or

■ FIGURE 6.12 ■

The electrode spark gap must be ⅛ inch, plus or minus
½₂ inch in furnaces with electronic ignition.

minus ½₂ inch (Figure 6.12). Bend only the side
electrode with needlenose pliers to establish the
correct gap.

☐ Cables that carry high voltages are subject to
breakdown. Make sure that the lead to the
electrode is free from cracks. There are also
ceramic insulators where the cable joins the
furnace combustion chamber; make sure that the
ceramic is not cracked. If cracks are found in
either the cable or insulators, replace the cable
and electrode assembly.

☐ If everything seems in order but still no spark
appears, the failure may be in the modular control
board itself. There are no on-the-road diagnostics;
the board is simply unplugged from its mounting
and replaced with a new one.

Catalytic Heaters

Catalytic heaters operate with a great deal of efficiency. Since there is no combustion chamber, heat
exchanger, or exhaust to the outside, nearly all the
heat generated is released to the inside. Catalytic
heaters radiate infrared rays that warm objects and
people without having to heat all the air in the enclosed area. The radiated heat is absorbed by objects
and people and is radiated back to heat the surrounding area.

Catalytic heaters require ventilation since they con-
sume oxygen. The minimum recommendation is that
not less than 1 square inch of open window area per
1,000 Btu's of heater output be provided. For example,
if the catalytic heater is rated at 8,000 Btu's, an
8-square-inch opening would be needed to supply the
heater without depleting the oxygen inside the RV,
assuming no air leaks.

Some catalytics are outfitted with Oxygen Deple-
tion Sensors (ODS), which will shut off the heater
when the oxygen content of air surrounding the heater
is below 17.9%. Normal air at sea level contains
20.9% oxygen. These heaters will not function at altitudes much greater than 5,000 feet since the oxygen
content of the atmosphere is not adequate to satisfy
the sensor. **Note:** Since there are no moving parts to
wear out other than the control valve assembly, manufacturers of catalytic heaters do not recommend that
owners attempt repairs. If a problem exists with the
heater, call the manufacturer to obtain the name of an
authorized repair station or return it to the manufacturer for necessary work.

■ Maintaining Catalytic Heaters

Here are a few tips on the care and maintenance of
catalytic heaters:

☑ CHECKLIST ■■■■■■■■■■■■■■■■■■

☐ Do not clean heater while it is hot.

☐ Keep the heater and the area around the heater
clean and dust free. A damp cloth wiped over the
grill and surrounding housing will keep it clean.
Do not attempt to clean the heater pad; it will be
damaged.

☐ Do not use a vacuum to clean the heater. The silica
wool element can be easily damaged by vacuum
suction.

CHAPTER 7

Air-Conditioning Systems

The ability to travel and live in a controlled inside environment during hot weather has been made possible by RV air conditioning. Not too long ago air conditioning was reserved for larger, luxury RVs; today the majority of rigs—including small travel trailers and campers—have air conditioning. Roof-mounted air conditioners are most common, although some high-end RVs are being equipped with central systems. RV air conditioners are compressor-type units and work on the same operating principle as those found in homes.

Compressor Air Conditioners

Because heat gravitates toward cold, *compressor-type air conditioners* are able to transfer heat from one area to another (see Figure 7.1). A *refrigerant* (R-22) is circulated through a closed system that includes an *evaporator*, where the refrigerant picks up heat from the interior of the RV and vaporizes. The refrigerant then is compressed in the *condensor*, where the heat is removed and is dissipated outside the RV.

As the air-conditioning system cools the air, it also dries it. This occurs when moisture in the air contacts the cold evaporator and turns to water droplets (like water condensing on a glass of cold water). The excess moisture drains from the air conditioner. The water you see dripping from the roof is moisture that has been removed from the interior of the rig (see Figure 7.2).

The use of high-pressure refrigerant and AC power dictates that the RV owner be especially careful before proceeding with any type of maintenance or repair of a compressor air conditioner. In fact, the entire sealed compressor/refrigerant system should not be opened or tinkered with by the consumer—leave that job to the experts. But, there are procedures that can allow the owner to detect problems, or better yet, prevent problems through proper maintenance.

■ Servicing Compressor Air Conditioners

The most important service procedure, other than monitoring voltage, is to keep thc roof air unit clean. The roof-top air conditioner should be kept covered in the off-season. This keeps out dirt, debris, and small animals.

Remove the cover shroud on a yearly basis and blow out the unit with compressed air, or give it the once-over with a vacuum-cleaner hose (see Figure 7.3). Inside the RV, the ceiling cover should be removed frequently and the intake filter pads washed or replaced. Most roof air manufacturers recommend that the intake filters be cleaned every two weeks during continuous use (Figure 7.4).

Checking for Air-Conditioner Operating Failures

Failure of the air-conditioning unit to operate may be caused by several electrical abnormalities.

CAUTION: 120-volt AC power can be dangerous and deliver a fatal shock. If you're not certain of the procedures, seek qualified help. Here's what you *can* do safely:

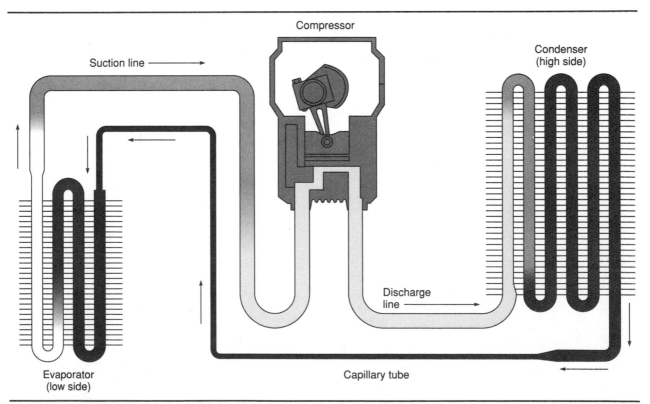

■ FIGURE 7.1 ■■■■■■

Operation and path of Freon in RV compressor-type air conditioners

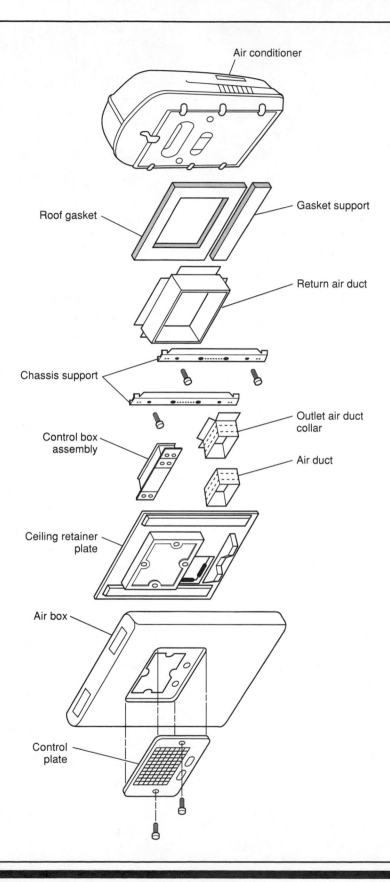

Air conditioner

Gasket support

Roof gasket

Return air duct

Chassis support

Outlet air duct collar

Control box assembly

Air duct

Ceiling retainer plate

Air box

Control plate

■ **FIGURE 7.2** ■

Exploded view of Dometic roof-mounted compressor-type air conditioner

■ FIGURE 7.3 ■

The cover shroud should be removed once a year in order to blow out the unit with compressed air.

■ FIGURE 7.4 ■

Intake filter pads are easily accessed from inside the RV and should be cleaned every two weeks during continuous use.

☑ CHECKLIST ■

☐ Check 120-volt AC voltage using a multimeter; insert the probe into any convenient outlet inside the RV. (See page 3.) It's always a good practice to check the incoming voltage from the available hookups or the onboard AC generator after arriving in the campground. The minimum voltage while the air-conditioner compressor is running is 100 volts. Most air conditioners are equipped with thermal-overload protection that will shut down the compressor if it becomes overheated. Overheating is caused by low voltage; as voltage drops, current rises and that creates abnormal heat. Most thermal-overload controls will shut down the compressor by the time voltage drops to between 100 and 103 volts. The newer electronically controlled air conditioners have electronic-threshold protection built into the circuit that automatically shuts down the compressor when voltage drops to between 103 and 107 volts. If voltage is in the 108- to 110-volt area, monitor the multimeter periodically because the voltage may drop further when other users get on the line. If the compressor is still running at 105 volts, the air conditioner should be turned off until proper voltage is restored. Most common extension cords are inadequately sized for their length and should not be used in conjunction with the RV's power cord (see Table 7.1).

☐ If there is no power present, insure that the power cord is plugged into its proper receptacle when using generator power (if your RV is so equipped). Usually this receptacle is located inside the same

■ TABLE 7.1 ■

Extension Cord Amperage Ratings

Gauge	Length (feet)	Maximum Amps
12	1–50	20
12	51–100	15
14	1–50	15
14	51–100	13
16	1–50	13
16	51–100	9.8
18	1–50	9.8
18	1–100	5.8

compartment as the power cord. Check the main breaker and the individual breaker for the air conditioner. If either is tripped, reset and try the air conditioner again. Continual tripping of the breakers is an indication of excessive amperage draw by the unit itself, low voltage, or a defective breaker. If the generator is the source of power, check the circuit breaker on the generator. If no power is available at the campground outlet, check the breaker unit in the power receptacle box at the campground. If there is a problem here, contact the campground personnel for assistance.

☐ If it is determined that 120-volt AC power is available and no breakers are tripped, the problem may be at the connector terminal under the air-conditioner ceiling shroud. To check this connection, turn off all power and remove the control knobs and retaining screws from the panel.

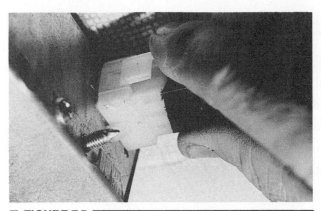

■ FIGURE 7.5 ■
Loss of 120-volt AC power to the air conditioner may be attributed to a loose connector terminal under the ceiling shroud.

■ FIGURE 7.6 ■
A manual-type main on-off switch can be checked with a multimeter.

Pull the panel down. A small nylon piece connects the control switches to 120-volt AC power. Make sure this connector is plugged in and tight. Turn on power. If the unit will not start at this point, seek qualified help (see Figure 7.5).

☐ If the main on-off switch is a manual type and not a solid-state electronic switch, it can be checked with a multimeter (ohms) (Figure 7.6). To check the switch, turn off the 120-volt AC power and remove the ceiling shroud assembly and wires from the on-off switch. Make a note of the proper wire location. With a multimeter, check the continuity from one side of the switch to the other. When the switch is in the "off" position there should be infinite resistance between the two points. When the switch is turned to the "on" position, the resistance should be zero. If not, a new switch should be installed.

☐ A new switch can be installed by removing the retaining nut and connection wires from the switch and pulling it free from its mount. Note the location of the wiring. Install a new switch in the reverse order.

☐ If all these checks fail, then the cause may be a shorted or burned-out motor. Seek qualified electrical help to determine the condition of the motor and compressor assembly.

Checking for Fan Operating Problems

If the fan runs at a slow speed, check these points:

☑ CHECKLIST ■

☐ Measure the amount of voltage present, as detailed on page 3. Low voltage will cause slow running speed.

☐ A tight fan-motor shaft can be tested by removing the outside cover shroud and spinning the fan by hand with the power turned off. Many fan motors have a small oil cup on the top of the motor. Remove the plastic plug from the cup and place three or four drops of an SAE 20-weight nondetergent oil in the cup once a year (Figure 7.7). Do not overoil. If the motor still is slow and tight, the bearings have failed and the assembly should be replaced by a qualified service technician.

☐ Dirty intake filters will reduce airflow, so periodic cleaning or replacement of the filters is necessary. Remove the control knobs and the ceiling shroud that hold the filters. The filters should be washed in warm, sudsy water, dried, replaced in the shroud assembly and the assembly returned to its location on the ceiling.

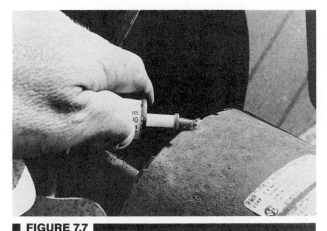

■ FIGURE 7.7 ■
The fan motor should be lubricated with SAE 20-weight oil once a year.

TROUBLESHOOTING the Compressor Air Conditioner

Problem	Possible Cause	Correction
Unit will not run	No 120-volt AC power	Connect to power source.
	Tripped 120-volt breaker	Reset circuit breaker.
	Defective on-off switch	Replace switch.
	Loose connector plug	Check connection integrity.
	Defective on-off switch	Replace main switch.
Fan runs too slowly	Poor electrical contact	Check all connections.
	Low line voltage	Check supply voltage.
	Undersize power cord	Replace with proper size.
	Tight motor shaft	Check shaft.
	Blower/fan misaligned	Check alignment.
	Intake filters clogged	Clean or replace filters.
Fan runs but compressor will not engage	Low voltage	Inspect supply output.
	Undersize power cord	Replace with correct size.
	Starting capacitor	Replace capacitor.
	Improper temperature setting	Reset thermostat.
	Defective thermostat	Replace thermostat.
	Defective time delay	Replace delay switch.
	High compressor pressure	Defective time-delay switch.
	Defective compressor	Replace compressor.
Compressor will not cycle off	Thermostat set too low	Set to warmer temperature.
	Clogged condensor coils	Clean condenser.
	Excess heat gain	Reduce heat-gain areas.
	Iced-over evaporator	Turn system off to melt ice.
	Stuck thermostat switch	Replace switch.
	Low refrigerant charge	Recharge unit.

Checking for Compressor Failure

Many times the fan motor will operate correctly, but the compressor will not engage and no cooling will result. This can be caused by several factors:

☑ CHECKLIST ▬▬▬▬▬▬▬▬

☐ The time-delay circuit may be defective. This circuit prevents the compressor from coming on before the head pressure is depleted. Failure to deplete the head pressure can damage the compressor. The time-delay circuit/switch should only be repaired by a qualified service technician.

☐ The air conditioner's thermostat determines when the compressor will start; make sure that it is set to a sufficiently cool temperature.

☐ If there are no results, the temperature-sensing bulb mechanism that sends a signal to the thermostat may be defective or improperly placed. The thermostat may also be defective. Seek qualified service to check these points.

☐ If the motor does not start easily and quickly, the capacitor (a storage device) may be defective. When a signal is sent from the thermostat calling for more cooling, the capacitor dumps its stored power to the motor, giving it an extra push for a few seconds to get it going. Seek authorized service to check the capacitor circuits.

☐ When the air-conditioning unit has been operating for a while, but the compressor fails to restart, the problem may be in the start-delay circuit. This circuit allows the compressor to rest for a few minutes between cycles so that the pressure in the system can equalize. If the compressor tried to start immediately after shutting off, there would be excessive pressure against the pistons, which would make starting difficult. The delay circuit allows this pressure to subside after each cycle. If the switch is defective, it may not close again when a signal from the thermostat calls for cooling. Seek authorized service for this difficulty.

☐ The compressor motor could be burned out. Seek qualified help to determine the condition of the compressor assembly.

■ FIGURE 7.8 ■
The condenser coils in an air conditioner must be kept clean to insure optimum efficiency.

Checking for Failure of Compressor to Shut Off

The opposite problem occurs when the compressor will not turn off. Several areas can be checked for this condition:

☑ CHECKLIST ■■■■■■■■■■■■■■■■

☐ Check to see that the thermostat is not set too low. If it is set on maximum cold, the unit will run excessively.

☐ Make sure the condenser coils are clean and unclogged. If not, the unit can't cool to its full potential, so it tries to run all the time to make up for the inefficiency. Remove the exterior cover shroud and vacuum or blow out the coils to remove dirt (Figure 7.8). Carefully straighten the cooling fins if they are bent (Figure 7.9). They are delicate, but the job can be done with a pocketknife blade.

☐ Continuous running may be the result of excessive heat gain. That is, the rate that the RV absorbs heat is faster than the air conditioner can remove heat. In this case the unit will never shut down. Make sure that all windows and doors are closed. If the RV is parked in direct sunlight, seek shade; sunlight causes a great deal of heat gain. If the condition persists, it is simply too hot, or the air conditioner is not large enough to deal with the volume of heat it is receiving.

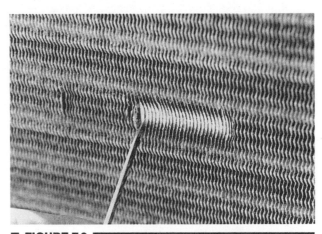

■ FIGURE 7.9 ■
Condenser coil fins that have become bent should be carefully straightened with a knife or screwdriver.

☐ During long-term operation in hot, humid weather the evaporator coils may freeze up, causing the compressor to run continually, but failing to cool adequately because the airflow over the coils is blocked with ice. To correct this situation make sure that RV doors and windows are opened infrequently. Do not release large amounts of heat and steam while cooking. If this cannot be avoided, set the thermostat to a slightly warmer temperature. This will allow the compressor to cycle off more frequently, which will melt any ice buildup. If the buildup is very heavy, the air conditioner should be shut down for a period of time until the ice melts (30 minutes is usually adequate).

TROUBLESHOOTING the Heat Strip

Problem	Possible Cause	Correction
No heat	No 120-volt AC power	Check for power.
	Tripped breaker	Reset breaker.
	Low voltage	Check voltage level.
	Loose connection	Inspect connections.
	Defective switch	Replace switch.
	Defective thermostat	Replace thermostat.
	Burned-out strip	Replace strip.

☐ Thermostat switch contacts can become stuck together, which will cause the compressor to run on. If this is suspected, seek qualified assistance in testing and replacing the thermostat assembly.

☐ The last possibility of compressor run-on is lack of refrigerant. This can only be determined with a pressure test by qualified service personnel. If the system is low on refrigerant, there is most likely a leak in the system requiring repair before recharging takes place. An air-conditioner service facility should deal with these problems.

■ Air Conditioner Heat Strips

Many compressor-type air-conditioning units are equipped with *heat strips*, grids of electrical wiring connected to a thermostat temperature control system within the air conditioner (see Figure 7.10). When the heat is turned on, the fan in the air conditioner circulates air; the heat grids heat the incoming air before returning it to the RV interior. Heat strips require 120-volt AC power.

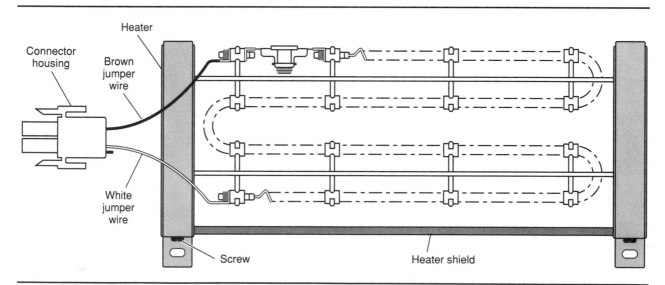

■ FIGURE 7.10 ■
Many air conditioners are equipped with heat strips that consist of grids of electrical wiring.

TROUBLESHOOTING *the Evaporative Cooler*

Problem	Possible Cause	Correction
Unit will not run	Blown 12-volt fuse	Test and replace fuse.
	Loose wiring connection	Check connection tightness.
	Dead battery	Charge or replace battery.
	Stuck fan shaft	Rotate by hand to free.
	Stuck pump shaft	Remove and clean pump.
Unit will not cool	High-humidity condition	No correction possible.
	Low water level	Replenish water supply.
	Stuck float valve	Free float valve.
	Inoperative pump	Check pump condition.
	Clogged water passages	Clean unit.
	Dirty evaporative mat	Clean or replace.
	Inoperative fan	Check fan motor.

Servicing Heat Strips

A limited amount of service on heat strips can be performed by the consumer. Using a multimeter, the incoming voltage supply can be checked. The same corrections can be applied to heat strips as to air conditioners.

CAUTION: Remember, 120-volt AC power can be dangerous. It is best to seek qualified help when in doubt.

Evaporative Coolers

Evaporative coolers force air through a water-soaked mat or screen, which cools the air as the water evaporates. The evaporative cooler fan is usually powered by a 12-volt electric motor. A 12-volt pump is used to distribute water to the absorbent evaporation mat while the fan blows air across the mat.

The cooler's reservoir is filled either by a connection to the RV's water pump via a flat control valve, or by manually filling with a hose from an outside fill point. Most reservoirs hold enough water for a day's cooling—about 5 gallons. Evaporative coolers are best suited to dry climates where the humidity is low.

■ Servicing Evaporative Coolers

Periodic cleaning of evaporative coolers is necessary to prevent operational difficulties. Algae can build up in the water pump, reservoir, and distribution lines, and dirt may accumulate on the evaporative mat, severely reducing airflow. It is good maintenance practice to keep the cooler covered during the off-season and when it is not in use. This prevents road dirt and grime from entering.

Checking for Failure of Cooler to Operate

If the unit refuses to operate, here is a step-by-step method of getting it cool again:

☑ **CHECKLIST**

☐ Check the condition of the RV battery. If the voltage is low, the unit may fail to run.

☐ Locate the 12-volt DC fuse panel in the RV and check the condition of the cooler's fuse. Use a multimeter to check the fuse (see page 2).

☐ Check the condition of the wiring connections; gain access by removing the ceiling cover on the cooler. The cooler wires are usually tied together with wire nuts. Make sure they are tight and free of corrosion. Check these connections with a multimeter to insure that current flows to this point. Make sure that there is a good ground and the electrical polarity (positive to positive, negative to negative) is correct.

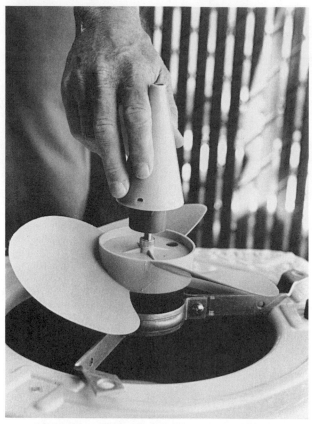

■ **FIGURE 7.11**
The fan motor shaft in evaporative coolers can be freed by hand to turn in most cases.

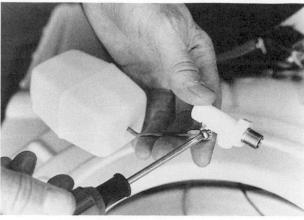

■ **FIGURE 7.12**
Evaporative coolers use a float-valve control that needs adjusting. If stuck, a few drops of oil may free the valve.

Checking for Failure of Unit to Cool

In the other condition, failure to cool, the fan operates, circulating air through the unit, but no cool air results. Take a look at these possibilities:

☑ **CHECKLIST**

☐ If the outdoor temperature (over 85°F) and humidity (50% or more) are high, it is likely the evaporative cooler is doing its best. The air simply does not feel very cold as it leaves the cooler because the evaporation rate is low during high-humidity weather, thus reducing the system's effectiveness.

☐ Check the water level in the reservoir. If it is low, cooling will be reduced.

☐ If the cooler is equipped with a float-valve control for the reservoir's water level, remove the outside cover from the cooler and check to see that the float drops, opening the water valve (Figure 7.12). A small amount of penetrating oil applied to the float-valve pivot usually will free it.

☐ The cooler will not function unless adequate water is supplied to the absorbent pad by the pump. Remove the exterior cover and insure that there are 12 volts present at the pump motor when the switch is in the "on" position. If the pump will not operate, it should be replaced.

☐ Locate the on-off switch and determine with the multimeter if power flows to that point. Then turn on the switch and check to see if power is available at the motor side of the switch. If power is not available, the switch needs replacing.

☐ If power is confirmed, check to see that the motor shaft is free to turn. If it is not, try to free it by hand (Figure 7.11). If it is tightly stuck, the motor may need replacement.

☐ If the pump is clogged or jammed and will not rotate, it could be drawing off enough amperage to prevent the fan motor from running. With the switch in the "on" position, make sure that 12 volts are present at the pump motor. If there is power to the pump motor and it will not rotate, it is probably seized and will require replacement. These pumps are usually a one-piece assembly with no provision for repair.

■ FIGURE 7.13 ■
Evaporative cooler pads must be kept clean and should be replaced every two years.

☐ If the pump runs normally, it may fail to pump adequately if any of the associated plumbing or hoses are kinked. When checking the pump, scrutinize the passages that the water must travel through to get to the pad. If there is any sign of clogging, the outlet hose from the pump can be removed and pressure-flushed with a garden hose to remove any debris.

☐ Failure to cool could be due to a dirty absorbent pad. The accumulation of dirt on the pad reduces its ability to hold water and to allow air to pass through, resulting in no cooling. Most pads can be cleaned by washing with a pressure (garden) hose to remove dirt. Since these pads are not expensive, it's best to replace them every few years. Pads are easily changed by removing the cover-retaining screws and the cover, then lifting the pad straight up and out of the cooler. Reverse the order to install the new pad (Figure 7.13).

CHAPTER 8

Refrigerators

RV refrigerators are completely different from household units. They live a relatively rugged life; they are asked to operate on a variety of energy sources, and withstand all the jostling and vibration of highway travel. Unless special care is given to them, it is understandable that they might someday complain or go on strike altogether.

The most common owner complaint is when the refrigerator simply doesn't perform very well: temperature inside the food compartment during hot weather approaches or exceeds 50°.

To comprehend the problems associated with RV refrigerators, it is necessary to understand the ingenious theory of *absorption refrigeration* (see Figure 8.1). Rather than applying cold directly, heat is drawn out (absorbed) from the refrigerator. Where there is an absence of heat, there is cold.

In absorption refrigeration there are no moving parts. The whole process is based on laws of chemistry and physics rather than mechanics. Here's how it works.

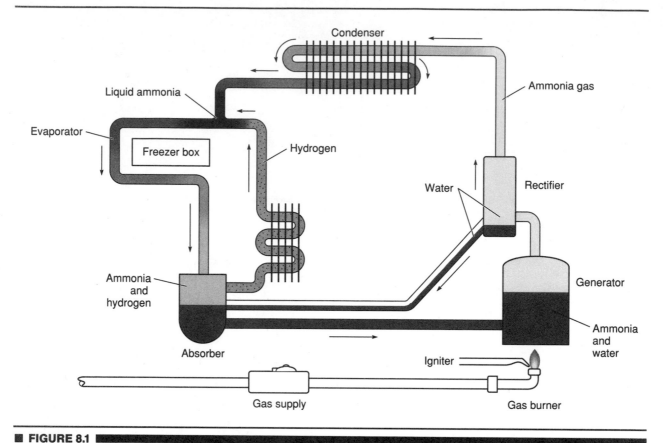

RV absorption refrigerators use ammonia, hydrogen, water, and sodium chromate under pressure to produce a cold food compartment.

Water, ammonia, hydrogen gas, and sodium chromate are combined under pressure in a containment vessel, sometimes known as a *generator* or *boiler*. Each of these elements plays an important role in the process of cooling or in the preservation of the equipment. The water, ammonia, and hydrogen gas are directly involved in the cooling process, but the sodium chromate's job is to prevent the heat from corroding the pipes.

As an electrical heating element or gas burner brings the solution to a boil, the liquid percolates up the pump tube. The ammonia is distilled out of the solution and continues to rise up the tube as a gas. A short way up the tube, the water and ammonia gas part company, and the water returns to the reservoir via a circuitous system of winding pipes. During the water's return, it is recombined with the ammonia at the far end of its voyage.

Meanwhile, the ammonia gas continues upward until it reaches the condenser, where it gives off its heat and returns to a liquid form. As the drops of pure liquid ammonia fall, they trickle into the *evaporator* (freezing unit) where they combine with hydrogen gas. This chemical marriage causes very vigorous evaporation, which results in cooling. Since this rapid evaporation process takes place in the freezer unit, that's where most of the cold goes, as the heat is literally sucked out.

Because of the evaporation, the liquid ammonia becomes a gas again and travels to a secondary evaporator in the refrigerator unit (the shiny fins inside) where it absorbs more heat. Then the gas enters a return pipe on its way back to rejoin the water and start the process again.

Leveling Problems in an Absorption System

It's a simple system, but problems can occur if the unit is operated severely off level. If the heating element or flame heats the boiler while there is not enough liquid in the right place, the heat may "cook" the sodium chromate. If that happens, the sodium chromate gets hard and can clog the tiny passages in the pump tube, or it can flake and float around until it finds a place to lodge. Eventually, it causes the failure of the refrigerator.

If the refrigerator is not relatively level, the liquid in the system readily accumulates, forming pockets that can impair the gas circulation or block it completely, in which case cooling will stop—permanently in most cases.

When the RV is stationary, it must be leveled to be comfortable to live in. If the refrigerator is properly installed (the freezer compartment parallel with the RV floor), the refrigerator will operate properly. To check this, use a bubble level to adjust the position of the RV front to rear and side to side until at least one-half of the bubble is within the center ring of the level.

When the RV is in motion, the continuous rolling and pitching movement will not affect the refrigerator as long as the movement breaks the plane of level, but when the RV is temporarily parked, the refrigerator should be leveled.

If you are in a situation in which the refrigerator cannot be leveled, such as a parking lot on a steep incline, no matter how short the time, shut the refrigerator off until it can be leveled or until you are once again on the road. The damage that occurs is cumulative, and each time you operate off level, the blockage becomes thicker until finally it blocks totally and the cooling unit is no longer functional.

In recent years, some RV refrigerator manufacturers have redesigned certain components of their units to prevent accidental damage due to off-level operation. The new refrigerators shut down operation before they can harm themselves. To know whether or not your unit is of a self-protecting design, check with the manufacturer. Otherwise, make sure your RV is level when the refrigerator is in operation.

■ Correcting Blockage in a Norcold Unit

If a Norcold refrigerator (Figure 8.2) suffers loss of cooling ability due to operation for extended periods of time in an off-level condition, a special procedure may restore function. The refrigerator must be removed from its compartment and placed on its left side for a minumum of one hour. This will allow the ammonia and water to mix with one another. Once the system has been relieved of its blockage, operation on AC should once again be initiated for a reasonable time to determine if the cooling process has been restored. If after this period the freezer plate has no indication of cooling, the cooling system must be removed and replaced.

■ Correcting Problems in a Dometic Unit

With certain models of Dometic refrigerators (RM360, RM460, RM660, RM760, Figure 8.3) if an excessive vaporization of the ammonia within the boiler occurs due to too much or too little heat input, either on electric or gas operation, or operating the refrigerator in an off-level position or with inadequate ventilation, the liquid mixture in the boiler becomes very weak. The circulation of liquid stops, and the evaporator inside the cabinet ceases to produce cooling.

Such a blockage of the unit in the liquid circuit is most often made evident by signs of overheating on the vapor pipe leading from the boiler to the condenser. The paint on this pipe may be blistered and the metal discolored.

To remedy this problem, remove the complete refrigerator whenever possible and allow sufficient time for the unit to cool down. Turn the unit upside down several times so that the liquid in the absorber vessel can be mixed with the liquid in the boiler. This procedure will restore the liquid balance to the unit. Sometimes a vigorous drive around the block will restore minor blockages.

Helpful Refrigerator Operating Hints

Even without understanding the technical details, there are many simple tricks that will make an RV refrigerator work better. Some of the procedures described here require a periodic visit to a service center

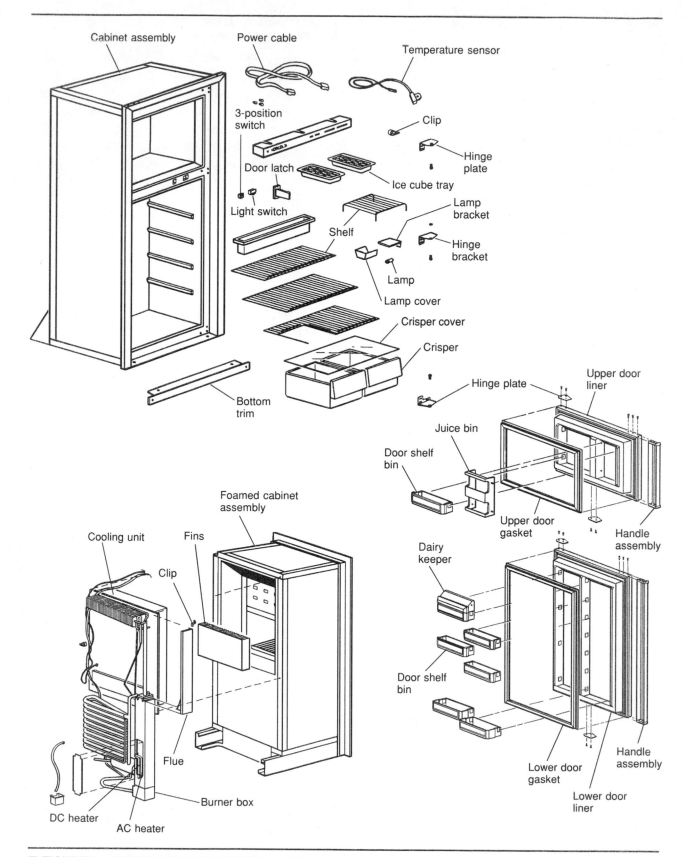

Cabinet assembly

Power cable

Temperature sensor

3-position switch

Clip

Hinge plate

Door latch

Ice cube tray

Light switch

Lamp bracket

Hinge bracket

Shelf

Lamp

Lamp cover

Crisper cover

Crisper

Bottom trim

Hinge plate

Upper door liner

Juice bin

Door shelf bin

Upper door gasket

Handle assembly

Foamed cabinet assembly

Cooling unit

Fins

Dairy keeper

Clip

Door shelf bin

Flue

Burner box

DC heater

AC heater

Lower door gasket

Handle assembly

Lower door liner

■ FIGURE 8.2 ■

Exploded view of Norcold RV absorption refrigerator

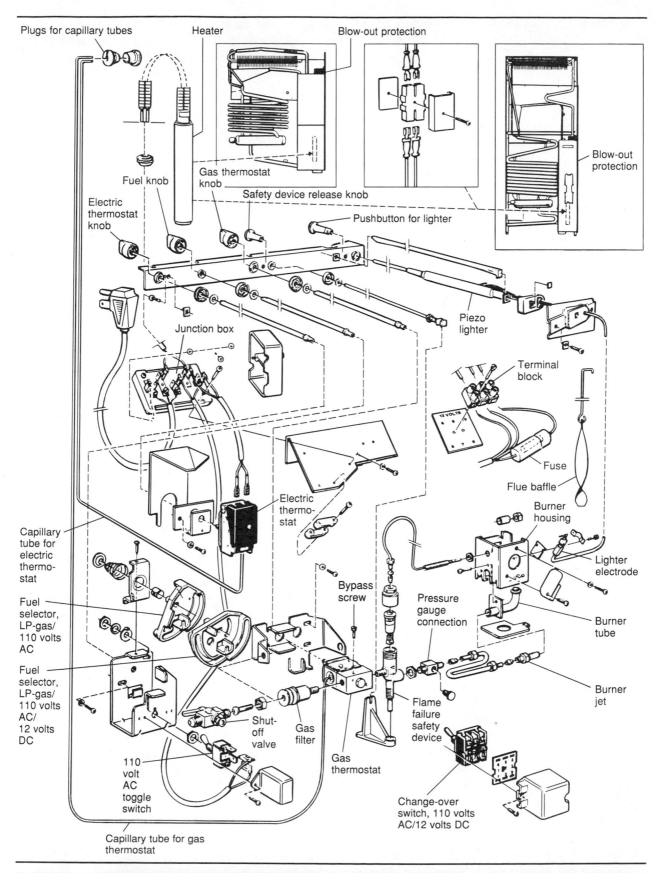

Plugs for capillary tubes
Heater
Blow-out protection
Gas thermostat knob
Fuel knob
Safety device release knob
Blow-out protection
Electric thermostat knob
Pushbutton for lighter
Piezo lighter
Junction box
Terminal block
Fuse
Flue baffle
Electric thermostat
Burner housing
Lighter electrode
Capillary tube for electric thermostat
Burner tube
Fuel selector, LP-gas/110 volts AC
Bypass screw
Pressure gauge connection
Fuel selector, LP-gas/110 volts AC/12 volts DC
Burner jet
Flame failure safety device
Shut-off valve
Gas filter
110 volt AC toggle switch
Gas thermostat
Change-over switch, 110 volts AC/12 volts DC
Capillary tube for gas thermostat

■ **FIGURE 8.3** ▬▬▬▬▬▬▬
Exploded view of Dometic RV absorption refrigerator

where technicians can test components with instrumentation if erratic refrigerator performance is noticed. But most of them are just everyday common-sense techniques.

- Pre-cool the refrigerator by starting it the night before the camping trip. This should be done with no food in the refrigerator. Wait until the unit is thoroughly cold before placing food inside.

- Pre-cool food in your home refrigerator. Pre-freeze foods to be kept in the freezer. This gives the unit a break by adding cold to it rather than adding heat and demanding more work to cool it down.

- Proper refrigeration requires free air circulation within the food storage compartment. Restricted air circulation within this compartment will cause higher cabinet temperatures. To remedy this situation simply rearrange the foodstuffs. It is essential that the shelves not be covered with paper or large storage containers because this inhibits free air circulation.

- To reduce frost buildup, cover stored liquids and moist foods and do not leave the door open longer than necessary.

- When buying food on the road that is intended for storage in the refrigerator, buy the coldest packages available and get them into the RV refrigerator as quickly as possible. This prevents its having to work extra hard to cool down warm packages.

- Always wipe moisture off the outside of containers before putting them in the refrigerator. If cold items are taken from the unit, they will have a tendency to sweat as they warm. Dry them off before putting them back into the refrigerator. This will help prevent a frost buildup, which consumes cooling power and insulates against efficient heat transfer.

- Make sure the unit is as level as possible. The more nearly level the unit, the more efficiently it will work. Continual off-level work eventually blocks circulation of the refrigerant.

- Periodically clean out the burner unit. LP-gas has a garlic or rotten-egg odor that becomes especially strong as the tanks run low. This scent attracts spiders, which will build nests in the burner.

  Special care must be taken when cleaning burner orifices; these parts are delicate. They cannot be cleaned by simply inserting a pin or thin wire. They must be removed, cleaned in alcohol, and then blown dry with compressed air. When reinstalling, insure that the burner flame is centered directly below the flue.

- Clean out the refrigerator's roof exhaust vent. Bird nests, leaves, twigs, or other debris can lodge there, choking the unit's efficiency. In extreme cases, they can even cause a fire.

- Do not overfill the LP-gas bottles or tank. This can damage the regular diaphragm, causing irregular delivery of the propane and resulting in erratic operation of the refrigerator.

- In the gas mode, the burners are designed for a specific Btu rating. The LP-gas pressure must remain constant or else the refrigerator will operate erratically (see pages 40–41).

  If you have noticed erratic cooling when operating on gas, check for kinks or clogs in the gas line. It is important to check LP-gas pressure at the refrigerator when other appliances are operating. Using a test manometer, pressure should read 11 inches of water-column pressure. Most RVers have a shop perform this test because of the equipment involved.

- Periodically have the regulator diaphragm replaced to insure maximum efficiency. The diaphragm can load up with a waxy substance after much use, which changes the way the pressure is controlled. If the pressure vacillates, the refrigerator will suffer irregular operation.

- Don't put any filters, covers, or plastic bags over the vents to the refrigerator unit. They are designed to be operated as they come from the factory, with nothing covering the vents. If the ventilation is restricted, a buildup of excess heat results, and the refrigerator cannot function properly.

- Don't open the refrigerator or freezer doors more often than necessary. Cold air in the refrigerator is just like a pile of sand. It falls to the bottom, and when you open the door, it runs out onto the floor. Every time the door is opened, the refrigerator gains a few degrees of heat. If it is opened six or eight times on an extremely hot day, it may lose most of its cool.

- In extremely hot weather, a small battery-powered fan (Fridgemate) in the refrigerator will help circulate the air faster than occurs by natural convection. This can help efficiency in unusually hot weather.

- Make sure an adequate electric cord is used when operating in the 120-volt AC mode. An extension cord with too small a gauge used with the RV power cord will cause inefficiency of the refrigerator heating element and result in a loss of cooling capacity.

TROUBLESHOOTING the Absorption Refrigerator

Problem	Possible Cause	Correction
Insufficient cooling	Wrong thermostat setting	Adjust thermostat to higher setting.
	Restricted air circulation over cooling unit	Remove any restrictions.
	Refrigerator not level	Adjust RV to level refrigerator.
	Air leakage into cabinet	Check door gasket; adjust or replace if necessary.
	Heavy coating of frost on evaporator	Defrost unit frequently.
	Faulty heater, wrong voltage or type	Install new heater of appropriate voltage.
	Intermittent power	Check for loose connections; repair as necessary.
	Voltage drop	Maintain voltage at full rate.
	Break in electric circuit	Check fuses, switches, wiring; repair as necessary.
	Faulty thermostat	Replace thermostat.
	Failed cooling unit	Replace cooling unit.
Excessive cooling	Wrong thermostat setting	Adjust thermostat to lower setting.
	Incorrectly located end of thermostat capillary tube	Reinsert capillary end of thermostat fully in the sleeve under the ice-tray compartment.
	Faulty thermostat	Replace thermostat.
	Improperly wired heater	Rewire heater according to unit wiring diagram.

- The flue, which is located directly above the burner flame, should be cleaned periodically to remove rust, scale, and soot. How often this is done is determined by frequency of use, propane quality, and region of the country. If the refrigerator is operated in areas with high humidity or salt air, it will require more frequent cleaning.

    After removal of the flue tube, the spiral baffle inside the tube must be carefully removed. Then a shotgun bore brush or a special brush available from the refrigerator manufacturer is used to clean the tube. When everything is clean, the baffle must be replaced exactly as it was. In order to perform this operation, you may have to remove the refrigerator from its recess. This cleaning is critical to get total efficiency. Generally, however, its benefits will only be noticed in extremely hot weather when maximum refrigerator cooling is needed.

- If possible, park so the refrigerator side of the coach is shaded.
- Clean the absorber coils and condenser fins to remove any buildup that can act as a heat-transfer insulator.
- The electric heating element should be checked periodically for proper resistance. It will deteriorate with age, leaving the refrigerator with a slowly diminishing capacity for cooling when used in the electric mode. Generally, owners have this test performed at a repair facility because of the instruments required.
- Defrost the unit regularly. A frost buildup insulates against thermal exchange, preventing the refrigerator from absorbing the heat from its contents. But don't use a hairdryer or high-heat source to speed

TROUBLESHOOTING the LP-Gas-Operated Refrigerator

Problem	Possible Cause	Correction
Insufficient cooling	Restricted air circulation over cooling unit	Remove any restrictions.
	Refrigerator not level	Adjust RV to level refrigerator.
	Insufficient LP-gas	Refill LP-gas tanks.
	Feeler point of thermocouple flame-failure device not heated enough by flame	Adjust position of feeler point in flame.
	Clogged bypass screw, clogged burner head, clogged burner jet orifice	Clean bypass screw with alcohol and by blowing through with air. If necessary, replace burner jet. Clean the head with a brush or toothpick.
	Flue baffle not inserted into central tube of cooling unit	Position baffle correctly. Consult manufacturer's specs.
	Baffle too low in flue	Position baffle correctly. Consult manufacturer's specs (see Figures 8.4, 8.5, and Table 8.1).
	Improper LP-gas pressure.	Have pressure checked. Pressure must not fall below 11 inches water-column pressure when thermostat is set on "max."
	Loose burner assembly	Refit burner assembly.
	Improper thermostat setting	Increase thermostat setting.
	Failed cooling unit	Replace unit.
Refrigerator too cold	Improper thermostat setting	Lower thermostat setting.
	Incorrectly located end of thermostat capillary tube	Reinsert end of capillary tube in clamp on fresh-food compartment.
	Incorrect size of bypass screw	Replace bypass screw.
	Dirt in thermostat valve	Clean valve and valve seat in thermostat.

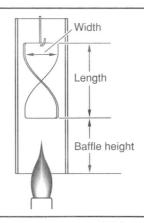

■ **FIGURE 8.4** ■
Baffle position for Dometic refrigerators

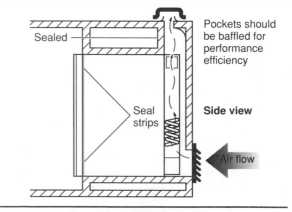

■ **FIGURE 8.5** ■
Baffle position for Norcold refrigerators

■ **TABLE 8.1**
Baffle Sizes and Heights

Model	Baffle Width x Length		Baffle Height	
	mm	inches	mm	inches
RM24	10 × 100	⅜ × 4	75	3
RM36C	20 × 100	¾ × 4	75	3
RM46, RM47	20 × 100	¾ × 4	75	3
RM66, RM67	20 × 100	¾ × 4	75	3
RM76, RM77	20 × 150	¾ × 6	75	3

defrosting. This can warp the cooling fins. Instead, use a pan of warm water and patience.

● Inspect the door gasket for proper sealing ability. Use the dollar-bill trick. (Shut the refrigerator door with a dollar bill halfway inside, then tug on the other half to see how difficult it is to remove. It should offer some resistance.) Or you can place a lighted flashlight inside the refrigerator at night and shut the door to see if light escapes.

● Since the interior refrigerator light (if so equipped) produces some heat, check to see that it goes out when the door is closed. To do this, use a thin butter-knife blade to spread the door gasket back a bit when the door is closed. This will allow you to look inside at night when the door is closed to see if the light is on.

● If your refrigerator can be operated in the 12-volt DC mode, make sure the connection uses an adequate gauge of wire and that there is no corrosion or damage to the wire.

   CAUTION: Do not operate the refrigerator on 12-volt DC unless the engine is running.

■ Checking for Overfreezing in Dometic Units

If your Dometic refrigerator freezes food in the lower compartment:

☑ **CHECKLIST**

☐ Make sure the gas thermostat knob is not stripped. If it is, replace it.

☐ Turn the knob up and down and watch for the flame to change. If it does not change, the thermostat is defective and must be replaced.

☐ Make certain the end of the capillary (sensing tube) is seated properly inside the refrigerator against the fins.

☐ If it changes from "high" to "low" (or vice versa) and still freezes in the lower section, change the bypass screw: shut off the gas. Remove the existing screw in the thermostat and replace it with a new one that has a lower number stamped on top. Finish by checking for gas leaks using soapy water.

■ Checking a Cooling Unit

Failure of refrigeration doesn't necessarily indicate that the cooling unit is defective. Other factors governing its operation must be checked.

If the refrigerator has been operating on LP-gas and a loss of cooling is noted, switch over to electric operation. If the unit has been operating on AC power, switch over to LP-gas. This will determine if component failure in the electric or LP-gas system is causing the cooling fault. After the refrigerator has been switched over from one power source to another, allow sufficient time to assure that the unit is cycling properly. The freezer plate should start to cool. The following are items to check before determining that a refrigeration cooling unit is faulty.

☑ **CHECKLIST**

☐ Evaporator plate is level in each direction.
☐ Controls have been properly set for the power source utilized.
☐ Power source is at the correct rating (11 inches water column for LP-gas, 120 volts for AC).
☐ 12-volt DC supply is present for mode selector control.
☐ Upper and lower vents are not obstructed.
☐ Refrigerator is properly leveled.
☐ Good ventilation.
☐ Clean proper-size burner orifice.
☐ Clean proper-size bypass screw.
☐ Clean thermostat valve.
☐ Proper LP-gas pressure.
☐ Correct flame.
☐ Correct position of baffle in boiler tube.
☐ No burnt-out element.
☐ Heating element in correct position.
☐ Correct size and wattage of heating element.

☐ Supply voltage corresponds to voltage stamped on heating element.
☐ No fluctuation in voltage supply.
☐ No loose electrical connections.
☐ Thermostat intact.
☐ No unit leaks.
☐ Safety valve intact.

CAUTION: Do not attempt to operate the system on 12-volt DC power when analyzing the system performance since this power source is designed for short-period operation only and does not power the system at its full capabilities.

General Maintenance

Once or twice a year, depending upon frequency of use, it is recommended to clean and adjust the burner assembly. This includes the burner jet, burner barrel, and flue system. On all LP-gas appliances, the cleaning solution used on the jets and associated parts should be one that dries without any residue. Rubbing alcohol and wood alcohol are appropriate cleaning agents. *Do not use a cleaner with a petrochemical base because it will leave a film on the inside of these parts and reduce burner efficiency. Never use a wire or pin when cleaning the jet. This will enlarge the orifice opening, damage the refrigerator, and create a fire hazard.*

Once a year the LP-gas pressure being delivered to the appliances should be checked by a qualified dealer or propane agency. Correct LP-gas pressure is 11 inches of water column. This should be checked at the test point in the refrigerator compartment.

When replacing a jet with a new one, make sure the replacement is correct for your refrigerator model. Too large or too small a jet can ruin the cooling unit. A jet that is too small will result in failure to maintain desired temperatures.

It is important to always check for LP-gas leaks after repair work has been performed. Do this with soapy water, not a match. (See also Chapter 2, "LP-Gas Systems," page 37.)

■ Replacing or Cleaning the Burner

For routine cleaning or replacement of the burner, follow this procedure as it applies to your particular unit:

1. Turn off the LP-gas supply at the tanks.
2. Disconnect the gas pipe from the burner assembly.
3. Disconnect thermocouple from safety valve.
4. Disconnect the igniter lead (if applicable) and loosen the screw.
5. Remove the burner housing.
6. Remove the orifice from the burner tube.
7. Clean both with alcohol and compressed air only.
8. Clean the burner tube and especially the gauze or slots with a brush. Blow out with compressed air.
9. At the same time, check the flue baffle to see that it is clean and free of soot. Heavy soot formation indicates improper functioning of the burner.
10. Clean baffle and flue.
11. Clean the cooling unit and the floor under the refrigerator.
12. Reassemble.
13. Turn on LP-gas supply.
14. The entire gas installation should be checked for leaks. Test all pipes with soapy water.
15. Check the burner with full flame ("max") and with bypass flame ("0"). **Note:** The thermostat will not close to bypass on setting "0" unless the refrigerator has been working for a few hours and the thermostat bulb is cooled to at least 40°F.

■ Cleaning the Refrigerator

The cabinet interior should be thoroughly cleaned on a regular basis. Remove the shelves and wash the interior walls with lukewarm water to which a small amount of baking soda or dishwashing detergent has been added. Dry the surfaces thoroughly, especially around door frames and door gaskets. Warm water only should be used to wash the cooling evaporator, ice trays, and shelves. Never use strong chemicals or abrasive materials on any part of the cabinet.

■ Defrosting the Refrigerator

Before defrosting the refrigerator, move food to another refrigerator if possible to prevent spoilage during defrosting. To defrost the refrigerator, turn the power selector switch off. Fill trays with hot water and place them in the freezer compartment. After all the frost has melted, empty the drip tray from beneath the finned evaporator (if not drained to the outside) and wipe up the excess moisture with a clean cloth. Replace the drip tray and all the food. Turn on the refrigerator, and turn the thermostat to "max" for a few hours for maximum cooling before returning it to its normal position.

■ Refrigerator Odors

Odors inside the refrigerator are caused by improper food storage. They may also be caused by infrequent cleaning of the food compartment or if the refrigerator has been shut off for some time with the door closed.

Checking for Gas Leaks

Odors outside the refrigerator may be caused by gas leaks. To check for leaks:

☑ CHECKLIST ▰▰▰▰▰▰▰▰▰▰▰

- ☐ Make sure that all gas appliances are closed.
- ☐ Test gas connections and all joints in the gas line with soapy water, up to and including the gas valve.
- ☐ Never look for a leak with an open flame. Use a flashlight when necessary to look for soap bubbles caused by leaks.
- ☐ Turn on gas valve and light burner, then test connections between the gas valve and the burner carefully with soapy water.

Odors outside the refrigerator may be caused by improper burner flame. If the flame touches the side of the boiler due to dislocation of the burner, relocate the burner. Burner dislocation may also cause smoke and discoloration of walls and ceiling. Remember:

- ● If the burner is damaged or faulty, replace it.
- ● If the flame touches the flue baffle, correct the position of the baffle.
- ● If the flue is dirty, clean it.

■ Flame Blow-Out

If the flame blows out under especially windy conditions, try to position the RV to avoid the wind blowing against the wall where the vent outlets are located. If the trouble persists, set the thermostat to "max." This measure can only be temporary because after a few hours foodstuffs in the cabinet will freeze. Do not cover the vents to prevent flame blow-out. Circulation of air is necessary for proper and safe refrigerator operation.

■ Setting the Burner Flame

Norcold refrigerators have burners with nonadjustable fixed orifices using primary air holes that control the flame (See Figure 8.6). A properly set flame in the burner of a Norcold refrigerator should be sharp blue with no yellow color.

Dometic refrigerators have used several different types of burners over the years, and setting the proper flame is different for each.

The Bunsen "B-" type burner has a ceramic head and a Klixon safety valve (Figure 8.7). When the thermostat dial is turned to "max," the flame must form a crown around the burner's inner stone and have upright streaks through its center holes. The flame must be blue and soft and may have a slightly luminous tip. Air adjustment rings on the burner are turned to adjust the flame.

The cylindrical "H-" type burner has adjustable primary air inlets combined with the Junker-type thermoelectric flame-failure safety device (Figure 8.8). Air-adjustment rings are employed for adjustment of the flame. The correct flame at "max" setting should have a bright-blue crown at the base of the flame and emit a slight buzzing noise.

The "E-" type burner has the jet and adaptor horizontally located, and the burner mixing tube is formed as a bend with a vertical outlet (Figure 8.9). The primary air inlets are preset and therefore not adjustable. The burner is combined with the Junker-type thermoelectric flame-failure safety device. The correct flame at "max" setting should have a bright blue crown at the base of the flame and emit a slight buzzing sound.

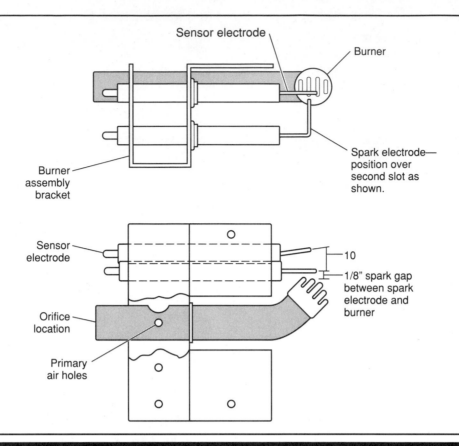

Sensor electrode

Burner

Burner
assembly
bracket

Spark electrode—
position over
second slot as
shown.

Sensor
electrode

10

1/8" spark gap
between spark
electrode and
burner

Orifice
location

Primary
air holes

■ FIGURE 8.6 ■
Norcold refrigerator burner has a fixed orifice; flame should be sharp blue with no yellow color.

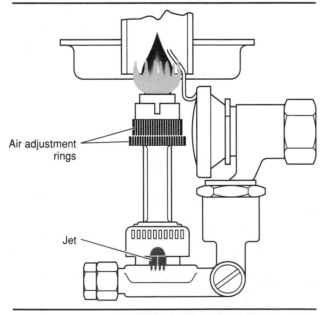

Air adjustment
rings

Jet

■ FIGURE 8.7 ■
The Dometic Bunsen "B-" type burner must have a flame that forms a crown around the burner's inner stone.

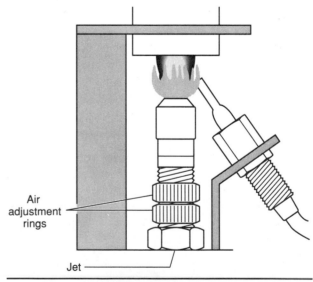

Air
adjustment
rings

Jet

■ FIGURE 8.8 ■
The Dometic "H-" type burner flame should have a bright-blue crown at the base of the flame and emit a slight buzzing noise.

boiler system. It is important to use the correct size of baffle and to correctly position it in order to obtain the best cooling performance.

Obstructions in the flue will reduce or stop flue draft, cause odors in the refrigerator, slow freezing, and raise cabinet temperatures. Flue stoppages may also cause the flame to burn outside the central tube.

To clean the flue tube, first loosen the burner assembly, drop it down, and cover it with a rag so no debris from the flue will fall into it. Lift out the spiral baffle on its support wire from the flue top. Working from the top of the flue, clean the tube with a suitable flue brush. Also clean the baffle before reinstalling it.

In some refrigerators it is not possible to reach the top of the flue tube to remove the spiral baffle. In this situation, cover the burner with a rag and then use air pressure from the bottom of the flue to loosen the rust.

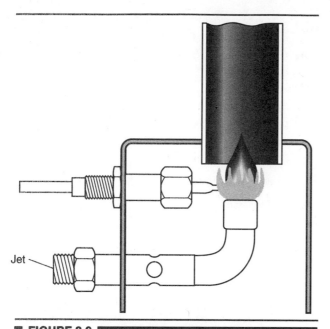

FIGURE 8.9
The Dometic "E-" type burner flame should also have a bright-blue crown at the base of the flame and emit a slight buzzing noise.

Cleaning the Flue Tube

The purpose of the flue system is to provide a draft that will pull the burner flame into the central tube and supply sufficient primary and secondary air to the flame. The baffle is inserted in the central tube to distribute the heat produced by the burner to the

Thermoelectric Flame-Failure Safety Device

The purpose of incorporating an automatic flame-failure device in the burner assembly is to prevent unburned gas from escaping from the burner and to avoid a fire if the flame has been extinguished or blown out (see Figure 8.10).

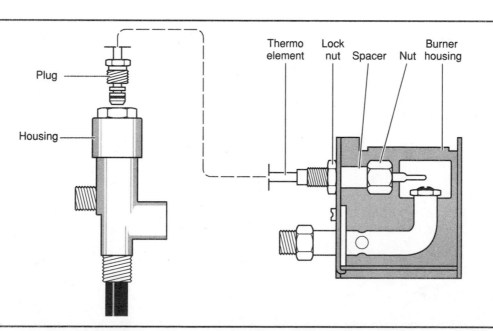

FIGURE 8.10
The thermocouple flame-failure safety device prevents unburned gas from escaping from the burner.

The device functions in this manner. By pressing the button, the gas valve is opened and gas can pass on to the burner. The thermocouple is located at the burner. When the gas flame of the burner is lit, heat is transferred to the thermocouple feeler. This heats the hot junction of the thermocouple feeler and an electric current is generated. This current passes through the copper wire to the electromagnet.

As soon as the electric current is generated, the electromagnet attaches the armature to the valve. The button can then be released. As long as current is flowing, the valve is kept open, allowing gas to pass to the burner. When the flame is extinguished, the heat transfer to the hot junction is interrupted and no electric current is generated. The armature with the valve is then forced back by a spring and the gas flow through the valve ceases.

Replacing the Thermoelectric Flame-Failure Safety Device

Replacement of the thermoelectric flame-failure safety device is simple:

1. Unscrew and remove the end of the thermoelectric unit from the valve housing of the LP-gas supply line.
2. Unscrew and remove the thermoelement from the burner housing.
3. Bend the new thermoelement to match the shape of the old one and screw the new unit

into place on the burner. Make sure the feeler is located properly over the burner.
4. Check that there are no burrs inside the valve housing that may cause leaks. Then install the end of the thermoelement into the valve housing of the LP-gas supply line. The plug must be properly tightened into the valve housing to insure contact between the thermoelement and the magnetic coil within the housing.

Replacing the Safety Valve Magnet

If the safety valve magnet is defective it must be replaced (Figure 8.11).

1. Unscrew the connecting plug on the thermoelement from the housing nut.
2. Unscrew the housing nut and remove the defective safety valve magnet from the housing.
3. Fit a new magnet valve and insure that it is properly inserted in the housing.
4. Fit the housing nut and the connection plug and check that a good contact between the contact plug on the thermoelement and the contact on the safety valve magnet is obtained.

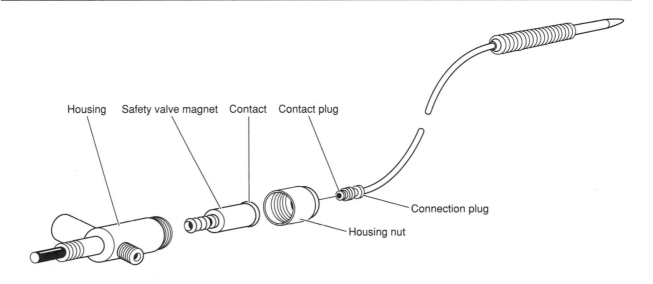

Housing   Safety valve magnet   Contact   Contact plug   Connection plug   Housing nut

■ FIGURE 8.11 ■

Replacing the safety-valve magnet in the thermocouple flame-failure safety device

■ Thermostat

If the thermostat control assembly loses its charge it will become inoperative. To test for a lost charge, while the flame is reduced to a minimum and the temperature control is set at a numbered position on the dial, remove the thermostat capillary tube from its clamp in the evaporator and warm the capillary end with the hand. If the flame fails to increase in size, the thermostat has lost its charge and the thermostat must be replaced (Figure 8.12).

Replacing the Thermostat

To replace the thermostat:

1. Shut off the gas supply.
2. Remove capillary from its clamp on the evaporator fins.
3. Remove sealing plugs on the outside and inside of the cabinet.
4. Straighten the capillary and pull it through the cabinet.
5. Remove the thermostat by unscrewing it from the gas filter and the flame-failure safety device.
6. Install new thermostat by reversing order of removal.

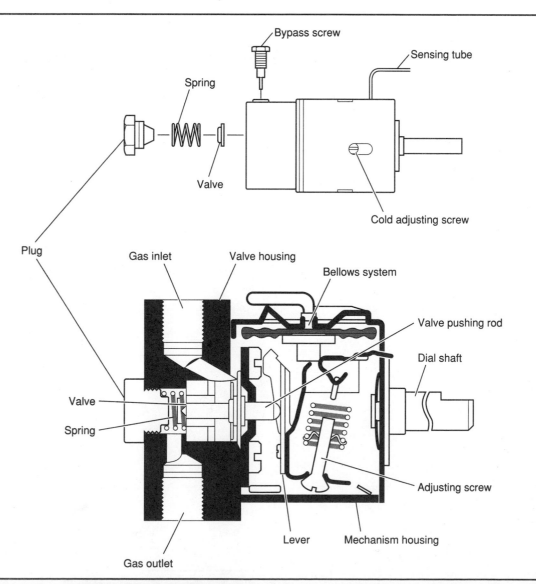

■ **FIGURE 8.12**
Exploded view of thermostat control assembly

■ Heater Elements

Some models are equipped for both 120-volt AC and 12-volt DC operation. The heat necessary for operation of an absorption cooling unit is supplied by an electric cartridge heater mounted in a pocket in the boiler system. If the heater is faulty, it must be replaced. Be certain that the replacement heater is of the proper wattage for your model refrigerator. If a unit of too low or too high a wattage is used, the refrigerator will not cool sufficiently.

Replacing the Heater

To replace the heater:

1. Unplug the unit from the 120-volt AC power supply and disconnect the wires leading to the 12-volt DC power supply.
2. Open the lid or door on the boiler cover.
3. Remove as much of the boiler insulation as necessary to give access to the heater unit.
4. Remove the defective heater unit.
5. Install the new heater unit and replace the insulation material.
6. Close the lid or door to the boiler cover.
7. Reconnect the 12-volt DC power supply wires and plug in the 120-volt AC power cord.

■ Igniters

Replacing the Flint-type Igniter

Refrigerator models with flint-type igniters require replacement of the flint after some time (Figure 8.13). To replace the flint, follow these steps:

1. Remove the outer burner shield.
2. Remove the lighter by loosening the screw retaining the lighter.
3. Remove cap and spring and tap out any remaining piece of flint.
4. Install a new flint and reassemble in reverse order.

Replacing the Igniter Wheel

If after several years of use the lighter fails to function properly even with a new flint, the serrated

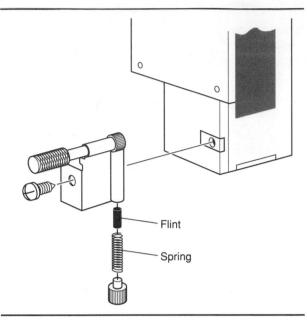

Flint-type igniters used in some refrigerator models require periodic flint replacement.

wheel may be worn and need replacement (Figure 8.14). Follow these steps:

1. Remove the lighter as described for flint-type igniter replacement.
2. Unscrew the rod from the serrated wheel and install a new wheel.

Replacing a Piezo-type Igniter

Piezo-crystal igniters create a spark over the burner when the igniting button is pushed in fully. They do not normally need any maintenance (see Figures 8.14 and 8.15).

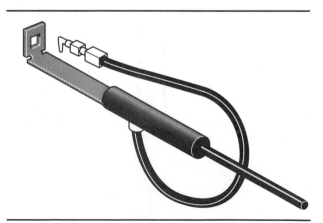

Piezo-crystal igniter used to light burner in Dometic RV refrigerators

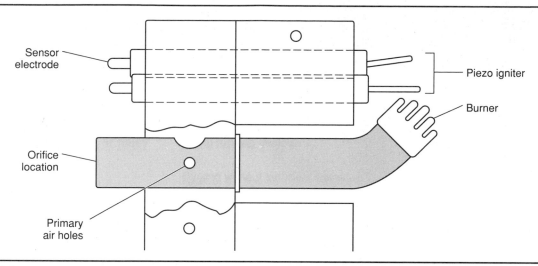

■ **FIGURE 8.15** ▬▬▬▬▬▬▬▬▬▬▬▬▬▬▬▬▬▬▬
Piezo-crystal igniter used to light burner in Norcold RV refrigerators

Replacement of Electrode Only (Dometic) If the electrode must be replaced, follow these steps:

1. Unscrew burner outer shield.
2. Loosen fastening screw holding the electrode against the side of the burner housing.
3. Loosen the electrode from its cable by unscrewing the electrode counterclockwise.
4. Install a new electrode. When fastening the electrode on the burner housing, make sure that the insulation plate is properly fitted between the burner housing and the electrode.

Replacement of Complete Piezo Igniter If the entire igniter must be replaced, follow these steps:

1. Release the piezo igniter knob inside the cabinet by pulling the knob outward.
2. Loosen outer burner shield and burner housing.
3. Loosen the two screws on holder. Now the complete igniter can be pulled out at the rear of the cabinet.
4. Install a new igniter by reversing the removal procedure.

Electrode Removal (Norcold) If the electrode must be removed, follow these steps:

1. Remove burner assembly.
2. Remove ignition-electrode mounting screw.
3. Remove ignition electrode.
4. Remove sensing-electrode mounting screw.
5. Remove sensing electrode.

Note: Always check spark gap after removing or replacing ignition electrode. Spark gap between electrode and burner must measure ⅛ inch.

CHAPTER 9

Ovens and Ranges

Top burners on RV ranges operate when LP-gas is routed via the supply line to the manifold that is located along the front of the top burner section. This manifold is continually pressurized as long as the LP-gas-tank valve is open. When a burner valve is opened, the gas is injected through the burner orifice into the venturi (mixing tube) where it mixes with primary combustion air and flows to the burner. At this point the gas-air mixture is evenly discharged through the ports in the burner cap. Here ignition occurs either by use of a lighted match or the pilot light, if applicable. The amount of primary combustion air may be adjusted on some stoves to modify combustion characteristics.

The fuel supply for the oven burner is taken from the manifold in the top section of the range. The tube leading from the manifold extends down and into the automatic oven safety valve. When this valve opens, gas passes through to the burner orifice. The orifice mixes

TROUBLESHOOTING the Magic Chef Oven and Range

Problem	Possible Cause	Correction
No gas to oven pilot	Improper control knob setting	Set oven control knob to "oven pilot on" position.
Oven slow to heat; poor baking; poor ignition of burners; pilots won't stay lit; popping sound from top burners; carbon on pilot shield; burner flame too low or too high	Defective gas pressure regulator	Have regulator tested.
Oven pilots won't light or stay lit	Incorrect pilot adjustment; damaged pilot tubing; defective pressure regulator; incorrect oven control knob setting	Adjust pilot; check pilot tubing for kinks or clogs; have pressure regulator checked; be sure oven control knob is not in "pilot off" position.
Top burners won't light	Top burners and flash tubing out of position; no pilot flame; air shutter improperly adjusted; clogged burner ports	Check and adjust position of burners and flash tubing; check and adjust pilot flame; adjust air shutter; clean burner ports with a toothpick.

the gas flow into the burner venturi, where it mixes with primary combustion air and enters the burner. The oven pilot ignites this mixture, resulting in flame evenly spread around the burner.

Pilot Burner (Magic Chef)

On Magic Chef units, the pilot burner is actually two pilots in one.

The *standby pilot* is the portion of the pilot light that burns constantly, provided that the LP-gas tank and manifold valve (if applicable) are open. It ignites the gas-air mixture at the burner when the oven valve opens. It also provides the base for the heater pilot.

The *heater pilot* is an extension of the standby pilot. It is on only when the oven thermostat calls for heat. The purpose of the heater pilot is to open the oven safety valve, thereby enabling gas to flow to the oven burner.

Thermostat

The *thermostat* is probably the most important component in the functioning of the oven. It regulates the oven to maintain the desired cooking temperature. The thermostat senses the oven temperature by means of a thermal bulb located in the top of the oven. This

bulb is filled with gas and connected to a bellows in the thermostat by a capillary tube. When the oven is on, the bulb heats up and the gas expands, causing the bellows in the thermostat to expand. A mechanical linkage within the thermostat shuts off the flow of gas to the pilot burner. The pilot flame ceases to burn at the heater position but continues at standby.

As the temperature decreases in the oven, the bulb cools, and the gas and the bellows in the thermostat contract. The mechanical linkage in the thermostat then causes an increasing amount of pilot gas to flow, and the pilot goes to the heater flame position.

On some newer ranges, the thermostat will have an "off" position (full clockwise rotation), where all gas is shut off to the oven main burner safety valve and to the oven pilot. At the "pilot on" position, standby pilot gas is admitted to the oven pilot.

Oven Safety Valve

The *oven safety valve* controls the gas flow to the main burner. The valve is operated by a thermal bulb in the heater pilot flame. This bulb is connected to a bellows in the valve by a capillary tube. When the bulb is heated, the mercury within it expands, in turn expanding the bellows and opening the valve. The opposite occurs when the heater pilot flame subsides.

TROUBLESHOOTING the Magic Chef Oven and Range (continued)

Problem	Possible Cause	Correction
Gas smell	Leaky gas line	Check all connections with soapy water; repair if necessary.
Cake rises higher on one side than other	Uneven heat	Pans set too close to side of oven; allow 2 inches from side. Level range.
Cake burns on bottom	Improper circulation	Oven too full for proper circulation; remove item. Do not use pan with dark bottom.
Oven will not operate	Pilot not lit	Relight pilot.
Oven door not closing properly	Misaligned door	Open oven door and slightly loosen four sheet-metal screws holding the door panel to the liner.
No constant pilot	No gas to range	Check gas supply; turn on LP-gas tank.
	Constant pilot selector key turned off	Adjust constant pilot selector key to LP position.
	Blocked tubing supply line	Disconnect tubing at source and at pilot end and blow out to clear passageway.
	Blocked orifice	Single tube pilot; disconnect tubing from pilot and blow out to clear orifice.
	Blocked pilot	Disconnect tubing from pilot. Remove orifice from pilot and clean out blockage or replace pilot.
	Pilot too close to oven burner flame	Adjust position of pilot assembly.
No heater pilot	Thermostat turned off	Turn thermostat knob to setting above oven temperature.
	Blocked tubing supply line	Disconnect tubing at source and at pilot end and blow out to clear passageway.
	Blocked orifice	Single tube pilot; disconnect tubing from pilot and blow out to clear orifice.
	Blocked pilot	Disconnect tubing from pilot. Remove orifice from pilot and clean out blockage or replace pilot.

TROUBLESHOOTING *the Magic Chef Oven and Range* (continued)

Problem	Possible Cause	Correction
Oven will not maintain proper temperature	Oven bulb not in proper location	Secure oven bulb in clips that hold it in proper location. Oven bulb should not touch any surface. Place approximately ½ inch away from surface of oven drum top.
	Oven bulb coated with foreign material	Use fine steel wool or scouring pad to gently clean surface of bulb.
	Oven bottom covered with aluminum foil	If foil blocks holes or slots in oven bottom, heat distribution will be affected; remove foil.
	Pilot flame not cycling off	High pressure can cause the constant pilot flame to act as a heater pilot flame. Check pressure and adjust as necessary. If that fails to solve the problem, replace thermostat.
	Safety device not closing. Flame-responsive element is being heated by oven burner flame due to either improper location or an overrated oven burner	Check flame-responsive element for proper location on burner pilot. Pilot burner must be properly located on bracket. Bracket must be in proper location. Check oven burner rate.
	Safety device not closing when flame-responsive element is not being heated	Replace safety device.
No main burner flame	Thermostat set lower then oven temperature	Reset knob to higher temperature.
	Closed oven burner orifice	Readjust to rated input.
	Flame-responsive element not hot enough	Check position of flame-responsive element. It must be enveloped in the heater pilot flame. Check gas pressure. Check pressure regulator; repair if necessary.
No main burner flame	Defective thermostat	Replace thermostat.
	Defective safety valve	Replace safety valve.
Yellow tips on burner flames	Improper gas-air mixture	Open the air mixture on units having adjustable air shutters. Orifice hoods may be out of alignment (see Figure 9.1).
Flames blowing off of ports	Excessive gas pressure; air shutter opened too much	Close air shutter slightly. Check gas pressure regulator.
Flames flashing back in mix tube	Gas–air mixture too lean	Reduce air shutter opening; check for sufficient gas pressure.

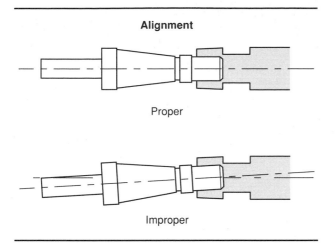

Alignment

Proper

Improper

■ **FIGURE 9.1**

Oven air-shutter orifice hoods must be aligned properly to produce a good gas-air mixture.

Lighting and Extinguishing Pilots

■ Magic Chef Ovens

To light pilot on Magic Chef ovens:

1. Turn off all burner valves. The oven thermostat dial should be in the "pilots off" position.
2. Turn on main gas supply to range.
3. Depress and turn the thermostat dial to the "off" position.
4. Lift main cook-top panel and light top burner pilot with a match or portable igniter.
5. Open oven door and light pilot. A small flame will be noted at the top of the pilot burner. If the range has not been operating for a long period of time, a longer waiting period for ignition of the pilot may be necessary due to air in the gas lines.

To extinguish top range and oven pilots; turn the thermostat dial to the "pilots off" position and turn off the main gas supply.

■ Wedgewood Ovens

To light pilot on Wedgewood ovens:

1. Verify gas supply is sufficient.
2. Turn all controls to "off."
3. Lift or remove range top.
4. Turn pilot supply valve on (Figure 9.2).
5. Light pilot.

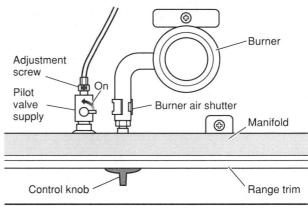

■ **FIGURE 9.2**

Location of pilot LP-gas supply valve in Wedgewood ovens

6. To light oven pilot, push in oven control knob and rotate counterclockwise to "pilot on" position.
7. Light oven pilot, located at back of oven to the left of the oven burner (Figure 9.3).

■ Spark Ignition Range Models

To light spark ignition range models:

1. Verify gas supply is sufficient.
2. Turn on desired top burner.
3. Wait approximately 7 seconds and push red igniter button.

To extinguish top range pilot, turn pilot supply valve off.

To extinguish oven pilot, push in oven control knob and turn clockwise to "off" position.

Pilot Adjustment

■ Magic Chef

For Magic Chef models' top burner pilots, remove the thermostat knob and turn the adjustment screw in the thermostat body with a screwdriver (Figure 9.4). The top pilot flame should be about $\frac{1}{8}$ inch above the lower edge of the flash tube.

For ranges without the "pilot off" or "pilots off" position on the thermostat knob, raise the main top and turn adjustment screw with a screwdriver.

The oven pilot has been preset and has no adjustment.

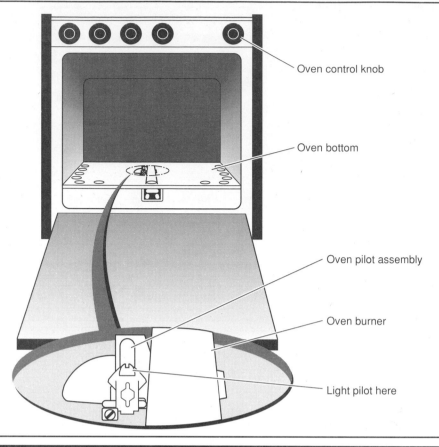

Oven control knob

Oven bottom

Oven pilot assembly

Oven burner

Light pilot here

■ **FIGURE 9.3**
The pilot light in the Wedgewood oven is located at the back of the oven.

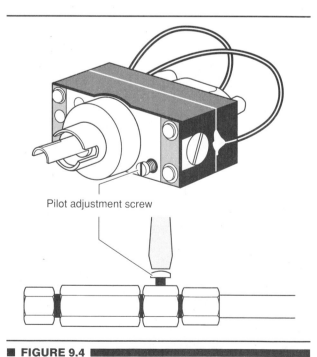

Pilot adjustment screw

■ **FIGURE 9.4**
Top burner pilots in Magic Chef models should be adjusted so that flame is ⅛ inch above lower edge of flash tube.

■ Wedgewood

For Wedgewood models' top burner pilots, the adjustment can be made with the brass screw on the pilot supply valve. Turn the screw clockwise to decrease flame, counterclockwise to increase flame. Pilot flame should extend ⅜ inch above the pilot assembly cup.

The oven pilot has been factory adjusted and requires no further adjustment. **Note:** The oven pilot may be slow in lighting due to initial air in the gas lines.

Burner Adjustment

The burner flame is adjusted by means of air shutters. If the air shutters are set too far open, the flame will lift away from the burner head and will be difficult to light. If the air shutters are set too far closed, the flame will look hazy and the distinct cone will be missing.

Open the air shutters to increase the air-to-gas mixture ratio until the flame has yellow tips but does not lift away from the burner head. Then close the air shutters until the yellow tips of the flame are eliminated. This provides the maximum flame efficiency without flame blow-out. **Note:** Top burner flames are preset at the factory on all Wedgewood models without optional range pilot.

Maintenance

Combustion problems are sometimes caused by an accumulation of dirt, grease, dust, or spider webs in the venturi or burner. Periodic inspection and cleaning of range and oven components will help prevent decreased operating efficiency.

When cleaning the burners or any orifice, care must be taken to prevent damaging or enlarging the openings. Never use a wire or other metallic implement to clean an orifice or burner port. Any enlargement of an orifice or the burner ports will affect the gas flow and burner function. Use a toothpick to clean orifices and burner ports.

Clean all surfaces as soon as possible after spills. Use only warm, soapy water. Never use abrasive or acid-type cleaners. Avoid the use of lye or caustic solutions on aluminum parts.

Chrome parts may be cleaned with a chrome cleaner to remove stubborn stains. In regions of high humidity and salt-air conditions, the chrome range top may show signs of rust on the underside directly above the pilot. To help eliminate this condition, the underside of the range top should be kept as dry as possible. If signs of rust are detected, spray the underside with a coat of high-temperature rust-inhibiting or silicone paint. Remove the range top and spray the paint in a well-ventilated area.

Never wash warm porcelain surfaces; allow them to cool first. Pitting and discoloration will result on stainless steel if spills are allowed to remain for any length of time.

Use an oven cleaner on the oven interior, following instructions on the product container. If a commercial oven cleaner is used, protect aluminum gas tubing, thermostat sensing bulb, and electrical components from the cleaner (masking tape is good for this). Thoroughly rinse oven with a solution of 1 tablespoon of vinegar to 1 cup of water.

Periodically have the LP-gas system checked to insure that the pressure regulator is functioning properly and delivering LP-gas at a pressure of 11 inches water column to the regulator at the oven. Modern RV oven gas pressure is regulated to 5 inches water-column pressure for safety reasons.

Component Replacement
■ Magic Chef Oven Thermostat

To replace the Magic Chef oven thermostat:

1. Shut off gas at LP tanks.
2. Remove main top and grates.
3. Disconnect pilot fuel lines and ¼-inch main fuel line at thermostat.
4. Remove two screws mounting thermostat to manifold pipe.
5. Open oven door and remove capillary bulb clips in top of oven.
6. Pull capillary bulb up through top of stove and remove thermostat.
7. To install, reverse the procedure. Be sure thermostat gasket is in place before installing thermostat.
8. Using soapy water, check for gas leaks at all connections.

■ Magic Chef Automatic Shutoff Valve

To replace the Magic Chef oven automatic shutoff valve:

1. Shut off gas.
2. Remove oven racks and oven bottom. Oven bottom is removed by pushing oven bottom toward back of oven. Then lift up front of oven bottom to release catches and pull oven bottom forward.
3. Remove mounting screw from oven burner and remove burner.
4. Disconnect ¼-inch supply tube from shutoff valve.
5. Loosen screw holding sensing bulb to pilot light assembly.
6. Remove sensing bulb.
7. Remove two screws attaching automatic oven shutoff valve support and remove automatic oven shutoff valve.
8. To install, reverse the procedure.
9. Using soapy water, check all connections for gas leaks.

TROUBLESHOOTING the Wedgewood Oven and Range

Problem	Possible Cause	Correction
Pilot won't light or stay lit	Closed supply valve	Turn valve on.
	Insufficient gas supply	Check gas supply.
	Insufficient gas pressure	Check for gas leaks and check regulator.
	Blocked pilot orifice or blocked flash tubes	Clean pilot orifice with toothpick; clean flash tubes.
	Pilot flame too high or too low	Adjust pilot flame.
	Pilot flame cover out of position and/or coated with carbon	Reposition pilot flame cover and/or remove carbon buildup.
	Pilot flame blow-out	If range is installed near an open window, the pilot may not stay lit on a windy day. **CAUTION:** Turn off gas and wait 5 minutes before relighting.
Burner won't light or stay lit	Insufficient gas pressure	Check for gas leaks and check regulator.
	Incorrect gas-air mixture	Adjust air shutter.
	Blocked burner ports, flash tubes, and/or burner orifice hood	Clean as necessary.
Burner lights but flame is too small	Improper gas pressure	Check for gas leaks and check regulator.
	Improper gas-air mixture	Adjust air shutter.
	Restriction in gas line.	Check gas line for kinks or blockage. Replace if necessary.
Burner flame lifts off burner head	Gas pressure too high	Check regulator.
	Incorrect gas-air mixture	Adjust air shutter.
Oven burner won't light or stay lit	Insufficient gas pressure	Check for gas leaks and check regulator.
	Incorrect gas–air mixture	Adjust air shutters.
	Blocked burner ports	Clean as necessary.
	Clogged oven pilot orifice	Clean oven pilot orifice.
	Defective oven safety valve or sensing element out of position	Check position of sensing element; replace safety valve if necessary.
	Defective thermostat	Replace thermostat.

TROUBLESHOOTING the Wedgewood Oven and Range (continued)

Problem	Possible Cause	Correction
Oven burner lights, but flame remains very small and oven heats very slowly	Improper gas pressure	Check for gas leaks and check regulator.
	Restriction in gas line	Check gas line for kinks or blockage. Replace if necessary.
Oven burner flame lifts off burner and oven cycles too frequently	Gas pressure too high	Check regulator.
Oven cooks unevenly and/or food burns on the bottom	Poor oven ventilation	Oven too full for proper circulation and/or ventilation holes in oven bottom are covered. Take steps to improve oven ventilation.

■ Magic Chef Range Top Burner Valve

To replace the Magic Chef range top burner valve:

1. Shut off gas supply at tanks.
2. Remove knobs.
3. Remove burner grates, main top, and top burners.
4. Remove two bolts from thermostat and raise slightly to permit removal of manifold.
5. Remove gas inlet tube from half union and move tube out of way.
6. Remove two screws, one from each end of manifold assembly.
7. Remove manifold assembly from range.
8. Remove defective valve (screw counterclockwise).
9. To install, reverse the procedure.
10. Before installing new valve, apply pipe sealant to threads.
11. Using soapy water, check all connections for gas leaks.

■ Magic Chef Range Top Pilot Light Adjustment

To adjust the Magic Chef range top pilot light:

1. Remove thermostat knob to provide access to adjusting screw. Adjusting screw is located at bottom right corner of thermostat. (Some models require raising the main top to turn the adjustment screw with a screwdriver.)
2. Adjust so that the tip of the flame is just over the edge of the inner cone and so that top burners light within four seconds.

■ Magic Chef Oven Burner Replacement

To replace the Magic Chef oven burner:

1. Shut off gas.
2. Remove oven racks and oven bottom.
3. Remove mounting screw from oven burner and remove burner.
4. To install, reverse the procedure.

■ Magic Chef Oven Pilot Light Assembly Replacement

To replace the Magic Chef oven pilot light assembly:

1. Shut off gas.
2. Remove oven racks and bottom.
3. Remove screw holding sensing bulb to pilot assembly.
4. Remove sensing bulb from pilot assembly.
5. Remove pilot fuel tube.
6. Remove nut and bolt attaching pilot assembly to support.
7. Remove pilot assembly.
8. To install, reverse the procedure.
9. Using soapy water, check all connections for gas leaks.

■ Wedgewood Range Top Replacement

To replace the Wedgewood range top:

1. Remove all burner grates.
2. Lift top upward by front end and pull out, away from rear vent trim.
3. To replace, insert lip on rear edge of range top beneath the rear vent trim.
4. Lower range top into place.
5. Apply a slight downward pressure on both sides to engage the retaining clips.

CAUTION: On models with a range pilot, be sure burner pilot flash tubes are in place and the pilot is burning before replacing top.

■ Wedgewood Top Burner Replacement

To replace the Wedgewood top burners (see Figure 9.5):

1. Remove range top.
2. Remove burner retaining screw.

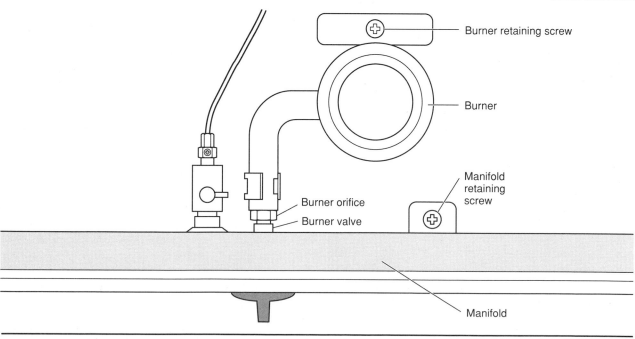

■ FIGURE 9.5 ■
Wedgewood range top burner assembly

3. Lift burner up and away from the burner orifice.
4. To replace, reverse the procedure.

Note: When cleaning top burners, be sure all ports are open before using. A toothpick is good for this purpose.

■ Wedgewood Top Burner Valve Replacement

To replace the Wedgewood top burner valves:

1. If range has an oven, set oven control to "off."
2. Turn off gas supply at tanks.
3. Remove range top and all top burners.
4. Unscrew the gas line input connection to the manifold.
5. Remove all control knobs.
6. Remove retaining screws that secure manifold to burner box.
7. Raise manifold just enough to remove defective burner valve.
   CAUTION: Do not raise manifold more than necessary because the interconnecting gas lines to the pilot(s) can be damaged.
8. Remove the bolts securing the burner valve to manifold.
9. Install new burner valve. Torque to 20 to 25 inch-pounds.
10. Replace manifold and top burners. Reconnect gas supply line.
11. Using soapy water, check all connections for gas leaks.

■ Wedgewood Oven Door Replacement

To replace the Wedgewood oven door (see Figure 9.6):

1. Open oven door and insert a nail or rod into the hole in each arm that connects the door to the range.
2. Push inward on the door as if trying to close it.
3. Using pliers, grasp the connecting arms close to the door liner and raise them upward. This will unlock the arms from the door. **Note:** Do not remove the nails or rods from the connecting arms until the door is replaced and the arms are engaged. The arms are spring loaded and will retract into the range if the nails or rods are prematurely removed. If this should happen, the entire range must be removed from the cabinet enclosure and the side panels removed to get the arms back in place.
4. Pull door outward until hinged arms clear the openings in the frame. **Note:** Due to tight tolerances, removal of the door requires a moderate amount of pressure.
5. To install the door, set door in position with the hinged arms placed into slots in the front frame.
6. Raise the door up and rehook the connecting arms into the door frame.
7. Make sure both connecting arms are securely rehooked, then remove nails or rods.

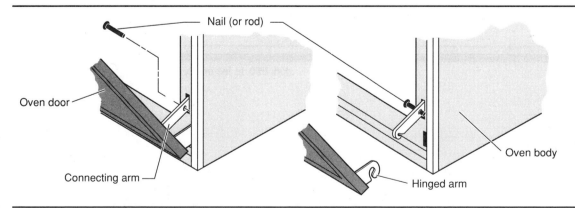

■ **FIGURE 9.6** ■
A nail or rod must be used to facilitate removal of the Wedgewood oven door.

Wedgewood Oven Burner Replacement

To replace the Wedgewood oven burner:

1. Set oven control to "off."
2. Turn off gas supply.
3. Remove oven rack and oven bottom.
4. Remove screw that secures burner to front support bracket. **Note:** Observe the position of the oven pilot assembly and routing of the sensing element (capillary tube) around oven burner and into pilot assembly. Return them to the same position when replacing the oven burner.
5. Lift and turn oven burner just enough to enable removal of the screw anchoring oven pilot assembly to the oven burner.
6. To replace, reverse the procedure.

Wedgewood Safety Valve Check

The Wedgewood safety valve is located in the rear of the oven behind a galvanized shield. To determine if it is defective:

1. Light oven pilot.
2. While watching pilot, turn the oven control to "broil" position.

3. The pilot flame should increase in size and cover the sensing bulb located at the front of the pilot assembly.
   a. If the flame increases and the oven burner doesn't light within 30 to 60 seconds, the safety valve is defective and must be replaced.
   b. If the flame doesn't increase, clean the oven pilot orifice and check thermostat.

Wedgewood Safety Valve Replacement

To replace the Wedgewood safety valve (Figure 9.7):

1. Turn off gas supply. Remove oven burner.
2. Remove safety valve's sensing element (capillary tube) from oven pilot assembly (Figure 9.8). The element is held in place by a single screw on the side of the oven pilot assembly.
3. Remove safety shield from rear of oven interior.
4. Remove mounting screws retaining safety valve to the rear panel of oven unit.
5. Pull safety valve forward into oven interior and remove gas input line on safety valve assembly.

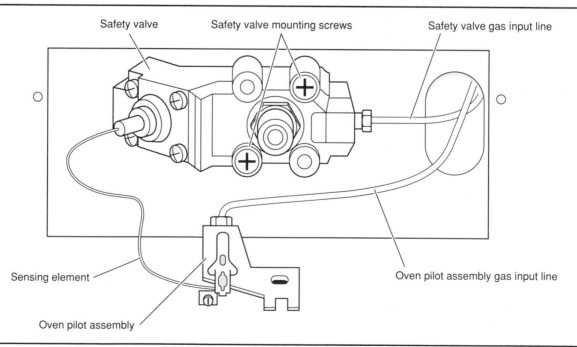

■ FIGURE 9.7 ■
Wedgewood range safety valve assembly

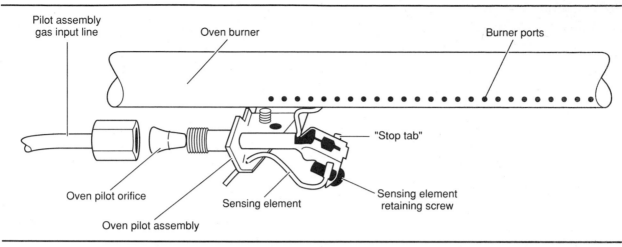

FIGURE 9.8
Wedgewood range oven pilot assembly

CAUTION: The safety valve can be pulled forward only a few inches. Use care to avoid damaging the gas input line.

6. Connect a new safety valve to gas input line.
   WARNING: Do not replace sensing element into oven pilot assembly while testing for leaks.

7. To verify that the connection is properly seated and will not leak:
   a. Turn on gas supply.
   b. Set oven control to "pilot on."
   c. Light pilot(s).
      WARNING: When lighting oven pilot, be sure the safety valve's sensing element cannot be heated by the pilot flame. This will prevent the safety valve from opening and allowing gas to flow through oven burner orifice.
   d. Set oven control to 400°F.
   e. Apply soapy water to safety valve's gas input line connections to check for leaks.
   f. When certain the connections are properly seated, turn oven control to "off."
   g. Turn off gas supply.

8. After performing the leak test, replace the various components by reversing the removal procedure. **Note:** When replacing the safety valve's sensing element, be sure it has been inserted through both holes and is resting against the stop tab of the oven pilot assembly before tightening the retaining screw. If the sensing element (capillary tube) is kinked or out of place, it will not function properly. Any damage to the sensing element will require replacing the entire safety valve. Individual parts of the safety valve cannot be repaired or replaced.

■ Cleaning the Wedgewood Pilot Orifice

The Wedgewood oven pilot orifice is a common area of blockage and should be cleaned periodically.

1. Set oven control to "off."
2. Turn off gas supply.
3. Remove oven rack and oven bottom.
4. Disconnect oven pilot assembly gas input line.
5. Remove oven burner.
6. Using a small screwdriver (inserted through the hole in the back of the pilot assembly), pop the orifice out of the pilot assembly.
7. Thoroughly clean soot and other foreign matter from the orifice. Use a toothpick to clean the small hole in the orifice and any clogged ports in the oven burner.
8. Make sure pilot assembly gas input line is clean and free of obstructions.
9. Replace orifice in pilot assembly.
10. Replace burner.
11. Reconnect pilot assembly gas line.
12. Turn on gas supply.
13. Turn oven control to "pilot on."
14. When certain no leaks exist, check operation of oven.

■ Wedgewood Thermostat Replacement

The Wedgewood thermostat is very difficult to replace. Check the safety valve and oven pilot orifice before deciding to change the thermostat. If the thermostat must be replaced (see Figure 9.9):

1. Set oven control to "off."
2. Turn off gas supply.
3. Remove range top and all top burners. **Note:** On models with range pilot, remove two screws that secure pilot assembly to burner box.
4. Disconnect gas supply line input connection to manifold.
5. Remove all screws that secure the range to the cabinet or wall.
6. At manifold, remove both gas lines to thermostat.
7. At rear wall of oven interior, just under flue opening, remove thermostat's capillary tube from tension clip.

8. Slide range forward enough to feed capillary tube through entry hole in oven's rear wall up through rear vent trim of burner box.
9. Remove manifold from burner box.
10. Remove bolts securing thermostat to manifold.
11. Connect new thermostat to manifold. Torque to 20 to 25 inch-pounds.
12. Reinstall manifold in burner box.
13. Carefully feed capillary tube back into oven and replace in tension clip so that it is directly centered beneath the flue opening. **Note:** If the capillary tube is kinked or out of place, it will not function properly. Any damage to the capillary tube requires replacing the whole thermostat. Individual parts of the thermostat cannot be repaired or replaced.
14. Continue reassembling the range by reversing the removal procedure.
15. After reconnecting the gas supply line to the manifold, replace all the top burners.
16. Turn on gas supply.

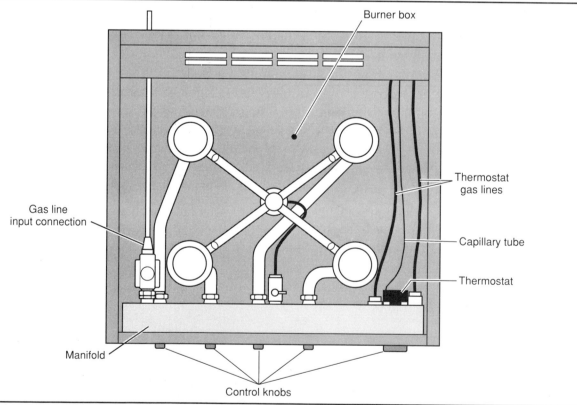

■ FIGURE 9.9

Both the top and the top burners must be removed from the Wedgewood range before proceeding with the removal of the thermostat.

17. Set thermostat control knob to "pilot on."
18. Light pilot(s).
19. Coat all connections with soapy water solution. Be sure to include thermostat-to-manifold, pilot(s), and oven safety valve gas lines, as well as gas supply input connection.
20. Check for indication of leaks.
    WARNING: If any leaks occur at any connection, turn thermostat control knob to "off" and gas supply off before tightening or reseating any connection. Repeat leak test after repairs.
21. When certain there are no leaks, check oven operation.

Range Hoods

Range hoods are fairly basic appliances, made of sheet metal, with a 12-volt DC light and ventilation fan assembly components as the only parts requiring periodic attention (Figure 9.10). Simple as the system may be, it is one of the areas of the RV that is quickest to become dirty with greasy cooking residue. Frequent cleaning is important.

■ Cleaning

All surfaces of the hood should be thoroughly cleaned on a regular basis with special attention given to the corners and more inaccessible recesses. As grease from cooking builds up, it attracts dust and dirt like a magnet, and it doesn't take very long for the hidden nooks and crannies of the hood to become quite dirty.

Warm, soapy water and a soft cloth or sponge are usually sufficient. But if grease has been permitted to build up over time it may be necessary to use a stronger solution, such as a grease-cutting ammonia cleaner.

Follow the cleaning effort with a soft cloth to dry the hood. This will help remove water spots and any residue that may be left.

The part of the hood that collects the greatest amount of grease is the aluminum-mesh filter element that is designed to trap grease as the ventilation fan is expelling the steam, smoke, odors, and greasy air from the cooking area. To clean the filter, remove it from the hood and soak it in warm, soapy water. Swish the filter back and forth in the soapy water to encourage the grease to dissolve. Don't try to scrub

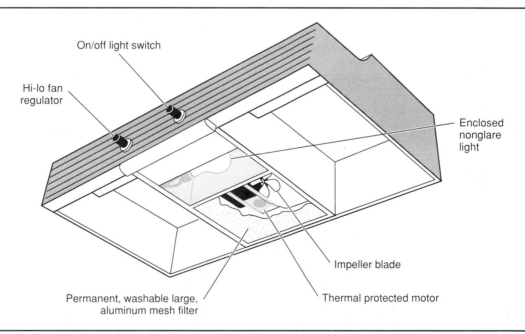

On/off light switch
Hi-lo fan regulator
Enclosed nonglare light
Impeller blade
Permanent, washable large, aluminum mesh filter
Thermal protected motor

■ **FIGURE 9.10** ■

Range hoods are usually equipped with a 12-volt DC fan, light, and filter.

TROUBLESHOOTING the Range Hood Fan and Light

Problem	Possible Cause	Correction
No power to fan or light	Blown fuse	Check the fuse. Replace if necessary.
	Faulty switch	Check switch for continuity. Replace if faulty.
Power to fan, but still won't work	Faulty fan motor	Replace fan motor.
Power to light, but still won't work	Faulty light bulb	Replace bulb.

the grease from the filter since this will only damage the expanded-aluminum screen. A soft brush may be of benefit if used gently. After washing, rinse thoroughly under a stream of clean water, shake dry, and then replace.

If, despite your best efforts, the filter is too clogged with grease and dirt to be cleaned, replace it with a new element. It is inexpensive and available at most RV supply outlets.

While the filter element is out of its holder, it's a good time to wipe the fan clean. This is a 12-volt DC appliance, so it offers no electrical shock hazard.

■ Fan Motor Replacement

If the fan motor is faulty, buy a new one before removing the old one. This will help prevent confusion during the replacement procedure because you can study the original and keep it fresh in your mind as you install the new unit.

1. Disconnect 12-volt DC power to fan by either removing the fuse from the fan circuit or removing cable from the battery positive terminal.
2. Remove grease filter from hood, exposing fan.
3. Remove screws holding fan in place.
4. Disconnect fan lead wires (cut if necessary).
5. Connect new fan wires. If the original wires were cut, use high-quality butt connectors to reinstall.
6. Install new fan by reversing the procedure.

CHAPTER 10

Microwave Ovens and Ice Makers

Small appliances, such as microwave ovens and ice makers, have made life so much easier at home that it made sense for the RV industry to pick up on this trend. The microwave oven has become almost as common as the kitchen sink in motorhomes and is showing up in more trailers. Although microwaves and ice makers require little maintenance, there are a few problems that can arise. Microwave maintenance is a very sophisticated science and should be left to a qualified service technician. Microwave ovens are very sensitive to voltage spikes due to erratic AC generators or surges in campground-hookup power and should be safeguarded by an electronic surge protector similar to those used for computers. Because microwave ovens mounted in RVs are in a much harsher environment than homes and are subject to vibrations and bouncing, they should be checked frequently for leakage. Commercial meters are available for this purpose. Ice makers should be equipped with an in-line filter to protect the system from harsh chemicals and the bad taste associated with treated water. Unless the RV has a power inverter, ice makers will only operate when the AC generator is running or when the rig is hooked to campground power.

Microwave Ovens

■ Theory of Microwave Cooking

Microwave ovens operate on radio frequency (RF). When the correct frequency is directed at food or liquid, it causes the molecules of food to oscillate, which produces heat. The radio frequency employed in a microwave oven is 2450 MHz, which falls within the radio broadcast band, not the X-ray band.

Food is cooked when the RF energy strikes molecules of food and causes them to agitate as the molecules try to align themselves with the 2450 MHz RF energy. Because the energy of 2450 MHz changes polarity every half cycle due to its half-wave double/rectifying circuit, the food molecules also change every half second. This makes the food molecules oscillate 4,900,000 times per second. Oscillation causes friction, which creates a substantial amount of heat energy for cooking.

Microwaves are reflected by metal (which is why the walls of the oven cavity are metal), but they pass through materials such as paper, glass, plastic, and ceramic. Food and liquids absorb microwave energy. Microwaves penetrate about ½ to 1½ inches of food, depending upon the food's density. Heat to complete the cooking process is transferred throughout the remainder of the food by conduction. Heat buildup takes place only within the food, but the oven cavity or the cookware may warm up as heat transfers from the food.

The oven cavity is made of metal so that it can contain and reflect microwaves back to the food. With a glass cooking shelf positioned above the oven floor on which food can be placed for cooking, microwaves can reflect from the oven floor to the underside of the food as well.

■ Microwave Components

Components typically found in a microwave oven include the following (see Figure 10.1):

- A cabinet to enclose all working parts of the oven.
- A door that swings either on a hinge system or on pins. The door must be precisely aligned and adjusted to prevent microwave leakage.
- A timer and cooking-level (temperature) control panel
- A magnetron, which produces the radio frequency for cooking
- A blower to cool the magnetron
- A stirrer to assure even distribution of microwave energy within the oven cavity.
- Interlocks to prevent the oven from operating when the door is open, and
- Various electrical components—a transformer, relay, diode, fuse, and capacitor.

■ Troubleshooting and Service

Because of the highly technical nature of microwave ovens, owners should seek professional service when problems with the oven arise.

CAUTION: The training and equipment necessary to properly troubleshoot and service microwave ovens are generally beyond the reach of the average owner; improper service can be very dangerous. The information in this book is designed to educate the owner to the various repair procedures so that he or she can better communicate with the service technician. *The microwave oven case should never be tampered with.* Owner maintenance should be limited to cleaning, checking for leakage, lubricating the door hinge, and changing the light bulb.

All procedures described and illustrated in this section apply to Magic Chef microwave ovens. Although the procedures may be similar for other brands, for specific details regarding the servicing of these brands, please refer to the manufacturers' service manuals.

■ Maintenance

Cleaning

Always unplug the oven before cleaning. Clean the outside and inside of the oven using a soft cloth and nonabrasive detergent and warm water; rinse well. With a soft cloth, dry the inside top, side, and back walls of the oven cavity, as well as the cooking shelf.

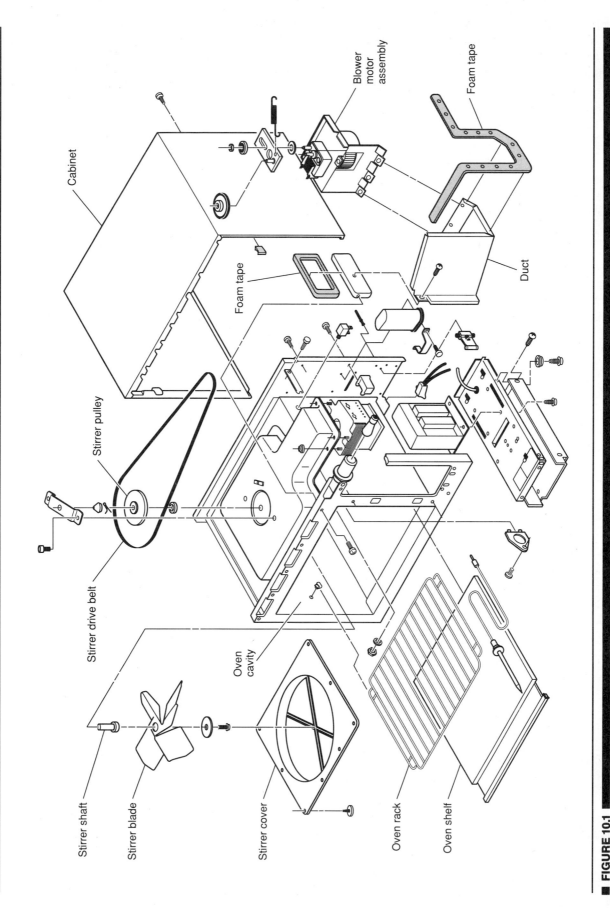

■ FIGURE 10.1

Exploded view of Magic Chef microwave oven

Never use chemicals, such as commercial oven cleaners or alcohol, and avoid the use of abrasives, such as cleansing powders, steel wool, or plastic scrubbing pads. Wipe spills off the interior components with a damp cloth as soon as they occur. If left unattended, accumulated spills will dry and become difficult to clean up. Spilled food can cause damage to some components. For example, the door seal plate and polypropylene cover in the oven cavity can burn if excess grease or food has carbonized on them.

Most foods can be removed easily with glass cleaner or soap and warm water. To remove dried-on foods, place ½ cup of water in the oven and heat it on "high" for 3 to 5 minutes. The steam will soften dried-on foods and they will wipe away more easily.

The glass oven floor can become scorched from the high temperature generated from the bottom of a browning dish. These stains can be removed by using Bar Keeper's Friend or Bon Ami cleanser. After using these products, rinse and dry thoroughly. Do not use cleansers on any other surface of the oven.

The probe should be cleaned by wiping it with a damp cloth as soon as possible after using. If food is baked on, rub very gently with a plastic scouring ball. Rinse and dry.

Lubrication

Twice a year, it is recommended that the door hinge be sprayed lightly with WD-40 or some comparable product. Also at this interval, the tip of the oven door latch should be lightly coated with Lubriplate. Apply lubricant sparingly and wipe up any excess. Never use any lubricant that contains silicone (Figure 10.2).

Oven Light Replacement

On all Magic Chef microwave ovens, the oven lamp is accessible through an access cover in the upper right rear of the oven cavity (Figure 10.3). To replace the bulb:

1. Unplug the oven.
2. Remove the access cover.
3. Remove the light bulb.
4. Replace with any similar 25-watt bayonet-base bulb rated for 115–130 volts.
5. Replace the access cover and secure with a ¼-inch hex screw.

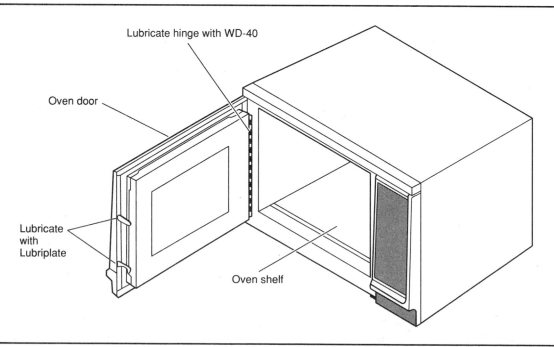

■ FIGURE 10.2
The microwave oven door should be lubricated with WD-40 (or similar product) twice a year; Lubriplate is used on latch.

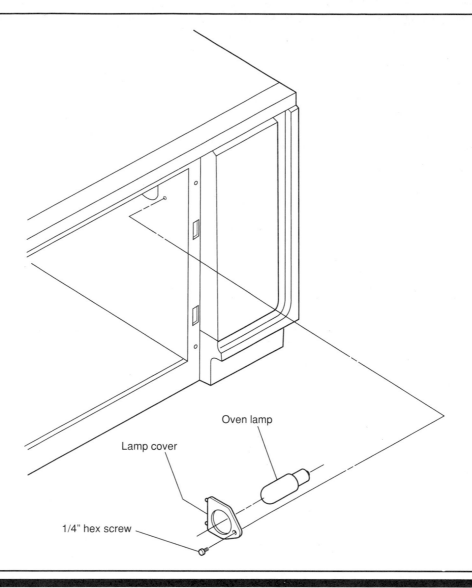

Oven lamp

Lamp cover

1/4" hex screw

■ FIGURE 10.3 ■
Removing microwave oven interior light bulb

Removing the Oven Cabinet

To remove the oven cabinet, follow these steps (see Figure 10.4):

1. Be certain the oven is unplugged.
2. Remove the screws from the back panel.
3. Spread the sides slightly from the bottom edge.
4. Slide the cabinet back to free the notched front edge from the front frame.
5. Lift the cabinet off.

Testing for Microwave Leakage

By using one of the following RF survey meters, you can test the oven periodically for microwave leakage.

Holiday Industries Model 1500
Holiday Industries Model 1501
Holiday Industries Model 1700
Holiday Industries Model 1800
NARDA Model 8100
NARDA Model 8200
Simpson Model 380

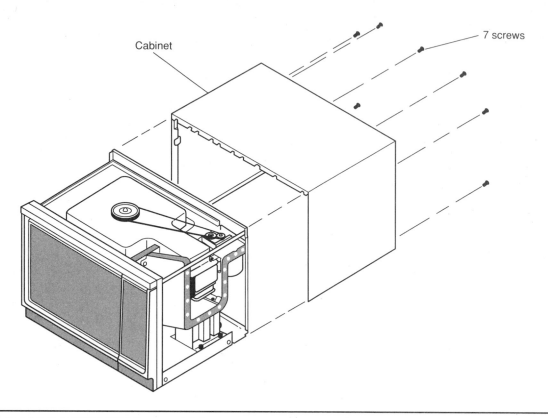

Cabinet

7 screws

■ **FIGURE 10.4** ▬▬▬▬▬▬▬▬▬▬▬▬▬▬▬▬▬▬▬▬▬
The microwave oven cabinet should only be removed by a qualified service technician.

To test for leakage, follow this procedure:

1. Fill an 8-ounce Styrofoam cup with water and place it in the center of the oven cavity.
2. Close the oven door; turn the oven on to a full (100% power) cooking mode.
3. While the oven is operating, check around the perimeter of the oven door and in the window area with the meter's probe. Move the probe at a rate of about 1 inch per second.
4. When the point of maximum leakage is located, rotate the probe until a peak reading is obtained. Then apply pressure to the door edge to see if the peak reading increases. The peak reading should not exceed 5 mw/cm2.
5. If the test indicates that the leakage is lower than the 5 mw/cm2 level, the oven is operating normally and no repairs or adjustments are necessary.
6. If the test indicates that the leakage is greater than the 5 mw/cm2 level, the oven should be repaired by an authorized service technician before any further use.

Door Adjustment

To adjust the microwave oven door (Figure 10.5):

1. Place the oven on its back.
2. Loosen the top and bottom hinge bracket nuts/hinge screws.
3. Align the top, bottom and left edges of the door with the front frame.
4. Jiggle the door slightly to be sure that it is lying flat against the front frame and that the secondary seal is not riding up on the sides of the choke.
5. Tighten the hinge bracket nuts/hinge screws.
6. Test for microwave leakage.

If the door leaks at or near a corner on the latch side, loosen the hinge bracket nut and hinge screws across the door diagonally from the leak and slide that pinned or hinged corner outward slightly, then retighten.

If the leak is on the pinned or hinged side of the door, loosen the hinge bracket nuts/hinge screws and

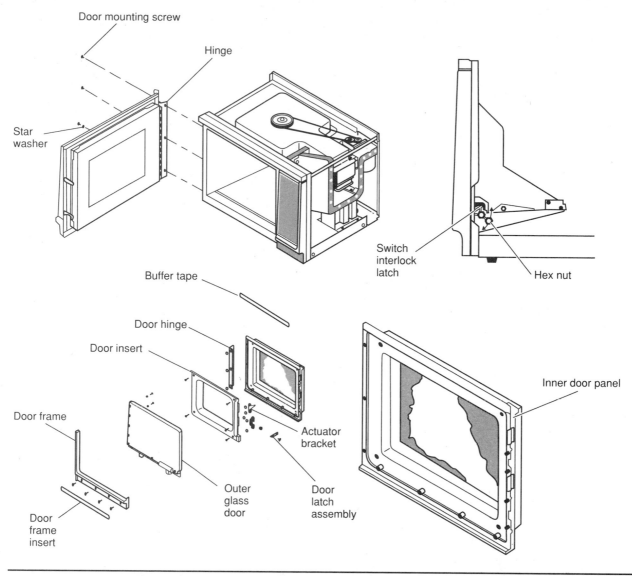

Magic Chef microwave oven door adjustment

adjust the door slightly closer to the front frame in that area; retighten.

If the leak is on the latch side of the door, add a latch bracket shim of appropriate thickness between the interlock switch bracket and the front frame. Recheck for leaks.

Replacing the Stirrer Cover

To replace the stirrer cover:

1. Open door fully.
2. Use a small flat-blade screwdriver to pry the plastic inserts loose from the stirrer cover through the oven cavity front opening.

3. Remove the stirrer cover through the oven cavity front opening.
4. To replace the stirrer cover, reverse the procedure.

Replacing the Stirrer

The stirrer is located in the top of the oven between the stirrer cover and the top of the oven cavity (Figure 10.6).

1. Unplug the oven.
2. Remove the oven cabinet.
3. Remove stirrer cover.

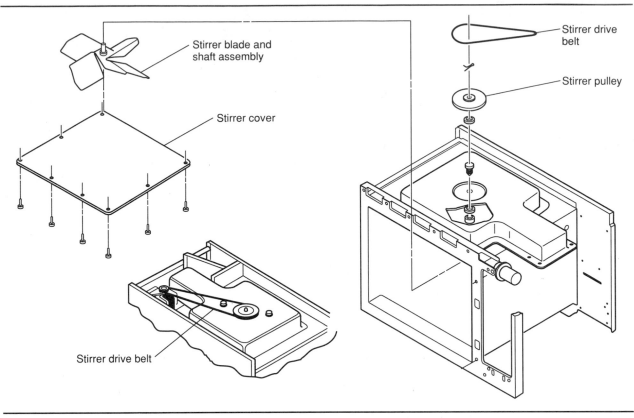

Stirrer blade and shaft assembly

Stirrer cover

Stirrer drive belt

Stirrer drive belt

Stirrer pulley

■ **FIGURE 10.6**

Magic Chef microwave oven stirrer assembly

4. Remove drive belt from pulley and fan motor shaft.

5. Remove cotter pin holding the stirrer in the oven cavity from the stirrer shaft.

6. Remove pulley and shaft, noting the positions of washer, spacers, and bushings.

7. When replacing stirrer, make certain that the blades are not out of line, causing them to hit the top of the oven or cover.

8. Be sure the stirrer and pulley turn freely.

9. To replace any component in the stirrer assembly, follow the procedure in reverse.

Replacing the Oven Shelf

Most often, shelf breakage is a result of improper use of the oven. This can occur if the oven is operated without being properly cleaned. Grease and food deposits can carbonize, causing the oven to arc. This results in extreme heat on some areas of the oven shelf, causing the glass to melt or crack. The same problem can be caused by improper use of aluminum foil or use of metal pans or containers in the oven. To replace the oven shelf, follow these steps (Figure 10.7).

1. Using a hook-type knife, such as a linoleum knife, cut the sealant all around the oven shelf.

2. Remove the old shelf and clean out all chips and debris that have fallen to the oven floor.

3. It is not necessary to remove all the old sealant from inside the oven.

4. Hold the edge of the deeply grooved plastic trim strip (supplied with the new shelf) over the turned-back flange on the edge of the oven front. Position the beveled edge up and toward the front.

5. Lay a small bead of RTV-102 White Silicone Rubber Adhesive behind the beveled edge of the plastic trim strip; then put the edge of the new shelf behind the beveled edge, forcing the RTV up along the edge, making a good seal.

6. Lower the new shelf onto the support studs in the back of the oven cavity.

7. Seal the shelf in place by applying a bead of RTV-102 White Silicone Rubber Adhesive around the back and side edges of the oven shelf.

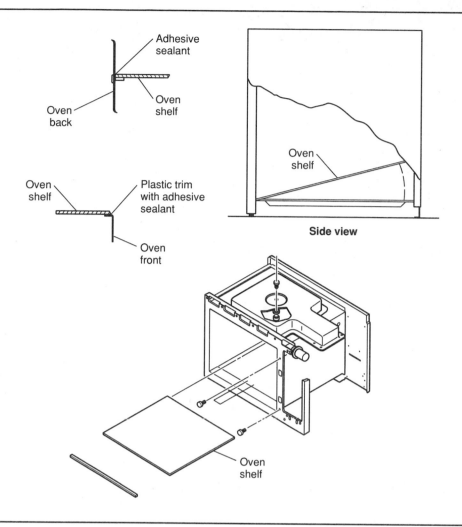

■ **FIGURE 10.7**
Replacing the oven shelf in a Magic Chef microwave

8. Wipe away any excess adhesive with a damp cloth so that a smooth fillet is formed between the shelf and the walls of the oven cavity on sides and back. Wipe away any excess adhesive on the front edge.

Ice Makers

Automatic ice-cube makers are designed to provide a continuous supply of ice cubes. Normally, these machines require very little attention, but routine care will insure that they function at maximum efficiency. The following information relates to the Dometic ice maker (see Figure 10.8).

■ General Operation

The unit must be installed level with the vehicle floor; otherwise the cubes will be larger at one end of the trough than the other and will take longer to eject into the ice bucket. Also, if the unit is tipped toward the rear, a condition known as frostback occurs on the suction line and the cubes will not be able to eject. To insure a level installation, the unit must be checked with a level gauge placed alongside the inside of the ice-maker mold itself, not on top of the cabinet.

The unit must have ventilation. If a free flow of air is not permitted through the grill, the compressor may run all the time, the cubes may stick together excessively, the unit may produce too few ice cubes, and the

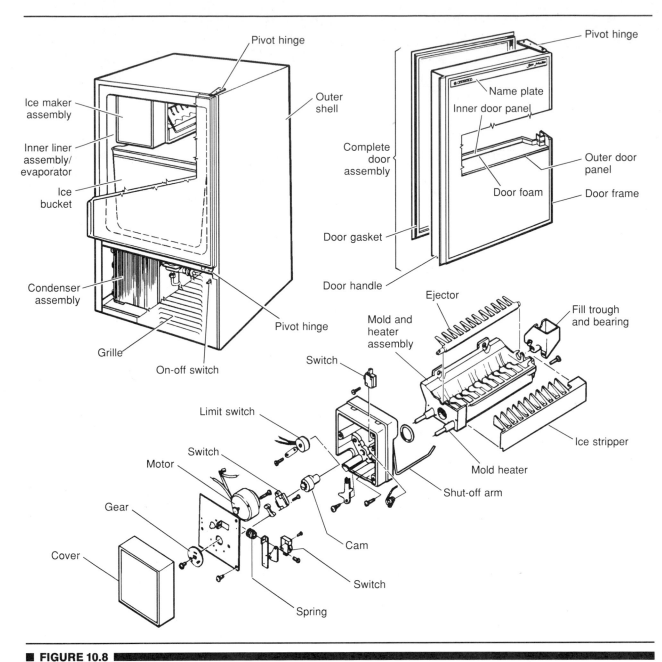

■ FIGURE 10.8 ■
Exploded view of Dometic automatic ice maker

machine may demand frequent defrosting. Do not limit air circulation by installing the unit behind closed doors.

Because the ice-cube maker is connected to a water supply line, it is possible that particles of scale or dirt may be dislodged from the line. This will produce dirty or discolored cubes. For this reason, it is recommended that all the cubes produced during the first two or three hours of initial operation of a new machine be discarded.

When the cube bin is full, the ice maker will automatically shut off, but the refrigeration unit will continue to operate to prevent the cubes from melting. Even though it is common for cubes to stick together, they are easy to separate by hand or by striking with a blunt object. Do not use a sharp object such as an ice pick or knife to separate the cubes, since damage to the plastic interior of the machine could result.

■ Maintenance

When cleaning the ice maker, do not use solvents or abrasive cleaning agents that can impart an odor or flavor to the cubes. The exterior may be treated with mild cleaners and furniture polish. Clean the interior with a soft, damp cloth. The ice bucket may be washed with warm, soapy water, but should be rinsed thoroughly and then dried to prevent the taste of soap in future cubes. Do not use hot water; this causes cubes to stick.

The condenser, behind the grill, should be cleaned three to four times a year.

If the ice maker is not used regularly, empty it periodically (every week to 10 days) to maintain a supply of fresh cubes.

The ice maker should be defrosted periodically. When defrosting, leave the door propped open a few inches to permit air circulation.

When the ice maker is shut down after a trip, the on/off switch should be turned to the "off" position. All remaining ice should be removed and the interior wiped dry. The door should be propped open a few inches to allow air to circulate inside the ice maker to prevent odors, mold, or mildew.

Once a year, or more often if necessary, shut off the water supply and remove the brass nut on the water inlet valve. Use a toothbrush to clean sediment from the inlet screen. This will help prevent sediment and impurities from clogging the water line.

■ Ice-Maker Adjustments

To set a colder temperature, move the adjustment screw one-quarter turn clockwise. To set a warmer temperature, turn the adjustment screw counterclockwise. When the temperature is colder, ice cube production slows down.

To adjust the amount of water permitted to enter the mold where the ice cubes are made, turn the water-fill adjusting screw (Figure 10.9). One full turn clockwise diminishes the amount of water allowed

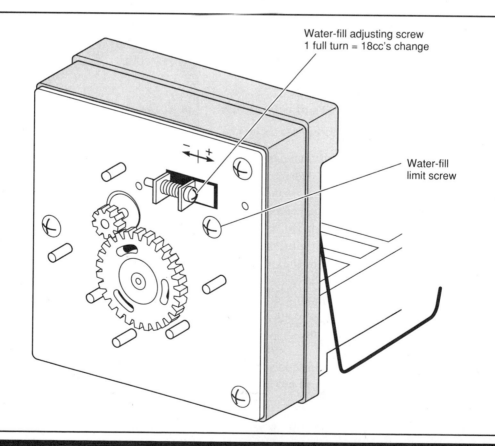

Water-fill adjusting screw
1 full turn = 18cc's change

Water-fill limit screw

■ FIGURE 10.9 ■
One full turn clockwise in the Dometic ice maker diminishes the amount of water into the mold by 18 cc's.

into the mold by 18 cubic centimeters. One full turn counterclockwise increases the amount of water allowed into the mold by 18 cubic centimeters. In this manner, cube size can be regulated. If the ice cubes do not eject easily from the mold, they may be too large; turn the water-fill adjusting screw to decrease the amount of water in the mold to a total of 120 cubic centimeters or 4.5 ounces.

■ Component Replacement

Before working on the ice maker, disconnect the appliance service cord from the power supply.

Ice Stripper Replacement

To replace ice stripper:

1. Remove ice maker from cabinet.
2. Remove retaining screw at back of mold.
3. Pull stripper back to disengage from front of mold.
4. Replace in reverse order.

Fill Trough and Bearing Replacement

To replace fill trough and bearing:

1. Remove ice stripper.
2. Push retaining tab away from mold.
3. Rotate counterclockwise until trough is clear.
4. Pull from back to detach from mold and ejector blades.
5. Replace in reverse order.

Ejector Blades Replacement

To replace ejector blades:

1. Remove ice stripper.
2. Remove fill trough and bearing.
3. Force back and up to detach from front bearing.
4. Place a small amount of silicone grease on bearing ends of replacement.
5. Replace in reverse order, insuring that blades are in same position as original.

Front Cover Replacement

To replace front cover:

1. Place coin in slot at bottom of mold support and pry cover loose.
2. To replace, be sure retaining tabs inside cover are located on top and bottom, then snap in place.

Mounting Plate Replacement

To replace mounting plates:

1. Remove front cover.
2. Remove the 3 retaining screws that hold plate in place.
3. Carefully remove plate, disengaging end of shutoff arm, noting relative position of shutoff arm spring.
4. Before replacing plate, be sure all wiring is orderly and shutoff arm spring is in place.
5. Replace in reverse order.

Motor Replacement

To replace motor:

1. Remove front cover.
2. Remove mounting plate (3 screws).
3. Disconnect wiring.
4. Remove 2 screws holding motor.
5. Replace in reverse order.

Water Valve Switch Replacement

To replace water valve switch:

1. Remove front cover.
2. Remove mounting plate (3 screws).
3. Disconnect wiring.
4. Remove switch (2 screws).
5. Replace in reverse order, making sure switch insulator is in place.
6. Check water fill and adjust if necessary.

Holding Switch Replacement

To replace holding switch:

1. Remove front cover.
2. Remove mounting plate (3 screws).
3. Disconnect wiring.
4. Remove switch (2 screws).
5. Replace in reverse order, making sure switch insulator is in place.

Shutoff Switch Replacement

To replace shutoff switch (see Figure 10.10):

1. Remove front cover.
2. Remove mounting plate (3 screws).
3. Raise shutoff arm.
4. Disconnect wiring.
5. Remove switch (2 screws).
6. Replace in reverse order.

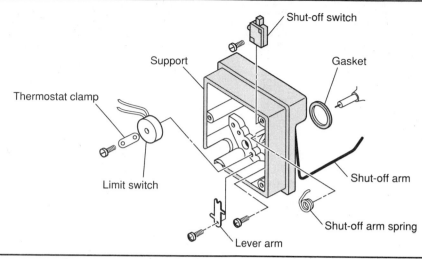

■ **FIGURE 10.10** ■
Dometic automatic ice maker shut-off switch assembly

Limit Switch Replacement

To replace limit switch:

1. Remove front cover.
2. Remove mounting plate (3 screws).
3. Loosen limit switch clip mounting screw.
4. Disconnect wiring and remove limit switch.
5. Apply Thermalastic (special gray putty substance) to sensing surface of replacement limit switch and bond to mold. **Note:** Do not use regular gray putty tape or similiar compounds. Contact appliance manufacturer for availability.
6. Replace in reverse order.

Mold Heater Replacement

To replace mold heater:

1. Remove stripper (1 screw).
2. Remove front cover.
3. Remove mounting plate (3 screws).
4. Detach limit switch from mold.
5. Detach heater leads.
6. Remove mold from support (4 screws).
7. With a flat-blade screwdriver, pry defective heater from bottom of mold.
8. Clean all Thermalastic from groove in bottom of mold.
9. Apply new Thermalastic to groove in mold.
10. Install replacement heater, using 4 screws in holes adjacent to heater groove.
11. Replace parts in reverse order of removal.

Control (Thermostat) Replacement

To replace control:

1. Remove rear panels from cabinet.
2. Remove mounting plate (2 screws).
3. Remove control from plate (2 screws).
4. Remove wires (3 terminals).
5. Remove control element from upper rear cabinet.
6. Straighten 12 inches of element on new control to insert into small-diameter aluminum tube control well. Control will not work if not inserted in control well.
7. Assemble in reverse order.

Solenoid Water Valve Replacement

To replace solenoid water valve:

1. Shut off water supply.
2. Remove water connections from valve.
3. Remove mounting screws (2).
4. Remove electrical connector.
5. Replace in reverse order.

TROUBLESHOOTING *the Ice Maker*

Problem	Possible Cause	Correction
Machine fails to operate	Lack of power	Check power supply.
	On-off switch	Check on-off switch for continuity in "on" position. Replace if defective.
Compressor fails to start	Temperature control	Check temperature control for continuity when cube maker contains water only. Replace if defective.
	Relay or overload	Bypass relay and overload by using test cord on compressor. Replace if defective.
	Control	Check control. Replace if defective.
Cube maker fails to fill with water	Water supply	Check water supply at inlet of solenoid water valve.
	Solenoid water valve	Check screen and clean if needed. Also check valve coil by energizing terminals with test cord.
	Water valve switch	Check switch for continuity.
Ice maker will not eject frozen cubes	Cubes too large	Defrost machine. Remove some water from tray. Adjust water fill to 120 cubic centimeters or 4.5 ounces.
	Faulty limit switch	Test switch for continuity. Replace if necessary.
	Faulty control	Test control for continuity. Replace if defective.
	Frost buildup	Defrost. Remove some water from cube tray with cloth. Check door gasket seal.
	Mold heater	Check for continuity. Replace if defective.
	Holding switch	Check for continuity. Replace if defective.
	Cube-maker motor	Use test cord to energize motor leads. Replace if motor is dead or internal gear is stripped.
	Shutoff-arm switch	Check for continuity. Replace if defective.
	Cam	Check if loose wire has jammed in cam.

TROUBLESHOOTING the Ice Maker (continued)

Problem	Possible Cause	Correction
Water fails to freeze	Fan motor	Check fan motor. Replace if not working while compressor is running.
	Temperature control	Test continuity through terminals 2 and 3 on control. Clean internal contacts or replace control.
	Refrigeration system	Have system serviced by authorized shop.
	Dirty condenser	Clean lint and dust from condenser.
Water in ice bucket	Unit not level	Level unit.
	Poor gasket seal	Check door gasket for proper seal.
	Water valve switch	Check switch. Replace if defective.
Ice maker freezes up	Poor door seal	Check door gasket for proper seal.
	Water splashing out of mold into bucket	Turn down water-fill adjusting screw.
	Leak through electric solenoid valve	Replace electric solenoid valve.
Failure to make ice	Frozen ejector blades	Defrost machine.
	Power supply off	Check power supply, including power cord to wall socket.
	Water supply off	Check water supply.
	Defective cold control	Check and replace if necessary.
Failure to stop making ice	Shutoff arm switch	Replace switch if defective. Free switch arm if frozen in ice or if stuck under freezing tray.
Not making enough ice	Improper cold control setting	Lower the cold control setting.
	Cubes too large	Turn down water-fill adjusting screw.
	Inoperative fan motor	Check and replace if necessary.
	Dirty condensor coil	Clean coil.
Excessive water	Water valve switch	Adjust downward.
	Faulty control	Check and replace if necessary.
	Leak through solenoid valve	Check solenoid valve and replace if necessary.
Water keeps running	Faulty water valve switch, solenoid valve, cold control	Check components and replace any that are defective.

TROUBLESHOOTING the Ice Maker (continued)

Problem	Possible Cause	Correction
Compressor knocks	Machine not level	Level unit.
	Faulty compressor	Replace compressor.
	Fan motor not running	Check fan motor; replace if necessary.
Compressor runs continually	Control setting too cold	Reset cold control to warmer setting.
	Dirty condenser	Clean condenser coils.
	Improper ventilation	Insure that grill is not blocked. Relocate ice maker if necessary.
Ejector motor runs, but ejector blades do not turn	Stripped gear in ejector motor	Replace ejector motor.
Ejector motor and blades turn continually	Defective cold control or holding switch	Check and replace control or switch, as necessary.

Ice Maker Replacement

To replace ice maker:

1. Remove formed rear panel.
2. Disconnect 6 wires.
3. Use Allen wrench to remove 2 screws holding ice maker to left-side wall.
4. Remove 3 hex head screws from bottom of ice maker.
5. Carefully pull ice maker out of cabinet.
6. Apply Thermalastic and assemble in reverse order.

Timing Cam Replacement

To replace timing cam:

1. Remove front cover.
2. Remove large white plastic gear.
3. Remove mounting plate.
4. Remove plastic timing cam.
5. Lubricate new cam with silicone grease.
6. Assemble in reverse order.

CHAPTER 11

Trailer Brakes

Trailer brakes are designed to reduce vehicle speed whenever the tow vehicle brakes are applied or whenever the brake controller manual switch is activated. This braking in concert helps prevent overheating of the tow vehicle brakes while maintaining speed control on long downhill stretches. Independent use of trailer brakes, using the manual switch, can reduce sway caused by severe winds or passing trucks.

There are two types of trailer brake systems: *electric* and *surge* (see Figure 11.1). Although they perform similar functions, they operate differently and require particular installation, maintenance, and repair routines.

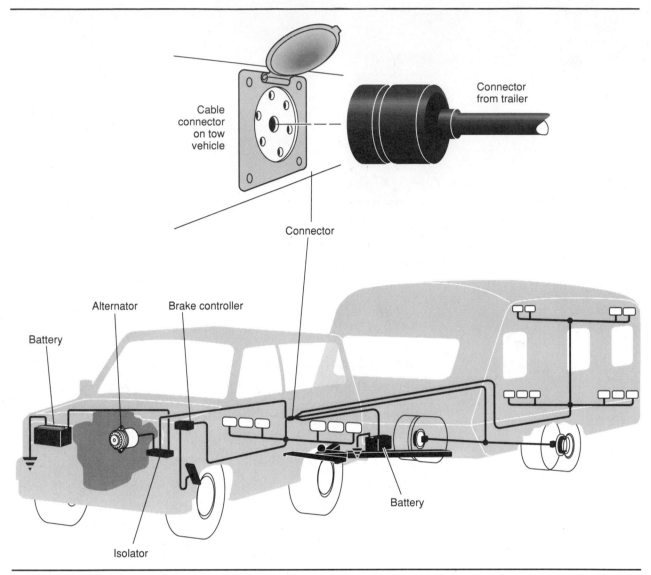

Cable connector on tow vehicle

Connector from trailer

Connector

Alternator

Brake controller

Battery

Battery

Isolator

■ FIGURE 11.1 ■
Electric brakes in travel trailers are activated by 12-volt DC current fed from the tow vehicle's battery through the brake controller mounted under the dash.

Electric Brakes

Electric brakes are the industry standard. They are designed to function in concert with tow vehicle brakes. The brake assemblies employ a revolving armature located in the brake drum. An electromagnet pivots on an arm with a cam that is attached between the brake shoes. When the magnet is energized, current flows through it, causing a magnetic attraction between it and the armature. The magnet attempts to follow the rotation of the armature. This causes the cam to rotate, actuating the primary brake shoe into the drum and energizing the secondary shoe, resisting the rotation of the drum. When the brakes are re-leased, the current ceases to flow through the magnet, releasing it from the armature. The return springs pull the shoes away from the brake drum.

Electrical current is directed from the tow vehicle's battery to the brake controller and modulated (in varying amounts) to the trailer brakes. The controller is usually mounted on the vehicle's dashboard beneath the steering wheel. Two types of controllers are used with electric brake systems: electronic and electric-hydraulic. In either case, the controller is the initial source for troubleshooting whenever there is difficulty with an electric brake system.

Surge Brakes

Surge braking is accomplished by the installation of an actuator in the tongue of the trailer. The system is hydraulic and includes its own master cylinder. The inertia or "push" of the trailer on the tow vehicle when slowing automatically synchronizes the trailer brakes with the tow vehicle braking action. As the trailer pushes against the tow vehicle during a stop or slowdown, the actuator pushes a piston in the master cylinder, which is integral to the A-frame; this in turn supplies hydraulic pressure to the brakes.

Surge brakes are usually found on boat trailers and on older, smaller trailers.

How the Controllers Work

■ The Electronic Brake Controller

Ideally, an electronic brake controller should be mounted in a level attitude because most of them operate with a swinging pendulum inside. However, if perfectly level installation is not possible, adjustment can be made to compensate for the out-of-level situation (see "Controller Adjustment," page 184.)

The Tekonsha electric controller, for instance, can be adjusted for level by turning the wheel located on the underside. A housing connected to the wheel holds a lamp and a light-sensitive device. Also inside the housing is the pendulum weight with a separating tab. When the pendulum is at rest, the separator tab is positioned between the lamp and the light-sensitive device, blocking illumination.

As the tow vehicle's brake pedal is applied (deceleration), the red wire is activated through the stoplight switch, which in turn activates the brake controller. Simultaneously, the pendulum weight moves forward, allowing light from the lamp to illuminate the light-sensitive device. This changes the resistance in the brake controller and activates the trailer-brake magnets. The natural G-force of deceleration moves the pendulum automatically in direct proportion to the amount of braking applied by the driver. Whether the tow vehicle brakes are applied smoothly or abruptly, the trailer should brake similarly because of the pendulum movement.

The Kelsey electronic brake controller utilizes a pendulum leveling arm and a system of magnets, hall device, and detector assembly. During braking, when the tow vehicle stoplights come on, the control module electronic circuit is activated by current on the red wire connected to the tow vehicle stoplight switch. As the tow vehicle decelerates, due to increased pedal effort, the magnet in the pendulum pulls away from the hall device and sends an electrical signal to the control module to increase amperage to the trailer brakes. The trailer brakes apply in direct proportion to the tow vehicle braking effort. The control module indicator light illuminates from dim to bright during the stop and goes dim at the end of the stop. When the tow vehicle pedal is released, the control module is turned off and the indicator light turns off.

Because electric current travels and activates the trailer brakes faster than the hydraulic system of the tow vehicle, the trailer should feel as if it is braking just slightly before the tow vehicle.

■ The Electric-Hydraulic Brake Controller

An electric-hydraulic brake controller utilizes an integral hydraulic cylinder to control the amount of braking effort directed to the trailer brakes. As the brake pedal of the tow vehicle is depressed, hydraulic fluid pressure from the vehicle's master cylinder moves the piston inside the brake controller's hydraulic cylinder. Movement of this piston pushes the controller's manual control arm toward the unit's wire-wound resistor assembly, activating the control automatically.

Testing Electric Trailer Brakes

A multimeter is required for testing electric trailer-brake systems.

■ Testing the Electrical Circuit

When testing the electric brake circuit and components, use a multimeter (amps). The following procedure indicates if current is flowing from the battery to the trailer brakes.

CAUTION: To prevent damage to the multimeter, connect one lead, then touch the other lead. If the

TROUBLESHOOTING the Electric Brake System

Problem	Possible Cause	Correction
Weak brakes	Loose connections	Check that all connections are clean and tight.
	Inadequate trailer ground	Check for proper grounding.
	Short circuit	Check electrical circuit.
	Incorrect variable resistor setting	Check for proper setting to avoid too much resistance.
	Worn or defective magnets	Replace magnets.
	Poor brake adjustment	Adjust brakes.
	Bent backing plate	Check backing plate flange. Correct if necessary.
	Contaminated lining	Check and replace badly contaminated linings.
	Inadequate gauge of wire	Refer to manufacturer's wiring recommendations.
	Stoplights connected in brake circuit	Stoplights must not be connected in the brake circuit. The graduation of the current changes as it passes through the controller, resulting in weak or grabbing brakes. Wire a separate circuit for the stoplight switch.
	Improper linings	Replace with proper linings.
	Worn linings	Reline with new linings.
	Worn brake drums	Inspect the brake drum surface; it should be free of scoring and excessive wear. Machine or replace drums as necessary.
	Out-of-round drums	Machine brake drums.
	Loose axle on springs or frames	Inspect and make necessary repairs.
	Loose lining on rivets	Replace brake shoes.
	Excessive load on trailer	Check to be sure trailer is not underbraked. Check the brakes on each axle to make sure they are working.
	Using trailer brakes only	Use of trailer brakes only can cause brake fade or loss of friction due to excessive heat.

TROUBLESHOOTING the Electric Brake System (continued)

Problem	Possible Cause	Correction
No brakes	Open circuit	Check for broken wires, loose connections, improper grounding, or faulty connector plug.
	Improperly wired or inoperative controller	Rewire controller. Check controller operation.
	Poor brake adjustment	Adjust brakes.
	Defective variable resistor	Check for loose or broken connections.
	Worn or defective magnet(s)	Replace magnets.
	Short circuit	Check electrical circuit.
	Defective connector plug	Check plug between tow vehicle and trailer for loose connections, dirty or corroded blades, or broken Bakelite insert in socket, shorting blades or pins.
	Burned-out resistor	Check resistor for continuity. Replace if necessary.
Intermittent or surging brakes	Out-of-round drums	Turn or replace drums.
	Inadequate trailer ground	Check for proper grounding. (**Note:** A ground through the coupler and ball is inadequate.)
	Broken magnet lead wires	Bench-check magnets and replace if necessary.
	Loose wheel bearings	Check and adjust bearings.
Noisy Brakes	Excessively worn lining	Check and replace shoes if necessary.
	Weak or broken springs	Check for weak or broken springs. Replace if necessary.
	Improperly located flange; bent backing plate	Check and repair if necessary.
	Contaminated linings	Check and replace badly contaminated linings.
	Improper bearing adjustment	Check and adjust wheel bearings. Check for worn or damaged bearings. Replace if necessary.
	Incorrectly adjusted brakes	Check brake adjustment.
	Improperly adjusted shoes	Adjust starwheel until there is a heavy drag, then back off adjuster slightly.
	Grease on linings	Replace leaky seal and linings.
	Worn magnets	Check for excessive or uneven wear. Replace if necessary.

TROUBLESHOOTING *the Electric Brake System* (continued)

Problem	Possible Cause	Correction
Breakaway switch fails to function	Weak or dead battery	Replace with new 12-volt DC battery. If brakes fail to function, replace breakaway switch.
	Faulty breakaway switch wiring	Check breakaway switch circuit for broken or frayed wires. Replace wire where necessary. Each splice must have a good connection.
	Faulty breakaway switch	Check breakaway switch by pulling pin and attempting to tow trailer. If switch works, brakes will engage.
	Only one brake working	Check the amperage at each brake. Where no amperage is indicated, check the wires leading to brake. If no defect is found, remove magnet from backing plate and check for amperage capacity, ground, or short. If brake is okay electrically, check for mechanical defects.
	Poor electrical connections	Check wiring for loose connections, broken wires, or worn insulation. Rewire as necessary.
Grabbing or locking brakes	Improperly installed flanges	Check flange locations. Refer to axle manufacturer.
	Contaminated linings	Check and replace badly contaminated linings.
	Controller too sensitive	Adjust brake controller.
	No variable resistor	A variable resistor is required when brakes have greater stopping power than is necessary for the weight on the axle. Install variable resistor when necessary. (**Note:** Not required on electronic controller.)
	Weak or broken springs	Check for weak or broken springs. Replace if necessary.

TROUBLESHOOTING *the Electric Brake System* (continued)

Problem	Possible Cause	Correction
Dragging brakes	Incorrectly adjusted brakes	Check brake adjustment.
	Insufficient gap between hydraulic controller contact pins and coil	Replace controller.
	Excessive residual pressure in the tow vehicle hydraulic system or a "gummed up" hydraulic controller cylinder	Purge tow vehicle hydraulic lines, replace fluid; replace controller.
	Improperly installed flanges	Check flange location. Refer to axle manufacturer.
	Badly corroded brake assembly	Check brake assemblies for corrosion. Be sure magnet levers operate freely. Clean and lubricate brake assemblies.
	Weak or broken springs	Check for weak or broken springs. Replace if necessary.
	Worn or bent magnet lever arm	Replace magnet and lever arm.

needle moves in the opposite direction on the scale, the polarity is reversed. To correct, simply reverse the leads.

1. Connect the trailer/tow vehicle electrical plug.
2. Connect the multimeter (amps) in series with the wire leading from the controller to the electric brakes.
3. Actuate the controller.
   a. *Electronic:* Set gain control to "maximum." Move manual lever to applied position.
   b. *Hydraulic:* Apply the tow vehicle brake pedal.

The amperage reading will vary as you apply more brake-pedal pressure or move the manual control arm to the fully applied position. The minimum low current will be 1 to 1¾ amperes. The maximum amount of amperes depends on the size and number of brakes on the trailer (see Table 11.1). Each electromagnet can draw about 3 to 4 amperes.

■ TABLE 11.1
Maximum Current Values in Amperes

Brake Drum Diameter	Two Brakes	Four Brakes	Six Brakes
7-inch	3.8–4.4	7.6–8.8	11.4–13.2
10- and 12-inch	6.0–6.5	12–13	18–19.5

Checking for Low Maximum Current

If a low maximum current is registered, use a multimeter (voltage and continuity) to check the following:

☑ CHECKLIST ▬▬▬▬▬▬▬▬▬▬

☐ Check the complete electric brake system for faulty wire connections.

☐ Check the male and female trailer plugs for corrosion. If there are any signs of bad contact points, replace connections.

☐ Check the electromagnets for wear or shorting.

☐ If no current registers on the multimeter, test the controller.

■ Testing the Hydraulic Controller

1. Check for open wires to the stoplight switch, battery, and service circuits with a multimeter.
2. Remove the controller from the vehicle:
   a. Remove cover from the unit (Figure 11.2).
   b. Check the resistor coil for burnout, using a multimeter (continuity).
   c. Check the hydraulic cylinder that actuates the lever for leakage. Replace if necessary.

■ FIGURE 11.2 ■
The resistor coil in the hydraulic brake controller is tested for burnout using a multimeter.

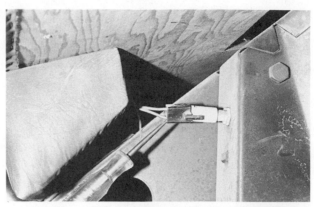

■ FIGURE 11.3 ■
The cold side of the brakelight switch can be determined by using a multimeter or a test light.

■ Testing the Electronic Controller

Check for open wires to the cold side of the stoplight switch, battery, ground, and service circuits with the multimeter (Figure 11.3). **Note:** If a short exists in the trailer-brake wire (blue), the electronic controller is designed to shut off. Once the short is corrected, the brake controller should function normally.

■ Inspecting the Electronic Brake Components

When inspecting the electric brake system, check the breakaway switch, magnet assemblies, and the brake drums.

Testing the Breakaway Switch

To test the breakaway switch, follow these steps:

1. Connect a multimeter (amps) or test light between the breakaway switch and the trailer brakes (Figure 11.4).
2. Pull out the breakaway pin. The multimeter should register current. If no current flows:
   a. Check for open wires.
   b. Check the battery for full charge.
   c. If the wires and batteries are okay, replace the switch.

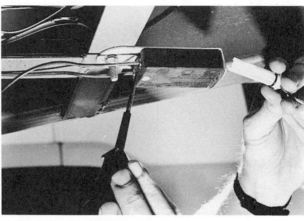

■ FIGURE 11.4 ■
The breakaway switch on a trailer can be tested by pulling the pin and checking the current with a multimeter.

Checking the Magnet Assembly

☑ CHECKLIST ■

☐ Check the magnet for wear (Figure 11.5). Replace the magnet if the brass screws that hold the friction element show wear.

☐ Check the magnet wearing surface for flatness by using a straightedge (Figure 11.6). Replace the lever arm, armpins, and magnet assembly if unevenly worn.

Testing the Magnet

To test the magnet, follow these steps:

1. Test for short circuits and open circuits by connecting the magnet in series with an ammeter and battery (Figure 11.7).

■ **FIGURE 11.5** ■
The trailer brake magnet must be checked for wear.

■ **FIGURE 11.6** ■
The trailer brake magnet wearing surface can be inspected for flatness by using a straightedge.

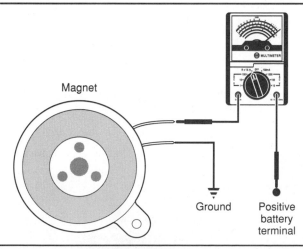

Magnet

Ground

Positive battery terminal

■ **FIGURE 11.7** ■
Short circuits and open circuits can be checked by connecting the magnet in series with an ammeter and battery.

■ **TABLE 11.2** ■
Amperage Values for Magnet Assembly

Brake Drum Diameter	Amperes
7-inch	1.2–2.2
10–12-inch	3.0–3.5

2. Test for short circuits within the magnet coil by connecting it in series with an ammeter and battery. When grounding the battery to the magnet case, the magnet should show no amperage value. If it does, a short circuit exists and the magnet must be replaced:
   a. Connect a test lead wire to a magnet wire.
   b. Take the other test lead wire to the positive post on the battery.
   c. Connect the other magnet wire to the negative post on the battery or ground the magnet case directly to the negative post and leave the remaining magnet wire open.
3. The average reading on the ammeter will vary with the magnet size (Table 11.2).

Testing the Brake Drum and Mechanical Components

The mechanical parts of the electric brake system should be inspected (See Figure 11.8). Brake shoes, drum, bearings, grease seals, and brake hardware need periodic service.

1. Inspect brake drums and armature surfaces for grooves.
   a. Replace brake drum armature if it shows excessive scoring due to contamination (mud, small stones, and sand). Armatures are either part of the drum, or will separate easily from the drum. **Note:** One-piece drum/armature can be machined on the lathe .030 inch. It is not recommended to machine the two-piece armature.
   b. Inspect the brake drum surface for heavy scoring. Check for excessive oversize with a drum micrometer. Replace the drum if it is more than .060 inch oversize compared to its original diameter.

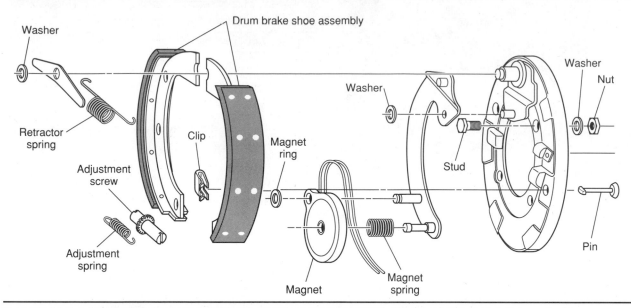

FIGURE 11.8
Mechanical parts of the electric trailer brake

CAUTION: If a drum is machined beyond .045 inch of its original diameter, use .030-inch oversize brake shoes. This maintains the correct shoe arc to the brake drum.

2. Replace linings if worn to $\frac{1}{32}$ inch from rivet heads or if contaminated with grease or oil.

Inspecting the Wheel Bearings

Clean and inspect wheel bearings to assure proper performance (Figure 11.9). If the bearings are in good condition, repack them with waterproof grease and put a new seal in the drum hub.

Using a torque wrench, tighten spindle nut to factory specification.

Adjusting the Brakes

For efficient braking, an electric-brake assembly must have the correct brake shoe-to-drum clearance. Brake adjustment must be performed regularly because it is not automatic.

1. Using a brake-adjusting tool, remove the plug in the backing plate. Turn the starwheel adjuster while rotating the wheel (Figure 11.10).
2. Continue adjusting until a heavy drag results.
3. Back off the adjuster slightly.

FIGURE 11.9
Wheel bearings from the trailer should be thoroughly cleaned and dried before repacking with new grease.

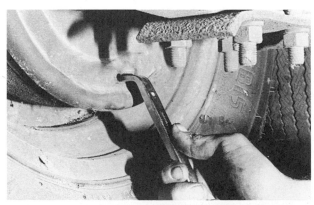

FIGURE 11.10
Trailer brakes must be adjusted after service by turning the starwheel that is accessed through the backing plate.

Mounting the Wheels

To properly mount the wheels:

1. Insure that the wheels are centered precisely on the axle flange.
2. Tighten the lug nuts in a star pattern to a torque reading of 85 to 95 foot-pounds.

Controller Installation

■ The Electronic Brake Controller

The controller must be mounted on a solid surface (normally beneath the dashboard) with the rear of the controller toward the front of the tow vehicle (Figure 11.11). Installation should place the controller within easy reach of the driver. Prior to final installation, hold the controller in the intended location and check to see that the pendulum can be adjusted properly. If the pendulum cannot be adjusted properly due to excessive controller angle, another location must be selected.

All electronic controllers are designed for use with 12-volt DC negative ground systems only. Reversing polarity or miswiring can cause permanent damage to the controller.

It is recommended that all connections be made with insulated, solderless, crimp-style connectors. Use a grommet where wires pass through the firewall for protection of the wiring and to seal against air leaks.

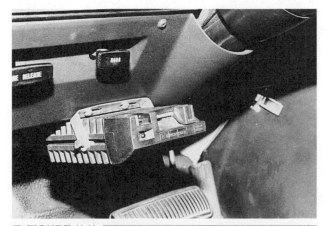

■ **FIGURE 11.11** ▬▬▬▬▬▬▬
The electronic brake controller should be mounted on a level plane, within easy reach of the driver.

Wiring the Electronic Brake Controller

Wiring should be done in the following order (Figure 11.12):

1. White wire to a clean metal ground.
2. Black wire to the positive side of the battery or starter solenoid. When routing this wire, keep it away from the radio antenna to reduce possible AM radio interference. Use 12-gauge stranded wire.

    CAUTION: Do not use a fuse. An automatic-reset circuit breaker may be used to protect this stranded wiring.

3. Red wire to cold side of stoplight switch.

    CAUTION: Some vehicles are equipped with separate switches for transmission converter and cruise control. Be sure the red wire is connected to the nonpowered side of the stoplight switch. If not properly connected to the stoplight switch, the indicator light and trailer brakes will not operate in conjunction with the vehicle brake pedal. To locate the nonpowered wire, use a multimeter 12-volt DC test light. Connect one test lead to the ground and the other lead to one of the two stoplight switch terminals. The nonpowered wire is the one that turns on the test light or registers voltage when the brake pedal is depressed and off when the brake pedal is released.

4. Blue wire to trailer brakes. This wire has electronic short-circuit protection.

Note: Some vehicle manufacturers, on certain models, have chosen to tie the wire coming from the four-way flasher circuit to the cold side of the brake-light switch. In this situation, every time the four-way flasher flashes, the brake control turns on, causing the brakes to pulse. Some trailer brake systems are so sensitive that this pulsing becomes objectionable. Installation of a Tekonsha Pulse Preventer (Part Number 2180-S), a semiconductor diode that isolates the brake-light current from the four-way flasher current, overcomes this problem. Brake-switch current can flow to the brake lights, but four-way flasher current cannot flow to the brake-light switch or the brake controller.

The Kelsey 81741 control module allows the four-way flasher lights to operate without affecting the trailer brakes, but the pendulum and load control knob must be adjusted properly. If the control module is not properly adjusted, the trailer brakes might pulse with four-way flasher lights.

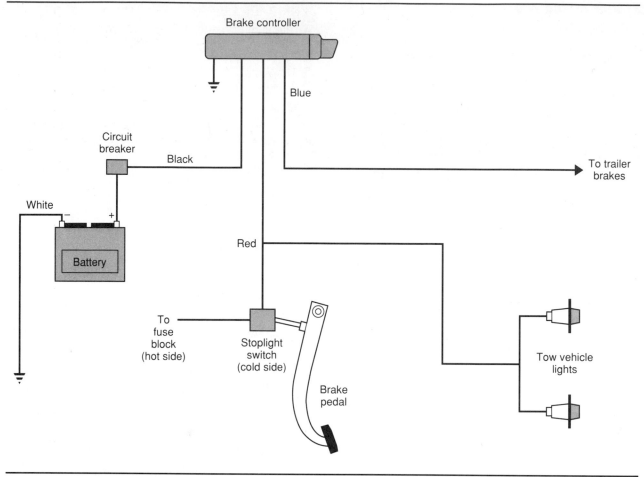

■ FIGURE 11.12 ■■■■■■■■■■■■■■■■■■■■■■■■■■■
Wiring diagram for Tekonsha electronic brake controller installation

■ The Electric-Hydraulic Brake Controller

CAUTION: Electric-hydraulic trailer brake controllers are not intended for use with some small vehicles. Master cylinders are too small in such vehicles, and the manufacturers will void the warranty if a hydraulic brake controller is installed. For these vehicles, install an electronic brake controller that does not tap into the tow vehicle's hydraulic brake system. Hydraulic brake controllers may not be used on certain vehicles with anti-lock braking systems (ABS). Check the tow vehicle owner's manual for recommendations concerning trailer brake controllers.

Install the controller mounting bracket at a solid location (normally beneath the dashboard).

Connect the hydraulic line from the brake controller to the tow vehicle's master cylinder. All late-model vehicles feature dual or divided master-cylinder systems with two outlets, one for front brakes and one for rear brakes. Select the proper brake control adaptor T-fitting for your particular vehicle. This T-fitting should be inserted at the outlet on the master cylinder serving the rear brakes. Be sure the rear-brake outlet is properly identified by referring to the vehicle manufacturer's manual or by following the hydraulic line from the rear brakes to the master cylinder.

CAUTION: Use only cadmium-plated adaptor T-fittings on aluminum master cylinders. Cadmium plating prevents electrolytic corrosion, which can severely damage the threads in the master cylinder over a period of time. With cast-iron master cylinders, either a cadmium-plated or a standard brass T-fitting can be used. Do not use a compression fitting to connect the hydraulic line to the master cylinder. A compression fitting has only a quarter of the design strength of an automotive brake line. Compression fittings will not provide the proper gripping force on steel brake lines.

To make the hydraulic connection:

1. Assemble the tube fitting to the T-connector.
2. Tube fitting should be turned hand-tight.
3. Tighten assembly with a wrench until it feels solid.
4. Apply ⅙ turn more. Do not overtighten since it may damage fitting and/or threads.

Important: Do not run the tubing in a straight line. Put a small loop in the line (to permit flexing) before running it through the firewall (Figure 11.13).

Bleed the hydraulic line by loosening the fitting at the brake controller. Press the brake pedal to allow the line to fill with fluid and dispel all air. Hold a rag below the fitting to catch brake fluid. *Keep pedal depressed until fluid flows continuously without sputtering. Tighten the fitting before allowing the brake pedal to be raised.* Check for leaks by depressing the pedal again several times and observing the connections at the master cylinder and at the brake controller. Check master cylinder fluid level and fill if necessary.

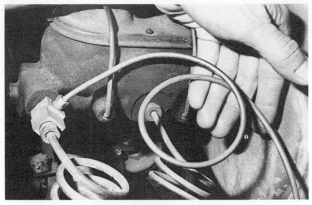

■ FIGURE 11.13

A loop in the hydraulic tubing between the master cylinder and firewall must be used when installing a hydraulic brake controller.

Wiring the Electric-Hydraulic Brake Controller

Use No. 12-gauge automotive grade wire or larger for wiring the electric-hydraulic brake controller (Figures 11.14 and 11.15).

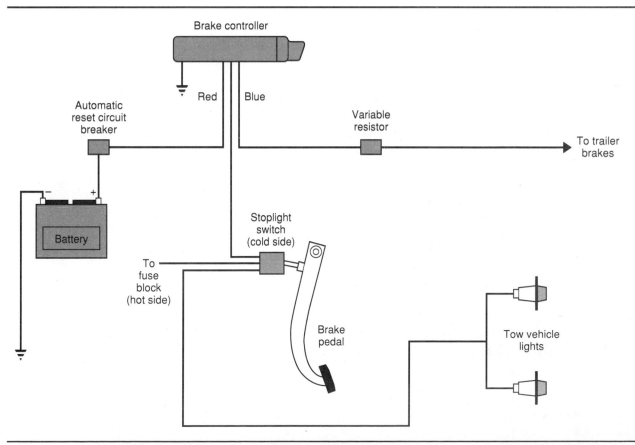

■ FIGURE 11.14

Wiring diagram for Tekonsha hydraulic brake controller installation

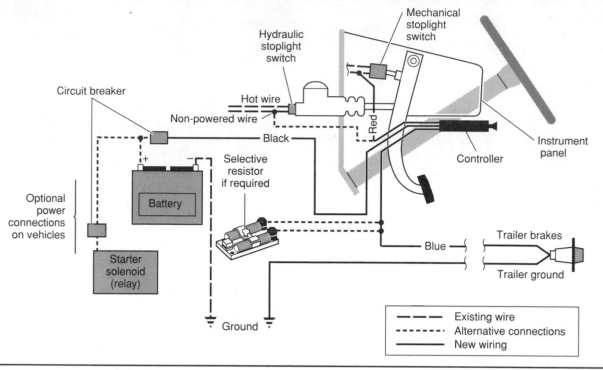

Wiring diagram for Kelsey-Hayes hydraulic brake controller installation

1. Connect the black wire to the positive terminal of the battery or to the positive side of the starter solenoid.
2. To protect the brake controller and vehicle wiring, an automatic-reset circuit breaker should be installed in the black wire between the battery and the brake controller. Use a 15-amp circuit breaker for two-brake trailers, a 20-amp circuit breaker for four-brake trailers, and a 30-amp circuit breaker for six-brake trailers.
3. Attach blue wire to brake system pin in tow vehicle/trailer connector plug. If necessary, install variable resistor in blue wire at this time.
4. Connect red wire to cold side of stoplight switch.

Controller Adjustment

■ Electronic Controllers

Adjustment of the brake controller to compensate for an out-of-level mounting position is accomplished by rotating the level-adjustment wheel (for Tekonsha, it's located underneath the controller) or the pendulum-leveling arm (for Kelsey it's on the left side of the controller).

Tekonsha Brake Controller Adjustment

With the Tekonsha controller, if the front is tipped too far upward, the pendulum may be out of position; the indicator light on the face of the unit will glow brightly. This indicates that the brakes are being activated even though there is no pressure on the tow vehicle brake pedal. To correct this condition, the tow vehicle must be resting on level ground with the engine running. The trailer does not have to be hitched. The adjustment steps are as follows:

1. Set the gain control to "minimum," depress the brake pedal, and hold.
2. Rotate the adjustment wheel toward the rear of the controller as far as it will go. As the wheel is being turned, the indicator light will begin to flicker.
3. Rotate the adjustment wheel toward the front of the unit until the indicator light glows steadily.

4. Again, rotate the adjustment wheel back toward the rear of the unit until the indicator light just begins to flicker.
5. Release the brake pedal. The adjustment wheel is now set.

The only other adjustment to be made is to set the gain control. This is done after the adjustment wheel is set. The trailer must be connected. Proper gain control adjustment is just before trailer brake lockup.

1. Set gain to ''minimum.''
2. Tow the trailer at low speed on a level, hard, dry road.
3. Slowly move the manual lever on the controller all the way to the left.
4. If the trailer brakes don't lock up, increase the gain control.
5. Repeat procedure until the maximum gain control setting without trailer-wheel lockup is found. Leave gain control there.
6. Use tow vehicle foot brake at low speed to check automatic operation. Tow vehicle and trailer should make a smooth, straight stop.
7. Gain control setting should be varied to compensate for great changes in trailer weight.

Kelsey Brake Controller

Adjusting the Kelsey Brake Controller Adjustment of the Kelsey controller involves setting the pendulum-leveling arm and the load-control knob.

1. Connect the trailer to the tow vehicle for this adjustment. If an equalizing hitch system is used, it should be operational and ready to go on the road. Make sure the tow vehicle and trailer are resting on a flat, level surface. Check to see if the tow vehicle stoplights are operating correctly, and disconnect all electrical connections between the tow vehicle and the trailer.
2. Adjust the load-control knob to its maximum brake position.
3. Depress the brake pedal far enough to turn on the vehicle stoplights. Hold this position.
4. Pull the pendulum-leveling arm toward the indicator light. The indicator light should illuminate brightly.
5. Push the pendulum-leveling arm away from the indicator light until the light just reaches minimum brilliance (or just goes off). The leveling arm should be approximately straight

down. Repeat this step several times to make sure the indicator light has reached minimum brilliance.
6. Release the brake pedal. The pendulum assembly is now initially adjusted. A readjustment may be necessary if the loading of either the tow vehicle or trailer causes a considerable change in the tow vehicle's front-to-rear position.
7. Move the control-module manual lever to the left and observe the control-module indicator light become increasingly brighter as the lever is moved.
8. If the indicator light does not illuminate, the tow vehicle has a short to ground in the trailer-brake circuit. Check and repair as necessary.
9. Connect the trailer to the tow vehicle and check the trailer to see if stoplights are operating correctly. Move the control-module manual lever to the left. If the indicator light does not illuminate, check the trailer-brake magnets and trailer-brake circuit (including trailer-to-tow vehicle connection) for a short. If a short occurs in the trailer brakes, plug, or wiring, the control-module circuitry will shut down and the indicator light will not illuminate or will glow extremely dimly. Locate and correct short. **Note:** It is normal to hear the trailer-brake magnets hum while testing the controller, or whenever the trailer brakes are activated.
10. Move the control-module manual lever to the left and observe the trailer stoplights come on. The trailer stoplights must illuminate when the manual lever is moved to the left. If they do not, check circuit and bulbs. Also check to see if the red wire connection at the brake controller is connected to the nonpowered side of stoplight switch.

Road-testing and Readjusting the Kelsey Controller To road-test and readjust the Kelsey controller, follow this procedure:

1. Adjust the load-control knob to the mid-range setting (center of knob travel).
2. At a moderate speed (20 mph or less) push the tow vehicle brake pedal in a normal manner. With the load-control knob set in the mid-range

setting, a firm braking action should occur. If more trailer braking is required, turn the load-control knob clockwise. If less trailer braking is required, turn the load-control knob counter-clockwise. The indicator light should illuminate from dim to brighter during the stop, and back to dim after stop is completed.

3. At a moderate speed (20 mph or less) energize the manual lever slowly to the left. A much harder stop can always be obtained since the manual lever is not affected by the load-control setting. The indicator light should illuminate from dim to bright during the stop.

4. The pendulum-leveling arm may be readjusted forward if the indicator light fails to glow, if there is delayed braking, or if there is no braking.

5. The pendulum-leveling arm needs to be readjusted backward if the indicator light glows steadily, if the trailer brakes grab, or if the trailer brakes pulse when the four-way flasher is turned on.

6. The pendulum-leveling arm is properly adjusted if the indicator light glows dimly when the vehicle is stopped on the level and the indicator light glows increasingly brighter as the pedal is pressed while stopping. There should be smooth braking action.

When properly adjusted, the Kelsey control module will allow a slightly greater amount of trailer braking going downhill and slightly less trailer braking going uphill. Normally, no control module readjustment is needed for towing in hilly terrain.

■ Adjusting Electric-Hydraulic Controllers

An adjustment spring can be set to change the amount of fluid displacement needed to move the hydraulic piston and activate the brakes. The amount of brake-pedal pressure needed changes slightly when the adjustment spring is altered, increasing or decreasing actuation of trailer brakes. This adjustment is made either with a fingertip adjustment wheel or by turning the knob on the manual control arm, depending upon the unit brand and model.

Variable Resistor

Some electric-hydraulic trailer brakes may be too harsh and aggressive during slow stops. The use of a

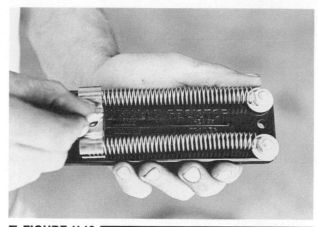

■ **FIGURE 11.16**
A selective resistor in the line to the trailer brakes can correct overbraking at slow speeds.

variable resistor will normally correct this problem (Figure 11.16). The variable resistor permits adjustment of the amount of resistance in the circuit feeding the trailer brakes. The unit is installed by wiring it directly into the electric wire leading from the brake controller to the trailer brakes. Adjustment is made by sliding a metal bridge toward one end or the other of the device to achieve more or less resistance.

Servicing Trailer Brakes

Servicing trailer brakes is within the capability of most do-it-yourself RVers. The job is messy but simple if all the proper tools and replacement parts are on hand.

Begin by jacking the trailer up and supporting it on jack stands. It is best to dismantle the trailer brakes one side at a time for two reasons. First, it is safer to have one side supported by wheels while the opposite side is up on jack stands; and second, if you become confused about the brake reassembly order, you still have at least one completely intact assembly to refer to.

■ Removing the Bearings

Begin trailer brake servicing by removing bearings as follows:

1. Remove the tire and wheel.
2. Remove the bearing dust cap (Figure 11.17).
3. Straighten and remove the cotter pin.
4. Remove the castle nut. It should be only finger-tight (Figure 11.18).
5. Remove the washer and lay it aside on a clean newspaper or rag.

6. Pull the brake drum toward you about an inch, wiggling it side to side slightly. This tends to force the outer wheel bearing toward the end of the spindle where it can be grasped easily.

7. Pull the outer wheel bearing off the spindle and lay it aside on a clean newspaper or rag (Figure 11.19).

8. Remove the brake drum assembly by pulling it straight out and place it open side up on a clean newspaper or rag. You may have to back off adjuster if drum will not pull off.

9. Remove the inner wheel bearing by running a wooden shaft through the hub interior until it contacts the grease seal. A gentle tap usually pops the seal out, and the bearing is then free to be removed (Figure 11.20).

Note: Always wear a protective surgical-type breathing mask when working on brake drums, and use water to clean the dust from the drums, linings, and hardware.

■ Cleaning the Bearings

All the old grease should be removed from the bearings before repacking with new grease in preparation for reinstallation in the hub.

CAUTION: Use parts-cleaning solvent rather than gasoline, which leaves a dangerous residue.

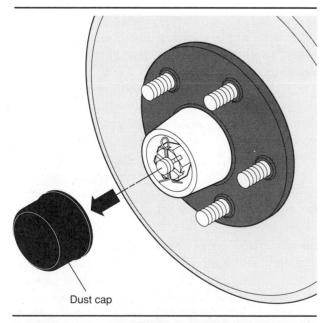

Dust cap

■ FIGURE 11.17
The bearing dust cap is removed to access the castle nut and cotter pin.

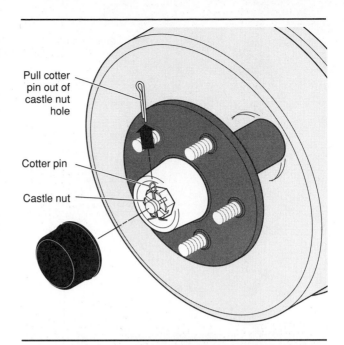

Pull cotter pin out of castle nut hole

Cotter pin

Castle nut

■ FIGURE 11.18
After removing the cotter pin, the castle nut should be only finger-tight.

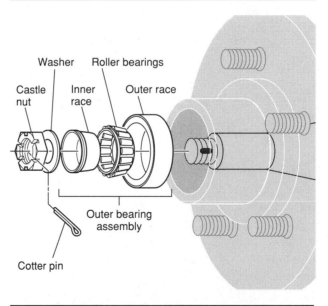

Washer   Roller bearings

Castle nut   Inner race   Outer race

Outer bearing assembly

Cotter pin

■ FIGURE 11.19
Outer trailer wheel bearing assembly

Clean the bearings until all the old grease is removed. Clean the bearing dust cap, castle nut, and bearing washer. When these parts are completely free of old grease, set them aside to dry. Do not use compressed air to dry bearings because the stream of air can spin them at a dangerous speed. Tap the bear-

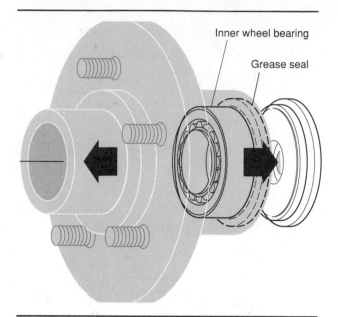

Inner wheel bearing

Grease seal

■ FIGURE 11.20 ■
A gentle tap is all that is needed to pop out the seal so that the bearing can be removed.

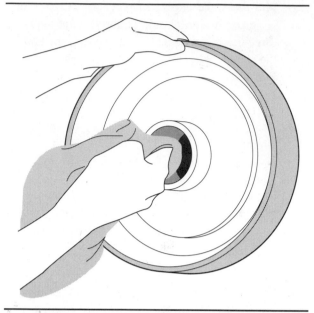

■ FIGURE 11.21 ■
The spindle and hub interior must be cleaned of all old grease before reassembly.

ings on a cloth in the palm of your hand to remove excess solvent, then dry all the rollers with the cloth. Remove all the solvent before repacking with new grease.

While waiting for the bearings to dry, clean the spindle and the hub interior of all old grease (Figure 11.21). This is a messy job; keep a roll of paper towels handy.

■ Inspecting the Bearings

Inspect the bearings and races with a critical eye. There is no sense reinstalling worn or damaged bearings; this only invites failure.

Signs of pitting, scoring, heat damage (indicated by discoloration), or uneven wear patterns are good reasons to discard a bearing and race set. If any of the rollers are imperfectly round, replace the bearing. If there are any signs of cracking, discoloration, or shiny spots (excessive wear) on the race, replace it. *Always replace bearings and races as a set.*

If you plan to reuse the old bearings, be sure to keep track of which race they mate with so you don't mismatch the bearings and races upon reinstallation. If new bearings and races are to be used, have a professional shop press the races into place.

■ Inspecting the Brake Drum

Before reinstalling bearings in the hub, inspect the brake drum. If it has been badly worn or damaged, it may need to be replaced or turned to renew the face of the drum. Damage is evident when the drums show cracks, scoring, excessive wear, or are out of round.

If oil or grease contamination has fouled the drums, use brake-parts solvent to clean the face of the drums.

If heavy scoring is evident, the cause may be excessively worn brake linings, loose lining rivets, or particles embedded in the linings.

Out-of-round drums have the appearance of uneven wear—as if the lining had not been contacting the face of the drum at some point. Drums in this condition need to be turned (bored) by a professional brake shop, or replaced. If the drums have been turned before or are so badly damaged that turning them will remove too much material, the new linings may not contact the drum when the brakes are applied. In such cases, new drums should be installed. Inside-drum measurements taken by the brake shop will determine if new drums are necessary or if the old ones can be reused. Linings should be arced at the same time the drums are turned, but many shops will no longer do this because of the dangers related to asbestos dust.

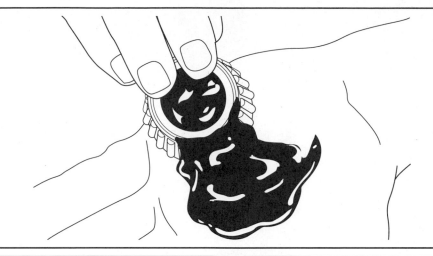

■ FIGURE 11.22
Wheel bearings can be packed by hand, using a good grade of high-temperature grease, if a wheel-bearing packer is not available.

The drum inspection should include the drum assembly bolts. If the bolts are loose, they may shear under hard braking conditions. Replace any bolts that are suspect.

Proceed with the next section only if the original drums are deemed usable.

■ Packing the Bearings

Use high-temperature wheel-bearing grease to repack the bearings. Unless you have a wheel-bearing packing device, you will have to do the job by hand (Figure 11.22).

Place a blob of grease about the size of a golf ball in the palm of one hand. Grip the bearing with the other hand. Force the side of the bearing (where there is an opening between the roller cages) down onto the grease. Do this repeatedly until the grease starts to ooze from the top side of the bearing and out the bearing face between the rollers. Continue forcing grease through the bearing until it is apparent that grease has filled every cavity between the rollers. Then, rotate the bearing to a new spot and begin the process again, forcing grease through the bearing. Continue with this process until you have rotated the bearing all the way around.

Lightly coat the races with grease and spread some grease inside the hub.

Reinstalling the Inner Bearing

Follow these steps to reinstall the inner bearing:

1. Lay the drum with the open (inner) side facing up.
2. Position the inner bearing on its race.
3. Place the new grease seal (never reuse an old seal) in position at the spindle opening on the inner side of the hub (Figure 11.23).
4. Place a block of hardwood over the seal and gently tap it with a hammer to drive the seal into the hub. Make sure the seal fits in the hub evenly all around. Drive the seal in until it is beyond flush and below the level of the surrounding hub.

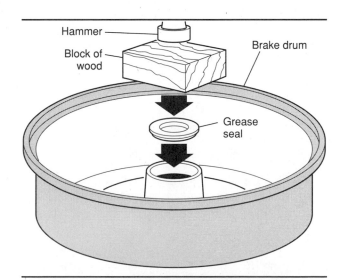

Hammer

Block of wood

Brake drum

Grease seal

■ FIGURE 11.23
New grease seals can be pressed into the wheel by using a straight block of wood and a hammer.

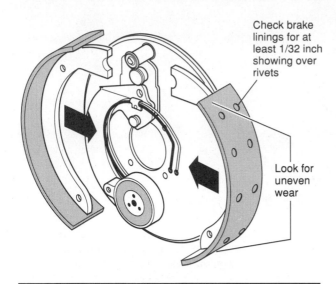

Check brake linings for at least 1/32 inch showing over rivets

Look for uneven wear

■ FIGURE 11.24 ■

Brake linings must be replaced if they have less than ¹/₃₂ inch of material showing over the rivets.

■ Inspecting the Brake Linings

Before proceeding, clean your hands of all grease. Grease or oil contamination can destroy the integrity of brake linings.

If the linings are worn down to within ¹/₃₂ inch of the shoe, replacement is in order (Figure 11.24). If the linings have worn unevenly, look for the cause rather than simply replacing the linings. The uneven wear may be caused by a broken return spring, out-of-round drums, grease contamination, or a shoe that has slipped out of position due to failure of a hold-down spring.

If the linings are due for replacement, replace the linings for all the brakes on that axle at the same time. Never replace the linings on only one side of the axle since this will cause erratic braking.

■ Removing the Brake Shoes

To remove the brake shoes follow these steps:

1. Remove shoe return springs (Figure 11.25) using brake tool or locking pliers. Be careful: The springs are under tension.
2. Remove the shoe hold-down springs (Figure 11.26).
   a. Reach behind the backing plate and hold the head of the hold-down pin to prevent its turning.

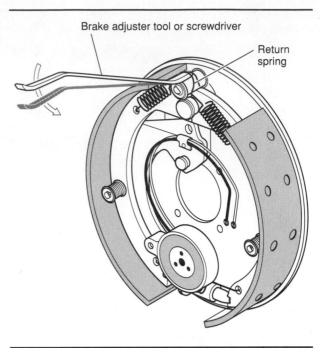

Brake adjuster tool or screwdriver

Return spring

■ FIGURE 11.25 ■

Brake return springs can be removed with a brake tool or screwdriver.

   b. Grasp the hold-down spring retainer (cup) with pliers. Push the retainer in against spring pressure and turn 90 degrees in either direction to align the end of the pin with the slot in the retainer. The retainer and spring will now separate from the pin.
3. Grasp the brake shoes at the top and pull apart. Remove them along with the adjuster mechanism and spring (Figures 11.27 and 11.28).
4. Remove the adjuster mechanism and adjuster spring from the shoes. If these parts are to be reused, clean them thoroughly. Give the adjuster a light coating of lubricant as recommended by the manufacturer.

■ Inspecting the Magnets

The magnet can be inspected by placing a straight-edge across the magnet's rubbing surface (Figure 11.29). If the rubbing surface is flat all the way across, it is contacting the armature correctly.

If the friction element isn't worn too thin, and if there is not excessive scoring from contaminants, the unit need not be replaced.

If the magnet is wearing unevenly, find the cause and correct it before installing a new magnet. The

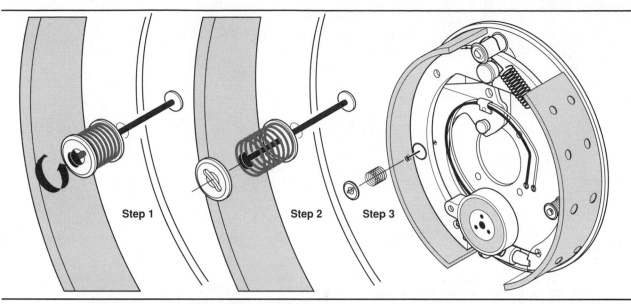

Step 1   Step 2   Step 3

■ **FIGURE 11.26**
Removing the brake shoe hold-down springs

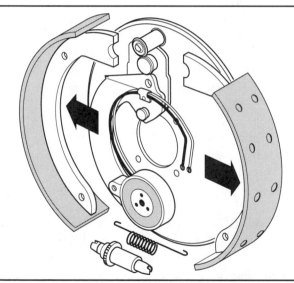

■ **FIGURE 11.27**
The brake adjuster mechanism and spring must be removed with the linings.

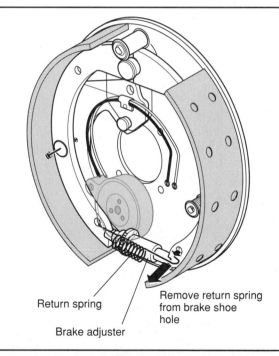

Return spring

Remove return spring from brake shoe hole

Brake adjuster

■ **FIGURE 11.28**
The brake adjuster mechanism and spring should be thoroughly cleaned and lubricated before reinstalling.

most common cause for uneven magnet wear is a worn lever pivot that allows the magnet to contact the armature at an angle. If this is the case, replace the entire lever assembly.

When replacing a magnet on one brake it is necessary to balance the brake system by replacing the counterpart magnet on the opposite end of the axle. Replacement of magnets on only one side of the trailer will result in erratic braking.

Installing New Magnets

If the magnet lead wires are plugged into a socket on the front of the brake assembly, disconnect by pulling the wires from the sockets (Figure 11.30).

If the leads run through the backing plate to a position behind the brake assembly, reach behind the

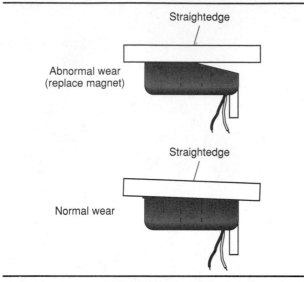

■ FIGURE 11.29 ■■■■■■■■■■■■■■■■■■■■■■■■■■

The most common cause for uneven magnet wear is a worn lever pivot, allowing the magnet to contact the armature at an angle.

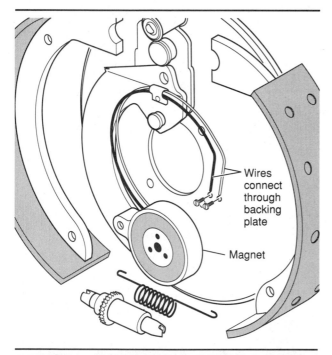

■ FIGURE 11.30 ■■■■■■■■■■■■■■■■■■■■■■■

Wires to the magnet that are routed through the backing plate must be cut before removal.

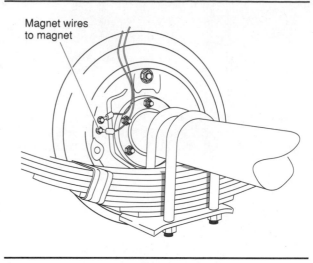

■ FIGURE 11.31 ■■■■■■■■■■■■■■■■■■■■■■■■

New grommets should be used when replacing the wires from the magnet through the backing plate.

backing plate to detach the wires or cut them, whichever applies.

If a grommet protects the wires as they pass through the backing plate, remove it with pliers before pulling the wires through. A new grommet will be needed in the same location on the wires of the new magnet prior to magnet installation (Figure 11.31).

The magnet can be replaced with the lever arm in place or removed (Figure 11.32). To remove the lever arm, first carefully remove the clip that holds it in position. Slide the lever off the stud. On Kelsey brakes, it is necessary first to remove the little spring clip from the positioning stud. On other systems, there is a detent ring inside the magnet assembly. This will slip off easily if the magnet is pulled toward you with a gentle rocking motion. Pay close attention to how the follow-up spring is positioned behind the magnet. The spring pushes against the magnet to maintain proper contact with the armature. This spring will frequently be wider at one end than the other. It must be reinstalled in the proper position. Normally, the wider end is toward the installer.

Install the new magnet, using the new clip included in the magnet kit. If necessary, squeeze the clip with pliers until it fits. Reinstall the lever mechanism if it was removed. Route the magnet lead wires and make the connections. If the wires plug into a socket, clean the socket prior to installation. If the wires were cut, make the connection either by soldering or by using quality crimp connectors. Use heat-shrink material or silicone to protect and strengthen the connection.

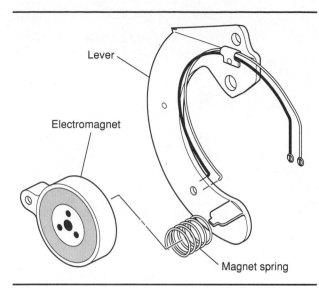

■ FIGURE 11.32 ▬▬▬▬▬▬▬▬▬▬▬▬▬▬
Brake magnets are attached to the lever arm, which can be
removed to facilitate magnet removal.

■ Installing Brake Shoes

With the magnets installed, brake shoes can be reinstalled. When installing new shoes, the primary
shoe must be installed toward the front of the trailer
and the secondary shoe to the rear.

1. Install an adjuster and adjuster spring on each
   set of new shoes. Make sure the adjuster nut is
   on the left side.
2. Position shoes and adjuster mechanism on
   backing plate.
3. Install shoe hold-down spring and retainer.
4. Install and shoe return springs.

■ Inspecting the Armature

Armatures generally last the life of the trailer, but
they are subject to rusting and scoring.

Light scoring is perfectly normal and is caused by
contaminants getting between the magnet and armature. To remove mild rust or scoring, use solvent and
steel wool. If the scoring is substantial, the armature
may need to be replaced.

Replacing the Armature

When replacing the armature it is *not* necessary to
also replace the counterpart armature on the other end
of the axle. However, it is wise to inspect all the

armatures and their magnets because they have all
been exposed to the same damaging conditions.

If the assembly is unicast, the entire unit must be
replaced. If the assembly was riveted, drill out the
rivets and replace them with nuts and bolts to install
the replacement unit.

■ Reinstalling the Drum Assembly

Follow these steps in reinstalling the drum assembly:

1. Carefully slide the drum over the spindle, taking care to avoid damage to the new grease seal
   as it slides over its mating ledge on the inner
   end of the spindle. Push the drum as far as it
   will go. The drum should entirely cover the
   shoes.
2. Install the outer wheel bearing over the spindle
   and press it up into the hub until it meets the
   bearing race.
3. Slide the bearing washer onto the spindle so
   that it fits snugly against the bearing.
4. Install the castle nut and finger-tighten it as far
   as possible.
5. While slowly rotating the drum counterclockwise, tighten the castle nut (to preload the bearings) with a wrench until it is snug or torque
   to 25 foot-pounds. Stop spinning the drum.
   Loosen the nut. Hand-tighten the nut and line
   up the holes in the spindle with the castle nut;
   install and bend a new cotter pin.
6. Spin the drum to see that it spins freely. If it
   doesn't, the shoes may be too tight against the
   drum. If so, back them off with the adjusting
   tool until the drum can spin freely.

■ Final Reassembly

1. Reinstall the bearing dust cap, taking care not
   to crush it against the nut when tapping the cap
   down tightly. If the cap is crushed against the
   nut, a hole will wear in the cap and allow dirt
   and water to enter.
2. Reinstall the wheels and torque the lugs according to manufacturer's specifications. Retorque
   the lugs after driving 50 miles.

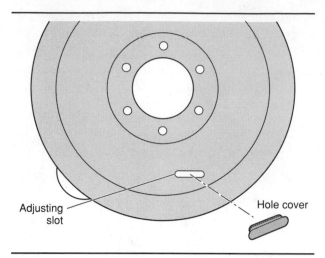

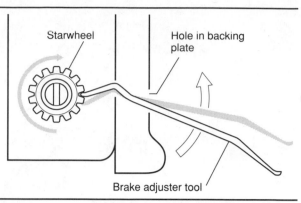

■ **FIGURE 11.33**
A rubber plug in the bottom of the backing plate gives access to the brake-adjuster mechanism.

■ Adjusting the Brakes

The brakes are adjusted by use of a brake tool or a large flat-blade screwdriver.

1. Remove the rubber plug at the bottom of the backside of the backing plate. This gives access to the adjuster mechanism (Figure 11.33).

■ **FIGURE 11.34**
A brake-adjuster tool works best for turning the starwheel between the linings, but in a pinch a screwdriver will work.

2. Insert the brake tool or screwdriver and locate the adjuster starwheel (a toothed wheel). See Figure 11.34.
3. While spinning the tire, turn the adjuster wheel up or down to adjust the brakes. Generally, moving the brake tool up loosens the brakes and moving the tool down tightens them. When the point is reached where the brakes drag, back off just enough to permit the tire to spin freely.

CHAPTER 12

Car Towing

The equipment used to tow small cars or trucks behind motorhomes typically does not need extensive maintenance. A bit of grease on the hitch ball usually will suffice when a tow bar is used. Wheel bearings should be repacked every year on a tow dolly or trailer, and if the dolly or trailer has brakes, they should be inspected annually.

The most important aspects for safe towing are the necessary equipment, installed and used properly, along with vigilance.

A prerequisite for safe towing is use of a proper combination of vehicles. Although even a relatively small motorhome may be able to tow a heavy car, the questions are, how far? how well? and how safely? Weight limits prescribed by manufacturers of motorhome chassis are intended to insure adequate performance and braking for the motorhome. Applying those limits to one's personal situation requires

■ TABLE 12.1 ■

Gross Combined Weight Rating (1989 Models)

Model	Weight (in pounds)
Chevrolet P30	19,000
Chevrolet G30	
5.7L Engine	Not suitable
Ford E-350	18,500
Ford F-Super Duty	25,000
John Deere	22,000
Gillig	
MHF460	20,000
MHM	30,000
MHA3208	36,000
MHHD6V92	40,000
Oshkosh	
V814	20,000
V815	23,000
V917	30,000
Roadmaster	27,500 for gasoline-powered chassis; no limit for diesels

knowledge of the motorhome's *curb weight* and the chassis manufacturer's *gross combined weight rating* (GCWR). The GCWR is the maximum total weight of the motorhome, towed vehicle, and all their contents (see Table 12.1). With knowledge of the motorhome's curb weight loaded for travel (including passengers), it's possible to calculate the weight allowance for a towed car or truck.

For example, if a 31-foot motorhome's curb weight, including supplies and passengers, is 14,000 pounds, the allowance for weight of a towed vehicle by Chevrolet is 5,000 pounds—a rather generous figure but nevertheless one that Chevrolet officially approves. As one might assume, less weight means better performance, better fuel economy, and improved braking.

These weight factors encourage motorhome owners to choose compact or subcompact vehicles weighing about 3,000 pounds or less. Popular exceptions are compact 4-wheel-drive vehicles such as the Ford Bronco II and Jeep Cherokee, which weigh 3,500 to 3,700 pounds. Even when the gross combined weight is within the manufacturer's limits, the ability to keep speed in check on steep downhill grades may require more braking than the motorhome can produce from the combined effect of downshifting the transmission (engine-compression braking) and application of service brakes. Additional discussion of braking will be included later in this chapter.

A variety of compact cars and trucks, including those with front-wheel drive and power steering, are approved by their manufacturers as suitable for being towed over long distances without speed restrictions (see Figure 12.1). In particular, Ford, Chrysler, and Toyota offer wide ranges of compact models with manual transmissions that are suitable. Check the

■ FIGURE 12.1 ■

A number of cars, trucks, and sport-utility vehicles have been approved by their manufacturers for towing behind motorhomes on all four wheels. Only a few are designated suitable for towing with automatic transmissions.

owner's manuals of the models you're considering to determine which is best for you.

Chevrolet/GMC S-10/S-15 Blazer/Jimmy vehicles were high on the list of popular vehicles until GM withdrew approval for towing long distances in 1985. Until that model year, owner's manuals had included specific approval for long-distance towing. The GM vehicles still can be towed, but, if the owner intends to stay within the confines of the GM warranty, only by using a cable-operated driveshaft-disconnect device (rear-wheel-drive vehicles only), a driveshaft-disconnect device (front-wheel drive), a dolly, or a trailer.

Only Honda offers an automatic-transmission-equipped car that can be towed on all four wheels without damage to the transmission. Other automatic-transmission cars must be towed on dollies or trailers unless one of the above-mentioned add-on items is used. Yet another option is an automatic-transmission lubrication pump system. Such systems, operated by 12-volt DC power from the motorhome, circulate the towed vehicle's transmission fluid to prevent bearing damage; they are available for many models of conventional automatic-transmission cars. Automatic transmissions made by Honda differ from others in that the input shaft from the engine need not turn to operate the transmission's built-in fluid pump. When

the Honda is towed, the transmission tailshaft operates the fluid pump, lubricating the tailshaft bearings.

Towing Equipment

Beyond maintaining a realistic weight situation, the choice of towing equipment is important for safety and convenience. Vehicles can be successfully and legally towed three ways: on their own four wheels utilizing a tow bar; with two wheels on a dolly (Figure 12.2); or on a trailer (Figure 12.3).

■ **FIGURE 12.2**
Tow dollies are very popular for pulling front-wheel drive, automatic, or manual-transmission cars behind motorhomes.

■ **FIGURE 12.3**
Car trailers can be used for towing cars, but the additional weight may strain the motorhome's gross combined weight rating.

Many motorhomers find that the extra weight of a dolly (310 to 600 pounds, depending on brand and model) or trailer (700 to 1,000 pounds) does not cause their gross combined weight to exceed the motorhome chassis manufacturer's GCWR, while others prefer the convenience and reduced weight of towing "flat" with a tow bar.

In either case, proper choice and installation of equipment is important—especially so with tow bars since they are mechanically attached to the towed vehicle, whereas use of a dolly or trailer only requires securing the vehicle on the dolly or trailer.

■ Hitch Platforms and Ball Position

Whether the towing method is a tow bar, dolly, or trailer, height of the hitch ball is important for proper handling and safety. Ball height will vary with the road clearance of the vehicle or trailer, which means that there is no precise ideal ball height, but the average will be around 18 inches. The proper ball height is one that places the tow bar or tongue of the dolly or trailer in a level attitude (see Figure 12.4).

When ball position is too high, coupler damage is possible if the motorhome is driven in an unusually high or low position relative to the towed vehicle.

A proper hitch setup for a motorhome includes a hitch receiver (Figure 12.5) that does not reduce the motorhome's rear ground clearance any more than necessary. The receiver should be positioned only slightly below the bumper. If the ball were positioned at the level of the receiver, it may be too high or too low depending on the towed vehicle's height. Ball mounts of different configurations are used to create

■ FIGURE 12.5 ■
A hitch receiver that does not restrict the motorhome's rear ground clearance is preferable. Receivers are usually rated for 3500 pounds.

proper ball height regardless of the position of the receiver (see Figure 12.6a and b).

The hitch receiver attached to the motorhome must be clearly rated for the total weight of the car and car/dolly or trailer you will be towing. (Ratings typically are stamped on hitch receivers and on ball mounts.)

Likewise, couplers must be clearly stamped with a load rating that is sufficient for the weight being towed.

In addition to heeding the ratings, use a mechanic's creeper to get under the motorhome and check the integrity of the hitch attachment to the motorhome frame. The hitch receiver should be bolted securely with Grade 5 or higher bolts and lockwashers or locking nuts. Also, Loctite thread sealant should be used. Check all nuts for tightness. Welding is not recommended.

Most motorhome chassis are not long enough to extend fully to the bumper of the motorhome; thus the coach builder typically adds chassis extensions. It is these frame extensions, sometimes hastily welded on the chassis, to which the hitch platform is attached. Inspect the quality of the welds that attach the extensions to the chassis.

Hitch balls are available in various quality levels and types. The ball should be stamped with a load rating equal to or in excess of the entire weight of your towed vehicle and dolly or trailer, if one of these is used. If the ball is not stamped with a rating, discard it and buy one that is. The ball should have a stem to

■ FIGURE 12.4 ■
If the ball height is correct, the tow bar will be in a level attitude when hitched to the motorhome.

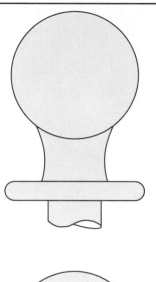

Correct style ball
Choose ball with tall, small diameter stem for maximum coupler arc movement.

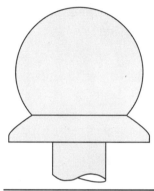

Incorrect style ball
Thick, short, stem; reduces arc movement.

■ **FIGURE 12.6** ■
Typical ball mounts can be used in two configurations (top and bottom) to achieve proper ball height.

■ **FIGURE 12.7** ■
Coupler movement flexibility depends on the type of ball. In all cases, a ball with a stem should be used.

allow the coupler full flexibility of movement (Figure 12.7). Don't use a ball without a stem because it restricts the range of movement of the coupler on the ball and in some situations can force the coupler off the ball.

■ Safety Chains

Federal law requires use of safety chains regardless of the towing method. Two chains should be used, rated for the equipment involved, either Class 2 or Class 3 chain rated for 3,500 or 5,000 pounds capacity, respectively. Steel cable can also be used and is more convenient, with less weight and bulk than chain.

The chains or cable should be attached to loops provided in the tow-bar baseplate and in the hitch platform. The chains or cables should be arranged in an X-pattern under the coupler and ball with enough slack so that they do not crimp the pivoting of the coupler on the ball, but not with so much slack that they drag in driveways. The purpose of crossing the

chains under the ball is so the tow bar or dolly/trailer tongue will be held off the ground if the coupler should ever become disengaged from the ball.

■ Tow Bars

Selecting and Installing the Tow Bar

Although rental yards offer tow bars that are designed for temporary installation using chains and partially relying on vehicle bumpers for support, we will limit this discussion to tow bars that are bolted to the frames of towed vehicles—the arrangement most commonly used by motorhome owners.

A variety of tow bars is available, ranging from universal, modern removable bars (Figure 12.8), to late-model telescoping self-aligning bars (Figure 12.9) that offer additional flexibility while positioning the car or truck for hitching. All tow bars should be iden-

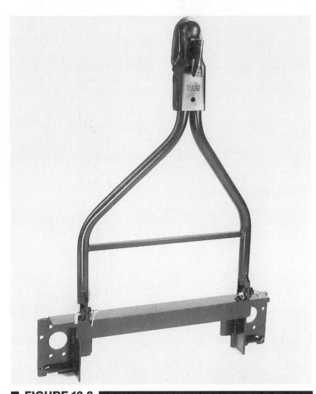

■ FIGURE 12.8 ■
The Hewitt tow bar is an example of a universal unit that is easily removable from the vehicle.

tified with ratings for maximum vehicle weight. Make sure your vehicle's curb weight does not exceed the tow-bar rating.

Locking pins make many tow bars easily removable; they're stowed in the vehicle or with the motorhome until needed. Special tow bars are designed so they can be swung to vertical positions and locked while the vehicle is driven (Figure 12.10).

All tow bars utilize a triangular structure for rigidity, whether the structure is steel tubing, flat steel bar, or two lengths of chain that form triangular support for a telescoping center bar. Rigidity is necessary because heavy stress can be exerted on a tow bar during sharp turns or when traveling over uneven terrain.

Tow-bar lengths vary, but length apparently is not critical to towing stability. With the possible exception of some of the Jeep-style universal bars, most bars are long enough to prevent jackknifing the towed vehicle into the rear of the motorhome during tight turns.

Most small trucks and 4-wheel-drive vehicles present no significant installation challenges for tow-bar manufacturers. These vehicles have body-on-frame design, offering a system of steel girders in the front

■ FIGURE 12.9 ■
Duncan's Eaz-Aligner is a telescoping, self-adjusting tow bar that remains on the tag-along vehicle.

Hewitt builds tow bars that are designed to swing up into a vertical position and lock in place while the vehicle is driven.

of the vehicle for attachment of the tow-bar baseplate (mounting platform). Ideally, the tow-bar manufacturer supplies a baseplate (mount) designed specifically for the vehicle so that few, if any, additional holes must be drilled in the vehicle's frame. The baseplate typically is bolted into place, using Grade 5 or higher bolts, lockwashers, and Loctite thread sealant as added insurance against loosening. Or, locking nuts may be used.

The design of baseplates for cars with unitbody construction presents a real challenge because such cars do not have conventional frames. The sheet-metal body itself provides the vehicle's rigidity, and designs do not allow stress loads of engine and suspension mounts to concentrate too heavily at single points. Unfortunately, front ends of unitbody cars typically are not designed with tow-bar attachment in mind, and the tow-bar baseplate designer must take care to distribute stress loads properly. Failure to do so can result in the baseplate mounting bolts being pulled out of the body, or, in extreme cases, major sheet-metal components may be torn off the car.

In situations where a prefabricated baseplate is not offered by the tow-bar manufacturer, a local welding or hitch shop usually is contracted by the tow-bar purchaser to build the baseplate. Master welders have an excellent understanding of stress loads and can come up with designs that offer acceptable durability. However, mediocre welders have been known to create unsafe designs. Unfortunately, the typical motorhomer may not be knowledgeable enough to choose a competent welder; thus it's best to choose a tow bar that is supplied with a prefabricated baseplate. If that's not practical or possible, at least choose a welding shop that does a large volume of tow-bar installations or hitches for vehicles that tow large trailers.

Visually Checking the Tow Bar

While traveling it's important that the motorhome owner visually inspect the tow bar every time the vehicle is stopped. The owner should perform a walk-around that includes these visual inspection points:

☑ CHECKLIST

☐ Coupler secured on hitch ball
☐ Pin (or bolt) securing coupler in locked position
☐ Hitch ball nut tight
☐ Ignition key positioned so steering column is unlocked
☐ Transmission shift lever and/or transfer case shift lever (4-wheel-drive only) still in neutral position
☐ Hand brake in "off" position
☐ All bolts, nuts, and pins on tow bar and baseplate tight
☐ Wiring harness connected
☐ Tires appear to have normal inflation pressure

Although it includes several points, this inspection takes less than a minute. The walkaround inspection should also include the motorhome's tires and a quick look underneath the chassis for signs of oil or coolant leakage.

Failure to see obvious problems developing is a primary cause of mishaps and costly damage that could be prevented. Many motorhome owners who do not regard themselves as mechanically adept do not take the time to check their equipment, assuming they probably won't recognize a problem. However, owners who take the time to make mental notes of how their rigs are set up may be able to notice when something changes. They may not know if the change presents a problem, but they could find out and possibly prevent an accident.

It's also best to check tail- and stoplights and directional signals once a day, preferably in the morning.

Mechanically Checking the Tow Bar

A more detailed mechanical inspection should be performed periodically, as common sense dictates, or once every week while traveling. It should cover these points:

☑ CHECKLIST

☐ Inspect all bolts underneath vehicle or otherwise out of sight that are used to attach tow-bar baseplate to car or truck. Inspect vehicle body or frame for deformation caused by stress on the bolts. All such bolts should have several threads protruding from nuts when installed; thus, a lower number of threads protruding will be a danger signal without having to retorque each nut with a wrench (although that should happen periodically). Deformation of metal components indicates improper design of baseplate.

☐ Inspect bolts securing hitch platform to motorhome.

☐ Check wiring for chafing or damage.

☐ Inspect all tow-bar pivot points for excessive wear.

■ Dollies and Trailers

Dollies (Figure 12.11) first became popular with motorhome owners when only a few manufacturers of small front-wheel-drive cars approved of their cars being towed—even those with manual transmissions. Many motorhome owners prefer automatic transmissions in their towed cars, and at this writing only Honda unofficially approves of unlimited towing of its vehicles on all four wheels with automatic transmissions (an alternative is use of an automatic-transmission lubrication pump). A dolly immobilizes the front (drive) wheels of the car, eliminating any concern about transmission damage while towing.

■ FIGURE 12.11 ■
Tow dollies immobilize the drive wheels of a towed car, preventing possible transmission damage.

Dollies are basically small trailers equipped with ramps that haul one axle of a vehicle. The dolly will tow either end of a car. For example, a rear-wheel-drive car can be backed onto the dolly. However, at least one manufacturer recommends against towing a car backward due to the possibility of sway (yaw) that may occur if the car's front suspension has worn components or is misaligned.

One of the most significant advantages of a dolly or a trailer is availability of brakes, either hydraulic surge-type or electric, which can make a sizable difference in braking capacity while traveling mountainous terrain.

Trailers are used by a small number of motorhomers who want the ultimate protection of the car against damage to the drivetrain as well as to the paint while towing—motorhomers who don't mind the inconvenience of parking a trailer after arrival at a destination. Trailers of various weight capacities can be purchased for towing a wide range of car sizes and weights. The weight of a towed car on a trailer is more apt to exceed the motorhome manufacturer's GCWR, which is still an important factor, even though braking is not a limitation. Gasoline-powered motorhomes typically are not capable of climbing steep mountain grades at acceptable speeds when gross combined weight approaches or exceeds the chassis manufacturer's GCWR.

Dolly Loading and Tie-down

Tie-down systems of several designs are used to hold the vehicle rigidly in place on the dolly or trailer. The owner should be sure that the tie-downs are not too large or too small for the tires of the towed vehicle. A tie-down that is too large will not hold the tire securely, and one that is too small may not be properly fastened. Be sure that nylon or other fabric tie-downs do not come in contact with metal parts that can cut the fabric.

Stop and recheck tie-downs after five miles of driving to make sure road vibration has not loosened any components. Regular rechecking about every 200 miles is advisable. Check the coupler locking mechanism as well.

Lubricating the Dolly

Some dollies have few lubrication points other than the hitch ball, while others have pivoting platforms that require oil.

To lubricate the Owens Classic Model CD2200:

1. Oil pivot pin. Under storage compartment lid, locate disc with four holes; add engine oil until excess runs out.
2. Grease tire-supporting platforms. Rotate car-dolly swivel in both directions to expose underside of platforms. Apply grease generously to underside.
3. Repack wheel bearings every 10,000 miles or 2 years under normal conditions.

To lubricate the Demco Kar Kaddy II:

1. Grease center pivot-pin zerk fittings every 1,500 miles.
2. Grease main frame platform skids every 1,500 miles. These fittings are accessible from under the front tire stop main platform.
3. An occasional drop of oil may be required on the moving parts of the tie-down winch.

Dolly and Trailer Brake Maintenance

Electric or surge brakes should be adjusted approximately every 2,000 miles of travel, or as needed to maintain good brake effectiveness. Since electric brakes can be actuated independently of motorhome brakes (via the trailer brake controller), it's possible to independently test dolly or trailer brake effectiveness periodically. However, effectiveness of surge brakes may be difficult to measure accurately because surge brakes function only in concert with the motorhome's brakes. Thus, it is necessary to adjust brakes on a regular basis.

Dolly and Trailer Brake Adjustment

Dolly and trailer surge or electric brakes require manual adjustment of brake shoe position—the same procedure used on cars and light trucks before the advent of automatic adjusters. To adjust brakes:

1. Hitch dolly or trailer to motorhome and set motorhome hand brake. Block wheels.
2. Jack up one wheel of the dolly or trailer so the wheel can be spun freely.
3. Remove plug from brake adjustment slot at bottom center of brake backing plate.
4. Using a flashlight, locate round toothed wheel (starwheel) just inside the slot. To determine which direction to turn the starwheel for tightening, use a brake-adjusting tool (available at auto supply stores) to turn the starwheel while spinning the tire. If after turning the starwheel at least half a turn you don't hear the brake shoes begin to drag on the drum, reverse direction.
5. Tighten the starwheel adjustment until the brake shoes make it impossible to spin the tire. Then loosen the adjustment until the brake shoes drag very lightly.
6. Reinsert the plug for the adjustment slot and adjust remaining brakes the same way. Remove jack and all tools when completed.

Checking Dolly and Trailer Hitching

Check dolly and trailer for the following:

☑ CHECKLIST ▰▰▰▰▰▰▰▰▰

☐ Coupler secured on hitch ball. Lift coupler to make sure. Install coupler locking pin or bolt. Check coupler fit. The coupler adjusting nut should be tightened to make firm contact with the ball, but it should not be so tight that latching the coupler is difficult.

☐ Safety chains attached (arranged in an X under ball)

☐ License plate in place

☐ Wheel platforms tilted into position; pivot platform in proper position (if applicable)

☐ Car/truck properly positioned on wheel platforms

☐ Wheel tie-downs tightened and locked

☐ Steering wheel locked with wheels straight ahead

☐ Wheel platforms locked (if applicable)

☐ Electrical plug connected; lights function properly

☐ Check wheel lug nuts. Torque to 75 pounds, or to the rating provided by the dolly or trailer manufacturer. Recheck once a week while traveling.

☐ Check tire pressure; inflate to dolly or trailer manufacturer's recommendation, if different from maximum inflation pressure stamped on tire sidewall.

■ Towing Lights

Most states require that towed vehicles have legal brake-, tail-, and turn-signal lights actuated by the motorhome's lighting system. Even in states that don't have the requirements, a full lighting system is necessary for safe towing (Figure 12.12). Dollies and trailers are fitted with appropriate lights by their manufacturers, and a four-wire plug can be installed at the rear of the motorhome to include the four lighting circuits necessary.

The motorhome owner who tows a vehicle on its own wheels with a tow bar must either use the towed vehicle's taillights, or add a *light bar*, an independent tail/signal light system (see Figure 12.13).

When using the towed vehicle's lights, the common wiring method is to splice three wires from the motorhome (tail, left turn, and right turn) into the wiring harness leading to the towed vehicle's rear lights. The splice point may be in the engine compartment or slightly to the rear, under the floor.

Electrical feedback problems can occur with late-model vehicles using transistorized ignition systems, however. Current from the motorhome may feed back through the towed vehicle's lighting system into ignition components or other control systems. This can be prevented by using a taillight wiring kit that includes diodes (one-way electrical valves), available from a variety of sources, including at least one manufacturer of widely used tow bar products. Light bars require a simple four-wire hookup that is identical to the system used for a dolly or trailer.

Motorhomes that use turn signals that are separate from brake lights require use of a solid-state converter to provide compatibility with the conventional lights of a dolly or trailer in which the same light is used for brakes and turn signals. Such converters are available from the same companies that make light bars and wiring kits.

Problems with intermittent loss of power to taillights and turn-signal lights involve poor ground connections, improperly crimped electrical connectors (see page 8), and deterioration of wiring due to vibration when crimp-on connectors are used. The connectors can become loose and cause intermittent open circuits.

■ Using the Brakes

With extra weight tagging along behind, it's always wise to allow an extra margin of stopping distance than normally would be required.

Any motorhome towing a vehicle should always have the capability of making an emergency stop on a downhill grade, even though service brakes have been used intermittently to retard speed. It's usually necessary to use service brakes frequently to retard speed on downhill grades in mountainous terrain, sometimes to the extent that partial brake fade occurs. Fade is caused by overheating of brake pads, rotors, shoes, and drums to the point where friction between the two is partially or fully lost. Although the brake pedal may feel firm, little or no reduction of speed occurs.

The RVer who is towing a vehicle on its own wheels must use lower gears to retard speed and minimize use of service brakes. If weight is too high to avoid excessive use of service brakes, additional braking in the form of a brake-equipped dolly, a brake-actuating tow bar, or an engine-braking (retarder) system for the motorhome is needed.

Brake-equipped dollies, such as those made by Dethmers Mfg. Co., Owens Mfg. Co., Trailex, Inc., and O-Rac Industries, can reduce braking loads on the motorhome. Also, Remco Recreational Equipment Mfg. Co. offers a brake-actuating tow bar with a cable system designed to actuate the towed vehicle's brakes. Decelomatic Corporation and Telma Retarder offer systems designed for installation in motorhomes to

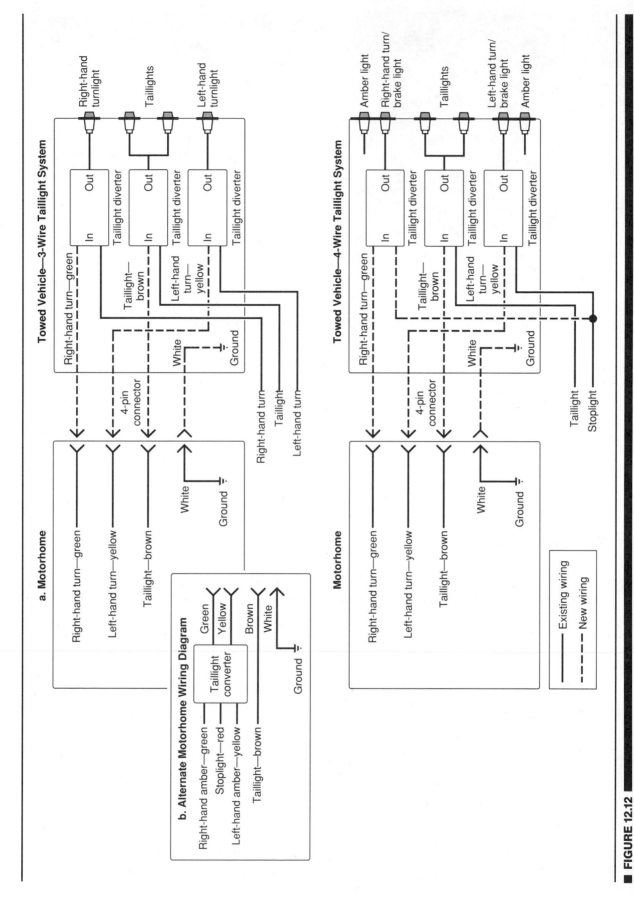

Towed Vehicle—3-Wire Taillight System

Right-hand turnlight

Taillights

Left-hand turnlight

Taillight diverter

Taillight diverter

Taillight diverter

In / Out

Right-hand turn—green

Taillight—brown

Left-hand turn—yellow

White

Ground

4-pin connector

Right-hand turn

Taillight

Left-hand turn

a. Motorhome

Right-hand turn—green

Left-hand turn—yellow

Taillight—brown

White

Ground

b. Alternate Motorhome Wiring Diagram

Green

Yellow

Brown

White

Taillight converter

Right-hand amber—green

Stoplight—red

Left-hand amber—yellow

Taillight—brown

White

Ground

Towed Vehicle—4-Wire Taillight System

Amber light

Right-hand turn/brake light

Taillights

Left-hand turn/brake light

Amber light

Taillight diverter

Taillight diverter

Taillight diverter

In / Out

Right-hand turn—green

Taillight—brown

Left-hand turn—yellow

White

Ground

4-pin connector

Taillight

Stoplight

Motorhome

Right-hand turn—green

Left-hand turn—yellow

Taillight—brown

White

Ground

——— Existing wiring

- - - - New wiring

■ **FIGURE 12.12**

Remco's kit for hard wiring three- and four-light systems between the motorhome and towed vehicle eliminates the need for external tail-, brake-, and turn-signal lights.

■ FIGURE 12.13 ■
Light bars are simple to use but can be unsightly if not removed from the vehicle.

retard speed either by causing the pistons to compress air during deceleration or the driveshaft to rotate against opposing magnetic forces.

■ Other Accessories

The myriad accessories available for towing include several mentioned earlier: the automatic-transmission lube-pump systems by Remco; a driveshaft-disconnect system and taillight wiring system, also by Hewitt Tubular, Remco, and Cosmos; and an axle-shaft disconnect system by Downey Off Road Manufacturing (Downey Disconnect).

Miscellaneous Towing Tips

Motorhome owners who tow a vehicle on its own wheels find that the miles on the odometer of the towed vehicle accumulate rapidly, reducing the resale value of the vehicle. Speedometer-tampering laws of recent years have made it very difficult or impossible to easily disconnect a speedometer drive cable from inside the engine compartment or the passenger compartment. Exceptions are vehicles equipped with cruise-control units that have separate cables from the transmission to the control unit and from the control unit to the speedometer. Either cable may be temporarily disconnected at the control unit when the car is being towed.

Some compact cars and trucks track better than others while being towed, due to differing steering geometry. If a vehicle does not track well, have an alignment shop set the front-wheel caster to the maximum factory-recommended setting. Always maintain maximum air pressure in tires to help reduce tire wear.

If the towed vehicle's front wheels have a tendency to reverse-steer (crank all the way in the wrong direction) in driveways, it may be necessary to use a stretch cord to anchor the steering wheel to a point behind the driver's seat so the wheel cannot make a full revolution. This is not ideal because it will accelerate tire wear, but will prevent an annoying lockup situation in driveways and on other uneven terrain.

Avoid sharp turns at slow speeds. Motorhomes have long rear overhangs, and sharp turns cause rapid lateral movement of the hitch ball. This tends to drag the towed vehicle sideways.

CAUTION: While towing with a tow bar or dolly, don't back up. The car or dolly will not steer in the motorhome's intended direction and the car will be dragged sideways.

Finally, be sure transmission lubricant is kept up to the recommended fill level to insure lubrication of the tailshaft during towing.

CHAPTER 13

Drivetrain Systems

An RV engine is the heart of the entire *drivetrain*, which consists of engine, transmission, driveshaft, differential, axles, and wheel bearings. The engine is a complex piece of machinery that requires proper lubrication and tune-up intervals to live up to its performance potential.

The types and varieties of engines range all the way from a small 1.5-liter four-cylinder type found in a compact car to a 7.5-liter V-8 under the hood of a 1-ton truck or motorhome. Because each type requires a systematic approach to both maintenance and troubleshooting, every RV owner should become familiar with the requirements of his or her particular engine. To identify the engine, check the emissions sticker that is attached under the hood or on the engine's valve cover. If the sticker is missing, check with the vehicle manufacturer to make positive identification of the engine. It is vital to know engine type and displacement (size) so that the proper parts and accessories can be purchased.

Engine Service and Repair

Most vehicles will be difficult to start without a fully charged battery that is in good condition. Make sure that connections are clean and tight. A battery can be charged with a trickle charger over a period of hours, or by using a fast-charger that can boost the battery in about 30 minutes. (See pages 11–12).

■ Fuel Filter Replacement

Most engines have a fuel filter installed in the system to prevent dirt and debris from reaching the carburetor (or fuel injectors). Periodic maintenance of this element can prevent many roadside difficulties. Depending on the vehicle, fuel filters are found in a variety of locations:

1. *The carburetor inlet.* The filter is located either behind the fuel-inlet nut on the carburetor or enclosed in a small canister that screws on the front of the carburetor bowl (Figure 13.1).
2. *The in-line filter.* A metal or plastic canister is located between the fuel pump and the carburetor (Figure 13.2). This type of filter is easily replaced by removing the hose clamps and replacing with a new element. Make sure that the flow-direction arrow is pointed toward the carburetor so that the filter will function correctly.
3. *On the fuel pump.* Many older RVs use a filter located on the bottom of the fuel pump, housed in a screw-on container. By simply removing the container, a new element can be installed in minutes.
4. *In-tank filters.* Many newer vehicles, especially those with fuel injection, utilize an in-tank filter that consists of a fine-mesh screen formed like a sock on the end of the fuel pickup. These screens require no periodic maintenance; however, if dirty fuel blocks the screen, fuel pressure will be low and performance poor. On many models, the fuel tank must be drained and dropped to facilitate cleaning of the screen.

■ Air Filter Service

Changing the air filter is probably the easiest maintenance operation to perform on any vehicle (Figure 13.3). Be sure to check for a correct type and size

■ FIGURE 13.1 ■
The carburetor inlet filter is usually located behind the fuel inlet nut.

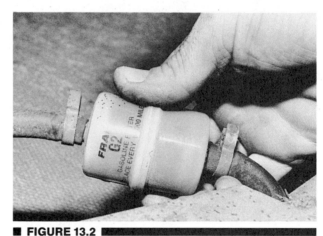

■ FIGURE 13.2 ■
In-line filters can be made of plastic or metal; all these filters are flow-directional.

■ FIGURE 13.3 ■
Clogged air cleaners can decrease performance and shorten engine life.

air-cleaner element. The wrong air-cleaner element can allow air to pass over instead of through the element, where dirt particles can be removed. Tests have shown that an engine's life is only about a third of what it could be when it is operated without an air-cleaner element. To change the air-cleaner element:

1. Purchase the correct size air filter for your engine.
2. Open the air-cleaner housing and lift out the old element.
3. Do not attempt to clean the old element. Air filters are inexpensive; use a new one.
4. Make sure the new element you are installing is exactly the same type as the old one.
5. Drop the new element in the housing and replace the cover. Tighten the cover securely.

■ Ignition Systems

Service and repair of ignition systems are becoming increasingly complex with the extensive use of electronic computer-controlled circuitry. Expensive, specialized testing equipment is needed to analyze most electronic ignition systems; this is best left to a repair facility. When these electronic systems go down, there is little that can be done by the average do-it-yourselfer except to replace suspected parts. If your RV utilizes a replaceable control unit (sometimes known as a "black box," or module), you can purchase and carry a spare. This may, however, prove to be expensive with some models of ignition systems. Replacement instructions vary widely; follow the replacement part manufacturer's instructions exactly.

Checking the Ignition System

If your rig has an older points-and-condenser-type system, you can easily carry spare parts for roadside repair. Here are the steps to checking ignition systems:

☑ CHECKLIST

☐ Remove a spark-plug cable and hold it about ½ inch from a ground source (Figure 13.4).
☐ Crank the engine and look for a spark jumping from the cable to the ground surface.
☐ No spark or a short yellow (weak) spark indicates ignition trouble.

■ **FIGURE 13.4**
Hold the spark plug cable about ½ inch from a ground source and crank the engine to check for ignition spark.

☐ With a points ignition system, remove the distributor cap and check to see that the points open and close when the engine is cranked.
☐ Points should open about .020 inch (about the thickness of 5 or 6 sheets of paper). If not, open them using a feeler gauge between the contacts when the point-rubbing block is on the peak of one of the distributor cam lobes.
☐ If you have a test light or a multimeter (DC volts), check to see if there is power to the movable contact of the points. Open the points and turn on the ignition switch. Place the positive test lead on the movable contact and the other lead to ground; there should be about 9 volts to the point's movable contact.
☐ If voltage is present, but there still is no spark, the problem is narrowed to the ignition coil or the condenser. The condenser can be tested with the points open using an multimeter (ohms). There should be infinite resistance between the body of the condenser and the pigtail lead leaving the condenser. If not, the condenser is internally grounded and must be replaced.
☐ If replacing the condenser does not result in spark from the coil, the coil should be replaced.

TROUBLESHOOTING the Engine

Problem	Possible Cause	Correction
Will not start	Low battery	Charge or replace.
	Out of fuel	Refill.
	Clogged fuel filter	Clean or replace.
	Faulty ignition	Repair.
	Wet ignition components	Dry ignition with hair dryer.
	Flooded carburetor	Wait 15 minutes, retry.
	Inoperative carb choke	Adjust and clean.
	Vapor lock	Let engine cool.
	Defective starter	Replace.
	Bad starter solenoid	Replace.
Hard to start	Inoperative carb choke	Adjust and clean.
	Damp ignition parts	Dry parts.
	Weak battery	Charge or replace.
	Incorrect timing	Check and reset timing.
	Dirty air filter	Replace with new filter.
	Worn spark plugs	Replace with new plugs.
	Faulty ignition cables	Replace with new cables.
	Contaminated fuel	Fill with fresh fuel.
	Clogged fuel filter	Clean or replace filter.
	Wrong oil viscosity	Replace with proper type for climate.
	Overheating engine	Check cooling system.
Lack of power	Clogged air cleaner	Replace.
	Worn spark plugs	Replace.
	Poor fuel delivery	Check fuel pressure.
	Wrong ignition timing	Check and reset timing.
	Incorrect fuel mixture	Repair or recalibrate carburetor.
	Poor engine compression	Check cylinder compression.
	Restricted exhaust	Examine exhaust components.
	Dragging brakes	Examine brake system.
	Worn cam timing chain	Replace.
Low oil pressure	Low oil level	Fill to proper level.
	Inaccurate gauge	Compare with good gauge.
	Incorrect oil viscosity	Replace with proper oil for climate.
	Aerated, level too high	Confirm dipstick reading.
	Worn engine bearings	Overhaul engine.
	Defective oil pump	Replace with new pump.
	Clogged pickup screen	Clean and replace.
	Diluted oil	Inspect for coolant contamination.

TROUBLESHOOTING *the Engine* (continued)

Problem	Possible Cause	Correction
Burning excessive oil	Clogged PCV or hose	Replace.
	Worn piston rings	Overhaul engine.
	Defective bearings	Overhaul engine.
	Worn valve guides	Valve job with new guides.
	External engine leaks	Replace defective gaskets.
	Vacuum leak	Replace intake-manifold gasket.
	Defective valve seals	Replace with new seals.
Engine overheats	Loose fan belt	Check belt tension.
	Low coolant level	Inspect for level or leaks.
	Dirty radiator fins	Clean radiator.
	Obstructed radiator	Remove obstruction.
	Clogged radiator core	Clean or replace radiator.
	Failed water pump	Replace.
	Bad radiator cap	Check holding pressure.
	Wrong ignition timing	Check and reset timing.
	Lean fuel/air ratio	Calibrate or adjust carburetor.
	Collapsed radiator hose	Replace soft hoses.
	Stuck thermostat	Replace thermostat.
	Broken fan shroud	Replace.
	Faulty thermostatic fan	Check for engagement.
	Improper coolant	Verify 50-50 ratio.
	Leaking head gasket	Perform cylinder-leak test.
	Blocked exhaust system	Inspect for obstruction.
	Cracked head or block	Perform cylinder-leak test.

Sometimes failure to start is caused by moisture in the coil or distributor. The only solution is to remove the moisture. Remove the distributor cap and dry the inside. A dry paper towel or rag works well. Or if you have an RV equipped with a generator, use an electric hair dryer to dry components quickly, especially in those hard-to-get-at locations.

■ Carburetor Flooding

Engine flooding is caused by an excessive amount of fuel entering the cylinders, resulting in an engine that is difficult or impossible to start. The situation also causes oil to be washed from the cylinder walls, causing rapid wear of piston rings. Ultimately the oil in the crankcase can become diluted, leading to early engine-bearing failure. Flooding is sometimes a prob-

lem at high altitudes, where gasoline boils more easily; this causes fuel to bubble over into the intake manifold. The most common causes are defective or improperly adjusted carburetor floats, defective needle and seat assemblies, dirty air-cleaner elements, and poorly adjusted carburetor chokes. Here are the procedures to start a flooded engine:

1. Wait 15 minutes before attempting to start a flooded engine. This time will allow some of the fuel in the cylinders to dissipate.
2. *Do not* pump the accelerator pedal. This only worsens the situation by inducing additional fuel into the engine.
3. After 15 minutes, press the accelerator to the floor and hold throttle wide open while cranking the engine. This allows the maximum

amount of air to enter the cylinders while adding a minimum amount of fuel.

4. If the engine still does not start, remove the air-cleaner cover and check the carburetor choke plate. When the engine is warm the choke plate should be open, standing in a vertical position. If it is not open it can be manually propped open and the engine then cranked over. Caution should be exercised here not to crank the engine with the air-cleaner cover off, which can result in a fire should the engine backfire upon starting. If it is stuck closed, the most likely cause is dirty or bent linkage or a defective choke-control unit. Commercially available carburetor cleaners can be used to clean dirty linkage. If this does not cure the problem, the control unit should be replaced and the choke readjusted.

■ Vapor Lock

Vapor lock is the opposite of flooding: no fuel is reaching the carburetor. This condition is common during warm weather when the fuel in the pump or lines becomes so hot that the fuel vaporizes and fails to reach the carburetor in sufficient amounts to allow the engine to function. Some RV engines are chronic when it comes to vapor lock.

1. Make sure all fuel lines are routed away from heat sources, especially exhaust components. If it is impossible to route lines away from heat sources, they should be protected by a shield.
2. An electric fuel pump mounted as near the fuel tank as possible and fitted with ⅜-inch-diameter hose barbs will keep the engine's mechanical pump supplied with sufficient fuel to reduce the incidence of vapor lock.
3. If vapor lock does occur, pull well off the road and allow the engine to cool. Pouring cool water over fuel lines and pump will cause the fuel to condense back to liquid form.
4. Fuel tanks must be properly vented either through the filler cap or by the evaporative emission system to allow air to enter the tank as fuel is drawn from it. If the tank cannot vent, the resulting vacuum will cause the engine to starve for fuel.
5. Proper maintenance of fuel filters (see page 210) will assure an adequate supply of fuel to the carburetor.

Electric Fuel Pumps as a Remedy for Vapor Lock

Vapor-lock problems can be difficult to correct, but the installation of an auxiliary fuel pump at the rear of the vehicle near the fuel tank is often an effective solution (see Figure 13.5). Since the engine-mounted fuel pump must draw fuel by suction from the fuel tank at the rear and lift it to the carburetor, the slightest bit of vapor developing in the fuel lines due to excessive heat will cause the pump to lose suction and fail to pump. An electric pump mounted near the tank is not as susceptible to heat absorption and will force a steady column of fuel to the suction side of the engine's mechanical fuel pump. Selection of a quality electric pump that will provide sufficient volume without restricting fuel is important. Installation should include ⅜-inch (inside diameter) fuel hose and connection barbs, an oil-pressure safety switch that will not allow the pump to operate if the engine stops running, and a pressure regulator that will not allow the pump pressure to exceed 5 psi.

The long-recommended Carter P-4070 pump had experienced a decline in quality at the time of this writing, making it a less-than-desirable choice, but the problem supposedly has been corrected. Two other brands to consider are the Holley Model 12-801 pump with a Holley 12-803 pressure regulator and the AC Delco pump Model EP 12S-6472381. The AC Delco and Carter pumps do not require the use of a pressure regulator.

Installing Electric Fuel Pumps The installation procedure for electric fuel pumps is as follows:

1. Select suitable mounting location as close as possible to the fuel tank. The pump must be mounted below the level of the tank.
2. Make sure that the pump and any fuel lines are not near any exhaust component that would induce heat into the fuel.
3. Drill mounting holes in the vehicle frame as recommended in the electric-pump manufacturer's instructions.
4. The vehicle's existing fuel line must be cut and the pump spliced in, using ⅜-inch fuel hose and connection barbs. If a pressure regulator is used, it should be installed at the electric pump's outlet.

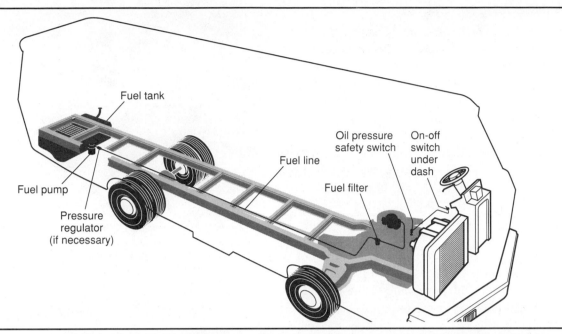

■ FIGURE 13.5 ■
Installation of an electric fuel pump should be as close to the fuel tank as possible. An on-off switch located under the dash and an oil pressure safety switch should be included in the installation.

5. An oil-pressure-sensitive switch must be installed on the vehicle's engine. The switch must be a "normally open" type that closes the switch contacts when oil pressure is detected.

6. Connect a wire of the proper gauge as recommended by the pump manufacturer to one contact of the switch.

7. Connect another wire with an in-line fuse of the proper amp rating from the other contact of the oil-pressure switch to a 12-volt DC circuit that is energized when the ignition switch is turned to the "on" position.

8. If a pressure regulator is used, a fuel-pressure gauge connected at the suction side of the mechanical pump should be used to set the pressure at 5 psi. Follow the regulator manufacturer's procedure for setting pressure. It is important to check pressure at the mechanical pump since checking the pressure at the electric pump and regulator will give a false reading. There will be a pressure drop due to line friction between the electric and mechanical pumps.

9. Start engine and check for leaks at all connections.

■ Defective Starter and/or Solenoid

Starters seldom are the cause of failure to start, although some engines have been known to ruin starters on a regular basis. If the starter is suspected, here are the steps to diagnose the problem:

1. Make sure the battery is fully charged and all terminal connections are clean and tight. A starter draws a very high amperage load; a marginal battery or poor terminal connections will not produce enough power to crank the engine.

2. If the starter motor spins but the engine does not turn over, the problem is in the starter-drive mechanism or the flywheel ring gear.

3. If the engine cranks slowly, and it is determined that the battery is fully charged and has clean, tight terminal connections, the problem could be caused in cold weather by too-high engine oil viscosity. Other causes may be starter drag caused by a worn starter motor or a defective starter solenoid.

Troubleshooting the Starter

As underhood temperatures soar, the starter and the starter solenoid absorb heat. When electrical components soak up heat, their internal resistance increases. If the battery, cables, and connections are not in perfect condition, the initial power requirement of a hot starter and solenoid may be more than the system can deliver. The problem is called, fittingly enough, "hot start." Battery cables should be the heaviest gauge possible, terminals should be kept clean, and if hot starts have been a problem, the starter should be replaced with a heavy-duty type that is free of aluminum parts, which conduct heat at a faster rate than cast iron and steel.

General Motors vehicles utilize a starter solenoid relay that is mounted on the starter (Figure 13.6). This design is especially susceptible to the hot-start problem. One remedy is to bypass the solenoid and install a fenderwell-mounted Ford relay (Figure 13.7). This removes the relay from the high-heat condition on the starter to a cooler location so that it is not affected by excessive heat gain.

■ Ignition Timing

Proper ignition timing is vital to engine performance and economy (Figure 13.8). Timing can be set accurately with a precision timing light. Timing settings vary widely among engine types, sizes, and year of manufacture. The correct setting can be found on the underhood emission sticker or by checking in a service manual for the model year and displacement of

■ FIGURE 13.7
Ford uses a fender-mounted starter solenoid that fares much better in hot temperatures. GM engines can be retrofitted with this type of solenoid.

■ FIGURE 13.8
Accessibility of timing marks in some vehicles is sometimes poor, but here the timing mark is fairly easy to view.

■ FIGURE 13.6
The GM starter solenoid is located on the starter, which makes it susceptible to hot-start problems.

engine. In some electronic fuel-injected engines, timing is controlled by the on-board computer and should not be set by the consumer.

It is often necessary to use a specially shaped tool called a *distributor wrench* to loosen the hold-down bolt because of poor accessibility to the bolt (Figure 13.9). One rule to remember: Rotating the distributor in the same direction that the distributor shaft turns will retard the timing; rotating the distributor in the opposite direction of shaft rotation will advance the timing (Figure 13.10).

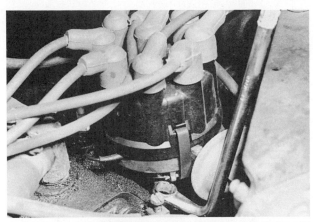

■ **FIGURE 13.9** ■

A distributor wrench is the best tool for loosening the hold-down bolt on the distributor.

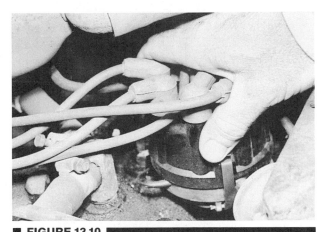

■ **FIGURE 13.10** ■

The distributor is turned to adjust the timing; rotation in the same direction of the distributor shaft retards timing.

Setting the Timing

To set engine timing:

1. Make sure crankshaft pulley is clean and timing marks are visible.
2. Connect timing light to the battery and number 1 spark-plug cable.
3. Loosen hold-down bolt until distributor moves under moderate pressure. Remove the vacuum hose that leads to the distributor-advance diaphragm and plug it (most engines).
4. Make sure all wires are clear of belts and fan; start engine and allow to idle at factory-recommended speed (off choke).
5. Aim light at timing marker. Make small corrections by moving the distributor slightly until the correct timing setting lines up with the marker (Figure 13.11).

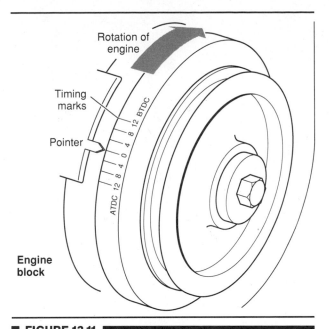

■ **FIGURE 13.11** ■

Once the timing setting marks line up with the pointer, the distributor must be tightened and timing rechecked.

6. Tighten distributor hold-down bolt and check setting again; repeat if the setting changed when the hold-down bolt was tightened.

■ Installing Spark Plugs

An engine's fuel economy and power potential are only as good as the spark plugs' ability to ignite the fuel in the cylinder (Figure 13.12). Spark plugs are inexpensive and their installation is not beyond the abilities of the do-it-yourselfer, although some engines are shoehorned into a very tight compartment, making plug changing a bit of a chore. Here are the necessary steps:

1. Purchase name-brand plugs that are recommended for the engine year and displacement. Many times this can be found on the engine emission sticker, in the owner's manual, or by asking an auto-parts dealer.
2. The engine should be cool.
3. Use only a proper-size spark-plug socket to remove plugs (Figure 13.13).
4. Pull off spark-plug cables by the boots; do not pull on the cables (Figure 13.14). A tool called a *boot puller* is available at auto-parts stores. Don't use pliers; they will cut the plug-cable boots, causing electrical leaks. It's a

■ **FIGURE 13.12**

Spark plugs can tell an owner the condition of the engine in several ways. (*a*) This is a nearly normal plug except for some ash buildup from additives in the fuel. (*b*) A broken electrode is caused by severe detonation. (*c*) Heavy residue buildup is due to excessive oil consumption. (*d*) Normal burning plug has no residue buildup and electrode will burn a light-colored tan. Gap has widened slightly in this plug. (*e*) Wet look of built-up oil is a sure indication that engine was using excessive oil. (*f*) Over-rich fuel mixtures or defective spark plug cable can cause plug to burn a dry flat-black color. (*g*) Gap bridging is caused by dirt that has entered the air intake, internal engine defects, or excessive oil consumption.

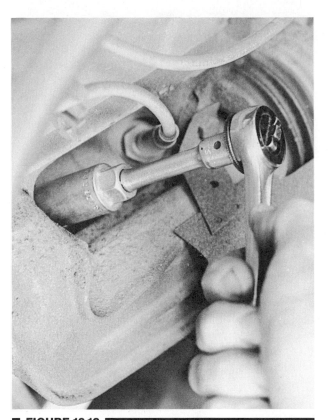

■ **FIGURE 13.13** ▬▬▬▬▬▬
A proper size socket must be used to remove spark plugs.

■ **FIGURE 13.15** ▬▬▬▬▬▬
Before removing spark plugs, clean the area with compressed air to avoid dirt from dropping into the cylinder.

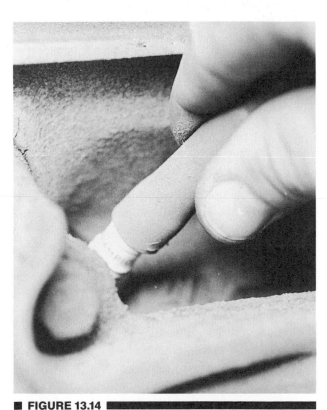

■ **FIGURE 13.14** ▬▬▬▬▬▬
Spark-plug cables should be pulled off by the boots, otherwise the connector can become damaged.

good idea to mark each cable as to its proper cylinder location. Failure to return plug cables to their respective spark plugs will cause the engine to run roughly or fail to start.

5. Using compressed air, blow off dirt from around the spark-plug base (Figure 13.15). A short length of vacuum hose can be aimed at the plug base while you blow through if compressed air is not available.

6. Spark plugs should be gapped to manufacturer's specifications. If there is a range of gap openings recommended, set them to the narrower setting; the gaps tend to open as the plugs wear.

7. Inspect plug seating surface on the cylinder head; any dirt, grease, or debris should be removed.

8. Thread new plugs into the cylinder head. Be careful that cross-threading does not occur.

9. Torque plugs to 20 foot-pounds.

10. Install spark-plug cables to the proper spark plugs.

■ Oil and Filter Changes

Changing the engine oil and filter, one of the most important maintenance procedures to prolong the life of an RV engine, is also easy and cheap to do in your own backyard. Use only top-quality oil and filters; bargain-basement lubricants may do more harm than good in the long run. Use only SF- or SG-rated oils for gas engines and CD-rated oils for diesels. (The new SG-rated oils are also rated CD for diesel use.) Follow the manufacturer's viscosity recommendations for the ambient outdoor temperatures you expect to encounter. Generally, 20W-50 works well for summer use and 10W-30 or 5W-30 for cold (consistently below 32°F) winter driving. Engine oil and filter changes can be accomplished by following these simple steps:

1. Check the owner's manual for the engine-oil capacity with a filter change. Purchase the correct quantity of oil and the correct oil filter for the engine.
2. Operate the engine until it is fully warmed. Most vehicles require 7 to 10 miles of driving to heat the oil in the crankcase.
3. With a proper-fitting wrench or socket, loosen the drain plug on the oil pan (Figure 13.16). **CAUTION:** This oil is hot; it can cause burns.

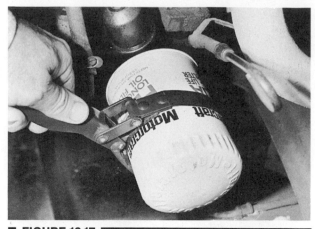

■ **FIGURE 13.17** ■
There are many tool configurations for removing oil filters.

4. Drain the oil into a suitable container for proper disposal. Used oil is accepted at most service stations for recycling.
5. While oil is draining, remove the oil filter with a filter wrench (Figure 13.17).
6. Clean the oil-filter base on the engine block with a rag. Make sure that the oil filter's O-ring gasket came off with the old filter and did not stick to the filter base on the engine.
7. Wipe a thin film of clean oil on the gasket of the new filter and screw it into place. Fill the oil filter with fresh oil if it mounts vertically to the engine and hand tighten with a three-quarter turn after the gasket contacts the filter base.
8. Next, replace the drain plug in the oil pan and tighten snugly.
9. Fill the crankcase with the proper number of quarts of oil and replace the fill cap.
10. Start the engine. Watch the oil-pressure gauge or light; if pressure is not attained after 15 to 20 seconds, shut off the engine before damage can be done. If pressure does not build, check for leakage. It is rare that the oil pressure fails to return after an oil change, but if it does fail, have a professional check the system before running the engine.
11. If the oil pressure is confirmed, check for any external leaks around the drain plug and filter gasket while the engine is running to assure that the job is leak free.
12. Repeat this oil-changing routine every 3,000 miles or according to the schedule in your owner's manual for severe service.

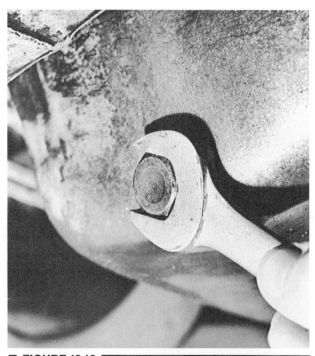

■ **FIGURE 13.16** ■
A proper fitting wrench or socket must be used to remove oil-pan drain plugs or the plug head can be stripped.

■ Cooling System Service

The cooling system must be in top shape to perform properly. With frequent inspection of hoses and belts and a regular coolant-change program, overheating is not likely to occur. Belts and hoses should be inspected frequently and replaced every four years or 50,000 miles. Coolant should be changed every year or 15,000 miles. Here is how to drain, flush, and refill the cooling system:

1. Purchase and install a simple backflush device in the heater hose. This device is found at most auto-parts facilities and makes cooling-system maintenance very easy. It is inexpensive, can be installed permanently in a few minutes, and enables a garden hose to do the flushing.
2. Open the petcock on the bottom of the radiator and allow coolant to start draining.
3. Remove radiator cap (coolant will drain faster) and inspect rubber gasket for defects.
4. Remove the lower radiator hose from the radiator.
5. Connect a garden hose to the backflush device and flush the engine block (Figure 13.18).
6. Run clean water through the radiator to flush.
7. Connect lower radiator hose and remove the garden hose from the backflushing device.
8. Consult the owner's manual to determine the total capacity of the cooling system.

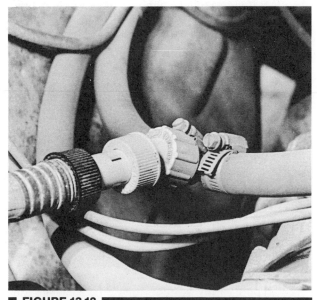

■ **FIGURE 13.18** ■
Simple backflushing devices that utilize garden hoses are available in most auto-parts stores.

9. Fill 50% of the system's capacity with ethylene glycol coolant; fill to capacity with water.
10. Run the engine until it reaches full operating temperature and recheck the level of the coolant in the system. Add a 50-50 mixture of water to coolant to top off the system.

The Transmission

The *transmission* transmits the entire drive force exerted by the engine to the rear differential assembly, and ultimately to the rear wheels. RV service should be considered severe; whether it is in a motorhome or a tow vehicle, the transmission undergoes a tortuous routine.

■ Description and Identification

Transmission configurations include three-speed automatic, four-speed overdrive automatic, three-speed standard shift, four-speed standard shift, and five-speed overdrive standard shift. The vehicle owner's manual will contain information on the type of transmission, service requirements, oil change intervals, and type of oil that should be used.

Because RVs place such heavy demands on the transmission, the oil should be changed at least every 25,000 miles, whether the transmission is standard or automatic. Heat is the main enemy of the automatic transmission. An automatic transmission should be outfitted with either a factory or aftermarket external oil cooler that is properly sized according to the gross vehicle weight of the motorhome or gross combined weight of a tow car/trailer. Standard transmissions do not require oil coolers because they do not generate excessive heat.

Transmission repair should be left to the experts, although the average RVer can perform service routines at home with a little effort.

TROUBLESHOOTING the Automatic Transmission

Problem	Possible Cause	Correction
Transmission overheats	Low fluid level	Replenish fluid.
	Foaming/overfill fluid	Lower fluid level.
	Low engine coolant	Replenish coolant.
	Inadequate oil cooler	Install larger cooler.
	Blocked oil cooler	Clear debris.
	Bent or crimped oil line	Repair restriction.
	Overloaded vehicle	Reduce load.
Transmission slippage	Low fluid level	Replenish fluid.
	Fluid level too high	Lower fluid level.
	Dirty fluid and filter	Change fluid/filter.
	Improper linkage adjustment	Seek professional help.
	Improper internal adjustment	Seek professional help.
	Defective internal parts	Seek professional help.
Incorrect shift points	Low fluid level	Replenish fluid.
	Incorrect linkage adjustment	Seek professional help.
	Incorrect internal adjustment	Seek professional help.
	Defective internal parts	Seek professional help.
Failure to engage a gear	Low fluid level	Replenish fluid.
	Dirty fluid and filter	Change fluid/filter.
	Improper linkage adjustment	Seek professional help.
	Defective internal parts	Seek professional help.

■ Transmission Service and Repair

Although transmission repairs are beyond the capabilities of the backyard mechanic, service is definitely not. Service neglect is the single largest cause of transmission failure; by changing the oil and filters frequently (25,000-mile intervals), transmission life can be improved significantly.

Be sure to check the owner's manual to find the correct type of lubricant for each particular transmission. There are many different requirements depending on the year, make, and model of transmission. The use of incorrect fluid can have a detrimental effect on the operation and life of the transmission.

Changing Automatic Transmission Fluid

The steps for changing automatic transmission fluid are:

1. Determine the refill capacity of the transmission. Repair and owner's manuals include these specifications. Most transmissions do not have a provision for draining the torque converter. Even though the capacity may be over 10 quarts, the most that can be drained from the pan in a fluid change is about 4 to 5 quarts.
2. Purchase the proper type and amount of oil required to do the job, plus one quart. This extra quart is ''just in case'' and can be carried in your RV as a spare.
3. Purchase a transmission pan gasket and new filter element for the transmission. Many auto supply stores sell transmission-oil-change kits that contain the gasket and filter plus a set of instructions.

TROUBLESHOOTING the Standard Transmission

Problem	Possible Cause	Correction
Slippage	Improper clutch adjustment	Adjust pedal free-play to 1 to 2 inches.
	Oil on clutch lining	Determine cause of oil.
	Worn clutch lining	Seek professional help.
Noise in neutral (clutch engaged)	Worn bearings	Seek professional help.
	Low oil level	Replenish oil.
Noise in neutral (clutch disengaged)	Defective throw-out bearing	Seek professional help.
	Low oil level	Replenish oil.
Noise while driving (all gears)	Defective gears/bearings	Seek professional help.
Noise while driving (selected gear)	Defective single gear	Seek professional help.
Hard shifting	Wrong oil in transmission	Replace with correct oil.
	Improper clutch adjustment	Adjust clutch.
Jumps out of gear	Worn syncro-mesh/gears	Seek professional help.

4. While the transmission is warm, drain by removing the pan and allowing the fluid to empty into a large container that will contain all of the spillage (Figure 13.19). **Note:** Dispose of used oil properly; most service stations will accept used oil for recycling.
5. Remove the old filter element and clean both gasket surfaces on the pan and the transmission case (Figure 13.20).
6. Install new filter element and gasket; tighten pan bolts evenly in a crisscross pattern to prevent distortion of the pan.
7. Refill the transmission with all but one of the number of quarts recommended.
8. Start the engine and allow it to idle for a few minutes; shift the gear selector through all gear ranges, then return it to ''park.''
9. Check oil level on the dipstick. If any is needed, add only small amounts at a time until the correct level is attained. Overfilling the transmission will cause oil to foam and possibly spew from the dipstick/fill tube onto hot engine parts.

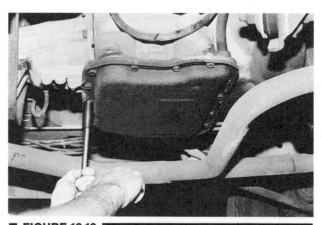

■ FIGURE 13.19 ■
If the transmission pan does not have a drain plug, it must be removed to allow the fluid to empty into a bucket.

■ FIGURE 13.20 ■
The old filter must be replaced when servicing the transmission.

Changing Standard Transmission Fluid

The procedure for standard transmissions is much the same except that refilling will require an oil gun to force oil into the fill hole on the side of the transmission. These are available at auto-parts stores.

1. Purchase the correct amount and type of oil recommended in the owner's manual.
2. Operate the vehicle until the transmission is warm. (Driving 5 to 10 miles is adequate.)
3. Remove the drain plug in the bottom of the transmission, allowing the oil to drain into a container.
4. After draining is complete, install drain plug and remove the fill plug on the side of the transmission.
5. Add the proper amount of oil until it seeps out of the hole or fills the transmission.
6. Tighten the fill plug in its hole.

Universal Joints

Universal joints (U-joints) are the links between the transmission, driveshaft, and rear-axle assembly. U-joints provide a flexible connection and allow the rear suspension to move up and down, improving the quality of ride. Many U-joints are permanently lubricated and require no service. If a joint fails however, the new U-joint should be equipped with a grease fitting. This fitting will allow clean grease to be added, extending the life of the joint.

■ Checking the U-Joint

If you suspect a U-joint may be defective, seek professional advice. Replacement of these joints is not difficult, but if not done precisely, severe driveline vibration can result. Here is a brief inspection/service routine you can perform:

☑ CHECKLIST

☐ Every other engine-oil change, check the driveshaft's U-joints by grasping the driveshaft near the U-joint. By using a back-and-forth-pushing action perpendicular to each of the U-joint's crosses, check for any play in the assembly. There should be little or none. Many RVs, especially motorhomes and long-wheelbase pickup trucks, will have a two-piece driveshaft supported by a center bearing mounted in a rubber collar. The

■ FIGURE 13.21 ■
U-joints that are equipped with fittings should be greased at the same time the suspension is being lubricated.

rubber collar will move, giving a floating action to the driveshaft. This is normal, but there should be no movement between the bearing itself and the collar or driveshaft.

☐ Using a grease gun, pump enough approved chassis lubricant into the U-joint so that the old grease is expelled past the seals and fresh grease just starts to appear (Figure 13.21).

☐ If your U-joints do not have a grease fitting, they are not designed to be lubricated.

Suspension Components

In recent years, many of the familiar suspension components that required lubrication have been replaced with permanently lubricated parts (Figure 13.22). All rear-suspension pivot points are rubber mounted and require no periodic maintenance. Even in front suspensions, the grease fitting is becoming a thing of the past. However, most heavy-duty vehicles still equip the *ball joints, tie-rod ends*, and *control-arm bushings* with grease fittings. A good practice is to lube these components at 10,000-mile intervals (Figure 13.23a and b). Most fittings are lubricated until fresh grease appears at the fitting. This practice forces out old grease, water, and road debris. You may discover that tie-rod ends and ball joints have a rubber bellows seal that does not allow grease to escape. If the bellows seems to contain grease, do not lubricate the fitting. The bellows may rupture if it is too full. This will allow entry of water and dirt, causing early failure of the joint. The bellows should appear to have a slight bulge and feel spongy when depressed with a finger.

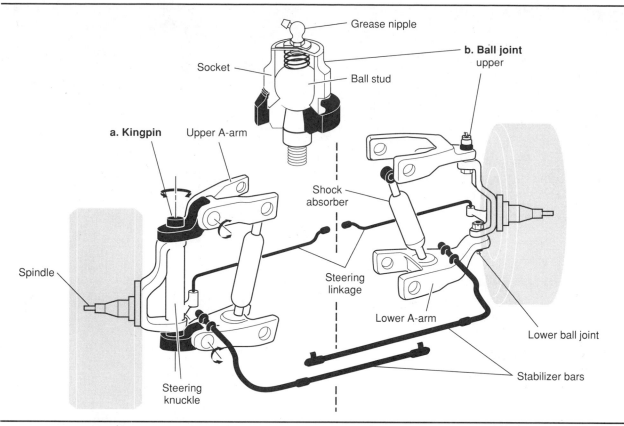

■ FIGURE 13.22 ■

Kingpins (*a*) or ball joints (*b*) are used in most suspension configurations in trucks, vans and sport-utility vehicles. Ball joints must be greased periodically.

■ FIGURE 13.23A ■

Before attaching the grease gun, the zerk fitting must be wiped clean of all old grease and dirt.

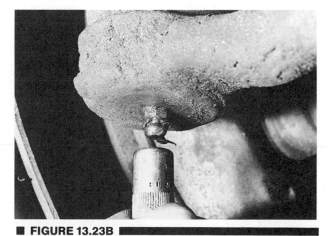

■ FIGURE 13.23B ■

Lubricate fitting only if the bellows seem low on grease; allowing the bellows to rupture invites water and dirt contamination.

There are two types of grease suitable for chassis lubrication. One is a general-purpose chassis grease that has a lithium base. This dark brown, slightly translucent grease has a high resistance to water wash-off and an excellent load-carrying capacity.

A grease with slightly better characteristics is a lithium-based "moly" grease. The addition of molybdenum disulfide, extreme pressure additives, and oxidation inhibitors makes this black-colored grease a good choice for heavily loaded components.

Rear Differential

The *rear differential assembly* consists of a housing that holds the rear wheel bearings and drive axles, ring and pinion gears, and differential side gears. The pinion gear is connected to the driveshaft and it, in turn, drives the ring gear that connects the differential side gears to the axles. The side gears allow one wheel to rotate faster than another during turning maneuvers so that the tires will not scrub.

The differential housing contains all these parts, as well as the gear oil that lubricates the entire assembly. Check your owner's manual for the type of gear oil required.

■ Changing the Differential Oil

Many manufacturers do not make a provision for draining the differential oil. The oil can only be removed by using a suction gun or by pulling the cover from the rear of the housing if it is so equipped. For RV service, changing the differential oil every 50,000 miles is recommended. Here are the steps:

1. Purchase enough of the correct grade and weight oil as noted in your owner's manual.
2. Drive the vehicle until the differential oil is warmed, about 5 to 10 miles.
3. If there is not a removable cover, the oil must be extracted through the fill hole by a suction gun. Remove all the oil possible (Figure 13.24).
4. If the cover is removable, you'll need to purchase a gasket to reinstall the cover so that leaks will not occur.
5. Remove the cover and drain the oil thoroughly (Figure 13.25).
6. Clean the cover gasket and housing surfaces so the new gasket will seal properly.
7. Replace the cover with the new gasket and tighten bolts evenly in a crisscross pattern (Figure 13.26).
8. Refill the differential until oil is level with the bottom of the fill hole.
9. Replace the plug.

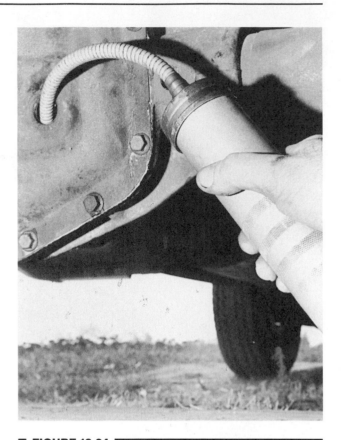

■ FIGURE 13.24 ■
Suction guns are used to extract oil from differential housings that do not have removable covers.

■ FIGURE 13.25 ■
Differential oil can be drained by loosening the top bolts, removing the bottom bolts, and prying the cover open slightly.

■ FIGURE 13.26 ■

After cleaning the old gasket material, use a new gasket and tighten the differential housing bolts evenly.

Wheel Bearings

Wheel bearings consist of precision-ground, hardened-steel, cylindrical rollers that are held together by a steel cage. These rollers rotate against a set of hardened-steel races. There is one race installed in the wheel hub (called the outer race) and one installed in the center of the roller/cage unit (called the inner race). It is upon these rollers and races that the entire weight of the vehicle is carried. The metallurgical quality of the steels used in bearing construction is of the highest quality. Combined with a clean, top-quality bearing grease, the lifespan of wheel bearings may exceed that of the vehicle itself (see Figure 13.27).

■ Troubleshooting Wheel Bearings

The first sign that a bearing is failing is a distinct grinding sound from a wheel assembly. The noise is usually noticed at low speeds first; as the condition of the bearing worsens, the noise is also heard at higher speeds. Wheel-bearing noises can be isolated from other noises because the sound of a defective wheel bearing keeps time with the rate of wheel rotation. Some tire defects may also show similar symptoms; therefore, check the tires for defects before delving into the wheel-bearing assemblies.

If you suspect a defective wheel bearing, drive only far enough to have the bearing replaced. Trying to make it over a few more miles may destroy expensive wheel hubs, spindles, and brake components.

■ Servicing and Repairing Wheel Bearings

A good maintenance program should consist of periodic cleaning and lubrication (every 25,000 to 30,000 miles). It is most convenient to perform wheel-bearing maintenance at brake inspection or service intervals when the bearings are removed to service the brakes. Wheel-bearing service can be done at home by the do-it-yourselfer, equipped with the proper tools. But be forewarned that access to bearings in motorhomes and heavy-duty pickups requires

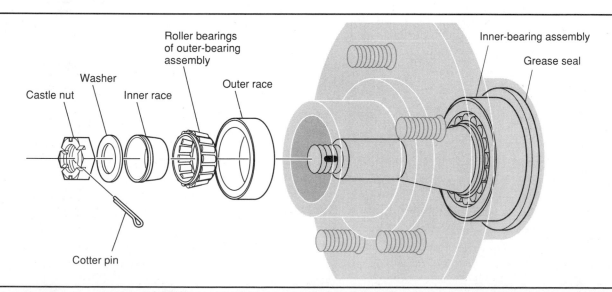

Castle nut • Washer • Inner race • Roller bearings of outer-bearing assembly • Outer race • Cotter pin • Inner-bearing assembly • Grease seal

■ FIGURE 13.27 ■

Exploded view of wheel bearings and races

removal of heavy wheels, tires, brake drums, calipers, and rotors. To service bearings:

1. Jack up the vehicle and use jack stands for safe support.
2. Remove the wheels and tires from the hub assembly.
3. If the vehicle is equipped with disc brakes, the caliper assemblies must be removed to allow the rotor to be slipped off the spindle.
4. Pull off the spindle dust cover to expose the bearing retainer nut and the locking cotter pin (Figure 13.28).
5. Remove the cotter pin and the locking nut, which will allow the outer wheel bearing and washer to be removed (Figure 13.29). Make sure that you have a clean rag to put the bearing on after removal.
6. The brake hub and drum (with disc brakes, the rotor) should now come off with a slight wiggling motion.
7. Turn the drum or rotor upside down over a clean rag or paper and drive the inner bearing and seal out of the hub with a hardwood dowel. (Using a metal device may damage the bearing beyond repair.) Keep left-side and right-side bearings with their respective hubs. A wear pattern develops differently on each bearing and matching race; swapping bearings and races could lead to early failure.
8. Meticulously clean the bearings, hub, retaining washer, and dust cap in cleaning solvent. It's best to clean the bearings separately, in solvent free of grit or grime (Figure 13.30).
9. Dry the components with a clean, lint-free rag. Make sure that all solvent is removed from the bearings since it will dilute the fresh grease that will be used to pack the bearings.
10. Carefully inspect the bearings and hub races for any sign of defects. Chips, scratches, and discoloration warrant replacement of bearings.
11. Bearings should be repacked with a top-quality wheel-bearing grease (Figure 13.31). Do not use standard chassis lubricants as they will liquefy at high temperatures.
12. To pack the bearings, force grease between the rollers and the inner bearing race surface. Place a small amount of grease in your hand

■ FIGURE 13.28 ■
Bearing retainer nut and cotter pin are exposed when the spindle dust cover is removed.

■ FIGURE 13.29 ■
The cotter pin must be pulled before removing the locking nut. Make sure a clean rag is used to store parts.

and force the bearing side against the grease so that hydraulic pressure will push the grease between the rollers. Continue around the entire circumference of the bearing until grease oozes out the top side. All bearings should be packed in this manner.

13. Wipe a layer of grease on the inside of the hub, filling the cavity and covering the bearing races with a light coating. Place the inner bearing against its race and carefully install a new grease seal by tapping it against its seat; use a hardwood block to prevent damage.

■ FIGURE 13.30 ■

Bearings should be cleaned carefully and dried thoroughly before installing new grease.

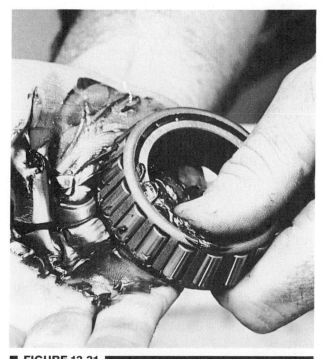

■ FIGURE 13.31 ■

When packing a bearing by hand, make sure all the gaps are fully filled with high-quality grease.

14. Place a light coating of grease on the new seal lip and install the hub/bearing assembly on the clean spindle.

15. Push the outer bearing into place and install retaining washer and nut.

16. Bearing-adjustment methods vary between manufacturers. If you use the following method (General Motors), it will work for virtually all vehicles:

    a. Tighten the spindle nut to 12 foot-pounds while turning the wheel assembly forward by hand to fully seat the bearings. This will remove excess grease from between the rollers that could cause excessive wheel-bearing play later.

    b. Back off the nut until the "just loose" position.

    c. Hand-tighten the spindle nut. Loosen the spindle nut until either hole lines up with a slot in the nut (no more than half-flat).

    d. Install a new cotter pin. Bend the ends of the cotter pin against the nut. Cut off any extra length so that the ends will not interfere with the dust cap.

    e. Measure the looseness of the hub assembly. There will be from .001 to .005 inch of end-play when properly adjusted.

    f. Install dust cap on the hub.

17. Reinstall the tires and wheels, torquing the lug nuts to the factory-recommended setting. After driving 40 or 50 miles, check the nuts again; loose lug nuts can cause wheel damage and possible wheel loss.

18. Torque values for studs are as follows:

    $\frac{1}{2}$-inch studs: 75 to 100 foot-pounds

    $\frac{9}{16}$-inch studs (single wheels): 90 to 120 foot-pounds

    $\frac{9}{16}$-inch studs (dual wheels): 110 to 140 foot-pounds

    $\frac{5}{8}$-inch studs: 130 to 180 foot-pounds

Tires

Tires are a marvel of today's engineering and manufacture. When you consider the job the tire must do—support weight, provide traction, stability, and a safe, smooth ride—it's a wonder they survive as well as they do. Tires are easy to maintain; you get a report of their condition every time you look at them. This allows you to spot trouble early.

■ Reading Your Tires

A tire's sidewall contains a wealth of information. Read the details that must appear on every tire by law to determine if the tire is right for your application. Tires are constructed in one of three ways: a bias ply, a bias/belted ply, and belted radial-ply construction. Each type has its advantages and disadvantages. A bias-ply tire has a stiff, strong sidewall but has a higher resistance to rolling; it does not contribute to fuel economy. A bias/belted tire is an improvement over the straight bias version because belts of either polyester or steel add a protective layer to help protect against road-hazard damage. The belts also stabilize the tread surface, allowing for slightly better wear characteristics. Radial-belted tires offer less rolling resistance, which increases overall fuel economy and performance. The belts surrounding the plies serve to protect them from puncture damage. But radials lack the sidewall strength and stiffness of bias-ply tires, making the sidewalls more vulnerable to damage.

The following information is contained on the sidewall of every tire (Figure 13.32):

Tire size The section width, aspect ratio, speed rating for some automotive applications, construction type (radial or bias), and the wheel-rim diameter.

Load range A letter identification system declares the load-carrying capacity; maximum recommended inflation pressure and maximum load in pounds are stated.

D.O.T. certification This simply means that the tire is certified as being built to Department of Transportation standards. Adjacent to this is the tire's serial number, which, in code, describes the location and date of manufacture.

Tube or tubeless This section spells out whether the tire should be used with a tube or without one.

■ FIGURE 13.32 ■
Load rating designation and weight ratings in pounds and air pressure are marked on the sidewalls of all tires (*top*).
Tire size is clearly marked on the sidewalls (*bottom*).

M+S rating If the letters M+S are molded to the sidewall, this means that the tire meets specifications that qualify it as combination highway, mud, and snow tire.

■ Tire Service and Repair

Tire service and repair should not be attempted by the amateur; your safety is at risk with less-than-perfect tire repairs. But the do-it-yourselfer can perform two important tasks:

1. Regular tire inspections for irregular wear patterns, defects, and inflation pressures.
2. Tire rotation at 5,000-mile intervals.

Inflation pressures should be checked a least once a month, more often if the vehicle is used on a daily basis. The pressure that you carry in your tires should be matched to the load of the vehicle without exceeding the load rating or inflation pressure on the sidewall of the tires.

The best way to determine the load is by weighing your vehicle. Motorhomes often operate at near (and some over) the chassis gross vehicle weight rating (GVWR). If in weighing the vehicle one determines that a tire is overloaded, change to a tire of proper load range. If the tire is within its capacity rating, inflation should be set to match the load (see Tables 13.1 and 13.2).

Inflation pressures should be checked and/or changed only when the tires are cold. A tire's pressure may climb 5 to 10 psi after driving some distance since heat causes the air to expand; measuring pressure in a hot tire will give erroneous readings. *Never* bleed air from a hot tire; it will then be operating in an underinflated condition. Light-truck tires with the LT designation stamped on the sidewall may be overinflated up to 10 psi over the manufacturer's recommendation.

■ TABLE 13.1

Tire Capacity Rating

Bias and Radial Tire Size and Load Limits (Lbs)

Tire Size	Tire Rev. Per Mile	Load Range	Inflation Pressure–PSI										
			30	35	40	45	50	55	60	65	70	75	80
Bias Tires Used As Singles													
7.50-16	652	C	1620	1770	1930	2060							
7.50-16	652	D	1620	1770	1930	2060	2190	2310	2440				
7.50-16	652	E	1620	1770	1930	2060	2190	2310	2440	2560	2670	2780	
8-19.5	652	D, E					2110	2270	2410	2540	2680	2800	
8.00-16.5	734	C	1360	1490	1610	1730							
8.00-16.5	734	D	1360	1490	1610	1730	1840	1945	2045				
8.75-16.5	712	D	1570	1720	1850	1990	2110	2240	2350				
8.75-16.5	712	E	1570	1720	1850	1990	2110	2240	2350	2470	2570	2680	
Bias Tires Used As Duals													
7.50-16	652	C	1430	1565	1690	1815							
7.50-16	652	D	1430	1565	1690	1815	1930	2040	2140				
8-19.5	613	D			1850	1990	2110	2230	2350	2460			
8-19.5	613	E			1850	1990	2110	2230	2350	2460	2570	2680	2780
8.00-16.5	734	C	1195	1310	1415	1520							
8.00-16.5	734	D	1195	1310	1415	1520	1620	1710	1800				
Radial Tires Used As Singles													
8R19.5	616	D			2110	2270	2410	2540	2680	2800			
Radial Tires Used As Duals													
8R19.5	616	D	1850	1990	2110	2230	2350	2460					
8.75R-16.5	712	E		1570	1720	1850	1990	2110	2240	2350	2470	2570	2680

Metric Radial Tire Size and Load Limits (Lbs)

Tire Size	Tire Rev. Per Mile	Load Range	Inflation Pressure–PSI						
			36	44	51	58	65	73	80
Metric Radial Tires Used As Singles									
LT215/85R16	682	C	1532	1742	1940				
LT215/85R16	682	D	1532	1742	1940	2127	2315		
LT235/85R16	653	D	1742	1984	2205	2425	2623		
LT235/85R16	653	E	1742	1984	2205	2425	2623	2844	3042
Metric Radial Tires Used As Duals									
LT215/85R16	682	C	1389	1587	1764				
LT215/85R16	682	D	1389	1587	1764	1918	2105		

TROUBLESHOOTING the Tires

Problem	Possible Cause	Correction
Wear bars showing	Tread worn to unsafe level	Replace tires.
Wearing on inside	Negative camber alignment	Align, increase camber.
	Worn ball joints	Inspect and replace.
	Worn A-arm bushings	Inspect and replace.
Wearing on outside	Positive camber alignment	Align, reduce camber.
	Worn ball joints	Inspect and replace.
	Worn A-arm bushings	inspect and replace.
Wearing in center	Overinflation	Reduce tire pressure.
Wearing on outside	Underinflation	Increase tire pressure.
Cupping or scalloping	Worn shock absorbers	Replace.
	Worn ball joints	Inspect and replace.
	Worn A-arm bushings	Inspect and replace.
	Worn steering components	Inspect and replace.
	Out-of-round tire	Check and replace tire.
	Out-of-round rim	Check and replace rim.
	Imbalanced tire	Balance tires.
	Grabbing brakes	Repair brakes.
	Inaccurate wheel bearing adjustment	Check and adjust.
Feathered wear pattern	Improper toe-in	Align front end.
	Bent suspension component	Inspect and replace.
Bulge in sidewall	Hitting road obstacles	Replace tire.
	Manufacturing defect	Replace tire.
Shaking	Improper balance	Balance tires.
	Out-of-round tire	Replace tire.
	Bent wheel rim	Replace rim.
	Worn suspension parts	Inspect and replace.
	Inaccurate wheel bearing adjustment	Adjust bearings.
	Worn shock absorbers	Replace shocks.
Hard/uneven steering	Low tire pressure	Inflate to correct psi.
	Incorrect front wheel alignment	Align properly.
	Worn suspension components	Inspect and replace.
Vehicle wander	Uneven tire pressure	Inflate to correct psi.
	Incorrect alignment	Align properly.
	Worn suspension parts	Inspect and replace.
	Vehicle overload to one side	Balance vehicle load.

TROUBLESHOOTING *the Tires* (continued)

Problem	Possible Cause	Correction
Squealing	Low inflation pressure	Inflate tires.
	Misalignment	Align properly.
	Differential problem	Inspect differential.
	Wrong load-range tire	Check and correct.
	Defective suspension parts	Inspect and replace.
Losing air	Puncture	Inspect and repair.
	Defective valve stem seal	Replace valve stem.
	Tire bead not seated	Reseat bead.
	Corroded internal rim	Replace rim.
	Flawed tire	Replace tire.
	Dirty rim flanges	Clean or replace rim.

■ TABLE 13.2 ■
Special Trailer Tire Load Ratings for Normal Highway Service

Tire Size	Load limits (pounds per tire) at various cold inflation pressures										
	15	20	25	30	**35**	40	45	**50**	55	60	65
6.00-13 ST	570	675	765	855	**935(B)**	1010	1080	**1150(C)**			
6.50-13 ST	650	770	875	975	**1065(B)**	1150	1235	**1315(C)**			
7.00-13 ST	715	845	965	1075	**1175(B)**	1270	1360	**1450(C)**			
6.45-14 ST	630	745	850	945	**1035(B)**	1120	1200	**1275(C)**			
7.35-14 ST	755	895	1020	1135	**1245(B)**	1345	1440	**1530(C)**			
7.75-14 ST	830	980	1120	1245	**1365(B)**	1475	1580	**1680(C)**			
8.25-14 ST	895	1060	1210	1345	**1470(B)**	1590	1705	**1815(C)**			
8.55-14 ST	980	1155	1320	1465	**1605(B)**	1735	1860	**1975(C)**			
6.85-15 ST	690	815	925	1030	**1130(B)**	1220	1310	**1390(C)**			
7.35-15 ST	780	920	1050	1170	**1280(B)**	1385	1480	**1575(C)**			
7.75-15 ST	830	985	1120	1245	**1365(B)**	1475	1580	**1680(C)**			
8.25-15 ST	905	1070	1220	1355	**1485(B)**	1615	1720	**1825(C)**			
8.55-15 ST	990	1170	1330	1480	**1620(B)**	1755	1880	**2000(C)**	2115	2225	2330(D)
8.85-15 ST	1035	1220	1390	1550	**1695(B)**	1835	1965	**2090(C)**			

Note: Letters in parentheses indicate load range for which **boldface** loads are maximum.

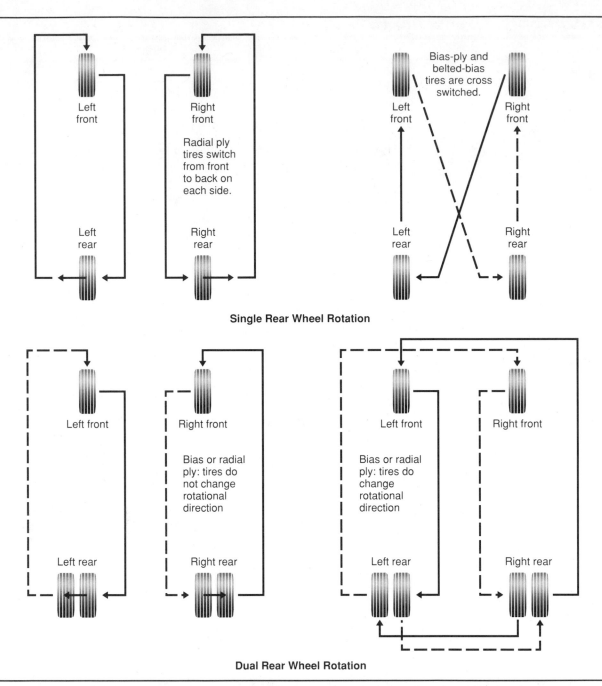

Single Rear Wheel Rotation

Dual Rear Wheel Rotation

■ **FIGURE 13.33** ■
Recommended tire rotations for single rear-wheel vehicles (*top*). Recommended tire rotations for dual rear-wheel vehicles (*bottom*).

A quick walk-around inspection should be made each day before the vehicle is driven. Check tires for odd wear patterns, sidewall defects, foreign objects that may be embedded in the tread, abrasions, and any other damage that may have occurred in the previous day's driving. By making this a regular habit, you'll avoid roadside failures.

Tire rotation is valuable in maximizing tire life. Different wear patterns develop, depending on the service the tire sees. (Drive tires develop patterns that differ from steering tires.) The rotation pattern will depend on the type of tire with which your RV is equipped. It's best to consult the owner's manual for your particular vehicle/chassis for specific recommendations regarding tire rotation (see Figure 13.33).

CHAPTER 14

Hitches

Hitches, and all the associated hardware that goes with them, are designed to connect a tow vehicle and a trailer in such a manner that safe towing results. As in every other aspect of an RV, proper equipment must be selected for the job, and then it must be maintained so it can perform its function successfully.

For conventional trailers, there are two different hitch types: *weight distributing* and *weight carrying*. The names are accurate descriptions of these types of hitches. Fifth-wheel trailers utilize a completely different type of hitch.

A weight-distributing hitch includes spring bars that attach between the ball mount and the trailer frame to distribute the tongue weight evenly to the front and rear axles of the tow vehicle and to all trailer axles (Figure 14.1). If used properly, a weight-distributing hitch maintains the tow vehicle and the trailer at level attitudes even after the full weight of the tongue has been imposed on the hitch. Sway-control devices are commonly used in conjunction with weight-distributing hitches.

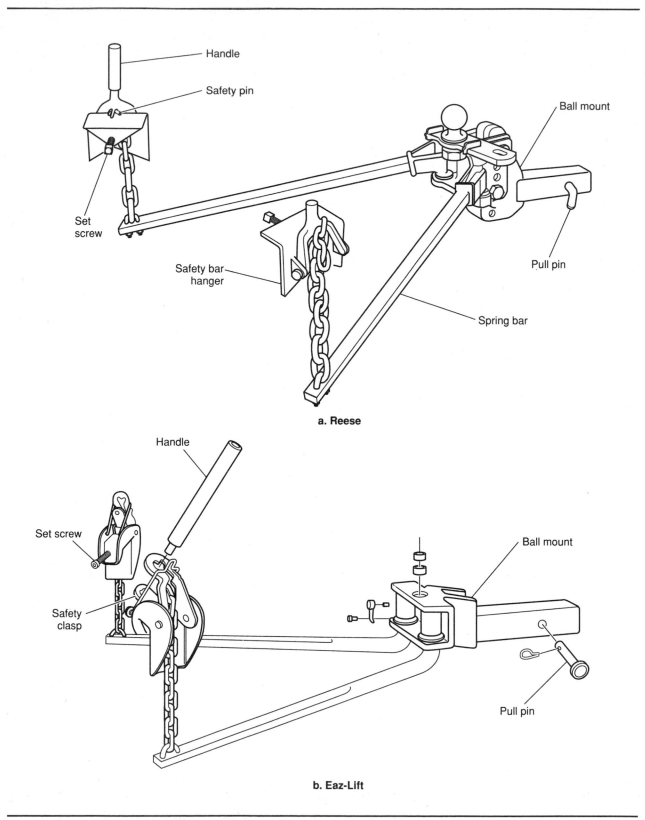

a. Reese

b. Eaz-Lift

■ **FIGURE 14.1** ■
Weight-distributing hitches are designed for towing heavier trailers. Reese (*a*) and Eaz-Lift (*b*) are the major suppliers to the industry.

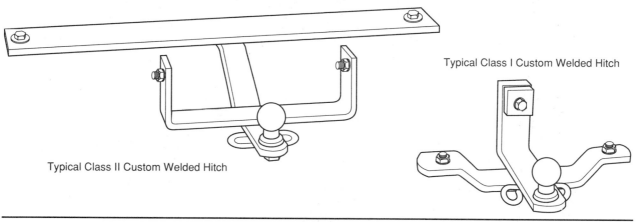

Typical Class I Custom Welded Hitch

Typical Class II Custom Welded Hitch

■ **FIGURE 14.2**

Class I (right) and Class II (left) weight-carrying hitches are available for towing lighter trailers.

A weight-carrying unit is designed to support the full tongue load on the hitch point (see Figure 14.2). Under this condition, the tow vehicle bears the entire weight of the trailer tongue at the point of hitch attachment. If the tongue weight is substantial, the rear of the tow vehicle will be forced downward and the front will rise. This can result in poor handling; weight-carrying hitches are rated only for lightweight towing. Sway-control devices are sometimes used in conjunction with weight-carrying hitches, depending upon the trailer being towed.

A *fifth-wheel hitch* consists of a platform that is installed in the bed of a truck above the rear axle (Figure 14.3). The uppermost part of the hitch is the saddle, which carries the weight of the pin box (the coupling system that is attached to the trailer). This is, in essence, a weight-carrying unit; the full hitch weight of the trailer is borne by the rear of the tow vehicle without being distributed fore and aft by hitch components. However, because the hitch point is centered almost directly above the rear axle, there is none of the leverage on the rear of the tow vehicle that a conventional trailer imposes. Some of the hitch weight is distributed to the front axle, so the tow vehicle maintains a fairly level attitude even though most of weight is being carried on the hitch. Because of the location of the hitch, fifth-wheel trailers can only be towed by pickup trucks with open cargo boxes. Sway-control devices are not necessary and cannot be employed in conjunction with fifth-wheel hitch systems.

Hitch Classifications

There are four classes of hitches. *Class I* is a weight-carrying hitch that is used for towing trailers up to 2,000 pounds gross weight. *Class II* is also a weight-carrying hitch, and it is rated for trailers up to 3,500 pounds. *Class III* can be either a weight-carrying or a weight-distributing hitch, rated for trailers up to 5,000 pounds gross weight. *Class IV* includes both weight-distributing and fifth-wheel hitches, rated for trailers between 5,000 and 10,000 pounds.

Conventional Hitch Hardware

■ Receivers

A conventional hitch platform is secured beneath the rear of the tow vehicle. The rearmost part of the platform is the *receiver*—a section of reinforced square-steel tubing into which the shank of a ball mount is inserted (Figure 14.4).

■ Shanks

For lightweight load-carrying service, there are ball-mount *shanks* made of square-steel tubing, but heavy towing requires solid shanks (Figure 14.5). In both cases, the shank has a hole through it that lines up with holes on opposite sides of the receiver. When the hole in the shank is lined up with those in the receiver, a hitch pin is held in place by a clip inserted through a hole or around a groove in the end of the pin.

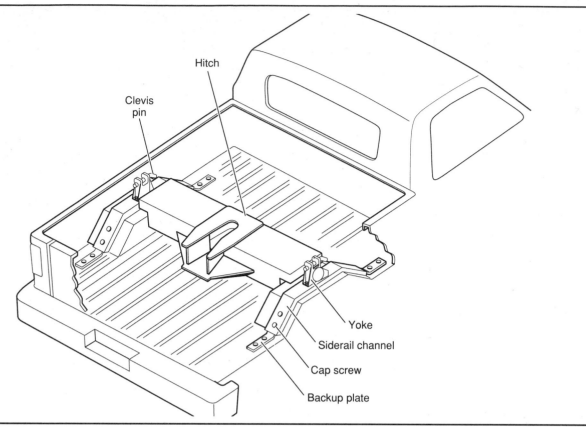

■ **FIGURE 14.3**
A fifth-wheel hitch platform is installed in the bed of the truck, over the rear axle.

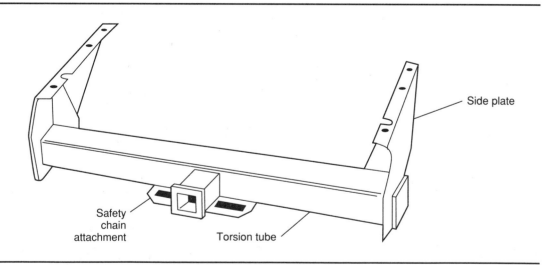

■ **FIGURE 14.4**
Receiver assemblies are secured, preferably using bolts, to the rear of the tow vehicles.

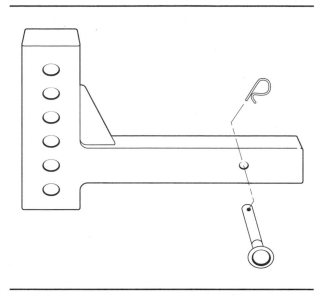

■ **FIGURE 14.5** ▰▰▰▰▰▰▰▰▰▰▰▰▰▰▰▰▰
Solid steel adjustable ball-mount shanks are available for heavy towing service.

■ Ball Mounts

A *ball mount* is attached to the end of the shank (Figure 14.6). Some ball mounts are adjustable to accommodate different styles of trailer tongues and couplers, as well as to permit fine-tuning of the hitch to optimize performance. Once the ball mount has been properly adjusted, it need never be readjusted unless it is to be used with a different tow vehicle or trailer. If no further adjustment is to be needed, the ball mount can be welded in place. However, an adjustable (bolt-together) ball mount offers flexibility for unforseen circumstances.

■ The Ball

A *ball* of appropriate size and rating is installed on the ball mount (Figure 14.7). Balls are available in sizes from 1⅞ inches to 2⁵⁄₁₆ inches, with a variety of risers to elevate the ball above the mount. Balls are rated for loads ranging from 2,000 to 10,000 pounds, but raised balls usually have lower ratings. It is vital that the ball rating be equal to or more than the gross vehicle weight rating (GVWR) of the trailer.

When using a Reese ball mount, if the ball has a 1-inch threaded shank, use bushing No. 55030 to reduce hole size in the ball mount to 1 inch. Place a lockwasher next to the nut. If the ball has a 1¼-inch threaded shank and a standard- (1 inch or more thickness) size nut, place a lockwasher on top of the ball mount. This reduces interference between spring-bar trunnion and ball nut during very tight turns. If the ball has a 1¼-inch threaded shank and thin nut (.72 inch thickness), place the lockwasher next to the nut. Torque the nut to 200 foot-pounds in all cases.

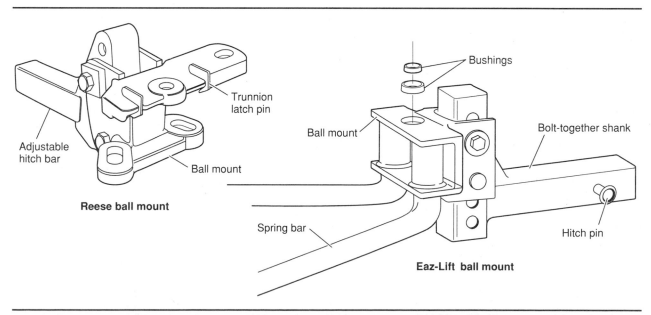

Reese ball mount

Eaz-Lift ball mount

■ **FIGURE 14.6** ▰▰▰▰▰▰▰▰▰▰▰▰▰▰▰▰▰▰▰▰▰▰▰▰▰▰▰▰▰▰▰▰▰
Adjustable ball mounts allow flexibility when setting up ball height and angle.

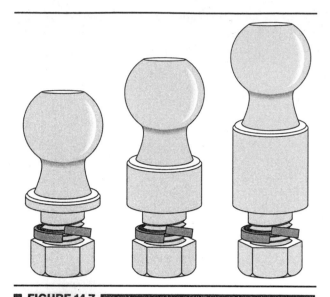

FIGURE 14.7
Hitch balls are available in 1⅞-inch, 2-inch and 2⁵⁄₁₆-inch sizes; heavier trailers require a 2⁵⁄₁₆-inch size.

Spring Bars

Spring bars are used with weight-distributing hitches to spread the tongue weight among all axles of both the trailer and tow vehicle (Figure 14.8). Spring bars are rated in various weight capacities, and the correct ones must be used to allow the load-distributing system to function properly. The rule of thumb is to employ spring bars rated slightly higher (up to 250 pounds more) than the tongue weight. If springs bars of insufficient capacity are used, the rear of the tow vehicle will sag under the weight of the tongue, or the spring bars will need to be overtensioned to maintain a level tow vehicle. If springs bars of excessive capacity are used, the ride will be harsh.

When the spring bars are attached between the ball mount and the trailer frame, tension adjustment is made by selecting different links in the spring-bar chains. This permits fine-tuning of the system for the proper amount of weight transfer. The chains are attached to frame brackets on the trailer tongue, and chain lifters apply tension to the spring bars as they are locked in position.

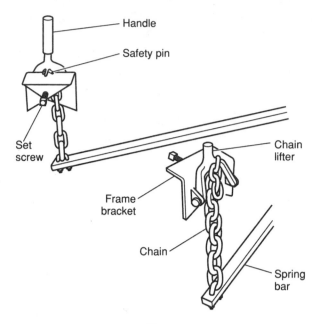

a. Reese

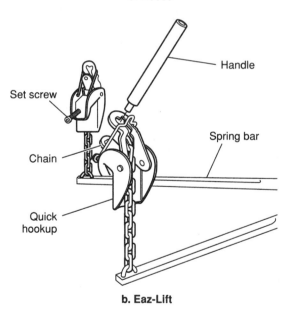

b. Eaz-Lift

FIGURE 14.8
Spring bars are used to spread the hitch weight to the front axle of the tow vehicle and axle(s) of the trailer. Shown here are the Reese *(top)* and the Eaz-Lift *(bottom)*.

■ Safety Chains

The final hitch-system components are the *safety chains* and their attaching devices. It is vital that the chains and hooks (or other attaching devices) are rated higher than the GVWR of the trailer. The chains should run from the trailer tongue to a set of safety-chain loops attached to the receiver. They should be adjusted so they are sufficiently loose to allow sharp cornering without interference, while being tight enough not to drag on the ground. Properly hooked up, the chains should cross beneath the coupler so that if the trailer were to come uncoupled, the tongue would be supported off the ground in the cradle formed by the crossed chains.

Installing the Hitch

In every installation, it is vital to insure that the platform is precisely aligned and solidly attached to the tow vehicle frame. High-grade bolts should be employed, and they should be torqued according to the manufacturer's installation instructions.

■ Conventional Hitches

Conventional hitch platforms are attached to the rearmost section of the tow vehicle frame. The platform can be welded in place, but it is preferable to use Grade 5 or higher bolts to fasten the platform to the frame. Care should be taken by the installer to insure that the strongest points of attachment are used. This is especially important when a custom installation is being performed and the platform is being fabricated on the spot. Most off-the-shelf platforms are designed for specific vehicles, and the bolt holes are predrilled to make installation easy and safe.

■ Fifth-Wheel Hitches

When installing a fifth-wheel hitch, it is important to bolt the platform directly to the tow vehicle frame rather than simply attaching it to the sheet-metal cargo box. Prior to installation of a fifth-wheel hitch, the height of the hitch point must be determined. Adjustment should be made to allow a minimum of 5½ inches of clearance at the closest points between

the top of the truck bed and the bottom of the trailer. Some applications (short-wheelbase trucks) may not allow the hitch to be installed in the ideal location due to clearance problems at the rear corners of the cab of the truck. In these instances a decision must be made as to whether it is preferable to lose the ability to maneuver the truck and trailer at a 90° angle to each other or to sacrifice some of the superior towing characteristics of a fifth-wheel hitch by locating it directly over or slightly to the rear of the rear axle.

Conventional Hitching Process

Successful use of weight-distributing hitch equipment depends upon proper adjustment of all components (see Figure 14.9).

1. Begin with the tow vehicle and trailer parked on level ground. Block the trailer wheels. Unhitch the trailer and use the tongue jack to adjust the trailer. Measure the distance between the trailer frame and ground at the front and rear corners and adjust until the frame is level. Note the following measurements:

   a. Distance from ground to top of inside of coupler socket.

   b. Distance from ground to lower corner of bumper at all four corners of tow vehicle.

2. The first adjustment to be made is the ball height. With the adjustable ball mount secured in the receiver, measure from the ground to the top of the ball. Depending upon the tongue weight and the type of tow vehicle, the ball height will need to be adjusted to be either equal to or slightly higher than the distance from the ground to the coupler socket in the trailer. Use the following as a guide:

   a. For trucks with extra-heavy-duty springs, set the ball height equal to the coupler height.

   b. For pickups with standard springs, raise ball height about $1/32$ inch for each 100 pounds of tongue weight.

   c. For passenger cars, raise ball height about $1/16$ inch for each 100 pounds of tongue weight.

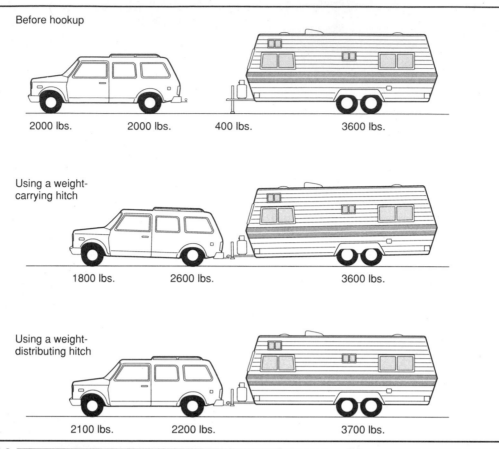

Before hookup

2000 lbs.   2000 lbs.   400 lbs.   3600 lbs.

Using a weight-carrying hitch

1800 lbs.   2600 lbs.   3600 lbs.

Using a weight-distributing hitch

2100 lbs.   2200 lbs.   3700 lbs.

■ **FIGURE 14.9** ■

Proper adjustment of a weight-distributing hitch will remove 50% of the tongue weight and spread 25% to the front axle of the tow vehicle and 25% to the trailer axle(s).

After the rest of the hitching process has been accomplished, it may be necessary to fine-tune the system by moving the adjustable ball mount up or down to achieve a perfect ball height. Adjustable ball mounts can also be tilted in small increments, raising or lowering the spring-bar tips in relation to the ground, allowing them to be placed under the proper amount of tension.

3. But this adjustment can't be made until the spring bars have been hooked up and examined for proper position. To obtain proper ball-mount tilt, insert the spring bars in the socket and swing them outward about 25°— the same angle as when hooked up to the trailer. Lift up on the spring-bar tips to take up slack. Tilt the ball mount to obtain the proper chain adjustment (Figure 14.10).

4. The next step is to lower the weight of the tongue on the hitch. Make certain that the coupler-locking mechanism grasps the ball securely. Raise the tongue jack to remove all weight from the hitch and continue upward until the rear of the tow vehicle rises a few inches. Insert the spring bars in their mounts and hook up the spring-bar chains to the chain-lift brackets on the trailer A-frame. The chains should be as close to vertical as possible, assuming the vehicle and trailer are aligned straight ahead. If necessary, move the brackets forward or backward until the chains are vertical. Insert the safety pins in the brackets to prevent serious injury from occurring after the load has been placed on the spring bars.

A little experimentation is necessary to discover which link of the chain to use, so start with a link that requires moderate force on the chain-lift brackets and then make adjustments

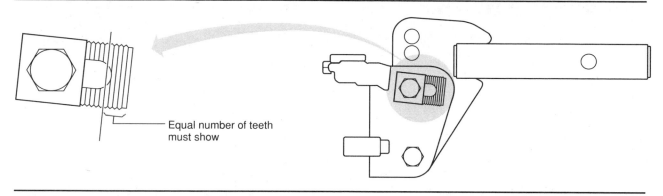

Equal number of teeth must show

■ **FIGURE 14.10** ■
Adjustable ball mounts allow the owner to regulate tilt when attaching spring bars.

up or down one link until the spring bars distribute the right amount of weight to keep the tow vehicle level. Make sure you have no fewer than four chain links under tension. Using fewer than four links can result in damage to the brackets when turning tight corners. If it is not possible to achieve a level tow vehicle without tightening the chains beyond the four-link limit, then the ball-mount angle must be adjusted or spring bars of a higher weight capacity must be employed.

5. Continuing, lower the tongue jack until all the weight is on the hitch. Measure again beneath the corners of the tow vehicle bumpers where you measured the first time to see if the vehicle has squatted equally front and rear, or if the hitching process has inflicted torque on the frame so that one side is lower than the other. If it isn't correct, readjust the links of the spring-bar chains until the tow vehicle squats equally front and rear and remains level side to side.

   Tightening the chains effectively transfers load from the rear to the front of the tow vehicle. Overtightening may result in loss of traction in a rear-wheel-drive vehicle and loss of rear-wheel braking effectiveness as the weight is removed from the rear axle. Undertightening results in light steering and poor handling of the tow vehicle.

6. After determining which are the correct spring-bar chain links for your trailer/tow vehicle combination, mark the link with paint for future reference.

7. Finish the hitching process by attaching the breakaway cable and plugging in the electrical cord. After removing the blocks from the trailer wheels, test the trailer lights and brakes.

Fifth-Wheel Hitching Process

Hitching a fifth-wheel trailer is somewhat easier than a conventional trailer because the hitch is fully visible to the driver at all times, so there is less difficulty in aligning the hitch and coupler pin.

1. Block the trailer wheels.
2. Lower the truck tailgate.
3. Raise the jacks until the pin box plate is slightly higher than the hitch saddle.
4. Remove the handle-locking pin, and rotate the handle to open the coupler lock. Return handle to closed position, but do not replace locking pin.
5. Slowly back up the truck until the kingpin is firmly seated in the coupler slot. When the kingpin engages the latch plate, the hitch will lock in place.
6. Set brakes on truck to hold slight pressure against kingpin.
7. Visually inspect to insure that the kingpin is solidly locked in place. If not, repeat steps 5 and 6.
8. Replace the safety pin to secure the handle.
9. Attach breakaway cable, plug in electrical cord, raise tailgate.
10. Remove blocks from trailer wheels and retract front trailer jacks.
11. Test trailer lights and brakes.

Sway-Control Devices

There are two different types of sway-control devices: the *friction* and the *Reese Dual Cam*. Because of the way friction sway-control units operate, they are not recommended for use on trailers with surge brakes or on trailer frames with less than .080-inch wall thickness.

Friction sway-control mechanisms consist of a bracket that attaches to the trailer frame, a friction assembly and a friction plate (that is adjusted by turning a screw-in handle), and a slide bar with a small ball socket on one end. For increased control, two units can be installed, one on each side of the trailer tongue.

In operation, the slide bar slips through the friction assembly, which is tightened until it acts as a brake on the slide bar, permitting the bar to slide in and out only under the influence of great force. The socket end of the slide bar fits over a small ball located to one side of, and to the rear of, the hitch ball on the ball mount. This sets up a triangle between the trailer frame, the sway control, and the hitch system. The sway-control unit acts as a variable-length side of the triangle. Its length is permitted to change when turning corners, yet the braking action of the friction assembly and slide bar resists any unwanted pivoting motion of the trailer and tow vehicle while traveling.

Reese Dual Cam sway controls are recommended only for trailers with tongue weights in excess of 250 pounds. They are a bit more complex than friction-type units, with more hardware involved. Once they are installed, however, no adjustment is needed. For even greater control, the Reese Dual Cam system can be used along with one friction-type unit. With the Reese Dual Cam system, vertical movement of the tow vehicle and trailer is permitted, but trailer sway is dampened by torsional action of the cam arms because they resist lateral movement.

■ Installing Sway-Control Devices
Reese Friction-type

1. Reese friction-type sway-control devices (Figure 14.11) are installed with the sway-control ball located 1⅜ inches forward of the hitch ball and 5½ inches outward. Install the ball using a toothed washer and nut. Place washer teeth toward adapter plate. Locate ball in outermost position and torque the nut to 100 foot-pounds.

2. Couple trailer for normal towing. Trailer should be directly behind tow vehicle in a straight line. If tow vehicle is not available, position ball mount in trailer coupler so hitch bar is on center line. Hitch bar should match tow vehicle hitch-box angle.

3. Check position of nylon pad. Correct position is inside the body between the friction-plate assemblies and with the hole aligned with body holes.

4. Install handle with washer into body. Lubricate handle threads, washer, and handle flange with oil or light grease before installing handle. Position slide-bar end 4¼ inches from body and parallel to body. Tighten the handle.

5. Place slide-bar coupler on ball. Hold bracket up to frame. Position bracket for best handle clearance. All four corner holes must be riveted to secure frame clamp bracket to frame.

6. Drill one ⅜-inch hole through bracket and frame side. Hole must be straight and round— drill must not walk. Holes in bracket are punched undersize—drill will match bracket and frame holes. Install drive rivet. Use washer on rivet if frame is less than .120 inch thick. Use a hammer to drive rivet pin flush with rivet head. **Note:** Use drive rivets for frames .080 inch to .188 inch thick. For thicker frames, use SAE Grade 5 bolts with nuts and lock washers.

7. Drill three remaining corner holes. Immediately after each hole is drilled, install a rivet or bolt.

8. Check for possible interference between slide-bar end and bracket rear end and between slide bar and snap-up bracket. Check for interference between bumper, bumper guards, coupler, and sway control. Have observer check for interference while trailer is slowly turned in both directions. If necessary, loosen and move sway-control ball inward to obtain clearance.

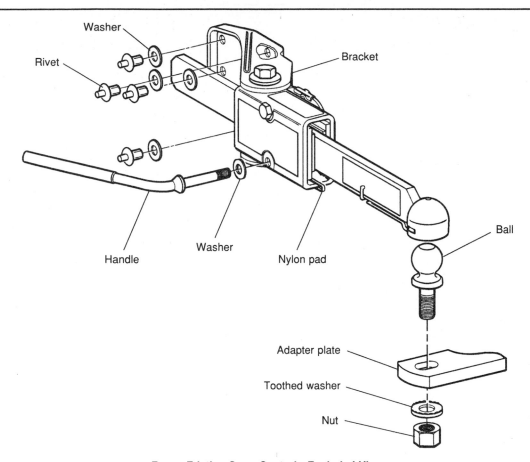

Washer

Rivet

Bracket

Handle

Washer

Nylon pad

Ball

Adapter plate

Toothed washer

Nut

Reese Friction Sway Control—Exploded View

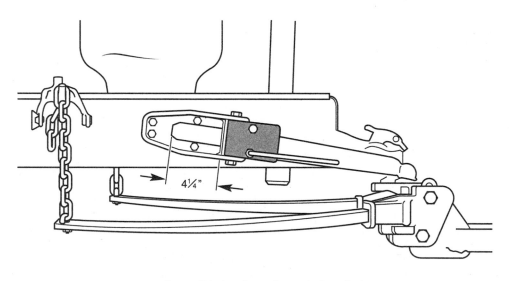

4¼"

Reese Friction Sway Control—Installed

FIGURE 14.11

Reese friction-type sway control device (two views)

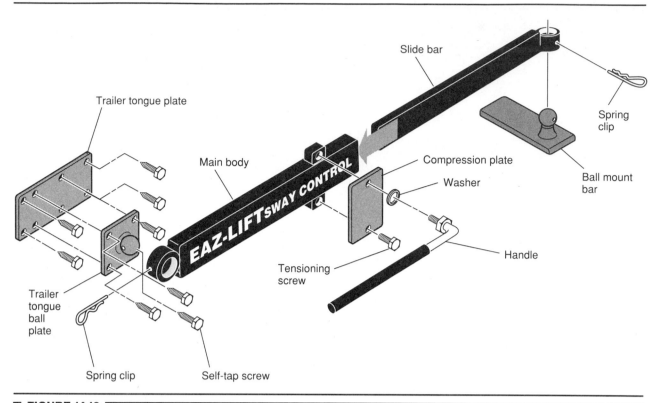

■ **FIGURE 14.12** ■
Eaz-Lift friction-type sway control device

Eaz-Lift Friction-type Sway-Control Devices

The Eaz-Lift friction-type sway-control device (Figure 14.12) attaches to a small ball on the ball mount, and another small ball on the trailer frame. A spring clip is employed to secure both balls in their respective sockets.

To position the ball for installation on the trailer frame, measure 24 inches back from the centerline of the coupler ball to locate the centerline of the frame-mounted sway-control ball. The sway-control ball can be either welded in place or secured with self-tapping bolts.

Reese Dual Cam Sway-Control Devices

Installation is fairly simple for the Reese Dual Cam (Figure 14.13). There are two separate units, each the mirror image of the other, one for the right side of the trailer A-frame and one for the left. Each unit consists of a frame U-bolt pivot bracket, a cam arm, and the cam. The frame U-bolt bracket attaches to the trailer tongue, and the pivot end of the cam arm is bolted to

the pivot point on the bracket. At the lower end of the cam arm, a clevis is used to connect the spring-bar chains to the cam arm. Using this system, the spring bars are no longer directly chained to the chain-lift bracket. Rather, the lower end of the cam arm fits up into the cam, which is attached beneath the trailing end of the spring bar. As the chain is tightened, the cam arm lifts the spring bar, thereby distributing the load.

Steps for installation are as follows:

1. Assemble clevis through chain. Attach clevis to cam arm with a ⅜-inch bolt and a ⅜-inch lock-nut. Assemble cam arm to pivot bracket using a ½-inch bolt. Assemble with bolt head to outside and tighten the nut securely against lockwasher.

2. Attach pivot brackets to each side of trailer A-frame using four U-bolts. Install eight ⁷⁄₁₆-inch tail nuts—leave nuts one turn loose.

   CAUTION: Be sure U-bolts are at least 2½ inches apart; 5 inches is preferred. **Note:** If frame is open on one side (C-channel), install a

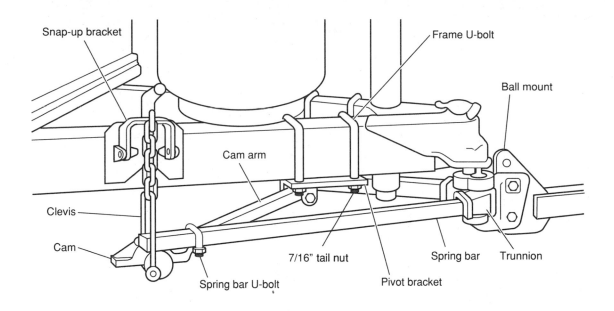

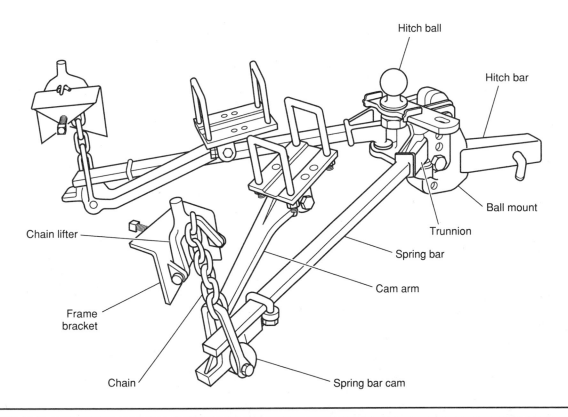

■ FIGURE 14.13 ■
Reese Dual Cam sway control (two views)

reinforcing plate in the open side where the pivot brackets are attached.

3. Attach snap-up bracket to trailer frame so the chain is vertical, if possible.

4. Attach cam to small end of spring bar using a ½-inch bolt and lockwasher, and a ⅜-inch U-bolt with two nuts and lockwashers. Torque the ½-inch bolt to 70 foot-pounds. Tighten U-bolt nuts. Rap each corner of U-bolt with a hammer, and torque nuts to 25 foot-pounds. **Note:** Cam must be mounted on bottom side of spring bar.

5. Measure from ground to top plate of ball mount. Connect trailer to tow vehicle. Raise trailer tongue and rear of tow vehicle with jack approximately 5 to 8 inches. Install spring-bar trunnion in ball mount. Place bottom trunnion into lower socket first. Spring bars may be used on either side. Mate spring bar and cam to cam arms. Pull chain vertical and place link on hook of snap-up bracket. Place snap-up in up position. Install safety pin. Install second spring bar using same number of chain links.

6. Lower jack. Again measure from ground to top plate of ball mount. Measurements should be the same or ½ inch less than before. If not, select the chain link that will bring tow vehicle to a level position. **Note:** Tow vehicle and trailer should be loaded and ready for travel before final leveling.

When hitching with the Reese Dual Cam system, the spring bars are positioned in such a manner that the lower end of the cam arm fits up into the cam beneath the tail end of the bars. The only adjustment made is to insure that the frame brackets are positioned so the system is self-centering. To do this, loosen the U-bolt nuts slightly and drive straight ahead with the trailer in tow for about 100 feet. Check mating of cam with arms and, if not correct, rap the pivot brackets with a hammer to jar them into place. Then tighten the U-bolt nuts. Periodic rechecking of alignment is part of standard maintenance.

■ Adjusting Sway-Control Devices

Adjusting a Reese sway-control friction assembly to work with a particular trailer requires some experimenting. After coupling the trailer to the tow vehicle and hooking up the sway-control device, it is necessary to find the zero-load point of the friction assembly. Do this by tightening the handle while at the same time moving the slide bar up and down in the friction assembly by hand. When the bar won't move any farther, the zero-load point has been reached.

Note the position of the handle, and tighten ½ to 1 turn for small trailers up to about 3,500 pounds. Tighten 1 to 1¾ turns for trailers between 3,000 and 7,000 pounds. (Overtightening can damage the unit.) This will give you a starting point, after which it is necessary to drive the vehicle in order to determine whether more adjustment is necessary. Make additional adjustments ¼ turn at a time until it feels right. An indication that the sway control is too tight is when the vehicle doesn't fully return to straight ahead after turning a corner.

Eaz-Lift's friction-type sway-control device is adjusted differently. Adjustments can be made by tightening or loosening the bolt below the handle, before tightening the handle itself.

Adjustment for the Reese Dual Cam sway-control system is accomplished by loosening the eight ⁷⁄₁₆-inch nuts. Drive the tow vehicle and trailer in a straight line. *This is important.* Sight down the center of the hood, and drive approximately 100 feet toward a distant point. Check mating of cam with cam arms. If not mated squarely, rap pivot brackets with hammer.

Tighten the eight ⁷⁄₁₆-inch tail nuts. Torque each nut to 60 foot-pounds, but do not distort frame.

Note: From time to time it may be necessary to use a different chain link to properly level tow vehicle and trailer due to weight changes in tow vehicle or trailer, or due to trunnion wear. Level tow vehicle, readjust dual cam, and recheck alignment periodically.

TROUBLESHOOTING the Hitch System

Problem	Possible Cause	Correction
Coupler separates from ball	Coupler ball clamp failure	Check ball clamp for breakage or excessive wear.
	Failure to properly connect coupler over ball	Double-check ball clamp when hitching up.
	Improper ball size	Check ball size and replace if necessary.
Spring bar falls out on ground	Broken spring-bar retaining clips	Inspect ball mount for broken or missing spring-bar retaining clips.
	Failure to properly insert spring bars	Double-check installation.
Spring-bar tension brackets open and release tension	Broken or missing bracket safety pins	Inspect bracket safety pins and replace if necessary.
Noise from hitch	Dry ball	Lubricate ball.
	Loose receiver bolts	Inspect bolts attaching receiver platform to vehicle frame. Tighten if necessary.
	Dry spring-bar ends	Inspect and lubricate trunnion ends of spring bars.
Poor tow vehicle handling	Improper spring-bar tension	Double-check hitching procedure.
	Improper ball height	Remeasure and adjust for proper ball height.
	Improper ball-mount angle	Adjust ball-mount angle to sustain spring bars level with ground and a minimum of four chain links under tension.
Loss of traction	Excessive spring-bar tension	Reduce spring-bar tension.
Light steering	Insufficient spring-bar tension	Increase spring-bar tension.
Steering plows through corners	Excessive sway control	Reduce sway control.
Trailer sways easily	Insufficient sway control	Increase sway control.
	Worn sway control	Inspect sway-control friction surfaces and replace if necessary.
	Insufficient tongue load	Increase tongue load to about 12% of total trailer weight.

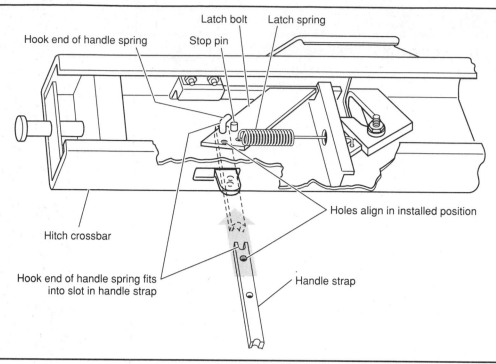

Hook end of handle spring

Latch bolt   Latch spring

Stop pin

Hitch crossbar

Holes align in installed position

Hook end of handle spring fits into slot in handle strap

Handle strap

■ **FIGURE 14.14** ■
Latch bolt and pivot point in fifth-wheel hitches must be lubricated with SAE 30-weight oil every six months.

Hitch Maintenance
■ Checking Hitch Systems

☑ **CHECKLIST** ■

☐ Inspect all fasteners for tightness at least every 2,000 miles of operation. This includes the bolts holding the receiver platform to the tow vehicle frame, the ball-mount bolts, spring-bar-tension bracket bolts, and sway-control mounts. On fifth-wheel systems, inspect the platform mounting bolts and the kingpin box mounting bolts. Torque all platform mounting bolts to 50 to 55 foot-pounds. Torque kingpin box bolts to 150 foot-pounds.

☐ Inspect ball clamp and coupler-latching mechanism for freedom of movement before each use. On fifth-wheel systems, inspect kingpin latch plate and latch bolt for freedom of operation.

☐ Inspect spring-bar trunnions and mounting sockets for wear before each use. On fifth-wheel systems, inspect the kingpin, pin-box plate, and saddle for excessive wear or damage.

☐ Inspect safety chains for signs of wear or stress before each use.

☐ Periodically clean and lubricate the coupler socket and ball clamp, the ball, the spring-bar trunnions, and the spring-bar sockets.

☐ On fifth-wheel systems (Figure 14.14), lubricate the latch bolt and pivot point of latch plate with SAE 30 oil at least every six months.

☐ Grease the load-bearing surfaces of the fifth-wheel hitch with a lithium-base grease every 2,000 miles of operation to reduce wear and provide easier turning.

☐ Inspect and clean fifth-wheel hitch latch plate before each use.

☐ On fifth-wheel hitches, grease the pivot points between the rails and hitch with a lithium-base grease every 2,000 miles of operation.

☐ Replace all worn or damaged parts.

■ Checking Sway-Control Devices

☑ CHECKLIST ▰▰▰▰▰▰▰▰▰▰▰▰▰▰▰▰▰▰▰▰

☐ For friction-type sway control, inspect and clean the components. Oil should be applied periodically to the handle and bolt threads, the trunnion bolts, and the ball. No oil should ever be placed on the friction surfaces or the slide bar.

☐ Reese Dual Cam sway-control-system maintenance consists of lubricating the ball-mount sockets and spring-bar trunnions to prevent rapid wear.

Trunnions should be lightly lubricated every towing day. Excess oil, dirt, and grit should be wiped out whenever the trailer is uncoupled. It's wise to oil the pivot-bolt joints occasionally at each end of the cam arms because the system was designed to utilize metal-to-metal friction. If the unit is noisy, it is permissible to lightly coat the cam surface with petroleum jelly.

CHAPTER 15

Interior Care

Soil and stains are the worst enemies of an RV interior. Routine, thorough cleaning is the most effective way to prevent damage to interior components. Periodic use of a vacuum cleaner on every dust-catching surface—blinds and drapes (employing a soft brush attachment on the vacuum nozzle), sofa and chairs, and carpet—will help keep the interior fresh and clean. This is especially important on the carpet, which is vulnerable to dirt tracked in from outside. Particles of dirt can work down into the pile and cut the fibers, gradually wearing out the carpet.

Routine cleaning should also include the countertops, inside cabinets, vinyl flooring, fiberglass tub/shower enclosure, porcelain or stainless-steel sinks, all appliance surfaces (both inside and out), and the wall paneling and woodwork. Allowing spills or water to sit may lead to permanent stains or water spots, so quick action is preferable.

Carpet and Upholstery Stain Removal

Care must be taken when removing stains from carpet and upholstery fabric. You can't just attack with hot water and strong cleaners or bleaches. The material has been dyed to give it its color, and you don't want to bleed out the dye. Also, most stains are set by hot water, so unless cleaning instructions specifically call for hot water to be used on a particular stain, use cold water.

The general rule is to act quickly, rather than to allow the spot or stain to dry and set. There are exceptions to this—drips of candle wax, for instance, which are more easily removed after the wax has hardened. But in most instances, spots need to be given immediate attention.

The other general rule is always to try out the cleaning product on a small test patch of the fabric or carpet before working on the main spots out where they are visible. How hard to scrub the spot depends upon the strength of the material being cleaned. The last thing you want to do is remove a patch of fabric along with the spot.

When cleaning a spot, always work from the outside edge of the spot toward the center. This prevents spreading the spot out into a larger area. Keep plenty of clean, absorbent materials (such as paper towels) on hand to soak up the moisture during the cleaning process. With carpeting, you can step on the paper towels to blot up the last of the moisture and residue after the cleaning is done.

Stubborn stains may have to be cleaned more than once in order to eliminate them completely. Some stains will never disappear altogether. A lot depends upon the fabric and the chemistry of the stain itself.

There are different remedies for different types of spots and stains. The following guide lists some of the most common types in alphabetical order. When the remedy calls for chlorine bleach, don't use it full strength; instead dilute it with four parts water to one part bleach. When peroxide is mentioned, use it in the full 3% strength, just as it comes from the bottle.

■ A Guide to Stain Removal

Blood Treat the blood stain with cold water. If it is safe for the fabric in question, follow up with hydrogen peroxide or chlorine bleach. If not, you may want to try an enzyme pre-soak product or unflavored meat tenderizer on the dampened spot. Finish up with a rinse of cold water, then dry with clean toweling.

Chocolate Several things will work well on chocolate spots: ordinary household detergent, ammonia, an enzyme pre-soak laundry product, or peroxide. Remember to test a small, hidden piece of the material before trying to clean the main spots.

Cigarette Burns in Carpet One solution is to carefully cut away the scorched fibers from the burned spot. Then locate a segment of the carpet that is never seen (in the corner of the closet floor, for example) and trim out some replacement fibers. Squeeze a little liquid glue into the area to be repaired, and set the fresh fibers in the glue.

Coffee This is one instance when you want to use hot water to remove a spot. Begin by soaking the stain with an enzyme pre-soak laundry product, or, if the fabric can handle it, a color-safe bleach or chlorine bleach. Then finish up by washing the stain out with hot water. Blot up as much of the moisture as possible with paper towels.

Fruit (including catsup) If you can catch it in time (before it dries), remove the fresh stain with cool water. Once the stain is dried into the fabric, soak it in a solution of cool water and a household detergent. Rinse and dry.

Milk, Cream, Ice Cream Soak the spot in a solution of warm water and an enzyme pre-soak laundry product. Then rinse and blot dry.

Mud Allow the mud to dry out first. Then you can brush it to knock loose as much of the caked-on dirt as possible and vacuum it up. Any mud that remains can be removed by soaking it in cool water. If there is a residual stain, use a household detergent, then rinse and blot dry.

Mustard One proven remedy for mustard stains is to use ammonia, another is peroxide. But always run a test on the material before cleaning to see if damage from the cleaning agents will occur.

Oil/Grease If we're dealing with freshly spilled oil or grease, try to sop up as much of it as possible with paper towels or other absorbent materials to prevent it from spreading. The next step is to pick out an inconspicuous little piece of the material on which to test cleaning agents. You can try using mechanic's hand cleaner on the greasy spot. Liquid detergent and dry-cleaning solvents also work. Finish up by washing the area with cool water and laundry detergent, then rinse and blot dry.

Tar Road tar can make a real mess of things inside a coach. You can try the remedies suggested for oil and grease, but if they don't work, try turpentine. Surprisingly, mayonnaise will also cut tar. As always, make sure you test a hidden little piece of the material before cleaning the main spots.

Urine These wet spots need prompt attention and a good wad of paper towels. Start by soaking up all the moisture possible until the paper towels don't show any dampness when you step on them. Then wash the area with an enzyme pre-soak laundry product, rinse, and blot dry.

Wine Begin with an enzyme pre-soak laundry product and hot water. If it's safe for the material, try an oxygen bleach and hot water. If the stains remain, and if the material can safely handle it, you can try a chlorine-bleach solution.

Drapes and Blinds

Periodically vacuum the drapes and blinds, using a soft-bristled brush attachment. Unless there are stains on fabric drapes, thorough vacuuming is the best maintenance. If stains occur, the drapes should be removed and either gently washed or dry cleaned according to the instruction tag on the fabric. If there is no tag containing cleaning instructions, contact the dealer or manufacturer to learn the recommended cleaning method.

Gentle care must be taken when working with aluminum miniblinds to prevent damage to the fragile blades. By lowering the blinds and then adjusting all the way in both directions, the broad surfaces of both sides of the slats can be vacuumed. Special miniblind brushes are available at many department stores; these make cleaning the blades easier. If spills or stains occur on the blinds, a soft damp cloth and mild detergent can be used. Gently wash the blinds and then dry thoroughly. Adjust the slats so they are separate and allow to air dry.

Vinyl Flooring

Today's vinyl floor coverings are exceptionally easy to care for. All they require is periodic sweeping or vacuuming and mopping. For stubborn dirt, mop with a solution of ammonia and warm water or one of the floor cleaners available in every grocery store. If serious scrubbing is necessary, use a plastic-bristle brush to prevent damage to the vinyl surface. Although most of the vinyl floor coverings used today have no-wax surfaces, a floor wax can be applied, if desired, to make future cleanup even easier.

Wall and Ceiling Paneling

Dust, fingerprints, and grease from cooking can coat the wall paneling and ceiling. Routine cleaning of these surfaces with a soft cloth and mild detergent solution will help prevent a heavy buildup of these elements.

Wood paneling can be treated with furniture polish or a preservative oil after cleaning.

Woodwork

Some of the most beautiful furnishings in an RV are made of wood; they will retain their beauty if treated as fine furniture in the home would be. A high-quality liquid or spray wood treatment can be used. Avoid the use of water-based waxes or polishes.

As beautiful as the woodwork is, it is vulnerable to damaging scratches, chips, and stains. Luckily, wood's characteristic is to have light and dark portions, a texture, a personality. Unlike paint, wood isn't meant to be monotone. When it comes to repairing wood, these characteristics help make the repair work less obvious.

■ Repairing Scratched Woodwork

Many different remedies have been suggested for making scratches and dings disappear. They don't mend the scratches, but at least they make them less visible. Read over this short list, then pick out the one that suits you best.

- One low-tech remedy is to use old motor oil as a staining medium for furniture. It renders a rich, dark color and oils the wood at the same time. A small amount can be rubbed into the scratches on wood to make them blend into the rest of the wood's grain.
- Instant coffee (one part) and water (two parts) can be rubbed into the scratches with a cotton ball. This solution can be used almost like a furniture polish to remove water spots and leave a soft sheen.
- Water marks can also be removed by the solid application of elbow grease and a soft cloth, if you catch them while they're still wet. Stubborn, dried-on marks may need an oil-based furniture polish to remove them.
- One fellow we heard of swears by Magic Markers as a scratch and ding mender. He just buys the color that most closely matches the woodwork and inks in the bad spot. Buffing over it with a soft cloth immediately afterward helps to soften the edges and make the repair less visible.
- Nut meats have been used to repair scratched woodwork. Just rub the broken nut meat over the length of the scratch, then wipe with a soft cloth.
- Paste shoe polish can be rubbed into the scratches to make them vanish. You can buy polish of different tones to match the woodwork. This serves not only to color the scratch, but to wax the surface as well.
- Of course, you can keep on hand a small dispenser of stain to match your woodwork. Just dab it on with a cotton ball, rub it in, wipe away the excess, and you're done. A little linseed oil mixed with the stain will help preserve the wood as you mend it.

Countertops and Sinks

Countertops take a great deal of abuse. Food is chopped up here, dishes drain here, everything spills here. It's an area that needs constant attention.

Some of that attention should be paid in advance. No matter what kind of material your countertop is made of, it can be damaged. Cutting should be done only on a cutting board. This will not only save the countertop, but the knife as well. If spills occur, they should be wiped up as soon as possible. Never use harsh abrasives on countertops since the surface may become damaged or dulled.

■ Some General Countertop Cleaning Tips

- Hard water can leave lime deposits on the counter. One way to remove them without resorting to abrasive cleansers is to use white vinegar and a soft cloth. For stubborn deposits, let the vinegar stand and soak the area for a few minutes.
- Toothpaste and a discarded toothbrush come in handy for cleaning the corners and the grout between tiles.
- Rather than spend time and energy scrubbing off dried-on food, lay a sponge or washcloth, wet with hot soapy water, over it for ten minutes to soak and loosen it up.
- If scrubbing is necessary, use a plastic scrub pad or brush to prevent damage to the countertop surface.

Corian Countertops

Corian is a high-quality material used for countertops in more expensive RVs. The material somewhat resembles marble and has a beautiful, smooth surface. However, Corian is soft enough to be damaged by a knife, leaving scratches and scars on the finish. Prevention is better than cure, and the use of a cutting board, pot holders, and ashtrays will prevent damage to a Corian countertop. To remove scratches or burn marks, use a very fine-grit sandpaper or a light abrasive rubbing compound. Work gently.

■ Stainless-Steel Sinks

Just because it's made of stainless steel doesn't mean that it can't get stains (one of the mysteries of life). Keep your steel sink looking nice and shiny by using a few of the following techniques.

- Most of the time, a stainless-steel sink only needs to be wiped out and dried with a soft cloth after each use in order to keep it looking spotless. This is especially important if you are using hard water.

- Vinegar will remove the buildup of lime deposits and water spots resulting from hard water.
- Rubbing alcohol or baking soda can be used to remove stubborn stains. Follow up with a good washing with hot water and detergent.
- Avoid using abrasive cleansers because they damage the surface of the stainless steel.

■ Porcelain Sinks

Durable as porcelain enamel is, it can still be damaged by abrasive cleansers. Use a spray-on foamy cleanser or one of the abrasive-free powders. Cleaning may require a bit of elbow grease, but it will save the porcelain finish. An alternate cleanser is dishwasher detergent. Wear rubber gloves when working with these cleansers to save the fine finish on your hands.

Fiberglass Sinks, Tubs, and Showers

Special care must be taken to prevent scratches or cracks in fiberglass. When they do occur, repair can be made by following the specific instructions on a fiberglass-repair kit, available at RV- and boating-supply outlets. Although it is possible to repair a scratch or crack in the fiberglass, it is difficult to match the original color. It may be necessary to paint the entire surface.

Everyday care and maintenance of fiberglass is similar to that of porcelain. Use only nonabrasive cleansers that state "fiberglass-safe" on the label. (There are cleansers on the market specifically for fiberglass. Look for these at RV-supply outlets, department stores, or supermarkets.) Before the initial use, and again after each thorough cleaning, apply a coat of paste wax to the fiberglass tub/shower and sinks to prevent the buildup of water deposits, discoloration, and stains.

Vinyl Shower Curtains

After each shower, use the hand-held shower wand to spray clear water over the surface of the curtain to remove soap residue. When it comes time to launder the curtain, either hand wash or machine wash on gentle cycle, using warm water and a mild soap. Do not use bleach. Remove the curtain from the machine before the final spin cycle and allow to drip dry.

Odor Eaters

Most of us already know about leaving an opened box of baking soda in the refrigerator, freezer, and oven to remove unwanted odors. But there are at least two other methods for removing odors from small enclosures or the entire coach.

- A pan of charcoal briquettes left sitting out in the open air will eliminate bad smells.
- Cat-box litter is quite effective as an odor eliminator. Fill a shallow pan and leave it sitting in the coach during storage. It takes care of the musty smells that can build up when the vehicle is not used for some time.

CHAPTER 16

Exterior Care and Repair

Mother Nature and the byproducts of our industrial society are rough on vehicles. The sun oxidizes the paint, bakes out the natural oils, and fades the color. It shrinks and cracks the vinyl, dries out and splits rubber, and deteriorates cloth upholstery. Rain can bring an acid or alkaline bath (essentially the fallout of industry) to mar the finish and makes mud to be tracked inside and splashed on the outside. The wind carries dust and dirt to deposit all over your vehicle. And while all this is going on, the bugs and birds are doing their part.

Gradual deterioration of the exterior is an ongoing process. Our aim here is to help define the symptoms of a vehicle in need of exterior care and discuss the job of providing that care.

When using exterior-care products, it is vital that the directions on the product package be followed exactly, because similar products may have totally different directions for use.

The Symptoms of Wear

■ Oxidation

When your paint takes on a dull, lifeless, chalky appearance, chances are it's suffering from oxidation. This is a gradual process in which oxygen combines with the paint to form new chemical substances. The process is speeded up by the bleaching action of the sun. The end result is slow deterioration of the paint.

The best method to slow down oxidation is to keep the vehicle covered or garaged, although this may not be practical for large RVs. While oxidation may not be entirely preventable, it is somewhat repairable by using products that remove the oxidized paint layer, thus exposing the fresh paint beneath. Cleaner-waxes and finish restorers will remove light oxidation. Glazes and rubbing compounds get even the heavy stuff. This, of course, eventually results in wearing the paint down to bare metal, at which time it becomes necessary to get a new paint job.

■ Acid/Alkaline Rain

Acid rain is a product of our industrial civilization. Emissions from industrial, vehicle, and natural sources introduce sulfur, sulfur dioxide, and nitric oxide into the atmosphere. These chemicals can be carried by wind for thousands of miles. When they combine with water, they form sulfuric and nitric acids, which can then fall as acid rain. Acid rain literally etches the painted surface of a vehicle.

Alkaline rain has a similar genesis and results in the same destruction of vehicle surfaces, accelerating the oxidation process and leaving ugly blemishes. Even waxed and poly-sealed surfaces are vulnerable.

Washing, waxing, and polishing won't help with acid/alkaline blemishes. Special products are formulated for this special problem.

■ Scratches

Minor scratches may be removed by using a cleaner or cleaner-wax, but deeper scratches will need a rubbing compound or glaze. These are abrasive products that remove top layers of paint, blending the scratch in so it becomes less visible.

■ General Grime

Depending upon where you live, your vehicle may stay clean for quite a while, or it may be covered with dirt every time you turn around. Only you can determine how often your vehicle needs a general cleanup, but certainly bird droppings, insects splattered on the outside, tree sap, and road tar and grime will be good indicators of the need for attention.

Once clean, how long is it going to last? That depends a lot upon the conditions where your RV is parked. If you're fortunate to have a garage for the rig, you may not need to attend to it very often. But if you're on the road a lot, or drive newly resurfaced roads or salted highways, or bake in the Sun Belt, or nest beneath a sappy forest, you may need to stock up on cosmetic products and keep a supply of clean rags handy.

Exterior Care

■ Washing the Vehicle

Before doing anything else to your vehicle's exterior, it must be thoroughly washed. But washing with household detergents containing alkali or ammonia can harm the surface. Special car-wash products have been developed that will remove the dirt and grime from a vehicle's surface without harming the previous wax job. Some products, in fact, combine a wash-and-wax job all in one process.

These products are liquid or powder concentrates that are made to be used diluted in a pail of water. A soft cloth or wash mitt should be used, and the vehicle should be washed in the shade. Gently dry with a soft, clean chamois or towel to avoid spots.

■ Finish Restorers

In preparation for waxing, the vehicle may need treatment with a finish restorer if the finish has become oxidized and dulled by grime. Milder than a true rubbing compound, these products remove stubborn grime and oxidation, thereby allowing the true color of the paint to show. Instructions for use vary with different products, so read and follow the directions carefully. Basically, these products are applied gently in a circular motion with a soft cloth. After drying, they are buffed to remove residue. Hard rubbing is not necessary.

■ Rubbing Compounds

For seriously deteriorated paint surfaces, rubbing compounds should be used. These products will remove layers of oxidized paint, minor scratches, and stains. Extreme care must be employed when working with rubbing compounds because if used too vigorously they will remove good paint. Rubbing compounds can also be used to remove scratches, stains, or rust from chrome finishes.

As always, work on clean, dry, cool surfaces. Apply compound sparingly and evenly, rubbing in a straight line, just enough to remove the oxidized paint, stains, or scratches. Buff lightly with a clean, dry cloth.

CAUTION: Do not use on flat black paint; on wood panels; or on vinyl, plastic, or fiberglass.

■ Waxes

Waxes are applied to the exterior of vehicles to protect the paint from the elements. The theory is to let the wax, rather than the paint, take the beating offered by sun, wind, blowing dirt, bugs, and all the rest. By keeping a healthy coat of wax between the paint and the elements, the paint will last longer and look better, and it's a simple job to renew the wax periodically.

All wax manufacturers agree that prior to waxing the vehicle should be well washed and cleaned of stubborn grime. If paint oxidation has taken place, some wax containers specify that finish restorers be used to prepare the surface for the final wax job.

Waxes should be applied in the shade to a cool vehicle surface with a clean, soft, damp or dry (according to package directions) terry cloth. They should be applied briskly and with a circular motion, laying down a thin, even coat to one section of the vehicle at a time. A separate soft, clean terry cloth should be used to lightly buff the wax after it has had time to dry to a haze. Turn the buffing cloth frequently, and shake out the residue as needed.

You can test the durability of your wax job by watching water bead on the surface. When rain or wash water no longer beads, it's time to freshen up the wax job.

■ Combination Cleaner-Waxes

Cleaner-waxes are far milder than rubbing compounds, yet can remove minor stains and oxidation. They offer a one-step process that leaves the painted surface cleaned of dull oxidation and stains, and coats it with a protective wax.

Begin with a clean, cool surface. Apply and finish as you would a regular wax, following specific directions for the product of your choice.

■ Polishes

Polishes are different from waxes. They are surface preparations that leave a glistening shine, but do not leave a wax layer over the paint. According to manufacturer claims, polishing a vehicle provides superior protection to waxing.

As with wax application, polish should only be applied with a circular motion to clean, dry, cool vehicle surfaces. Oxidized paint will be removed by the polish and retained in the polishing cloth, so it may be necessary to keep several cloths on hand to permit working with a clean cloth at all times. Overlap areas being worked to insure thorough coverage of all body panels.

After the polish dries to a haze, remove residue by buffing with a clean cloth.

■ Polymer Sealants

Secret formulas and claims of spectacular results circulate in this area of the automotive-product market. Polymer coatings are claimed to seal the vehicle finish against everything from smog to bird droppings. In theory, the formula actually bonds to the painted surface of any vehicle, whether it be metal, chrome, or fiberglass. It is not, however, intended for use on vinyl, flat paint, plastic, decals, or synthetic or painted wood.

Wash and dry the vehicle, but don't use household detergents or cleaners, since they may cause streaking. Apply poly sealant in a circular motion to the entire vehicle surface. Allow to dry thoroughly, until a haze appears. Wipe off. Then, with a fresh, dry cloth, buff vigorously.

■ Metal Polishes

To remove tarnish and minor corrosion, a metal polish is the product of choice. While there are similarities between some of these products, directions for use vary, so it is important to follow instructions on the package.

Generally, these products are rubbed gently onto the metal surface being treated, and then buffed off. Some products specify that care must be taken to prevent the polish from drying on the surface before being removed.

■ Tire Dressings

To restore a newer look to aging tires that may have rubbed against a curb or are just losing their snappy appearance, there are products for both whitewall and blackwall use.

Black-tire dressings are applied to clean, dry tires with a paint brush, being careful to avoid getting the dressing on wheels or any white lettering on the tire. Allow the dressing to dry for about an hour. In cases of old tires with porous rubber, a second coating may be necessary.

Whitewalls and white lettering can be restored to a newer appearance using products specifically for that job. Follow directions on the container because they vary between products. Basically, the whitewall restorer is sprayed or wiped on and scrubbed or rinsed off, with a short curing duration in between.

■ Wheel Cleaners and Polishes

Wheel cleaners come in liquid or paste form. The liquid ones are easier to use because all you do is spray them on the wheels, wait about a minute, and then hose off with a strong stream of water. Paste cleaners are applied much like paste wax and require some rubbing and buffing. However, stubborn grime may demand scrubbing even with the spray-on/hose-off liquid cleaners. And some of the liquid cleaners employ a two-stage system in which two solutions are used—the second neutralizing the action of the first.

CAUTION: Not all types of wheels can be cleaned with all brands of wheel cleaners. Some chrome cleaners will damage aluminum or magnesium wheels, while other products are specifically formulated for these materials. Read the labels carefully before you buy.

■ Degreasers

Some degreasers on the market are specifically formulated to work on the warm surfaces of an engine, to melt the grime away so working under the hood isn't such a messy job. Others are "all-purpose" degreasers and cleaners that can be used to clean up small areas wherever they are needed.

Labels offer directions for specific use. Often the products will be used full strength, but sometimes they need to be diluted. Most often they are sprayed on, then hosed or wiped off.

■ Glass Cleaners

The numerous glass cleaners on the market are all used the same: spray on and wipe off with a lint-free cloth or paper towel.

But normal glass cleaners should not be used on windows to which a film-type window tint has been applied. For this application, there are special non-abrasive plastic polishes formulated for use on window-tint film, Plexiglas, and convertible windows. To apply, spray on clean, dry surface; spread evenly with soft, dry cloth; buff to a shine.

To remove bugs and other stubborn dirt from the windshield when normal glass cleaners fail, use white vinegar on a clean cloth. To remove tree sap, try baking soda. It isn't as abrasive as cleanser, but it will cut through the sap.

■ Tar and Bug Removers

There is no substance as stubborn as road tar, but bugs come close. Bug and tar remover is designed to clean grease, bugs, and road oil from glass, paint, and polished metal surfaces without damaging the standard automotive paint. It is also effective in cleaning tree sap from the finish.

Dampen the cloth with the bug and tar remover and rub briskly over the grimy surface until it is clean. Wipe with a clean, dry cloth to remove residue. To restore the finish, reapply wax or polish.

An alternate method of removing road tar is to use laundry pre-wash solution. It cuts the tar like magic.

Aluminum Care and Repair

Aluminum RV exterior skin can be either raw metal or painted. Care of the two surfaces is different in some respects. Harsh abrasives should not be used when cleaning the unpainted aluminum because the raw metal surface can become marred by fine scratches. However, a painted aluminum surface can be treated just as a painted steel surface because it is the paint that is being treated, not the aluminum.

To care for and restore the luster of an unpainted aluminum surface, wash thoroughly with a warm solution of automotive wash product. Do not use strong detergents, solvents, or abrasive cleansers. Wash during the cool of the day, in the shade, or on an overcast day. Never wash the aluminum skin in direct sunlight.

Check to see that all windows, vents, compartment doors, and entry doors are closed tightly before washing. Use a large sponge or soft cloth. Begin with the roof. Wash one section at a time, then rinse to prevent the cleaning solution from drying on the surface. Dry with a chamois or soft, clean towels to prevent water spots.

Road tar, sap, and bugs should be cleaned off as soon as possible, before they can harden in place. Use kerosene, turpentine, or naphtha with a soft cloth, taking care not to scratch the surface. Rinse thoroughly with clear water. Wax the affected areas.

The aluminum skin should be waxed every three to six months, or more often if necessary, as determined by exposure to the elements.

A painted aluminum skin should be washed and cleaned of road tar, sap, and bugs using the methods for unpainted aluminum. When necessary, oxidized paint can be treated by using a polish, combination cleaner-wax, or, in extreme cases, a polishing compound. A good grade of automotive wax should be applied every three to six months, or more often if necessary.

If the coach is in storage, a soft cloth cover can be used to help protect the surface. The tires should also be covered to protect against the harmful effects of the sun.

Aluminum skin that has been damaged cannot be repaired and must be replaced. Because the aluminum skin is made of large panels of material, considerable work must be done to remove the damaged panels and replace them with new material. Emergency repairs can be made to prevent moisture or dirt from entering the coach through a damaged exterior wall. Use duct tape to close a puncture or tear. If a panel has come loose, use sheet-metal screws or wood screws (appropriate for the type of coach framework) to secure the panel to the framework until professional repairs can be made.

Fiberglass Care and Repair

Fiberglass comes in two varieties: painted and gel coat. Gel-coat fiberglass has the pigment applied as the fiberglass panels are manufactured. Routine maintenance of both types of fiberglass is the same: periodic washing (always in the cool of the day or in the shade) with an automotive wash product. Rinse thoroughly to remove soap residue. Dry with a chamois or soft, clean towels to prevent water spots. Apply a coat of good automotive wax every three to six months (or more often if necessary) to protect the surface.

If damage occurs to a fiberglass surface, repair is fairly easy. A repair kit can be purchased at RV- and boating-supply outlets.

Deep scratches can be repaired by applying a coat of fiberglass resin, allowing it to cure, then sanding it until it blends with the surrounding surface. If the original fiberglass was painted, a coat of touch-up paint will be necessary to make the repair invisible. If the original surface was gel coat, the color layer may not have been breached and the clear resin used for the repair may permit the original color to show through, so no further touch-up is necessary. However, if the gel-coat layer is damaged, it may be repaired with a gel-coat repair kit, available at most marine- and RV-supply outlets.

■ Touching-up Gel Coat

To perform touch-up work on gel coat, follow this routine:

1. Select the proper color gel coat.
2. Brush or spray it on the damaged area.
3. Catalyze it with MEK (methylethyl ketone) peroxide, according to the directions on the container.

4. Cover the repair area with a sheet of plastic food wrap to seal off oxygen penetration. This is necessary because gel coat will not cure in the presence of oxygen. Leave the plastic wrap in place for six to eight hours (or overnight, if desired) at a temperature of 70°F.

5. After curing, remove the plastic wrap and wet-sand the area with 320- or 400-grit sandpaper. Follow this by buffing, polishing, and applying paste wax.

To paint over a gel-coat surface, remove any wax, sand the surface, and apply a coat of primer surfacer. Sand the surfacer. Finish by applying paint in a color to match the rest of the coach.

■ Repairing Severely Damaged Fiberglass

Severe damage, such as cracked or broken fiberglass, is also easy to repair. Follow these steps:

1. Trim away excess broken pieces and restore the remaining fiberglass to its original shape as much as possible.

2. Grind, sand, and clean the surface of the area to remove road grime, oil, and dirt.

3. Mix the fiberglass resin according to instructions on the product container.

4. Cut the fiberglass cloth large enough to cover the area to be repaired and to overlap onto surrounding solid fiberglass by a few inches. If possible, apply a layer of fiberglass to the backside of the damaged area to serve as reinforcement. Then work on the exterior repair.

5. Soak the fiberglass cloth in the resin and then apply the cloth over the surface of the area to be repaired. Smooth it down with a roller to help make it adhere well to the surface and to eliminate bubbles. The resin will begin to cure immediately, so work swiftly, but carefully. Allow the resin to cure the full amount of time specified in the product instructions.

6. After the resin has fully cured, grind and sand the area to make the repair patch blend with the surrounding surface. Apply additional layers of fiberglass as necessary until the repair is built up to the original contour and strength.

7. Grind and sand each layer before applying the next, taking care to maintain the proper body-panel contour. Use a block sander to prevent ripples. After the final layer of fiberglass has been applied, cured, and sanded, body filler may be used to blend the repair work. To make the repair match the rest of the coach, the area must be painted.

Caulking and Sealing

Age and the elements can dry and crack seam-sealing caulk material, making it unsightly or even resulting in leaks. Periodically inspect all seams and joints to check on the condition of the caulking compound. These areas are found on the roof, around vents, where roof and sidewall panels meet, around the screws used to secure accessories such as roof ladders, along molding strips, and around windows and door frames, for example. If chunks of caulk are missing or badly deteriorated, replacement is advised.

Original-equipment caulk compound is available in ribbon form and can be purchased at RV-supply outlets. Silicone sealer can also be used to replace damaged caulk. When replacing caulk, completely remove the old compound prior to installing the new caulking material.

Moldings and Doors

Exterior trim moldings are often secured to the coach with a double-sided adhesive tape. If the molding begins to pull loose, it can often be repaired by simply replacing the tape and pressing the molding strip back into place.

When cleaning the coach, take a moment to wipe the dirt from the rubber weatherstrip gasket surrounding the door. A shot of silicone lubricant helps keep this gasket fresh.

Periodically inspect the hinges for loose screws. Tighten if necessary. If the hinges squeak, lubricate them with a light oil and wipe away any excess. An occasional drop or two of lock lubricant with graphite will help keep the locks operating freely.

■ Realigning a Door

Door misalignment can occur as a result of abuse, improper installation at the factory, or normal wear and tear. To realign a door:

1. Determine the cause of misalignment by removing the inside door molding and making a visual inspection to locate where the door frame has shifted in relation to the coach wall.
2. Loosen the screws that hold the aluminum door frame to the coach framework. Work on the hinge side of the door rather than the latch side when making these adjustments.
3. Using ⅛ inch by 1-inch plywood shims, return the frame to square by driving the shims into the appropriate spaces between the door frame and stud. Continually check the way the door fits in relation to the frame, and make adjustments with the shims until the fit is perfect.
4. Complete the job by tightening the screws to secure the door frame to the coach wall, then replace the molding.

Windows and Screens

Windows need to be kept clean, and the tracks in which they glide should be kept free of dirt. Use a toothbrush or clean paintbrush with short bristles to sweep the tracks clear of dust and accumulated dirt. A vacuum with a long nozzle may also be used here. Clean the glass with an ammonia glass cleaner to eliminate spots and streaks. If a film-type window tint has been applied to the glass, wash only with soapy water, then rinse and wipe dry.

Window screens may be removed for thorough cleaning. Using soapy water and a soft brush, gently wash the screens and then thoroughly rinse. They may be replaced immediately and allowed to air dry.

Replacement of screen material is easy. The screen is held in the frame by a round rubber gasket that is pressed over the edge of the screen and into a groove in the frame. Remove the gasket by prying it out of the groove with a flat-blade screwdriver. Use the old screen intact as a pattern to cut a new piece of matching screen material. Spread the new screen material over the frame and reinstall the gasket, gently pressing it into the groove to secure the screen material. Take care to apply just enough tension on the material so that it doesn't tear but is tightly stretched across the frame.

Ladders, Roof Racks, and Roof Vents

Periodically check the mounting hardware for tightness and to insure that no cracks or breaks have occurred. Inspect the caulk material used around the mounting hardware, looking for possible breaches in the seal. Repair as necessary.

Roof vents are subject to damage from wind, overhanging branches, and from being stepped on, kicked, or having items dropped on them when loading the roof. They also suffer the natural effects of age and sunlight.

Periodically inspect the roof vents for cracks, splits, or breakage. Check the caulking compound around the seams and repair as necessary to prevent leaks. Clean out pine needles, leaves, and other debris that naturally collect there.

Replacement of a vent cover is easily accomplished. Simply remove the screws that hold the vent cover to the hinge and the lifting mechanism.

Trailer A-Frames

There is very little that can go wrong with trailer A-frames. Periodically inspect all the hardware attached to the frame and tighten if necessary. The frame should be washed to prevent the buildup of road grime and dirt. Touch-up paint should be used on all scratches and paint chips to prevent rust. A coat of paste wax will help keep an A-frame clean and protected from the elements.

And What about the Driveway?

We might as well not stop until we've discussed ways to clean up after a vehicle that drips an occasional drop of oil or grease on the driveway.

Cat-box litter, spread out over the oil or grease drip, will help absorb it. Spread it evenly over the oil spot, sweep it back and forth to work it into the spot, and leave it for a few days to do its work. Cat-box litter also helps remove odors from the garage.

Another solution is to use dry cement. Scatter it over the spot, sweep it around to work it in, then let it sit for a few days. The cement will absorb the grease and oil, and when you sweep it up the spot will be gone. Not gone entirely? Give it another try. It'll gradually disappear. There are also commercially available grease, spot, stain, and rust removers specifically formulated to work on concrete and asphalt.

CHAPTER 17

Exterior Accessories

Accessories that are added to the outside of a motorhome, trailer, or camper not only add character, but make RVing more comfortable. An RV with an extended awning is much more inviting, especially during the heat of the day. If an awning is properly maintained, it is less likely to give the owner fits when operating the mechanism. Hydraulic electric levelers and tongue jacks take much of the work out of leveling and hitching up an RV—they certainly beat using boards and rocks! But hydraulic electric levelers are complex pieces of equipment and require periodic service to insure operational efficiency. Television antennas are as common as kitchen sinks and are obviously necessary if the RV is equipped with a television set. Simple care of the mechanism is all that is needed. Be sure to lower the antenna before driving the rig. Searchlights and air horns are two other items that find their way to the rooftops of many RVs. One lets you see, the other lets you be heard—not a bad combination. With a little care, these options will last the life of the RV.

Awnings

Awnings are the RV counterparts to patio covers, but they are more complex because they are retractable. Awning systems are sized to fit all types of RVs, ranging from the largest motorhomes to the smallest tent trailers. In addition to the main awning that covers the entire side of an RV, smaller awnings are available for use on individual windows.

The typical RV awning system consists of an awning rail attached to the top edge of the RV sidewall, adjustable rafters and lower support arms to stiffen the awning when extended, brackets for attaching the rafters and support arms to the side of the RV, a roller tube onto which the awning fabric is rolled, and some type of locking mechanism to prevent the awning from unrolling while traveling.

The awning manufacturers have designed their products to operate slightly differently from one another. One of the keys to successful use of an awning system is to study the owner's manual and learn the proper steps to setting up and taking down the awning so that there will be no confusion at the campsite.

■ Maintenance

Fabric Awnings

Some awnings are made of fabrics that are resistant to rot and mildew, while others need special care to prevent this type of damage. Rot and mildew result from moisture being trapped in the fabric. Although instructions from manufacturers using rot- and mildew-resistant fabrics state that their awnings can be rolled up wet if necessary, even these awnings should be opened and allowed to dry thoroughly as soon as possible. If the fabric is not rot- and mildew-resistant, even greater care must be taken.

It is important to keep the awning material as clean and dry as possible. Even on mildew-resistant material, pollen or dust can support mildew growth, which results in a stain. In areas of the country prone to salt spray or road salt, the awning fabric and hardware should be washed frequently to prevent damage. Air pollution has been found to damage the fabric, and it is recommended that during prolonged exposure to air pollution the awning should be washed at least twice a month.

Cleaning Fabric Awnings To clean the fabric, carefully follow the manufacturer's recommendations. The following are the typical recommendations, although the procedure may be different for some brands.

1. Periodically (as the need demands) loosen hardened dirt with a dry, soft brush.
2. Hose off dirt, both top and bottom.
3. Using a mixture of ¼ cup of dish soap and ¼ cup of bleach with 5 gallons of warm water, wash both the top and bottom of the fabric.
4. Roll up the awning for anywhere between 5 minutes to 2 hours (depending upon the stubbornness of the dirt) to allow the cleaning solution time to work on both sides of the fabric.
5. Unroll the awning and rinse thoroughly.
6. Allow the fabric to air dry completely before rolling it back up.
   CAUTION: Never use a strong detergent or stain remover on the awning because it will destroy the fabric's water repellency. Avoid the use of hard-bristle brushes, petroleum-based chemicals, or abrasive or caustic household cleaners on the awning fabric.

To remove stubborn mildew, wipe the affected areas with white vinegar, which will kill the mildew. Rinse the fabric with clear water. The fabric may require rewashing after this cleaning procedure.

Checking for Leaks Leaks in the fabric may be the result of several causes:

- If the leaking occurs after washing, the cause may be insufficient rinsing. Rinse more thoroughly and allow to dry, then check for water repellency.
- If water drips through the needle holes in the stitching, use a commercial seam sealer (available at canvas and RV-supply outlets) or apply a layer of paraffin wax to the top of the seams.
- A pinhole leak can develop if a spot of water-repellent on the top of the fabric has flaked off. To fix the hole, apply a small dab of VLP (Vinyl Liquid Patch) with the end of a cotton swab. By

TROUBLESHOOTING the Awning

Problem	Possible Cause	Correction
Awning won't roll up or needs help rolling up	Insufficient spring tension	Follow suggested procedure in owner's manual to increase spring tension.
Awning fails to roll up completely	Insufficient spring tension	Increase spring tension.
	Crooked awning rail	Straighten awning rail.
	Bent roller or shaft	Straighten or replace roller or shaft.
Awning won't roll down	Unreleased lock device	Release lock device.
Awning wrinkled	Crooked awning rail	Straighten awning rail.
	Overstretched or understretched fabric	Loosen fabric and restretch.

gently rolling the VLP around the hole, the paint will melt and fill in the pinhole with a perfect color match. Be sure to allow the VLP to dry before rolling up the awning.

- If water leaks through the fabric where a pool of water has collected on the awning, lower one of the support arms to promote drainage.

Awning Hardware

As with the fabric, different manufacturers recommend various procedures for maintenance of the awning hardware. Carefully read the owner's manual before proceeding. Following are typical recommendations for some awnings.

- Clean all the hardware with a solution of warm, soapy water.
- Rinse and allow to dry.
- Lubricate the rafter arms and support arms using paraffin wax or silicone spray.
- Lubricate the threads on knobs in the same manner.
- A stubborn push button or lift handle can be lubricated with silicone spray. Also lubricate the bottom bracket release tab for easier disengagement.
- A light oil may be used on the latch section of the base brackets, the threaded portion of the security knobs, and the spring-loaded adjustment knob in the lift handle. After lubricating, wipe excess oil from all parts.
- Periodically extend all telescoping arms as far as possible and wipe away any accumulated dirt.

Prior to and again at the end of each season, check all fasteners for tightness. Replace any missing parts with factory-authorized replacement parts. If streaks appear or water is seeping behind the awning rail, check for loose screws or damaged sealant at the rail.

Levelers

Hydraulic levelers are used on motorhomes to provide a firm, level foundation when parked in a campsite. When traveling, the levelers ride in a horizontal position beneath the chassis. When activated, the levelers pivot to a vertical position and the hydraulic rams extend downward until they contact the ground. With a leveler positioned at each corner of the coach (or with one centered in the front and one at each corner of the rear), the chassis can be raised a different amount fore and aft, side to side, until the coach is level.

Some models are automatic, employing a computer-controlled sensing device that operates the system and automatically brings the coach to level. Other systems are manual, requiring that the driver control the leveler for each corner individually.

In this section, we will cover the care and maintenance of both manual and automatic systems. Because of the complexity of installation, we recommend that these systems be installed by experienced personnel.

■ Leveler Maintenance

A & E Mark V Levelers

Check the following items on A & E Mark V levelers.

☑ CHECKLIST ▬▬▬▬▬▬▬▬

☐ Inspect the spring assemblies of each leveler to be sure they are free of road hazards and dirt buildup prior to every trip.

☐ Make sure the routing of electrical wires avoids sharp edges of undercarriage components and heat-producing portions of the coach or generator exhaust system.

☐ Keep the 12-volt battery system charged. If it is necessary to start the engine prior to operating the Mark V Levelers, it could indicate a battery drain or insufficient charging of the battery.

☐ The following owner maintenance checklist should be employed before, during, and after any extended use of the leveling system.
   ☐ Condition of battery terminals
   ☐ Battery electrolyte level (if appropriate)
   ☐ Inspection of all leveler units
   ☐ Check of spare 30-amp MDL fuse
   ☐ Lubrication of gear box
   ☐ Lubrication of inner tube

Note: When inspecting each unit, check if any wires have been pulled loose during the previous trip.

■ Lubrication

Once a year, the top cover of the gear housing should be removed (this can be done without removing the leveler) and the exposed gear assembly cleaned, then repacked with heat-resistant grease. A moly-based chassis grease is recommended.

At the same time, lube the inner tube assembly through the existing slot of the outer tube assembly (Figure 17.1). After lubrication, cycle each leveler to distribute grease evenly.

■ Leveler Repair

Reduced Lifting Capacity

If the lifting capacity of the levelers is reduced over a period of time, the original capacity can be restored by following this procedure:

1. With the leveler in the retracted position, remove the gear housing assembly.
2. Remove the 5/16-inch 24-socket head screw and the spigot.
3. Clean and grease the spigot and add a .005-inch-thick washer.
4. Reassemble in reverse order.

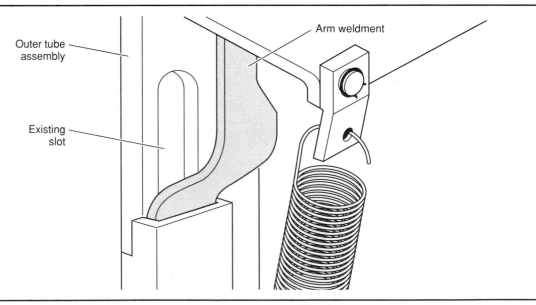

■ FIGURE 17.1 ▬▬▬▬▬▬▬▬▬▬▬▬▬▬▬▬▬▬▬▬▬▬▬
Inner tube of leveling jacks should be lubricated through the slot in the outer tube assembly.

Jammed in Retraction

If the leveler jams in the retracted position, this may be a result of relay failure or mechanical jamming between the underside of the brake and the ball screw nut (see Figure 17.2). To repair, follow this procedure:

1. With the leveler in the retracted position, remove the gear housing cover.
2. Remove the ⁵⁄₁₆-inch 24 x 1¼-inch-long cap screw.
3. Remove the clutch gear, disc springs, and spigot. Remove the washer.
4. With an adjustable wrench, turn the drive spindle in a counterclockwise direction to free the jam.
5. Remove the retaining ring and the inner tube assembly.
6. Add the split nylon washer between the brake and nut, around the ball screw.
7. Clean and grease all parts, then reassemble.

■ Automatic Hydraulic

Automatic Hydraulic Maintenance

When the vehicle is serviced, and while the four leveling units are in the retracted position, check the supply of oil in the hydraulic oil reservoir. To check the oil supply, remove the breather plug from the top of the hydraulic oil reservoir. The oil level should be one inch below the top of the reservoir. Fill as necessary using Dextron II automatic transmission fluid.

Periodically clean the levelers of mud or road grime. In cold weather, clear away ice from the levelers.

Do not move the vehicle while the levelers are still in contact with the ground. However, if this should accidentally happen, reset the master switch and follow the automatic retract procedure, then visually inspect to see if the leveling units have returned to the travel position.

Periodically inspect all electric and hydraulic lines to insure that they are away from sharp edges or heat sources. Inspect for oil leaks and have repairs performed as necessary.

If the motorhome is stored, the levelers should be extended with some vehicle weight on them, and the operation cycle performed once a month.

Insure the integrity of the 12-volt DC system. Low voltage can cause leveling-unit problems.

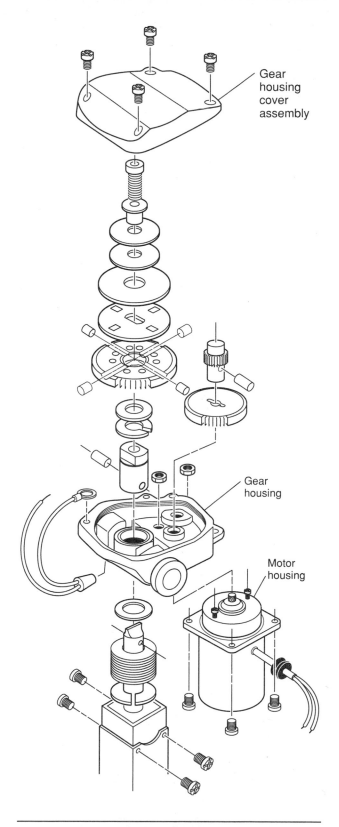

Gear housing cover assembly

Gear housing

Motor housing

■ FIGURE 17.2 ■

Exploded view of the gear housing for disassembly if the leveler becomes jammed in retraction

TROUBLESHOOTING *the Leveler*

Problem	Possible Cause	Correction
Main power light does not illuminate and no levelers operate	Blown or missing fuse	Replace fuse.
	Dead battery	Charge battery.
	Poor battery or ground connection	Repair connection.
	12-strand cable not connected to console	Connect plug to console.
	Broken wires in 12-strand cable	Disconnect cable plug from console, check voltage between pins 10 and 12 in plug. Pin 10 should be 12+ volts and pin 12 should be ground.
30-amp fuse blows when main control switch is turned on	Wrong fuse	Replace fuse with 30-amp Slo Blo.
	Short in control console	Isolate and repair short or replace control console.
	Short in relay box	Isolate and repair short or replace relay box.
30-amp fuse blows when leveler is activated	Wrong fuse	Replace fuse with 30-amp Slo Blo.
	Short in relay box or wires between relay box and leveler	Isolate short; repair or replace faulty component.
	Leveler is damaged and binding	Repair or replace.
	Shorted motor	Replace motor.
Levelers operate, but very slowly	Low battery	Start engine, then operate levelers.
	Poor battery or ground connection	Tighten or repair connection.
	Levelers caked with mud or road grime	Clean and lubricate.
Green light will not light regardless of position of motorhome	Disconnected 5-strand cable	Reconnect plug to control console.
	Faulty component	Disconnect 5-strand plug from control console. Resistance between each pin 1, 2, 3, and 4 and ground (pin 5) should show 0 as appropriate corner of sensor is tilted down to simulate unlevel vehicle, and "open" when same corner is tilted up. If not, replace sensor. If resistance is okay, replace control console.
	Burned-out bulb	Replace bulb.

TROUBLESHOOTING *the Leveler* (continued)

Problem	Possible Cause	Correction
Green light flickers with main switch on	Motorhome at border line of level	Extend all levelers slightly to stabilize motorhome.
	Sensor not secured	Secure sensor.
	Faulty sensor	Check sensor as above; replace if necessary.
	Faulty ground	Check ground connection.
Green light stays on regardless of position of motorhome	Damaged or improperly mounted level sensor unit	Replace or resecure level sensor.
	Faulty component	Disconnect 5-strand plug from console. If light goes out the problem is in cable or sensor. If light stays on, replace console.
Red position indicator will not light, but leveler is vertical	Mercury switch	Rotate mercury switch 45° in its mount. If that fails to correct problem, replace switch.
	White wire from ignition switch to control console not connected	Connect white wire to accessory position of ignition switch that supplies 12-volt DC power when ignition is on.
	Poor wiring connection to mercury switch	Disconnect 12-strand plug from control console. Using a multimeter, check resistance between pin 6, 7, 8, or 9 and pin 12; it should be 0 when leveler is vertical and "open" when horizontal. If resistance values are okay then replace console. If values are not okay, check wire, crimp joints and mercury switch.
	Blown ignition accessory switch fuse	Replace fuse.
	Burned-out bulb	Replace bulb.
Red position light will not go out, but leveler is retracted	Short in wire to mercury switch	Disconnect 12-strand plug from console and with multimeter check resistance as detailed previously. If not "open" when leveler is horizontal, check wiring and mercury switch for shorts. If "open" when leveler is horizontal, replace control console.

TROUBLESHOOTING *the Leveler* (continued)

Problem	Possible Cause	Correction
Individual leveler motor fails to operate	Faulty leveler, relay box, wiring, control console	Check voltage between red and black wires near leveler (should be 12 volts when switch for that leveler is activated). If voltage is present, replace leveler. If no voltage is present, remove 12-strand plug from console. Connect pin 2, 3, 4, or 5 one at a time to pin 12. Corresponding leveler should operate. If all operate, problem is in control console; replace console. If one or more fail to operate, check voltage between red and black wires near relay box. If voltage is present, problem is in wiring between relay box and leveler; repair wiring. If no voltage is present, replace relay box.
Motor operates, but leveler fails to move in either direction	Jammed leveler, weak clutch, or stripped gear	If rapid clicking is heard, leveler is jammed or clutch is weak; repair or replace leveler. If no rapid clicking is heard, but motor is heard, spur gear, pinion gear, or drive is stripped, drive spindle pin is sheared, or motor shaft is stripped. Replace as necessary.
Leveler motor runs but leveler moves only in one direction	Faulty wiring; bad relay or control console	Read voltage at red and black wires at motor. If voltage is 10-12 volts and black is positive with extend switch activated and negative with retract switch activated, problem is in the leveler. If polarity does not reverse, problem is in relay box or control console. If other levelers operate, problem is in control console. If no levelers operate, disconnect 12-strand plug and connect plug pin 1 and either 2, 3, 4, or 5 to ground. If leveler operates properly, problem is in control console. If leveler does not operate, problem is in relay box.
Leveler fails to retract fully	Bent or broken weldment arms	Replace weldment arms.
Leveler fails to swing to true vertical position	Tight pivot bearing	Clean and lubricate, or replace if necessary.
	Tight weldment arm pivot point	Clean and lubricate, or replace if necessary.

Checking the Leveling System Before, during, and after any extended use of the leveling system, check the following items:

☑ CHECKLIST ▰▰▰▰▰▰▰▰▰▰▰▰▰▰▰▰▰▰

☐ Fluid level in reservoir
☐ Condition of battery terminals
☐ Inspect each leveling unit
☐ Inspect hydraulic-line routing
☐ Inspect for fluid leaks

Note: When inspecting each unit, check if any hydraulic lines or electrical wires have been pulled down or pulled loose during any previous trip.

Automatic Hydraulic Adjustments

Standard and High-Profile Levelers To adjust standard and high-profile levelers:

1. *To perpendicular position:* If the unit does not reach the vertical position, loosen the lower adjusting nut and tighten top adjusting nut. If the unit goes past the vertical position, loosen the top adjusting nut and tighten the lower adjusting nut.
2. *The stop:* The position of the leveler in the travel position can be lowered by adjusting the stop. To lower the stop, put in additional ½-inch washers. **Note:** It is important when making this stop adjustment to provide clearance for the leveler to extend fully without swinging down. It is possible for this to happen, so clearance must be made for the various undercarriage parts of the vehicle.

Heavy-Duty Levelers To adjust heavy-duty levelers:

1. *To perpendicular position:* The proper position of the leveler when fully extended is perpendicular to the vehicle's floor. If any leveler is not in this position, it needs readjustment.

   If the unit does not reach the vertical position, loosen the set screw and turn the adjusting cap clockwise. If the unit goes past the vertical position, turn the adjusting cap counterclockwise. Do not turn the adjusting cap more than one turn before recycling unit.

2. *The stop:* The position of the leveler in the travel position can be lowered by adjusting the stop. To lower the stop, put in additional ½-inch washers. **Note:** It is important when making this stop adjustment to provide clearance for the leveler to extend fully without swinging down. It is possible for this to happen, so clearance must be made for the various undercarriage parts of the vehicle.

Level-Sensing Unit To adjust the level-sensing unit:

1. Level the coach using a conventional bubble level.
2. Adjust the three screws on the sensing unit until all green lamps on the light panel are out. Try adjusting a half-turn at a time to start, then a quarter-turn for fine adjustment. **Note:** After each adjustment, lightly tap the screws to let the mercury settle into the new position.

Hydraulic Pump Relief To adjust the hydraulic pump relief:

1. To check and set the relief, disconnect the pressure line from the outlet port and connect a pressure gauge to the outlet port.
2. Remove the cap that covers the relief screw and turn the master switch on.
3. Activate the pump by grounding the second solenoid. This is the solenoid from which a cable goes directly to the pump motor terminal. Ground the solenoid by attaching an insulated wire to the small terminal that has a gray wire connected to it. This wire must be insulated to prevent electric shock. Then touch the wire to a good ground. The correct relief pressure is 3,500 psi. Do not ground the solenoid for more than 30 seconds or the pump may be damaged by overheating.
4. If the relief needs adjustment, turn the relief screw clockwise to increase the relief pressure and counterclockwise to decrease the relief pressure.
   CAUTION: Do not turn the relief screw more than a quarter-turn before rechecking the relief pressure.

TROUBLESHOOTING *the Automatic Hydraulic Leveler*

Problem	Possible Cause	Correction
Side of master switch will not light	Blown fuse	Replace fuse.
	Burned-out bulb	Replace bulb.
System stops during leveling or retracting and "low volts" light illuminates	Low battery power	Recharge battery.
One side of master switch illuminates but levelers will not retract	Bad battery cable connection or other connections	Check connections and repair.
	Bad solenoid pump	Replace solenoid pump.
	Damage to leveler	Repair or replace.
Hydraulic pump will not activate	Bad battery cable connection	Repair battery cable connection.
	Bad solenoid on pump	Replace solenoid valve.
	Low oil in reservoir	Fill oil reservoir.
Hydraulic pump activates but levelers do not extend	Broken hydraulic line	Replace line.
	Bad solenoid valve on main hydraulic manifold	Replace solenoid valve.
Levelers extend when they should swing vertically	Levelers were not fully retracted before they received the vertical signal	Retract levelers before sending vertical signal.
	Bad solenoid valve on main hydraulic manifold assembly	Replace solenoid valve.
	Damaged leveler	Replace leveler.

Note: If the coach must be moved and the normal methods of retracting the levelers have failed, proceed as follows:

The drain valve is located on the underside of the coach, usually close to the solenoid manifold. The drain valve is a 2 x 2 x ¾-inch block with a T-handle. (On some coaches with air suspension or levelers that do not fold horizontally, a 3-port drain valve is provided.) Place a container under the drain valve. Slowly open the drain valve by turning each T-handle approximately 3 turns. Drive the coach forward off the levelers. Stop and check that all levelers have returned to the horizontal position.

CAUTION: Oil may squirt out of the drain valve when first opened and will squirt out when the coach is driven off the levelers.

Alternate procedure (If drain valve is not present): Go to the left front jack and slowly loosen the hose fitting at the actuator cylinder until oil begins to drip. When oil stops, loosen more until oil drips again. Repeat procedure until hose is completely disconnected. **Note:** Do not loosen the hose fitting at the main cylinder.

After the hose to the actuator is off, move the vehicle off the levelers. Stop to make sure the levelers have returned to the horizontal position.

Solenoid Manifold To adjust the solenoid manifold:

1. After the coach has been leveled, the system extends the remaining levelers to stabilize the coach. The units will extend until they touch the ground. If the units do not touch the ground, or the units reach the ground and lift the coach, the solenoid manifold relief needs to be adjusted. The manifold relief is located between the right rear and right front solenoid valves.

2. If the units do not touch the ground, loosen the lock nut and turn the top adjusting nut clockwise. Do not turn the adjusting nut more than a quarter-turn. Follow the automatic retract and automatic leveling procedures.

3. Check to see if the units touch the ground during stabilizing. If not, repeat procedure until the units touch the ground to stabilize the coach but do not lift it. Tighten lock nut.

4. If the units touch the ground and lift the coach, loosen the lock nut and turn the top adjusting nut counterclockwise. Do not turn adjusting nut more than a quarter-turn. Follow the automatic retract and automatic leveling procedures.

5. Check to see if the units touch the ground to stabilize the coach but do not lift it. Tighten the lock nut.

Hydraulic Fluid

Dextron II transmission fluid is recommended for automatic hydraulic levelers. Alternate fluids include:

SAE 5W nondetergent motor oil
SAE 10W nondetergent motor oil
SAE 5W light hydraulic oil
Type A transmission fluid
Type B transmission fluid
Type F transmission fluid

Warning: Never use brake fluid or hydraulic jack fluid.

Servicing Automatic Hydraulic Levelers

To service automatic hydraulic levelers, follow these steps:

1. Occasionally while driving, one of the leveling units could extend for no apparent reason. This situation is usually caused by the improper routing of the hydraulic lines in the system. A line could be too close to a component of the exhaust system, causing the fluid to be heated and the pressure to rise, which extends the leveler. Checking and rerouting the hydraulic lines or protecting them with a heat shield should eliminate this condition.
CAUTION: Temperatures of 220°F will melt hoses and create a possible fire hazard.

2. If nuisance leaks develop at various fittings or at seal locations, it could be possible the relief pressure is set too high, causing higher outlet port pressures that could damage the seals, fittings, or hoses. Prior to readjusting the relief pressure, make sure the reservoir is filled correctly and all fittings are tight. The relief pressure adjusting valve is located on the side of the pump/motor assembly closest to the outlet port with the flare fitting. To check the relief pressure:
   a. Disconnect the pressure hose on the pump outlet port and install an appropriate pressure gauge.
   b. Remove the cap that covers the relief screw.
   c. Start the pump motor by activating the leveler farthest from the control unit.
   d. The correct relief pressure should be 3,500 psi.
   e. Adjust the pressure by turning the relief screw clockwise to increase the pressure, or counterclockwise to decrease the relief pressure.

3. The leveling system may not retract if the solenoids or control panel malfunction. Should these problems occur while the vehicle is on the leveling units, the leveling units must be returned to the horizontal position. To return the leveling units to the horizontal position, go to the left front leveling unit and slowly loosen the hose fitting at the actuator cylinder until oil begins to drip. When the oil stops dripping, loosen the fitting until oil drips again. Repeat procedure until the hose is completely disconnected.
   CAUTION: Do not loosen the hose fitting at the main cylinder. After the hose to the actuator cylinder is off, move the vehicle off the leveling units. Stop to make sure the leveling units have returned to the horizontal position.

Prior to troubleshooting the automatic hydraulic leveler, check to make sure the battery system is in working order. This system can draw as much as 300 amps; thus the battery must supply at least 13 volts. This system will not operate from a converter or battery charger. Its energy source must be a battery. It's best to run the engine while operating the leveling system.

Also make sure the reservoir is full of oil. It is important that all four leveling units be retracted prior to checking the oil level. To check the oil level, remove the breather plug from the top of the hydraulic oil reservoir. The oil level should be approximately one inch below the top of the reservoir.

■ Manual Hydraulics

Maintenance

When the vehicle is serviced, and while the four leveling units are in the retracted position, check the supply of oil in the hydraulic oil reservoir. To check the oil supply, remove the breather plug from the top of the hydraulic oil reservoir. The oil level should be one inch below the top of the reservoir. Fill as necessary using Dextron II automatic transmission fluid.

Periodically clean the levelers of mud and road grime. In cold weather, clear away ice from the levelers.

Do not move the vehicle while the levelers are still in contact with the ground. However, if this should accidentally happen, retract the leveling units, then visually inspect to see if the leveling units have returned to the travel position.

Periodically inspect all electric and hydraulic lines to insure that they are away from sharp edges or heat sources. Inspect for oil leaks and have repairs performed as necessary.

If the motorhome is stored, the levelers should be extended with some vehicle weight on them, and the operation cycle performed once a month.

Manual Hydraulic Adjustment

Adjustment of Level-Sensing Unit To adjust the level-sensing unit:

1. Level the coach using a conventional bubble level.

2. Adjust the three screws on the sensing unit until all the green lamps on the light panel are out. (Figure 17.3a and b). Try adjusting a half-turn at a time to start, then a quarter-turn for fine adjustment. **Note:** After each adjustment, lightly tap the screws to let the mercury settle into the new position.

Adjustment of Standard and High-Profile Leveling Units To adjust standard and high-profile leveling units (Figure 17.4):

1. If the unit does not reach the vertical position, loosen the lower adjusting nut and tighten top adjusting nut. If the unit goes past the vertical position, loosen the top adjusting nut and tighten the lower adjusting nut.

2. The position of the unit in the travel position can be raised or lowered by moving the stop up or down in the slot. This adjustment can be used to provide the necessary clearance of the leveler to the vehicle when horizontal.

Adjustment of Heavy-Duty Leveling Unit To adjust heavy-duty leveling units (Figure 17.5):

1. If unit does not reach the vertical position, loosen set screw, turn adjusting cap clockwise. If unit goes past the vertical position, turn the adjusting cap counterclockwise. Do not turn

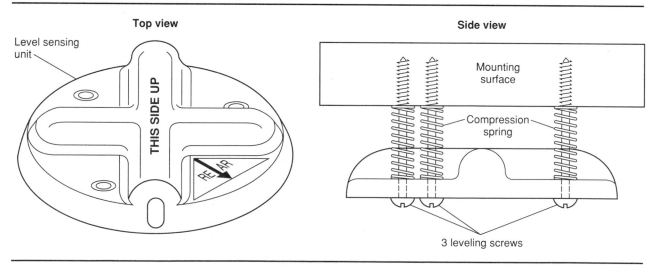

■ **FIGURE 17.3** ■

The level-sensing unit must be adjusted by turning the three screws until the green lights in the monitor are out.

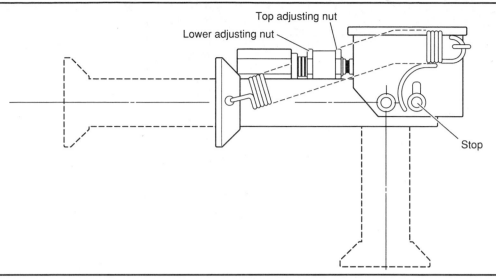

■ FIGURE 17.4 ■

Standard and high-profile leveling jacks have top and lower adjusting nuts to fine tune vertical position.

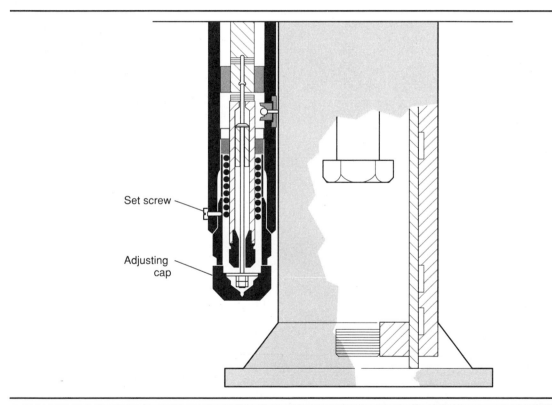

■ FIGURE 17.5 ■

An adjusting cap is used to position the vertical profile of the heavy-duty leveler.

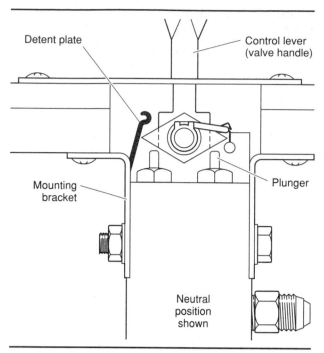

■ **FIGURE 17.6** ■■■■■■■■■■■■■■■■
Detent plate must be adjusted if the hydraulic control handles fail to hold in the retract position.

the adjusting cap more than one turn before recycling the unit.

2. The horizontal position is fixed and cannot be adjusted.

Adjustment of Hydraulic Control Valve Two parts of the control valve are adjustable. The proper adjustments are made at the factory and readjustment is rarely necessary. The following procedures are recommended to adjust them if the need arises:

1. *Detent Plate:* Adjustment of the detent plate is necessary if it fails to hold the control levers in the retract position or if the plunger is not depressed sufficiently by the valve handle in the retract position (Figure 17.6). To adjust the detent plate, loosen the nuts that hold the valve-mounting bracket and the detent plate to the valve assembly. The proper adjustment can be made by moving the detent plate up or down to a point where the valve handle is resting solidly on the detent plate in the retract position, yet holding the plunger down to its fullest extent or no less than 1/16 inch of this extension.

2. *Microswitch:* If the activating rod does not fall directly upon the nipple of the microswitch, the problem can be corrected by either of the following methods:

   a. Carefully bend the activating rod until it is properly aligned with the microswitch.

   b. Remove the mounting bracket and the detent plate. Remove the snap rings on the pivot rod and then carefully slide off the valve handles, spacers, and spring, noting where each part must go during reassembly. The microswitch is adjusted by loosening the small hex nuts that hold the microswitch to the pivot plate, and then making the proper correction. Finally, reassemble the control valve, remembering to properly adjust the detent plate as it is replaced (Figure 17.7).

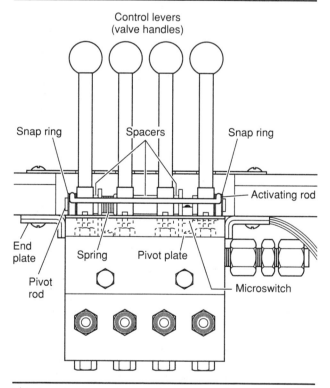

■ **FIGURE 17.7** ■■■■■■■■■■■■■■■
View of the hydraulic control valve and handles

Tongue Jacks

For raising and lowering the trailer tongue (of fifth-wheel), a *tongue jack* (or set of fifth-wheel jacks) is used. They are available in both manual and electric models. While manual tongue jacks are simpler, the electric counterparts are popular because they are easier to operate.

■ Tongue Jack Maintenance

Basic maintenance of all types of jacks consists of keeping them clean and lubricated. Lubrication should be performed at the beginning of each season, or more often as conditions demand.

Lubricating the A & E Tongue Jack

The A & E electric tongue jack requires annual lubrication of the motor gear box assembly. To perform this maintenance procedure:

1. Remove the top cover of the gear housing to expose the gear assembly.
2. Clean the gear assembly of all old lubricant.
3. Repack with heat-resistant grease. The manufacturer recommends a moly-based chassis grease
4. The lower assembly where the power head meshes with the slot in the top of the jack shaft should be cleaned and greased at the beginning of each season.

Lubricating the Atwood Power Jack

Atwood recommends the following procedure for its power jacks:

1. Before each use, inspect the jack tubes and replace if bent or damaged.
2. If wiring is connected to battery terminals, inspect frequently for corrosion. Clean with a solution of baking soda and water, then apply a thin coating of petroleum jelly.
3. Periodically, extend the jack as far as possible and clean the inner ram tube. Coat the tube with a light coating of silicon spray lubricant.

■ Emergency Manual Operation for Electric Jacks

In case of electrical failure, the electric jacks can be operated manually by following these procedures:

A & E Power Tongue Jack

For the A & E power tongue jack (Figure 17.8):

1. Disconnect the fuse holder.
2. Loosen the ⅜-inch socket-head screw.
3. Lift off the motor head and turn the slotted shaft with the hand crank (supplied by manufacturer) clockwise to lower the trailer and counterclockwise to raise the trailer.
4. After use, line up the motor housing so that the switch is facing the front of the A-frame. Retighten the socket-head screw.

Atwood Power Jack

For the Atwood power jack (Figure 17.9):

1. Remove hex nuts and lockwashers from lower side of motor and cover assembly.
2. Lift motor and cover assembly off jack.
3. Turn hex drive nut with wrench or optional manual drive handle.
4. When reinstalling electric motor on jack, rotate hex drive nut so that the pin in the hex drive nut is aligned with slot in motor drive shaft.
5. Tighten hex nuts to 25 inch-pounds torque.

TROUBLESHOOTING the Electric Tongue Jack

Problem	Possible Cause	Correction
Motor fails to operate in either direction	Blown fuse	Replace fuse.
	Dead battery	Charge battery.
	Poor ground connection at base plate	Remove jack and clean mounting surface.
	Internal open circuit in 12-volt DC motor	Replace motor.
	Faulty toggle switch	Replace switch.
	Poor ground wire connection at motor case bolt	Reconnect ground wire.
	Open condition in the 12-volt DC circuit	Find and repair open circuit; use multimeter.
	Loose connection at battery	Repair connection.
Motor runs, but no jack movement	Stripped motor shaft	Replace motor.
	Stripped drive, clutch, or pinion gear(s)	Replace gears.
	Sheared jackscrew pin	Replace pin.
30-amp fuse blows when toggle switch is activated	Short in red or black wire between switch and motor	Repair or rewire.
	Internal short in motor	Replace motor.
	Load limit exceeded	Reduce load.
	12-volt DC source wire too small	Rewire with heavier-gauge wire.
Jack operates, but utility light fails to light	Open condition in the 16-gauge black wire between the motor switch and the utility light	Repair or rewire.
	Faulty light switch	Replace switch.
	Poor ground connection at utility light	Repair connection.
	Faulty bulb	Replace bulb.
Jack operates, but 30-amp fuse blows when utility light is switched on	Short in 16-gauge black wire between light switch and utility light	Repair or rewire.
	Wrong bulb in light	Replace bulb.
Grinding noise when jack is activated	Damaged or bent leveler	Replace leveler.
	Worn thrust bearing	Replace thrust bearing.
	Dry gear housing	Lubricate.
Jack will not lift trailer	Low battery condition	Recharge battery; start engine.
	Jack overloaded	Reduce load.
	Too small 12-volt DC source wire	Rewire with heavier-gauge wire.
	Jack has extended the maximum length	Use blocks under the jack.
Jack travels in only one direction	Faulty switch	Replace switch.

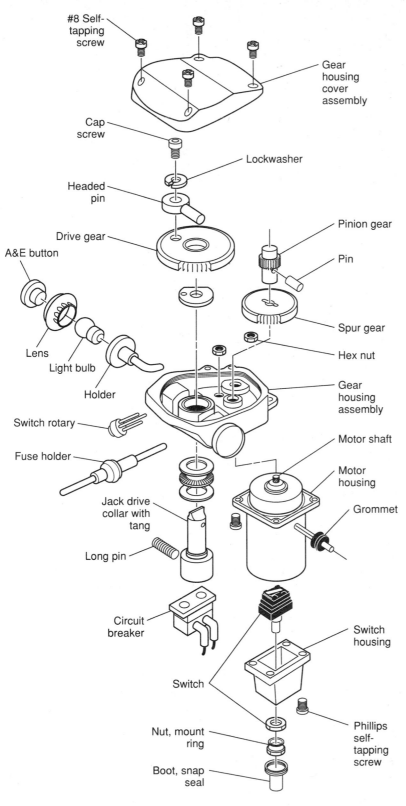

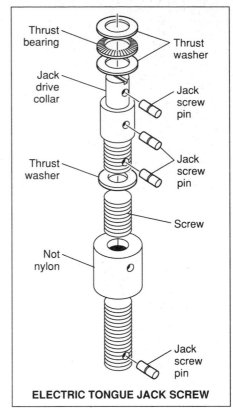

ELECTRIC TONGUE JACK SCREW

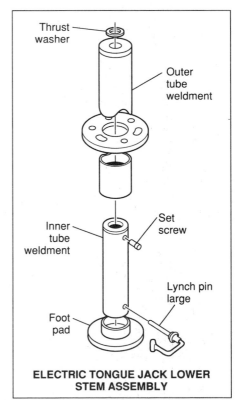

**ELECTRIC TONGUE JACK LOWER
STEM ASSEMBLY**

■ **FIGURE 17.8** ■

Exploded view of the A & E power tongue jack

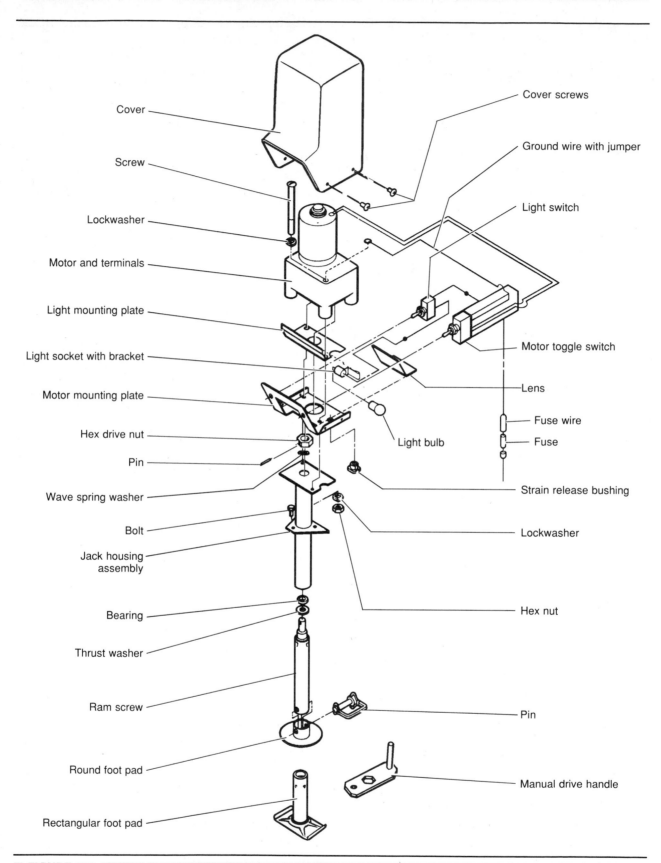

Cover

Screw

Lockwasher

Motor and terminals

Light mounting plate

Light socket with bracket

Motor mounting plate

Hex drive nut

Pin

Wave spring washer

Bolt

Jack housing assembly

Bearing

Thrust washer

Ram screw

Round foot pad

Rectangular foot pad

Cover screws

Ground wire with jumper

Light switch

Motor toggle switch

Lens

Light bulb

Fuse wire

Fuse

Strain release bushing

Lockwasher

Hex nut

Pin

Manual drive handle

■ **FIGURE 17.9**

Exploded view of the Atwood power tongue jack

Antennas

In this section, we'll examine the Winegard Television Systems antenna that is widely used on both motorhomes and travel trailers. This antenna is controlled from inside the RV by use of a manual crank that both elevates and rotates the antenna for optimum reception.

■ Antenna Maintenance

Periodic lubrication of the elevating gear assembly is the only routine maintenance procedure. To lubricate the elevating gear, apply a liberal amount of silicone spray lubricant to the elevating gear with the lift in the down position. Then run the lift up and down a few times to distribute lubricant over the gears (Figure 17.10).

If rotating the antenna becomes difficult, normal operation can be restored by lubricating the bearing surface between the rotating gear housing and the baseplate (Figure 17.11). Use silicone lubricant spray for this purpose.

1. Raise the antenna.
2. Remove set screw from rotating gear housing.
3. Spray lubricant into hole and around edges of gear housing.
4. Rotate gear housing until lubricant coats bearing surfaces and antenna rotates freely.

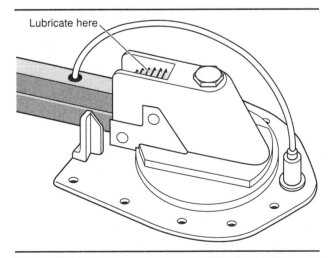

Lubricate here

■ **FIGURE 17.10**
Silicone is used to lubricate the elevating gear in the Winegard television antenna.

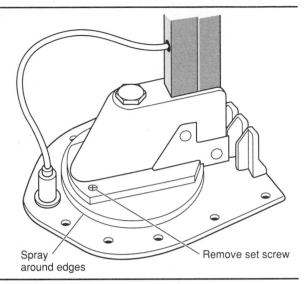

Spray around edges   Remove set screw

■ **FIGURE 17.11**
If rotating the antenna becomes difficult, the bearing surface must be lubricated with silicone.

■ Replacement of Antenna Components

In the event that the elevating shaft and worm gear assembly become worn or broken and require replacement, follow this procedure (Figure 17.12):

1. Loosen set screw to release the elevating crank, spring, and directional handle.
2. Remove the RGH-2 plug from the top of the gear housing. This will expose the top of the worm gear assembly.
3. To remove the worm gear assembly, remove the top pin.
4. Disengage elevating gear from worm gear.
5. Remove the elevating shaft and worm gear assembly.
6. Cut the replacement elevating shaft to match the length of the original.
7. Install the new assembly by reversing the procedure. The two gears will automatically realign themselves after all items have been put back together by turning the elevating crank half a turn.

To remove the lift assembly from vehicle without breaking the seal between baseplate and roof, the

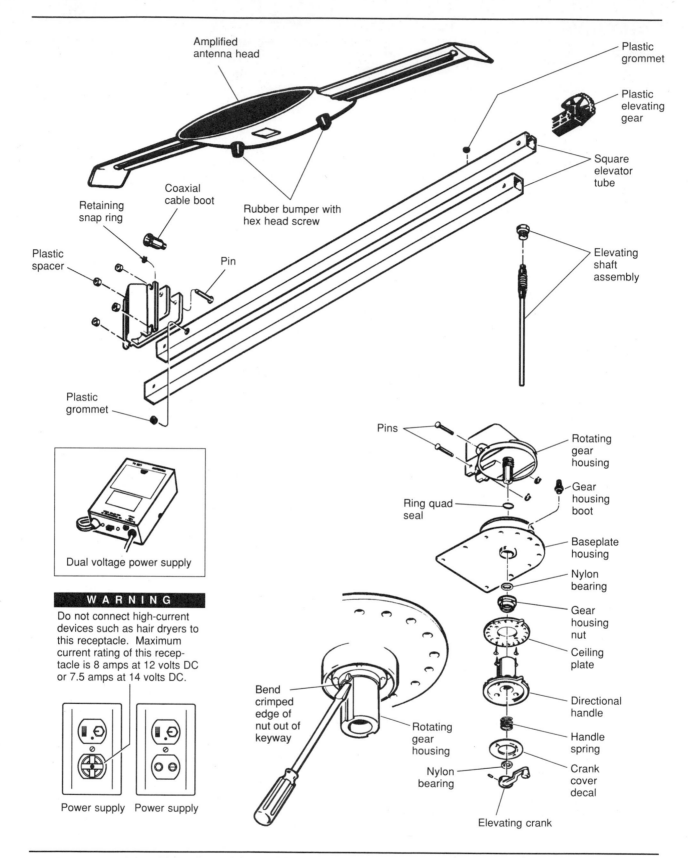

Amplified antenna head

Plastic grommet

Plastic elevating gear

Square elevator tube

Retaining snap ring

Coaxial cable boot

Rubber bumper with hex head screw

Pin

Plastic spacer

Elevating shaft assembly

Plastic grommet

Dual voltage power supply

WARNING

Do not connect high-current devices such as hair dryers to this receptacle. Maximum current rating of this receptacle is 8 amps at 12 volts DC or 7.5 amps at 14 volts DC.

Power supply   Power supply

Pins

Rotating gear housing

Gear housing boot

Ring quad seal

Baseplate housing

Nylon bearing

Gear housing nut

Ceiling plate

Bend crimped edge of nut out of keyway

Rotating gear housing

Directional handle

Handle spring

Nylon bearing

Crank cover decal

Elevating crank

FIGURE 17.12

Exploded view of Winegard television antenna

TROUBLESHOOTING the Antenna

Problem	Possible Cause	Correction
12-volt DC power not getting to antenna	Short in cable, broken cable, or connectors improperly installed	Check cable and replace if faulty. Check connectors for proper installation.
12-volt DC power not present at power supply "Ant" jack, but red light on	Faulty power supply	Replace power supply.

rotating gear housing and baseplate must be separated.

1. Loosen Allen set screw in elevating crank.
2. Remove crank directional handle and spring.
3. Using a small flat-blade screwdriver, with a blade the same width as the keyway in the rotating gear housing, bend the crimped area of GHN-1 nut out of keyway.
4. Using a $5/32$-inch drill, clean threaded portion of GHN-1 nut out of keyway.
5. Insert spanner wrench over shaft and rotate until pins engage holes in nut (Figure 17.13. **Note:** A spanner wrench may be constructed from a $7/8$-inch deep socket or 1-inch EMT conduit. Grind the face of the socket down about $1/8$ inch, leaving pins to engage the GHN-1 nut.
6. Unscrew nut counterclockwise.
7. Rotating gear housing and all parts connected to it may now be lifted from the baseplate on roof.
8. To reassemble, reverse procedure. Use new GHN-1 nut and tighten only enough to remove side play in lift. Make certain the lift rotates freely. Bend edges of GHN-1 nut down into keyway with a punch when properly adjusted.

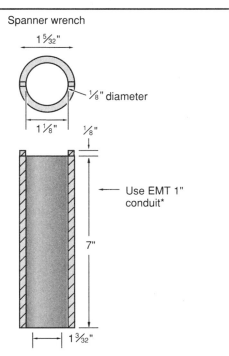

Spanner wrench

$1\frac{5}{32}$"

$\frac{1}{8}$" diameter

$1\frac{1}{8}$" $\frac{1}{8}$"

Use EMT 1" conduit*

7"

$1\frac{3}{32}$"

*Spanner wrench may be constructed from a $\frac{3}{8}$" deep socket or 1" EMT conduit. Grind face of socket down about $\frac{1}{8}$" leaving pins to engage GHN-1 nut. Remove elevating shaft if necessary.

■ **FIGURE 17.13** ▮

A spanner wrench is used to rotate the shaft when removing gear housing in the Winegard antenna.

Remote-Control Searchlights

A *remote-control searchlight* is generally installed on the roof of the vehicle and controlled from inside the vehicle by a four-way toggle switch or set of toggles for up-down and left-right operation. The system consists of the control panel, wiring harness, and searchlight assembly. Within the searchlight assembly is a 12-volt DC electric motor with a gearset to move the searchlight head up and down or left and right.

■ Maintenance of Remote-Control Searchlights

Soapy water and a soft cloth should be used to remove grime from the searchlight head and prevent water spots from forming. Otherwise, there is not much routine service required unless the bulb needs replacement.

■ Bulb Replacement

There are two types of bulbs: dual-filament (spot/flood) and single filament (Figure 17.14).

To replace a faulty bulb:

1. Loosen the bulb-retaining ring screw and pull retaining ring away from searchlight housing.
2. Disconnect the wires from the faulty bulb.
3. Connect wires to new bulb.
4. Reinstall bulb-retaining ring in reverse order from removal.

Bulb Replacement
Loosen screw and remove ring. Disconnect wires from faulty bulb. Connect wires to new bulb as shown below. Install bulb and fasten with bulb retaining ring.

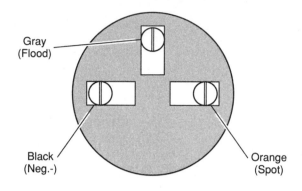

Dual-filament spot-flood
61022–Series   61026–Series
61025–Series   61040–Series

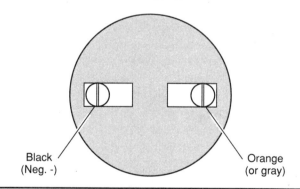

Single filament
61041–Series
61042–Series

■ FIGURE 17.14
Bulb-replacement procedure for remote-control searchlight

TROUBLESHOOTING the Remote-Control Searchlight

Problem	Possible Cause	Correction
Dual-filament bulb works in reverse (up is spot, down is flood)	Improper wiring	Reverse wiring as follows: orange from light to gray from switch or gray from light to orange from switch.
Control level works in reverse in all directions	Improper wiring	Reverse red and white battery connections.
Control lever works in reverse in horizontal direction only	Improper wiring	Disconnect yellow and blue wires. Reconnect as follows: yellow from light to blue from switch or blue from light to yellow from switch.
Control lever works in reverse in vertical direction only	Improper wiring	Disconnect green and violet wires. Reconnect as follows: green from light to violet from switch or violet from light to green from switch.
Light moves in only three of four possible directions, one horizontal direction is inoperative	Improper wiring	Reverse connection. Disconnect yellow and blue wires. Reconnect as follows: yellow from light to blue from switch or blue from light to yellow from switch. If opposite horizontal motion becomes inoperative, replace the switch. If problem persists, return light for service.
One vertical direction is inoperative		Reverse connection. Disconnect green and violet wires. Reconnect as follows: green from light to violet from switch or violet from light to green from switch. If opposite vertical motion becomes inoperative, replace switch. If problem persists, return light for service.
Dim light	Low voltage	Check voltage at power source. Check for proper wire gauge and length. Rewire if necessary.
Bulb operates but no light movement, or light moves but bulb does not light	Blown fuse	Check fuses. Replace if necessary.

Air Horns

A popular accessory on motorhomes and some tow vehicles is an *air horn*. Air horns operate on compressed air that is delivered by a 12-volt DC air compressor. A small storage tank is part of the system and holds compressed air in reserve until needed. When the horn is activated, a valve opens to permit compressed air from the storage tank to flow to the horn assembly.

■ Maintenance of Air Horns

An air horn system is so simple and durable that it requires a minimum of maintenance (Figure 17.15). Though the horns are fairly impervious to weather, to prevent possible freeze damage to the horn assembly diaphragm, tilt the horns downward slightly to permit drainage of moisture.

Periodically check tubing connections for leaks. While the system is charged, use soapy water at the connections and watch for any bubbles indicating an air leak.

Clean the horns with soapy water and dry with a soft cloth to prevent spotting.

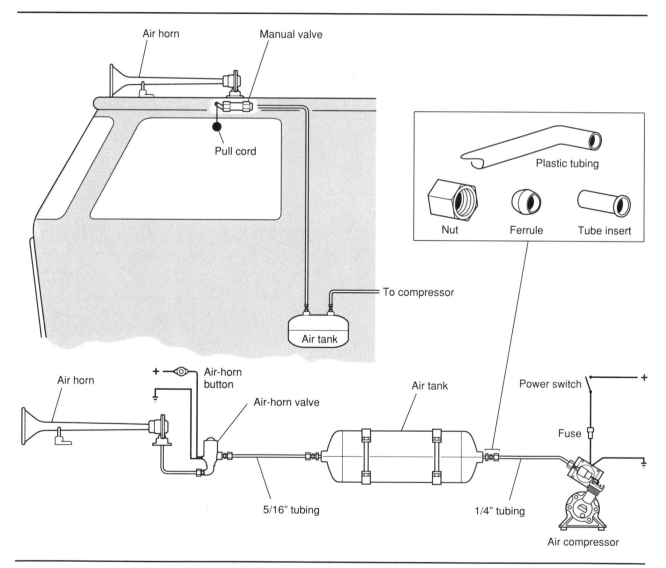

■ FIGURE 17.15 ■

Air-horn kits are made from extremely durable components and require little maintenance.

TROUBLESHOOTING the Air Horn

Problem	Possible Cause	Correction
No power to compressor	Blown fuse	Check fuse and replace if necessary.
	Poor electrical connection	Repair electrical connections.
Inoperative compressor	Failed motor	Replace compressor.

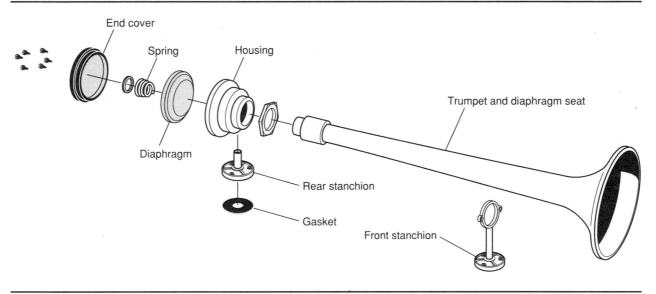

■ FIGURE 17.16 ▬▬▬▬▬▬▬▬▬▬▬▬▬▬▬▬▬▬▬▬▬▬▬
Replacement of the air-horn diaphragm is a simple procedure.

■ Diaphragm Replacement

Replacement of the horn assembly diaphragm typically involves four steps (See Figure 17. 16):

1. Remove the end-cover screws. When doing this, hold the end cover down to compress the internal spring.
2. Remove end cover and pull spring from recess.
3. Install new spring. Replace diaphragm in housing and press end cover against the diaphragm.
4. Install end-cover screws, tightening them evenly by moving around the cover to apply equal pressure.

■ Wiring Information

When wiring the compressor to the vehicle battery, use the following as a guide to wire gauge:

10 feet = 14 AWG
14 feet = 12 AWG
30 feet = 10 AWG

Index

Page numbers appearing in **bold faced** type refer to illustrations in the text.

Reader
Survey

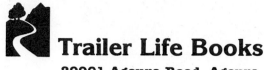

Trailer Life Books

29901 Agoura Road, Agoura, California 91301 (818) 991-4980

Dear Repair Manual Owner:

Thank you for purchasing the all-new edition of <u>Trailer Life's RV Repair and Maintenance Manual.</u> In an ongoing effort to improve this book, we are relying heavily upon our readers to share with us their experiences in using it. We are as eager to learn about any negative experiences as we are to hear about positive ones.

We've made it easy for you to be our consultant on this and future versions of the Repair Manual: Your answers to specific items we need to know about will only take a few minutes. However, a questionnaire cannot possibly cover all aspects of critique, so feel free to amplify your comments on any questions asked, or add any comments on topics not covered.

It's important to us that we hear from you. After you've had a chance to look the book over, please send us your completed questionnaire. We want to make a good manual even better, and we need your help to do it.

Sincerely,

Rena Copperman

Rena Copperman
General Manager
Trailer Life Books

1. For what purpose do you use the *Repair Manual?*

   _____ To make your own repairs

   _____ To use as an aid in diagnosing problems in your RV

   _____ To use as an aid to communicate with your mechanic

2. How often do you think the *Repair Manual* should be updated?

   _____ Every 6 months   _____ Every 3 years

   _____ Every 12 months   _____ Every 5 years

   _____ Every 2 years

3. Is the present way the material is presented satisfactory?

   _____ Yes _____ No

   Comment _____

   _____

   _____

   _____

   _____

   _____

   _____

   _____

4. Should we publish a loose-leaf updated supplement periodically?

   _____ Yes _____ No

   Comment _____

   _____

   _____

   _____

   _____

   _____

   _____

5. If yes, would you be willing to pay:

_____ $5 to $10   _____ $13 to $18

_____ $10 to $13   _____ Over $18

6. Which chapters in the *Repair Manual* do you feel are the most helpful?
   (Rate from 1 [least helpful] to 5 [most helpful])

   _____ Electrical Systems   _____ Exterior Accessories

   _____ Water Systems   _____ Refrigerators, Ranges, Ovens, Microwaves, and Icemakers

   _____ Generators   _____ Air Conditioning Systems

   _____ Interior Care   _____ LP-Gas Systems

   _____ Towing Cars   _____ Trailer Brakes

7. Which additional systems or areas would you like to see covered?

   _____

   _____

   _____

   _____

   _____

   _____

   _____

8. Which areas or chapters would you like to see deleted?

   _____

   _____

   _____

   _____

   _____

   _____

   _____

9. Which areas or chapters would you like to see expanded or added?

     _____

     _____

     _____

     _____

     _____

     _____

     _____

10. Do you feel a companion videocassette would be useful?

     _____ Yes _____ No

11. Would a list of manufacturers' hotline telephone numbers be helpful to you?

     _____ Yes _____ No

12. Of the many new features in the revised *Repair Manual,* which of the following did you find
    the most helpful (rate from 1 [not helpful] to 5 [extremely helpful])?

     _____ Troubleshooting Guides

     _____ More extensive use of photographs and artwork

     _____ Checklists (as seen on page 250)

     _____ Expanded Table of Contents and new Index

     _____ The step-by-step instructions for repairing, replacing, or maintaining systems
             (see page 244)

13. Do you use any other repair manuals?

     _____ Yes _____ No

    If yes, which do you find the most helpful:

     _____ Automotive repair manuals designed specifically for the vehicle

     _____ Owner's manual

     _____ Other RV repair manuals (Please list) _____

14. Would you be interested in separate, expanded versions of individual chapters or systems described in the manual?

_____ Yes _____ No

Which chapter or chapters would you like to see sold in an expanded version?

_____

_____

_____

_____

_____

_____

_____

15. Are you familiar with the original *Trailer Life's RV Repair and Maintenance Manual?*

_____ Yes _____ No

16. Additional Comments:

_____

_____

_____

_____

_____

_____

_____

_____

_____

_____

_____

_____

_____

_____

Thank you for your help. Please remove the survey and send to:

Repair Manual Survey
Trailer Life Books
29901 Agoura Road
Agoura, CA 91301
Attention: Rena Copperman

Name _____

Address _____

_____

Are you an RV owner? _____ Yes _____ No

What year, make, and model RV do you own? _____

Age (optional) _____

Have you purchased any other Trailer Life books? _____ Yes _____ No

If yes, which ones? _____

_____

_____

Comments _____

_____

_____

_____

_____

_____

_____

_____

_____

_____

_____

_____

_____

_____

_____

RV Repair and
Maintenance Log

RV REPAIR AND MAINTENANCE LOG

DATE	TYPE OF SERVICE	COST	COMMENTS

RV REPAIR AND MAINTENANCE LOG

DATE	TYPE OF SERVICE	COST	COMMENTS

RV REPAIR AND MAINTENANCE LOG

DATE	TYPE OF SERVICE	COST	COMMENTS

RV REPAIR AND MAINTENANCE LOG

DATE	TYPE OF SERVICE	COST	COMMENTS

RV REPAIR AND MAINTENANCE LOG

DATE	TYPE OF SERVICE	COST	COMMENTS

RV REPAIR AND MAINTENANCE LOG

DATE	TYPE OF SERVICE	COST	COMMENTS